THE COLOUR DICTIONARY OF

HERBS & HERBALISM

THE COLOUR DICTIONARY OF

HERBS & HERBALISM

Edited by
MALCOLM STUART

ORBIS PUBLISHING · LONDON

First published in Great Britain by
Orbis Publishing Limited, London 1979
as part of *The Encyclopedia of Herbs and Herbalism*

© Orbis Publishing Limited,
London and Istituto Geografico de Agostini,
S.p.A., Novara 1979, 1982

Printed in Czechoslovakia

ISBN: 0-85613-413-9

Title page photograph: the old-world charm of a formal
herb garden at Gaulden Manor, near Taunton, Somerset.
Opposite: German or Wild Chamomile (*Matricaria
recutita*).

CONTENTS

INTRODUCTION

Herbalism has long been thought to consist almost exclusively of the light-hearted study of early printed works which dealt with the supposed medicinal action of plants or their use in cookery. The study of herbs has only recently begun to lose its association with quack medicine and become part of the return to a more natural way of life with the rediscovery of our pre-industrial heritage. The study of herbs cannot be slotted into a narrow botanical niche, either, since the development of man's relationship with plants has always been inextricably linked with economics, religion and science.

In defining the term 'herb', 'herbaceous' plants are those which lack a woody stem and die down to the ground at the end of their growing season, or life if the plant is an annual. Yet this definition cannot accommodate some of the first herbs that come to mind such as Sage, Rosemary or Lavender. These are among the most commonly used herbs which are woody and do not die down. As the dictionary restricts our study to the use of stems and leaves from plants whereas herbalism can involve the use of lichens, fungi and innumerable other plants whose fruit, roots, bark and gums are of value to us, we must simply define herbalism as the study of those plants which are of use to man. The definition of a herb is further complicated by the inclusion of such

Left: The old-world charm of a formal herb garden showing the use of a focal point and plants with foliage of various colours (Gaulden Manor, near Taunton, England).

plants as certain onions, beetroot, celery, olives and chicory, which we now term vegetables. Originally herbs were divided into three different types: pot herbs, which included onions, for example; sweet herbs, such as thyme, which we now call culinary herbs; and salad herbs such as wild celery. In the seventeenth century pot herbs began to be called vegetables since they were no longer thought of as suitable only for the pot but were also used at table. The horticultural breeding of these plants led to the development of their structure and their flavour away from the wild plant to the larger and less bitter modern equivalents.

Until comparatively recently herbs were an integral and quite clearly a necessary commodity in life. In medieval Europe, for instance, their cultivation, collection and distribution were essential to the smooth maintenance of any household. In the kitchen Ash twigs (*Fraxinus excelsior*) and Horsetail (*Equisetum arvense*) served respectively as egg whisks and brushes. Such herbal implements are to be found today only in exclusive chandlers. Soapwort or Bouncing Bet (*Saponaria officinalis*) was used as a soap for delicate fabrics, and Pennyroyal (*Mentha pulegium*) as a flea-repellent. Mullein (*Verbascum thapsus*) and other herbs served as tapers or emergency candles, and almost every daily task involved one herb or another. For cheesemaking Lady's Bedstraw (*Galium verum*) provided a juice which acted as the rennet. Herbs still play a vital role in the tobacco and brewing industries, in the manufacture of wine and liqueurs, as

Above: This ancient painting of healing drugs was used to illustrate a book by Galen, whose accounts of botanical drugs were undisputed until the Middle Ages.

Below: A page from an eleventh-century herbal. It illustrates an Ivy and describes the herb's medicinal applications. (This one was written at Bury St Edmunds, England.)

flavourings and colourings in the confectionery trade and in the manufacture of dyes. With their lovely natural scents and oils, herbs are once again becoming as essential to the modern cosmetic business as they have always been to perfume manufacturers.

In order to understand the present revival of herbalism, the development of man's relationship with plants through the centuries should be examined. History from the emergence of Homo sapiens to the present day can be divided into three broad epochs: the hunter-gatherer period, the agricultural period and the present agricultural-industrial period with its beginnings some four hundred years ago.

Our knowledge of the very early history of man and his evolution is still very vague. We can know very little for certain about early man's diet and way of life, and our assessment of his dependence on plants must, therefore, be a combination of surmise and deduction from the remains discovered by archaeologists. While tools and artifacts commonly survive to give an indication of economics and technology, plants and foods are only preserved in ideal conditions, such as particularly dry regions and, often, caves. Plant remains comprise a variety of forms, mostly seeds, some flower and fruit stalks and leaves. A skilled botanist can identify plants from these remains, and even fossilized faeces can provide clues.

As a hunter-gatherer, man hunted animals, fished, gathered wild fruits and leaves and grubbed up the edible roots of wild plants. He may or may not have reacted instinctively in his rejection of poisonous plants. Certainly he must have experimented with and come to know the many plants within the limits of his nomadic wanderings. Most were innocuous and bland; some nourished him; a handful were particularly pleasant to taste and some equally unpleasant. By trial and error he discovered that some could relieve pain, some proved fatal and a few had a strange unearthly effect on his mind and body. In this period man was able to develop techniques for neutralizing or rendering palatable the parts of plants which he discovered to be of any value to him.

Plants were chopped, leached, dried, roasted and cooked. There is even some evidence that the hunter-gatherer may have experimented with fermentation.

Right: Marjoram was cultivated in medieval times not only as a food flavouring but also for its medicinal qualities, particularly as an antiseptic.

The hunter-gatherer period was the longest clinical trial in history which eventually produced the herbs that provided the best foods, the poison to destroy enemies, the finest fuels and weapons, soporific drinks, medicines, the plants that produced colour for body and cave paintings, and the 'magic' plants which carried primitive man away from reality.

This last group consists, of course, of those herbs causing visual, auditory, tactile, taste or other hallucinations. They are variously described as hallucinatory, psychedelic, narcotic or psychoactive, and their effect can vary from mild euphoria to the inducement of artificial psychoses. Their importance cannot be overemphasized since the effects they have on the human mind and body led to the powerful role they played in primitive society. To early man such herbs offered temporary relief and an escape from the severity of his environment. When sick they provided a direct palliative or cure for his ills, though often we must suppose that the psychic effects of these plants were of more importance than their purely physical effects. This is especially significant when we consider that to early man the modern divisions between science, medicine, art and religion would not have had any meaning. Sickness, in primitive societies, is often attributed to supernatural forces entering the body and from the earliest times, therefore, medicine was linked with the supernatural.

The early doctors and herbalists were invested with an appropriately high social status and indeed, they often enhanced their social position by guarding the 'secrets' of their herbal remedies and stage-managing superstition. Mandrake, a herb with anciently appreciated anaesthetic and purgative properties, was imbued with many forbidding superstitions. In the first century A.D., Josephus the Jewish historian said that Mandrake had the power to expel evil spirits from sick persons but that it was certain death to uproot it casually. The Paeony, too, had to be dug at night, for if a woodpecker caught a gatherer by day, woe to his eyes! Hallucinatory herbs and their products have been used for thousands of years in all civilizations. Today their abuse is a topic of much contention in what is known as the drug problem. Opium, hashish, cannabis, morphine, and cocaine are the most frequently misused. The long historical associations of such herbs with the supernatural and primitive religion have been incorporated into modern attitudes to herbalism. Much of the valuable knowledge our ancestors accumulated about herbs has been dismissed because of superstitious contamination.

The second period in history witnessed the birth of agriculture, not as was once supposed in the fertile valleys of Mesopotamia, but in the Near East. One of the earliest archaeological sites is at Jarmo in Iraq where excavations have revealed evidence of wheat and barley which have been dated at 6750 B.C. Agriculture began a few thousand years later in the New World and probably started independently. Maize, gourds, beans and squashes have been found in early sites in Mexico. The discovery of agriculture or the Neolithic revolution, as archaeologists term it, was to change man's whole existence. Whereas the hunter-gatherer needed a good deal of land to sustain him, agriculture meant that relatively smaller areas of land under cultivation could sustain a whole community. Man began to make permanent settlements and the prerequisites for the growth of science commenced. Instead of subsisting man could open up the forests to make suitable environments for the herbaceous sun-loving crops he favoured.

By 3500 B.C., the Egyptians were making ropes from Papyrus and palm fibre, they had begun to make cosmetics and

Left: The frontispiece of a compendium of plants, which was published in France in 1774. It describes the plants' range of uses to man.

INTRODUCTION

perfumes and in their treatment of disease they became less reliant on magic. By 2700 B.C. the Chinese had started to cultivate tea and to approach healing with the use of herbs on a more scientific basis. Everywhere those species most useful or highly prized for domestic, medicinal or religious employment were brought into cultivation, planted nearer to human dwellings and stored. The Persians gave man the first gardens by planting aromatic and scented herbs together with shade-offering trees in beautiful and peaceful sites. In some early cities like Nineveh, municipal herb gardens were planted for popular use. State-run medicinal herb gardens can be seen in Nepal.

Slowly scholarship and trade developed and flourished. Ideas were exchanged as communication grew and with the great civilizations of Greece and Rome the foundations of modern science and medicine had been laid. The classical works of the Greeks and Romans provided standard reference sources right up to the seventeenth century, but nevertheless the most useful herbs included in them can be traced back to the hunter-gatherers and Neolithic man. Herbalism and our understanding of the benefits of plants did not stop developing with the Greeks and Romans, however, neither has its study been limited to Europe. The discovery of the New World brought many new plants which were added to European herbals and pharmacopoeias. But even so we only have records of a mere fraction of the world's 342,000 estimated species of plant life. Wild products and plants are still gathered in large quantities even in the most economically advanced countries; new species of wild plants are still being taken into cultivation in exactly the same way as the first agriculturalists did, while more uses are being found for well-known plants.

Yet our initial enthusiasm for the chemical and synthetic alternatives to herbs made available by modern science has had the effect of blindfolding us to our real and continued need for herbs. Removed from the basic processes of production, we know little or nothing about the raw materials or stages involved in the commodities we buy – we cannot tell whether the dye in blue jeans is from Indigo or India. Efficiency had dictated that of the 200,000 species of flowering plants, only 12 or 13 are widely cultivated, and most of us

have a far more restricted vegetable diet than the Roman conquerors of Europe. Sadly, industrialization has meant the loss of much of the valuable herbal knowledge of our ancestors and the misconception that we can manage without herbs.

This is clearly a very great misconception if one thinks of the massive quantities of crude herbs used today even in the most sophisticated of societies.

After a decline of about two hundred years, herbalism is now experiencing a revival of both public and professional interest. The professions which so ridiculed medical herbalism as ineffective and superstitious 'old wives' tales' are once again turning to nature in an attempt to discover methods and materials free from the undesirable side-effects frequently experienced with the modern 'chemically tailored' synthetic drug. New methods of reappraisal are being used to judge the beliefs produced by centuries of practical experience. There are signs that the revival of interest in herbs will be extremely profitable to man and the herbal practices of our ancestors are being increasingly vindicated.

Herbalism has become part of the new concern in our society for an ecological balance and an unpolluted 'natural' way of life. This late twentieth-century appreciation of herbs and their immense value in food and medicine truly represents the

rediscovery of old wisdom indicating that the biblical expression 'all flesh is grass' is as true today as it always has been.

Medicinal Uses

The correct use of medicinal plants is central not only to effective medication but also to personal safety. Just because herbs are natural things it does not follow that all can be used indiscriminately without causing harm, indeed many *can* be harmful when used incorrectly and should never be employed by unqualified individuals, while others probably should never be used even by qualified medical personnel.

This is emphasized by the fact that modern herbalists rarely, if ever, use any of the poisonous or powerful plants which were common in the armamentarium of the Medieval physicians. Instead, they use safe remedies, of proven effectiveness, which slowly but surely assist in restoring the body's natural healing propensity, without jolting it into action or reation as do powerful and toxic plants or modern synthetic drugs.

Knowledge of the correct application and combinations of various herbs in any given patient's condition is very complex – and far beyond explanation in this book – but suffice it to say that it is the use of certain combinations of plants which often leads to the success of the herbal practitioner. These combinations act in a way which is somewhat different from that of the individual components of a conventional prescription.

On the other hand, it should be made clear that even qualified practitioners do not mix several herbal components haphazardly, since the outcome of such so-called polyphytopharmacy cannot be predicted. Some things may counteract the effect of others, just as some foods are known to counteract the beneficial effect of herbs. The best examples of this are the negation of the effects of Devil's Claw by apples, and of Ginseng by ordinary tea!

In some cases herbalists do not employ combinations but single plant species as a remedy. This is known as the use of simples. Throughout the *Dictionary*, therefore, all the actions of herbs refer to their effect when used as simples, and not in combination – although some classic combinations are referred to. Often therapeutic indication alludes to historical usage, now obsolete, and in many cases reference is made to known contra-indications. Such species should be avoided completely, and in addition, it should be borne in mind that there is always the possibility of an individual allergic-type reaction or sensitivity to any plant; note the allergic character of Cowslip (*Primula veris*) and its relations, for example.

There are also many special cases in which certain herbs should never be used – pregnant women cannot ever take Rue (*Ruta graveolens*) or Pennyroyal (*Mentha pulegium*) which may act as abortifacients; those with renal or urinary calculi should not take Rhubarb (*Rheum officinale*) as a laxative; and Juniper berries (*Juniperus communis*) are to be avoided both by the pregnant and by those whose kidneys may be inflamed. Many such examples exist.

Generally speaking, children should not be treated herbally, nor indeed with any other form of home medication, since in children ordinary symptoms, such as those of the common cold, may develop into a potentially serious complaint in as little as 24 hours. This raises the whole question of mis-diagnosis. Certain commonplace symptoms such as vomiting, a stiff neck, headache, fever and earache may seem in themselves trivial complaints, but considered in the perspective of other associated symptoms and the patient's predispositions and case history, it may indicate a much more serious problem which warrants medical attention. Since any complaint is best treated immediately, it is important to remember that if symptoms do not disappear very quickly, proper qualified advice must be sought. Mis-diagnosis is one of the strongest arguments against self-medication today!

Other problems to face when using herbs concern which part of the plant to employ (often the root, leaf, bark, fruit or flower have differing properties), what dosage should be employed, how and when the dose should be administered, and the length of time a remedy should be taken.

Individual herbal remedies may be prepared in several different ways, some being directly related to their form of administration – poultices, ointments, salves and creams, for example, are obviously for external application only. Other methods are related to the extraction of specific groups of active materials from a plant, so that alcoholic or acidic (vinegar) solutions may be needed to remove therapeutic chemicals which would not be released or solubilized in water.

Still other methods are related to the physical nature of the herb itself. Pouring boiling water over a thick hard root may extract only a fraction of its constituents, whereas the same procedure is perfectly satisfactory for most leaves and flowers. A complete understanding of all the different methods of preparation of herbal remedies requires a fairly extensive knowledge of pharmacy and is obviously not relevant to the home use of herbs, which is confined to preparations in infusion, decoction and as a poultice.

These processes, which should always be undertaken freshly, and never kept for more than 12 hours in view of possible deterioration, are simple methods for extracting the active substances from a range of harmless medicinal plants of value in straightforward conditions such as lack of appetite (Agrimony, Gentian, Sweet Flag, Caraway), colds (Yarrow, Elder, Peppermint, Boneset, Hyssop, Horehound), constipation (Psyllium seed, Fennel seed, Yellow Dock, Turnera), dyspepsia (Lemon Balm, Sweet Flag, Marshmallow, Meadowsweet, Chamomile, Angelica), indigestion (Peppermint, Dandelion, Lime, Parsley) and insomnia (Valerian, Hops, Lime, Passion Flower).

Infusion: This method is used to extract the water-soluble substances from the less dense parts of such as the leaves, stems and flowers, and is also sometimes employed for thin, small chopped roots and fruits. The method consists of pouring 500 ml (20 fl oz) of boiling water onto 30 g (1 oz) of the finely cut material contained in a porcelain, stone or glass vessel, fitted with a tight lid. The lid keeps in the volatile substances which would otherwise be lost during the 10 or 15 minutes normally required for infusion. After straining, the liquid is allowed to cool to just below blood heat before the dose is taken (normally a wine-glassful), or it may be allowed to cool completely. Normally three doses are taken each day, usually before meals.

Decoction: Hard plant parts such as roots, rhizomes and barks, seeds, and woods release their water-soluble constituents only after more prolonged hot-water treatment. This requires adding 30 (1 oz) of the herbal remedy to 500 ml (20 fl oz) of cold water in an enamel or glass vessel and allowing it to soak for 10 minutes. The temperature is raised to boiling point and the mixture then simmered for 10 to 15 minutes. This is followed by a further 10 minutes steeping. During the entire process the vessel should be kept covered. After straining and cooling the dose (normally a wineglassful) is taken.

Poultice: This method may utilize either fresh plant material which is bruised and crushed to a pulp, and is then mixed with a small quantity of hot water; or dried herbs which are softened by mixing them with some suspending material such as flour, bran, corn meal or other suitable vehicle. Both fresh and dried plant poultices are best applied indirectly to the skin by sandwiching the paste between thin cloth prior to application to the affected part of the body.

There is no doubt at all that the herbal world can provide a wealth of help in a number of very different medical conditions. In disease that help is achieved only by the use of the right herbs prepared and administered in the correct way, which generally is through the agency of a practitioner who has made a careful and prolonged study and practice of the art of herbalism. In a range of simple and straightforward conditions the average individual can also obtain benefit from using the well-known and harmless herbs himself. It should be borne in mind by the reader, though, that much information contained in modern works on herbalism may also include data on former usage of medicinal plants which are not suitable to the disposition of modern man, and that all the variations of the precautions mentioned here must be carefully considered before attempting to treat one-self for any condition. With the exception of the best known herbs it is wise always to seek advice before use.

HERBS A-Z

The following pages include a detailed list of 420 of the most important herbs, each illustrated with a photograph or drawing and with its characteristics and constituents described in full. The enormous variety and extent of the powers of plants is amply demonstrated in these entries. The practical information included gives ideas on how to cultivate those herbs that interest you, together with a concise indication of their uses, whether culinary, medicinal or otherwise. Once again, however, we must stress that the medicinal use of plants requires expert knowledge. In this respect, the book is a reference work rather than a guide to practical application. Under no circumstances should readers use the information in these pages for home treatment without first taking expert advice.

The cultivation section states whether the species is found in the wild state (as most are), or whether it is found wild only as an escape from cultivation, and also gives details of commercial and horticultural cultivation where applicable. Related varieties which are of greater horticultural importance have been noted, and, in addition, those closely related species that are cultivated as medicinal or economic plants for the same purpose as the species in question are also mentioned.

Left: A mass of different herbs growing in the wild. Many of the herbs described on the following pages – over 420 species – can be collected easily and put to a variety of different uses, which include culinary, medicinal and cosmetic.

Each entry lists the parts of the plant, together with their uses, most commonly employed. In some cases, it has been necessary to list different parts of the plant for different uses, as the effects of different parts of plants can vary widely – to the extent of being contradictory.

The naming of herbs often causes problems. We have used the Latin botanical names of the plants (the most accurate system), followed by the preferred common name in bold type with some of the alternatives. The Latin names have particular significance, and it is as well to know how they are made up. The following example is of a relatively complex name, as the herb is a hybrid, although the principles apply to all other species:
Mentha x *piperita* var. *citrata* (Ehr.) Briq. LABIATAE

Bergamot Mint Eau de Cologne Mint/ Orange Mint
In this example, *Mentha* indicates the genus and *piperita* the species; (Ehr.) stands for Ehrhart which is the name of the botanist who first classified the species and Briq. (the abbreviation of Briquet) is the name of the person responsible for the accepted reclassification – thus without brackets. Originally this plant was classified by Linnaeus simply as *Mentha piperita*, but it was then reclassified by Ehrhart as *Mentha* x *piperita* var. *citrata*; the x indicates that the plant is a cross between *Mentha spicata* and *Mentha aquatica*, and the 'var.' means that this is a variety of mint which is not sufficiently distinct to be classified as a separate species. Labiatae indicates the family to which the plant belongs.

Abies alba Mill. PINACEAE
Silver Fir
This conifer was once the source of 'Strassburg Turpentine', first described in detail by Belon in *De Arboribus coniferis* (1553). It was retained in the London Pharmacopoeia until 1788. It is now rarely collected, and the leaves, buds and fresh resin are only used in folk medicine.
Description Coniferous evergreen tree to 50 m; trunk straight, branches brownish and pubescent; leaves simple, needle-like, glossy and dark green above, rounded at apex; to 3 cm long. Monoecious, the male cones small; female to 16 cm long, erect, becoming reddish-brown, with deciduous scales. Appearing late spring to early summer.
Distribution Native to central and southern Europe; mountainous regions from 400–2000 m altitude. Introduced elsewhere.
Cultivation Wild. Employed horticulturally, especially the cultivars *Columnaris*, *Compacta* and *Pendula*. Dislikes polluted air.
Constituents Oleo-resin comprising turpentine; essential oil; a sugar, abietite; provitamin A.
Uses (leaves, fresh resin, oil of turpentine occasionally) Antiseptic; diuretic; expectorant; carminative. Employed in the treatment of bronchitis, cystitis, leucorrhoea, ulcers and flatulent colic. The oil is an irritant and can be applied externally, diluted, as a rubefacient in neuralgia.
Contra-indications The oil should only be used externally, and may cause skin reactions.

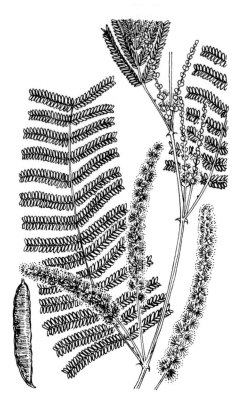

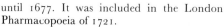

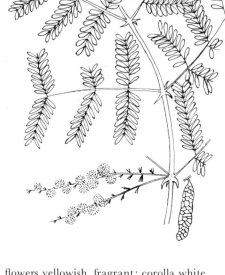

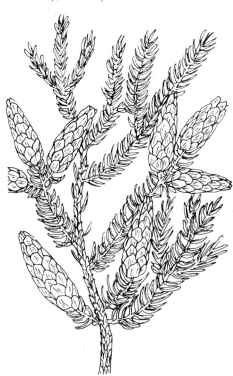

Acacia catechu (L) Willd. LEGUMINOSAE
Catechu Black Cutch/Kutch
This herb was known as *Cacho* or *Kat* and was an important export from India to China, Arabia and Persia in the sixteenth century. It was introduced to Europe in the seventeenth century from Japan. The dark brown extract was not recognized as a vegetable substance until 1677. It was included in the London Pharmacopoeia of 1721.
Description Moderate sized tree, 9–12 m high; trunk short, not straight, 1.5–2 m in girth; straggling thorny branches; light feathery foliage; rough, dark grey-brown bark; pale yellow flowers.
Distribution Indigenous to eastern India, Burma; common in hotter, drier parts of Ceylon, plains of Burma, forests of tropical east Africa.
Cultivation Not cultivated; trees felled and processed.
Constituents Astringent action due to catechu-tannic acid. Also contains quercetin, catechu red, catechol.
Uses (boiled and strained extract of heartwood chips, forming very dark brown solid mass) Powerful astringent, useful for inflamed conditions of throat, gums and mouth; used diluted as a gargle. Used to treat diarrhoea and externally for ulcers and boils. Wood for posts, heating and charcoal. Catechu and bark for tanning and dyeing.

Acacia Senegal (L) Willd. LEGUMINOSAE
Gum Arabic Acacia Gum/Gummi acaciae
When the Egyptians brought gum from the Gulf of Aden in the seventeenth century B.C., they called it Kami and used it mainly for painting and as an adhesive for lapis lazuli or coloured glass. Theophrastus mentioned Kami, in the fourth century B.C., and Celsus called it *Gummi acanthinum* in the first century B.C. Arabian physicians at the medieval school of Salerno used it and it was liable for customs duty at Pisa and Paris. It reached London by 1521 via Venice. Gum Arabic is still used pharmaceutically.
Description Low tree, 3–6 m high, bending grey branches, grey bark; leaves pale green, smooth; flowers yellowish, fragrant; corolla white.
Distribution Indigenous to east and west Africa. Common in Arabia and India.
Cultivation Not cultivated; trees incised and gum collected early winter.
Constituents Consists mainly of calcium, magnesium and potassium salts of arabic acid (arabin). Forms a mucilage in water.
Uses (dried gummy exudation from stems and branches) Soothing for inflamed tissue. Used in mouth lozenges, cough mixtures, emulsions. Highly nutritious taken as gruel. Adhesive.

Acanthus mollis L ACANTHACEAE
Bear's Breech Brank Ursine
The specific name, Acanthus (from the Greek *akanthos*, *ake* meaning thorn, *anthos* meaning flowers) occurs frequently in Greek and Roman

writings referring to different prickly plants. The beautiful leaves stimulated designs for the decoration of columns in classical Greek architecture.

Description Hardy perennial; leaves oblong with undulating margins, dark green and glossy, 30–60 cm long; stems straight to 150 cm high; white or lilac pink flowers on spikes, summer.

Distribution Native of southern Europe. Now widely distributed.

Cultivation Tolerates ordinary soil; prefers deep loam, either full sun or partial shade. Propagate by division in spring or autumn; root cuttings, or seed, in spring. May be cultivated as house plant in large pot in full light.

Uses Crushed leaves once used for burns and scalds.

Achillea millefolium L COMPOSITAE
Yarrow Milfoil/Woundwort/Carpenter's Weed

From ancient times this herb has been associated with the healing of wounds and the stemming of blood-flow, hence the generic name; Achilles, for example, was supposed to have cured his warriors with its leaves.

A. millefolium has traditionally had a wide medical use.

Description Aromatic perennial, far-creeping stoloniferous herb; erect furrowed stem, 8–60 cm high; white or pinkish flowers (early summer to autumn) and slightly hairy bipin-nate leaves, 2–10 cm long, divided into fine leaflets.

Distribution Widespread in temperate zones; native to Europe; on all but poorest soils.

Cultivation Increase by division spring or autumn. Grows in any soil in sunny position.

Constituents Volatile oil containing azulene; and a glycoalkaloid, achilleine.

Uses (dried aerial parts, including flowers) Diaphoretic; antipyretic; hypotensive; diuretic and urinary antiseptic. Combines with Elderflowers and Peppermint for colds and influenza. Of use in hypertension and coronary thrombosis, dysentery and diarrhoea. Fresh leaf alleviates toothache. Regulates menstrual

periods. Stimulates gastric secretion.

Fresh herb in salads. Can substitute Hops in brewing.

Cosmetic cleanser for greasy skin.

Snuff; tobacco substitute. 'I Ching' sticks.

Contra-indications Large doses produce headaches and vertigo.

Aconitum napellus L RANUNCULACEAE
Aconite Monkshood/Blue Rocket/Wolfsbane

This lethal herb was widely employed as an arrow poison by the ancient Chinese and its generic name comes from the Greek *akontion* meaning a dart. *Napellus* means 'little turnip' – a reference to the shape of its tuberous root.

Aconitum napellus was an important herb among the thirteenth-century Welsh physicians of Myddvai but was not introduced into medicine generally until the eighteenth century.

Description Hardy herbaceous perennial; essentially biennial as roots produced one year, flower the next; stem erect reaching 150 cm; leaves dark green, glossy, 3–8 cm wide, divided; flowers (summer and autumn) violet blue, 2 cm high, helmet shaped, in terminal clusters.

Distribution Indigenous to Alps and Pyrenees; mountainous districts of northern hemisphere. Prefers moist soils in shade.

Cultivation Root division in autumn; selected daughter roots are stored in a warm place and then planted mid-winter in moist loam. Seeds sown in spring flower in 2–3 years. Attractive garden decoration; blue, white and violet cultivars include Blue Spectre, Sparks Variety.

Constituents Sedative and toxic action due to

alkaloid, aconitine. Also contains picraconi-tine, and aconine.

Uses (dried root tubers, whole plant fresh or dried) Sedative; pain killer; antipyretic. Once used for feverish conditions, now only externally for neuralgia and sciatica.

Contra-indications All parts intensely POISONOUS. To be used only by medical personnel.

Acorus calamus L ARACEAE
Calamus Sweet Flag/Sweet Sedge/Myrtle Flag

Acorus calamus was an ancient herb of the East and is also mentioned in the Bible in the book of Exodus. It was probably introduced into Russia by the Mongolians in the eleventh century, and into Poland by the thirteenth. At the end of the sixteenth century it was widely distributed by the Viennese botanist Clausius.

Description Hardy, vigorous, aromatic perennial; much branched rhizome, 3 cm thick, bearing sword-shaped leaves with wavy margin, 1 m high and 15 mm wide. Small flowers

(early summer), on inflorescence 4–8cm long.

Distribution Indigenous to central Asia, eastern Europe; now native in northern temperate zones, in marshy regions.

Cultivation Needs moist soil and frequent watering, best by water margins. Divide clumps early spring or autumn, cover well. Only flowers in water.

Constituents Bitter, aromatic, volatile oil; bitter principle, acorin.

Uses (dried rhizome) Carminative; vermifuge; spasmolytic; diaphoretic. Stimulates salivary and gastric glands. Slight sedative action on central nervous system. Best used in flatulent colic, dyspepsia.

Beer flavouring and liqueur. Candied rhizomes used as sweetmeats. Young leaf buds in salads. Insecticide; powder repels white ants.

Perfume additive similar to orris root. Toothpowder, hair-powders and dry shampoos. Snuff.

Contra-indications Oil of acorus has reputed carcinogenic properties.

Adiantum capillus-veneris L POLYPODIACEAE
Maidenhair Fern Venus Hair

The generic name *Adiantum* is from the Greek word *adiantos* or unwetted, since the foliage repels water and the plant's natural habitat is a wet environment. The specific and common names refer to the hair of the pudenda after the fine, shiny, black petioles. This was once the most important herbal ingredient of a popular cough syrup called *Capillaire* which remained

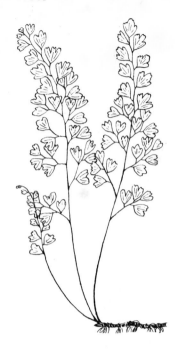

in use until the nineteenth century.

Description Perennial fern 10–40 cm tall; petioles thin, delicate, black and shiny. Leaves ovate to narrowly triangular, finely pinnate, pinnules fan-shaped and toothed; sori reddish-brown on the underside of leaf tips.

Distribution Native to Great Britain, central and south Europe. Now world-wide in temperate and tropical regions. Especially near the sea, in caves, wells, on damp walls; cliffs, on chalky soils; but also to 1300 m altitude.

Cultivation Wild. Cultivated as a pot plant in loam and leaf mould mix; requires moist atmosphere. Propagate by division.

Constituents Mucilage; tannins; gallic acid; sugars; various bitter principles; capillarine; minute quantities of an essential oil.

Uses (fresh, or dried, leafy fronds occasionally) Weak expectorant; bechic; weak emmenagogue; weak diuretic.

Principally employed in chest complaints such as respiratory catarrh, and coughs. Once used in the treatment of both pleurisy and asthma but with little effect in the latter.

Adonis vernalis L RANUNCULACEAE
False Hellebore Pheasant's Eye/Spring Adonis/Ox-eye

The name is derived from the legend of Adonis, who was killed by a wild boar and from whose blood the herb sprang. It is still retained in several European pharmacopoeias. There are two varieties, *A. vernalis* with yellow flowers and *A. annua* with red flowers.

Description Perennial herb, 10–30 cm high; sparingly branched, leaves numerous and much divided; flowers (early spring) solitary, terminal, rich yellow, 3–6 cm wide.

Distribution Central and south-east Europe. Occasionally wild in temperate zones; can be grown in the garden.

Cultivation Grows in moist soils in full sun or shade; flowers best in sunny position. *A. vernalis* suits rockeries. *A. annua* cannot be transplanted.

Some white or double flowered varieties are cultivated.

Constituents Glycosides, including cymarin.

Uses (dried herb) Valuable heart tonic, not cumulative and less toxic than Digitalis. Dilates coronary arteries. Not widely used due to irregular absorption. Vermifuge.

Contra-indications POISONOUS even in very small amounts; to be used by medical personnel only.

Aegopodium podagraria L UMBELLIFERAE
Ground Elder Goutweed/Bishops-weed/ Herb Gerard

The name suggests both the leaf shape and the specific use of this herb in ancient times, from the Greek *aigos* meaning goat; *podos* meaning foot and *podagra* the Latin for gout. In the Middle Ages it was cultivated as a pot herb or vegetable.

Description Perennial weed with creeping rootstock; hollow stem reaching 20–40 cm bearing umbels of white flowers (summer), 2–7 cm wide; leaves 10–20 cm long with stalks, sub-

divided into 3 leaflets.

Distribution Native to Europe, naturalized in eastern North America; often near habitation, hedgerows.

Cultivation Wild; too vigorous for garden cultivation, although *A. podagraria variegatum* is used for edging.

Uses (dried herb, fresh root and leaf) Diuretic; sedative. Traditionally taken as a drink for gout and sciatic pains. Boiled root and leaf in hot poultice applied to joints.

Young fresh leaves cooked in spring as vegetable; taste similar to spinach. Used in salads.

Aesculus hippocastanum L HIPPOCASTANACEAE
Horse Chestnut

Aesculus was the classical name of an oak tree but the origins of the common name are uncertain: it was used extensively in the East as cattle and horse fodder; alternatively the prefix 'horse' may have differentiated it from the edible Sweet Chestnut, *Castanea sativa*.

Description Deciduous tree up to 35 m high; very resinous buds, bark smooth when young and becomes scaly; leaves subdivided into 5–7 leaflets, 8–20 cm long; flowers (early summer) white, pink or yellowish, on erect conical inflorescence; fruit spiny, green, containing brown seed.

Distribution Native to Balkan peninsula; now widely cultivated.

Cultivation Grows in many soils; often self-sown.

Constituents Saponin; aescine; flavones; coumarin; tannins.

Uses (fresh seed without seed-coat, branch bark) Tonic; narcotic; antipyretic. Bark employed traditionally in intermittent fevers. Combined action of constituents of seeds strengthens arteries and veins, preventing thrombosis. Seed extract relieves haemorrhoids. Fruit mash for cattle and sheep fodder.

Contra-indications Seed POISONOUS. To be used by medical personnel only.

Aethusa cynapium L UMBELLIFERAE
Fool's Parsley Lesser Hemlock/Dog Poison

Known to sixteenth-century apothecaries as *apium rusticum*, this is a highly poisonous herb, as indeed the common names suggest. Care is required when collecting edible plants from the wild. Fool's Parsley, for example, can easily be taken for an edible Parsley.

Description Annual, flimsy looking, rarely more than 30 cm high, thin, hairless, hollow stem; leaves triangular, segments ovate, pinnatifid; umbels of white flowers (summer) 2–6 cm wide with 3 or 4 long pendulous bracteoles.

Distribution Native to Europe; common, widely distributed; weed of cultivated ground.

Cultivation Wild plant.

Constituents Toxic principle an alkaloid, cynopine.

Uses (dried herb) Stomachic; sedative. Once used for gastro-intestinal complaints of children, convulsions, summer diarrhoea.

Contra-indications Very POISONOUS. Small amounts cause pain, confusion of vision, vomiting.

Aframomum melegueta Rosc. ZINGIBERACEAE
Grains of Paradise Melegueta Pepper/ Guinea Grains

The name *Melegueta* is derived from the ancient African empire of Melle which extended over the Upper Niger region. It was originally transported from the African west coast across the desert to ports on the Tripoli coast. It served as a spice in medieval European cuisine and was one of the ingredients of the spiced wine, hippocras. Known as *grana paradisi* because it was imported from distant lands, it was sold at Lyons in 1245. At the same time the Welsh physicians of Myddvai called it 'grawn Paris'.

Description Herbaceous reed-like plant, 1–2.5 m high, long leaves producing delicate wax-like, pale purple flowers, succeeded by pear-shaped scarlet fruit, 6–10 cm long, enclosing

pulp and brown seeds, 2 mm wide.

Cultivation Wild; cultivated particularly in Ghana.

Constituents Essential oil; pungent resin.

Uses (seeds) Stimulant. Hot and peppery condiment; used as pepper substitute. Traditionally used in veterinary medicine.

Agathosma betulina (Berg.) Pillans. RUTACEAE
Buchu Bucco/Short Buchu/Round Buchu
One of the few indigenous plants of southern Africa to find a place in both traditional and

orthodox western medicine, the use of Buchu was learned from the native Hottentots by the colonists of the Cape of Good Hope. It was first introduced to Europe in 1821. Until recent legislation most of the leaf production was used as a cordial flavouring in the United States. Buchu is still used by herbalists and African tribesmen. Originally classified as *Barosma betulina* (Bergius) Bartl. & H.L. Wendl.

Description A small shrub 1–1.5 m high bearing smooth rod-shaped branches with leathery, glossy, pale yellowish-green leaves 1–2 cm long, 5 mm – 1 cm wide. Young twigs and toothed margins of leaves have conspicuous oil glands. White flowers.

Distribution Cape province of South Africa: mountain-sides and hillsides on dry soil.

Cultivation Wild plant; cultivated on hillsides.

Constituents Volatile oil comprising up to 40% diosphenol; limonene and menthone.

Uses (dried leaf) Urinary antiseptic; of use in cystitis and urethritis. A weak diuretic.
Used to flavour brandy (Buchu brandy).
Used as a blackcurrant flavouring.
Black South Africans use the leaves mixed with oil as a body perfume.

Agave americana L AGAVACEAE
Century Plant Agave/American Aloe
Agave is from the Greek for admirable, after the plant's appearance; the common name refers to the mistaken belief that it flowers only after a hundred years' growth. In many tropical countries the Agave provides one of the cheapest and most effective cattle fences available.

Description Succulent monocotyledon, eventually flowering after 10 years or more, after which it dies, although frequently leaving suckers at the base. Leaves are very thick, 15–20 cm wide, 1–2 m long, grey, smooth, and spiny-edged. Flowers to 3 cm long, pale

yellowish on horizontal branches of a 6–12 m tall stalk.

Distribution Native to tropical America, especially Mexico. Introduced and established in southern Europe, India, central and south Africa, and elsewhere. On arid soils.

Cultivation Wild. Cultivated as an ornamental or hedge plant in tropical countries; propagate from seed or suckers.

Constituents (leaf) acrid volatile oil; agave gum; phloionolic acid; oxalic acid and oxalates; saponoside; cutin; hecogenin, a sapogenin; a sugar, agavose.

Uses (fresh or dried leaf, juice, root, gum) Purgative; emmenagogue; diuretic; insecticide; counter-irritant.

Wide folk-medical use in tropical countries, particularly for external application to burns and contusions.

The juice is fermented to yield the Mexican alcoholic drink, pulque.

Powdered leaf employed as snuff; root used in washing clothes.

Used for fencing in tropical countries.

In veterinary medicine it is only used as a purgative.

Agrimonia eupatoria L ROSACEAE
Agrimony Church Steeples/Sticklewort

The specific name of this herb refers to Mithradates Eupator, ancient king of Persia, who was renowned as a herbalist. 'Agrimony' is a corruption of the Greek word *argemon*, a white speck on the cornea of the eye. This herb was once famous for the healing of wounds, and it was an ingredient of *eau de arquebusade*, used to treat wounds, from the fifteenth-century word for musket or arquebus. Still used in European folk medicine.

Description Perennial herb; erect downy, reddish stems, 30–60 cm high; compound pinnate leaves, up to 20 cm long. Flowers (summer-autumn) yellow, 5–8 mm wide and numerous.

Distribution Throughout Asia, Europe, North America; common on roadsides, waste-ground, hedgebanks.

Cultivation Wild, but easily propagated by root division in autumn. Tolerates varying conditions.

Constituents Tannin; volatile oil; resin. The combination is anti-inflammatory, antibiotic, astringent.

Uses (dried flowering plant) Mild astringent; possibly diuretic. Used for acute sore throats, chronic catarrh, children's diarrhoea, cystitis, and externally as a lotion for wounds. The whole plant yields a yellow dye.

Agropyron repens (L) Beauv. GRAMINEAE
Couch Grass Twitch Grass/Witch Grass

A well-known and troublesome weed to gardeners, Couch Grass has played a long and important role as a medicinal herb, and was promoted by Dioscorides and Pliny. European country people still drink it as a tisane and it is one of the plants eaten by sick dogs to induce vomiting.

Description Perennial grass; long jointed, branching, yellowish rhizome 1–3 mm diameter; erect glabrous stems; bright greenish-grey leaves up to 15 mm wide; small purplish flowers in spikes appearing mid-summer to early autumn.

Distribution Widely distributed native of Europe; naturalized in United States and troublesome in eastern states. Northern Asia, Australia and S. America. Weed of arable and wasteland.

Cultivation Wild plant.

Constituents Triticin (a carbohydrate which resembles inulin); sugar; inositol; salts of potassium; mucilage; acid malates; a volatile oil with antibiotic properties.

Uses (dried rhizome) Diuretic; urinary antiseptic. Useful in cystitis. Underground parts once used as cattle food.

Ailanthus altissima (Mill.) Seingle
SIMAROUBACEAE
Tree-of-Heaven Copal Tree/Varnish Tree

Introduced to England in 1751 from Nanking in China, and then in 1800 to the United States where it rapidly became a popular ornamental. The medicinal value of the bark was discovered in France in 1859. *Ailanthus* is from the Indonesian for tree of heaven, a name first given to another species. The alternative common names 'copal' and 'varnish' tree are misnomers, as the tree does not provide a varnish (or copal) material.

Description Rapidly growing deciduous tree reaching 10–20 m; leaves 30 cm–1 m long, subdivided into 11–14 oblong, lanceolate or ovate, gland-bearing leaflets 7.5–11.5 cm long. Flowers small, greenish in terminal panicles 10–20 cm long followed by reddish-brown indehiscent winged fruit called samara.

Distribution Chinese native. Naturalized in eastern North America.

Cultivation Wild. Introduced horticulturally to urban areas as a shade-tree due to its rapid growth, and resistance to pollution and disease. Easily grown from seed.

Constituents Fixed oil; volatile oil; gum; oleo-

resin; sugars; oxalic acid; possibly alkaloids and glycosides.

Uses (fresh or dried root and stem bark) Emetic; cathartic; antihelmintic; astringent. Formerly used in the treatment of dysentery and diarrhoea, asthma, epilepsy, palpitations and as a douche in gonorrhoea and leucorrhoea.

The remedy is unpleasant causing nausea, vomiting and debility, and is therefore no longer employed.

Ajuga reptans L LABIATAE
Bugle Common or Creeping Bugle/Bugle Weed

One of the common names of Bugle is the Carpenter's Herb, which reflects its original importance as a plant used to stop bleeding. Known to apothecaries as 'bugula' the herb is rarely used today, but it possesses other properties which as yet have not been fully researched.

Description Perennial with leafy stolons or runners; basal spatulate leaves form rosette; stem square, hairy on two sides and bearing 6–12 small blue flowers in early to late summer. Occasionally white or pink flowered mutants.

Distribution European native; introduced elsewhere. Common on damp ground in loamy soil, rich in nutrients. Mixed woodland, meadows.

Cultivation Wild plant; horticultural varieties *purpurea* and *variegata*.

Constituents Tannins; unknown digitalis-like substances.

Uses (dried whole herb) Astringent; bitter; aromatic. Formerly used to stop haemorrhages; for coughs, and ulcers. Thought to possess heart tonic qualities.

Alchemilla alpina L ROSACEAE
Alpine Lady's Mantle
The historical associations of Alpine Lady's Mantle are similar to those of *Alchemilla vulgaris*. Traditionally the alpine species was

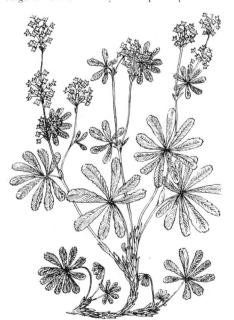

considered more effective although this has not been proven.

Description Perennial herb 10–12 cm high; leaves 3–7 cm in diameter divided into 5–7 leaflets white and silky beneath, glabrous above; small yellow-green flowers in clusters on branched, erect, thin stems. Flowering from mid-summer until early autumn.

Distribution Mountain ranges of Europe and mountain pastures of northern Europe.

Cultivation Wild plant.

Constituents Similar to *Alchemilla vulgaris* (Lady's Mantle).

Uses (dried leaves) As for Lady's Mantle but considered more effective.

Alchemilla vulgaris agg. ROSACEAE
Lady's Mantle Lion's Foot
This is an example of a herb which acquired a

reputation far greater than its therapeutic action would have suggested. Although unknown by ancient classical writers it became an important northern European magical plant on the discovery that overnight dew collected in the funnel-shaped folds of its partly closed nine-lobed leaves. To alchemically minded sixteenth century scientists dew was strongly magical, and so in turn was Lady's Mantle. Hieronymus Bock emphasized this by ascribing the name *Alchemilla* or the 'little magical one' to the herb.

Description Perennial herb, 10–50 cm high, branched stems bearing few round or reniform leaves 3–8 cm in diameter, with 7–11 lobes; flowers not prominent, 3–5 mm in diameter, greenish-yellow, in terminal panicles; upper flowers small and without petals. Appearing early spring to mid-autumn. (At least 11 closely related species are aggregated under the name *Alchemilla vulgaris*).

Distribution Northern Europe and mountainous areas of central and southern Europe. Prefers deep loamy moist soil in meadows, pastures, open grassy woodland, paths. Calcifugous.

Cultivation Wild plant.

Constituents Tannins. Unknown anti-inflammatory substances. Action anti-diarrhoeal.

Uses (dried leaves, rarely dried flowering

plant) Astringent and styptic. Prolonged use relieves discomfort of menopause and excessive menstruation.

Used in veterinary medicine for diarrhoea.

Alkanna tinctoria Tausch. BORAGINACEAE
Alkanet Dyer's Bugloss/Spanish Bugloss
Although several colouring plants are now called Alkanets, *Alkanna tinctoria* probably was the first to be used. Its name is derived from the Spanish *alcanna* which came from the Arabic *al-henna*, the well-known Henna dye. Alkanet means the 'little alcanna'. It was exported

from Spain, Germany and France for centuries as a dye for pharmaceutical and cosmetic use. It was also used by victuallers. It is now often replaced by the Evergreen Alkanet, *Pentaglottis sempervirens*, and the Common Alkanet, *Anchusa officinalis*.

Description Thick root up to 10 cm long with purplish root bark, bearing numerous stalks reaching 30 cm high; leaves are long and narrow alternate, somewhat hairy, many clustering around root crown. Attractive funnel-shaped, purple-blue, sometimes white or yellow, flowers; appearing late summer to early autumn.

Distribution Central and southern Europe. At roadsides, dry sandy soil. Calcifugous.

Cultivation Wild plant.

Constituents Possibly an alkaloid poisonous to mammals.

Uses (root, root bark) Not used medicinally. Used variously as a colouring agent. A red colour is released in oils and waxes but not in water.

Alliaria petiolata (Bieb.) Cavara & Grande
CRUCIFERAE
Garlic Mustard Hedge Garlic/Jack-by-the-hedge
A common European herb which has never

been of much importance medically. Also known as *A. officinalis* Bieb., the generic name is derived from *allium* or garlic after the smell of the crushed plant.

Description Garlic-smelling biennial or perennial reaching 30–100 cm; stem erect, simple. Leaves thin, pale green, petiolate, coarsely crenate, cordate above, reniform beneath. Flowers small white, 6 mm diameter, in a false umbel; appearing mid-spring to mid-summer.

Distribution European native. In open wasteland, moist woodland, on well-drained nutrient-rich soil.

Cultivation Wild plant.

Constituents Essential oil; a heteroside, sinigrine, which in water yields the aglycone, allyl isothiocyanate.

Uses (fresh, or dried flowering plant occasionally) Antiseptic; vulnerary; stimulant; rubefacient; expectorant; diuretic.

A dilute poultice, applied to ulcers and cuts or abrasions, cleans and aids healing; undiluted, it is of use externally to relieve pain from neuralgia, and rheumatism. Leaf may be used in small quantities as a salad herb, boiled, or in sauces. The crushed seed can be taken as a condiment.

Allium cepa L LILIACEAE
Onion

The Onion has been in cultivation for so long that its country of origin is uncertain and it is now rarely, if ever, found wild.

The plant is recorded in the works of the Chaldeans, Egyptians and Greeks, and as early as A.D. 79 Pliny described in detail its cultivation and the varieties to be used.

Columella in A.D. 42 introduced the word *unionem* from which the common name is derived. Modern classification groups the

Shallot, formerly *A. ascalonicum* L, with this species and numerous cultivars of *A. cepa* now exist, including some bred to crop within a limited range of day-length and temperatures. The unusual top Onions, (Egyptian or Tree Onions) were recorded by Dalechamp in 1587, and are usually grown as herb garden novelties.

Description Variable biennial or perennial to 120 cm, characteristically with 4–6 aromatic, cylindrical, hollow leaves and hollow scape. Flowers sometimes absent or replaced by bulbils. When present they are greenishwhite, small, numerous, in rounded umbels, appearing late summer.

Distribution Probably native to central Asia or south-west India. Now world-wide.

Cultivation Cultivated plant, or wild very rarely. Numerous cultivars exist which are now subdivided according to major characteristics into 3 groups: the Cepa group, the Proliferum group, the Aggregatum group. The first group contains the common culinary Onion and its members have single bulbs and are usually propagated from seed sown in spring or autumn or from sets sown in summer. The second group contains the Tree Onion and its members produce swollen bulbils in the inflorescence, and are propagated from these bulbils in late spring or late autumn, or by division every 3 years. The last group contains the Shallot, usually sterile but producing a crop of bulbs at the base and grown from these in early spring or late autumn. All onions prefer a very rich, deep soil.

Constituents Similar to those of garlic; also containing glucokinins; pectin; flavonoid glycosides; vitamins A, B_1, B_2, B_5, C, E; nicotinamide.

Uses (fresh bulb, fresh juice) Antibiotic; diuretic; expectorant; hypotensive; stomachic; antispasmodic; hypoglycaemic.

Useful in the treatment of coughs, colds, bronchitis, laryngitis and gastro-enteritis. Reduces the blood pressure and the blood-sugar level.

Used externally as a local stimulant, on cuts, to treat acne, and to promote hair growth.

An important vegetable and flavouring.

Allium sativum L LILIACEAE
Garlic

Garlic, a member of the onion family, is one of the most common flavourings and is used daily in cooking in most of the warm climates of the world. The flavour of the cloves develops best in sunny countries, and may be rank when grown in northern Europe.

It has been cultivated in the East for centuries and was widely employed medicinally by the Egyptians and Romans. The slaves that constructed the pyramid of Cheops were given garlic cloves daily to sustain their strength as were Roman soldiers. The common name is derived from the Anglo-Saxon *leac* meaning a pot-herb and *gar*, a lance, after the shape of the stem.

Description Perennial or biennial; sub-globular bulbs consisting of 8–20 cloves (partial bulbs) surrounded by silky pink-white skin. Several flat, erect, long pointed leaves 1–2.5 cm wide, to 15 cm long arising from base or crown. Unbranched stem (spathe) 7.5–10 cm long, pointed, bearing apical, small, dense umbels of rose-white or greenish flowers, often displaced by sterile pinkish bulbils 4 mm long.

Distribution Asian native; introduced in all warm climates. Prefers rich, light, well-drained soils.

Cultivation This plant has been grown from the Mediterranean to Central Asia for centuries. Several varieties exist including small cloved and giant forms, and white, pink, or mauve skinned forms. Flavour varies from sweet to nutty, mild to strong. Plant individual cloves in spring or preferably autumn in rich, dry soil, in a sunny position, 15 cm apart and 4 cm deep.

Constituents Essential oil, comprising mainly allyl disulphide and allyl propyl disulphide; vitamins A, B_1, B_2, C; antibacterial substances comprising allicin, allicetoin I and II; also an enzyme alliinase.

Uses (fresh bulb) Antibacterial; hypotensive; expectorant; weak anthelmintic; weak fungicide. Employed in the treatment of hypertension and arteriosclerosis; as a carminative and an expectorant in bronchial catarrh. Provides protection against the common cold, amoeboid

dysentery, typhoid and other infectious diseases. Garlic also increases the flow of bile and the fresh juice was once used as an inhalation in the treatment of pulmonary tuberculosis. Wide culinary use; both fresh and cooked, when the flavour varies. Employed in butters, vinegars and salt. Parsley reduces the aroma on the breath.

Contra-indications May be slightly irritant to the skin.

Allium schoenoprasum L LILIACEAE
Chives

Chives is the only member of the onion group found wild in both Europe and North America, and although used for centuries was not cultivated until the Middle Ages. It cannot be dried with any success but may be quick-frozen and stored.

Description Perennial in clumps; small bulbs produce grass-like cylindrical hollow dark green leaves, 20–30 cm long, 2–3 mm diameter, bearing in the summer an inflorescence of pink or purple flowers in a compact spherical capitulum.

Distribution Native to cool parts of Europe; introduced and naturalized in North America. Tolerates a wide range of conditions from dry, rocky places to stream banks, damp grassland and wood edges.

Cultivation Wild but cultivated commercially

and horticulturally in northern Europe and America. Variable in form depending on the environment. A large leaved type exists. Chinese chives (*A. tuberosum*) is larger, coarser-flavoured and has flat solid leaves. Propagate by sowing seed in mid-spring, or by division of clumps in spring or autumn. An excellent decorative edging plant for herb gardens.

Constituents Very similar to garlic (*Allium sativum*).

Uses (fresh or quick-frozen leaf) Used only for culinary purposes, chopped in sauces, soups, salads and as a garnish.

Alnus glutinosa (L) Gaertn BETULACEAE
Alder English or Common Alder/Owler

The common name derives from an old Germanic word meaning reddish-yellow, since the trunks change from white to reddish-yellow after felling. A supposed colour simi-

larity with blood led to the tradition that felling Alders was unlucky. The tree is an inhabitant of wet environments and coincidentally its main use was as a support under bridges or buildings. Venice is largely constructed on Alder posts.

Description Medium sized tree or large shrub, reaching 25 m; leaves stalked, obovate, 5–10 cm long, downy veins underneath, sticky when unfolding; small flowers appear before leaves in early spring; female catkins referred to as 'berries' almost spherical, formed in autumn.

Distribution North Africa, Europe, parts of Asia. Introduced and locally naturalized elsewhere. Prefers moist, swampy sites beside streams.

Cultivation Wild plant.

Constituents Tannins.

Uses (Bark, leaves) Tonic, astringent. Bark decoctions once used as gargle and for external inflammations. Formally used in bitters.

Used as a wool dye, the bark produces reds and blacks, the young shoots yellow, fresh wood pink and the catkins green.

Once extensively used by tanners.

Aloe vera L *A. perryi* Baker *A. ferox* Miller
LILIACEAE
Aloes Curaçao/Socotrine/Cape

One of the most important crude drugs of history, *Aloe vera* is still extensively used in modern medicine. Known to the Greeks at least as early as the fourth century B.C., a legend claims that Aristotle requested Alexander the Great to conquer the inhabitants of Socotra – the island which produced Aloes – and install Greeks. In the tenth century, however, Moslem travellers reported that Socotra was still the only place cultivating Aloes. Curaçao or Barbados Aloes were offered by London druggists in 1693, and Cape Aloes were exported first in 1780.

Description Several species of succulent liliaceous plants forming clusters of very fleshy leaf blades, usually prickly at the margin and tip; stemless or producing woody branching stems; from 45 cm–15 m tall, bearing erect spikes of yellow, orange or red flowers. Appears most of the year.

Distribution Natives of dry, sunny areas of south and east Africa; naturalized in north Africa, Spain, Indonesia and the Caribbean islands.

Cultivation Wild plant; cultivated commercially in Africa and the Caribbean. Grown as a house plant.

Constituents Barbaloin and isobarbaloin, forming 'crystalline' aloin; 'amorphous' aloin; aloe-emodin; resin; volatile oil. Action on large intestine largely due to purgative effect of aloins and aloe-emodin.

Uses (the brownish crystalline solid, resulting from drying the liquid which exudes from cut leaf blades) Purgative. Used normally in combination with carminatives to prevent griping. Fresh juice used to heal burns.

Contra-indications Excessive use induces haemorrhoids.

Aloysia triphylla Britt. VERBENACEAE
Lemon Verbena

This South American plant was introduced to Europe by the Spaniards and was once used to give a lemon scent to fingerbowls at banquets. The former botanical name *Lippia citriodora* (HBK) and the common name reflect the strong lemon scent of the plant's leaves. Lemon Verbena's modern generic name, *Aloysia* comes from the name Louisa, after Maria Louisa, wife of King Charles IV of Spain. Although half-hardy this herb makes a good indoor plant, as well as providing attractive and aromatic stems and foliage for flower arrangement.

Description Aromatic shrub to 3 m, but rarely more than 1.2–1.5 m in cooler northern temperate zones. Branches striate and scabrous, bearing whorls of 3–4 leaves which are entire, 5–7.5 cm long, short-petioled, glabrous, lanceolate and dotted on the underside with oil-bearing glands. Flowers white or pale lavender, small (6 mm long) in axillary spikes or terminal panicles.

Distribution Native to Chile and Argentina; widely distributed in tropical zones.

Cultivation Wild. Cultivated horticulturally and as a greenhouse plant in temperate zones. Half-hardy in cool temperate countries and requires frost and wind protection; plant against a south facing wall on light, well-drained soil; protect with straw and cut back at the end of the growing season.

Propagate from woody cuttings in early summer or from seed sown under glass in early spring.

Constituents Essential oil, comprising mainly citral.

Uses (fresh or dried leaf) Antispasmodic; stomachic; aromatic.

As a tea it is of benefit in the treatment of nausea, indigestion, flatulence, palpitations, vertigo.

Leaf may be used sparingly as a lemon flavouring in cakes, fruit dishes and sweet foodstuffs, or in drinks.

The dried leaf is employed in pot-pourris and scented sachets.

The oil is used in perfumery.

Contra-indications Prolonged use or large internal dosage may cause gastric irritation.

Alpinia officinarum Hance ʐɪɴɢɪʙᴇʀᴀᴄᴇᴀᴇ
Galangal East India Root/Galanga

This root was introduced into European medicine by the writings of the Arabic physicians Rhazes and Avicenna; it was first recorded by Ibn Khurdadbah in 869 who listed it with Musk, silk and Camphor as an article of trade from the Far East. It was commonly used in the Middle Ages as a culinary spice with Cloves, Nutmeg and Ginger. The plant from which the root came was not described until 1870, when it was named after Prosper Alpinus the sixteenth-century 'teacher of drugs' at Padua University.

Description Perennial rhizomatous herb of flag-like form; stems reaching 1.5 m, covered with long narrow lanceolate leaves; bearing racemes of orchid-shaped flowers, white and veined red; rhizome 3–9 cm long, 2 cm thick; pleasantly aromatic when dried.

Distribution South China, tropical south-east Asia, Iran.

Cultivation Wild; grown commercially.

Constituents Essential oil and resin, both stimulant. Also galangol; galangin; kaempferide.

Uses (dried rhizome) Carminative, stimulant. Similar to Ginger. Of use in flatulent dyspepsia. Once used for seasickness. Snuff for catarrh. Culinary spice. Vinegar and cordial manufacture; brewing. Popular in east European, Russian and Indian cuisine.

Althaea officinalis L ᴍᴀʟᴠᴀᴄᴇᴀᴇ
Marshmallow Sweet Weed/Schloss Tea/Althea

The name is well known as a confectionery; the original *pâte de guimauve* was a soothing paste containing the powdered root. The plant has a long medicinal and culinary history; the Romans considered it a delicious vegetable, and in the ninth century the Emperor Charlemagne promoted its cultivation in Europe. Today it is widely used both in folk and modern medicine.

Description Erect hardy perennial reaching 1–1.25 m high; stem and leaves hairy, latter with 3–5 lobes or undivided and short petioles; 5-petalled white or pink flowers, 3–4 cm in diameter, clustered in leaf axils, appear in late summer until early autumn.

Distribution Moist places throughout Europe from Norway to Spain; temperate parts of western and northern Asia; Asia Minor, Australia, and eastern North America. Prefers saline areas, salt marshes and damp land near to sea or estuaries. Often wild.

Cultivation Wild and commercially cultivated. Propagation by seed sown spring or summer, or division of root-stocks in spring or autumn. Succeeds on light soil if compost introduced below root level to keep cool.

Constituents 30% mucilage comprising glucosan and xylan; responsible for demulcent action. Also sucrose; lecithin; phytosterol; asparagin.

Uses (dried root, 2 years old; leaves, flowers) Demulcent; emollient. Relieves inflammations of mouth and pharynx, and gastritis and gastric ulcers. Externally as poultice for leg ulcers. Powdered root used to bind active ingredients in pill manufacture. Roots boiled and then fried with butter, or young tops eaten in spring salad.

Althaea rosea (L) Cav. ᴍᴀʟᴠᴀᴄᴇᴀᴇ
Hollyhock Common or Garden Hollyhock

Now a well-known and widely distributed decorative garden plant it first reached Europe from China in the sixteenth century, after which it was used both as a medicinal herb and a pot-herb. Turner gave it the name Holyoke in 1548 indicating the blessed mallow, and Lyte in 1578 called it the 'beyondsea rose'.

Description Tall biennial producing in second year spire-like, hairy, flowering stem up to 3 m tall; large, rough, long-stalked 5–7 lobed leaves, in the axils of which are formed flowers, up to 10 cm in diameter on short peduncles. Colour from pale pink or yellow to purple-black. Flowering mid-summer to late autumn.

Distribution Native of China. Now widespread.

Cultivation One of the oldest cultivated plants;

easily raised from seed. Tolerates most soils.
Constituents Mucilage; volatile oil; tannin and anthocyanin pigment.
Uses (dried double purple flowers) Anti-inflammatory, emollient, mildly purgative. Used as tisane for chest complaints or as a mouthwash. Colours wine.

Amaranthus hypochondriacus L AMARANTHACEAE
Amaranth Love-lies-bleeding/Red Cockscomb
This herb is one of a number of Amaranthus species or varieties which have been taken into horticultural cultivation. Most were native to tropical countries where they are predominantly coarse looking plants usually used as pot-herbs. The name derives from the Greek *amaranton* meaning 'not fading' since the crimson flowers do not fade with the death of the plant, and thus the plant came to symbolize immortality. The bright red colour led to the

belief that the plant stopped all kinds of bleeding – part of the seventeenth-century school of thought known as the Doctrine of Signatures.
Description Tall glabrous annual to 2 m; erect, upper parts branched; leaves dull green, spotted with purple, 3–15 cm long, 15 mm to 1.75 cm wide, on thin petioles; the small greenish or usually crimson flowers, borne on erect terminal clusters, to 20 cm long, appear in late summer.
Distribution Native of tropics and American central states. Prefers waste-grounds, cultivated fields.
Cultivation Wild or grown horticulturally from seed sown in spring.
Constituents Mucilage; sugars.
Uses (dried flowering herb) Astringent. Of use in diarrhoea. Externally as wash for ulcers; as gargle for ulcerated mouth; to reduce tissue swelling, and also as douche for leucorrhoea. Young leaves of Amaranthus species widely used as a vegetable.
The related *A. retroflexus* (L) once used as an alternative to soap, due to high saponin content. It was also used as a vegetable; seeds made into flour.

Anacardium occidentale L ANACARDIACEAE
Cashew Nut
Although only the nut or kernel is widely known this tropical tree provides a wide variety of uses and products, and is of some importance in native medicine in Africa and the Americas.
Description Spreading attractive evergreen tree reaching 12 m, bearing alternate oval leaves 10–20 cm long, 3–10 cm wide, and scented panicles 20 cm long of yellow-pink flowers each 1 cm across. Flowers followed by fleshy edible receptacle (cashew-apple) partly enclosing kidney shaped nut.
Distribution Native to tropical American zones; naturalized and cultivated in tropical countries.
Cultivation Commercially in groves and occurs infrequently in the wild.
Constituents Protein; niacin; magnesium; iron; anacardic acid; cardol.

Uses (nut, oil, tree bark, fruit) Nut or kernel nutritive, high protein content. Tree bark once used in certain malarial fevers and fresh shell juice removes warts and corns. Juice from fruit made into wine and spirit. Milky secretion from incised tree makes indelible marking ink. Non-drying lubricant oil from nut. Ammonium salts of resin form hair dye.
Contra-indications Oil from fresh shell strongly vesicant, causing skin blisters.

Anagallis arvensis L PRIMULACEAE
Scarlet Pimpernel Poor Man's Weatherglass
This is an interesting herb which merits modern research. It was held in high esteem from the time of the earliest Greeks until the nineteenth century and is now rarely used, even in folk medicine. Evidence suggests that it is of benefit in melancholia and diseases of the brain; its Latin name derives from the Greek 'to delight', a term given to the herb by Dioscorides; another common name is 'laughter bringer'. The flowers are sensitive, and close if rain threatens.
Description Annual herb; prostrate creeping

square stems up to 30 cm long, thinner branched ascending stems bearing opposite leaves, ovoid and spotted black on the underside; scarlet flowers, often with purple centre, single, long-stalked, appearing in leaf axil from early summer to early autumn. There are two varieties of *Anagallis arvensis*, one red and one blue.
Distribution Widely distributed in temperate zone, especially Europe. Found in loamy soil with high nutrient content; vegetable and cornfields; rare on wasteland.
Constituents Saponin. Active principles not fully understood.
Use (leaf, whole herb, fresh or dried). Diuretic, diaphoretic. Once used in epilepsy, hydrophobia, depression following liver disease, dropsy, and rheumatic conditions. Leaves once used in salads. Cosmetic herb as 'pimpernel water' for freckles.
Contra-indications POISONOUS; there is evidence the plant causes anaemia. Leaves can cause dermatitis.

Anemone alpina L RANUNCULACEAE
Alpine Anemone
Previously classified botanically as *Pulsatilla alpina* Schrank. and *Anemone acutipetala* Hort., this herb formerly enjoyed only local European folk-medical use, and is not mentioned in either classical or modern works.
Description Perennial on thick rhizome; stems reaching 10–40 cm, soft-hairy. Leaves large, long-petioled, ternate then 2–pinnate. Flowers with 6 sepals, solitary, 5–7.5 cm wide, white tinged with violet; appearing mid-spring to early summer.
Distribution Native to the mountains of Europe. Introduced elsewhere.
Cultivation Wild. The subspecies *sulphurea* (L) Hegi, which is characterized by yellow flowers, is found in alpine collections. Propagate by division or root cuttings in autumn or early spring; or from seed as soon as it is ripe.
Constituents Protoanemonine; anemonine.
Uses (whole, dried flowering plant) Irritant; alterative; anodyne.
Formerly used in the treatment of toothache

and rheumatic pain, but due to its toxicity it has fallen into disuse.

Contra-indications POISONOUS; not be taken internally.

Anemone hepatica L RANUNCULACEAE
Kidneywort American Liverwort

This delicate looking herb possesses individual flowers which last for little more than one week but which in that time have the ability to double in length. Its name comes from the Greek *heparatos* meaning liver; in folk medicine it is still used for treating the liver.

Description Small perennial; much branched root-stock; almost evergreen; produces on

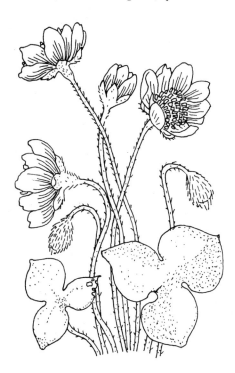

petioles reaching 30 cm kidney-shaped 3-lobed leaves, green above, reddish-purple beneath. Light blue flowers, 4 cm in diameter, born singly on hairy scapes reaching 40 cm; from mid-winter to early autumn.

Distribution North temperate zone; mainly in moist deciduous woodland, preferably calcareous, with loamy soil.

Cultivation Wild plant. Propagate by division soon after flowering; in sheltered position on ordinary soil with good drainage; or from seed gathered and sown in mid-spring. In shade. Seed dispersed by ants.

Constituents Mucilage; tannin; sugar. Action uncertain. Fresh leaf contains the poisonous protoanemonine.

Uses (dried leaves and flowers) Demulcent; pectoral; tonic. Tisane used for liver congestion, kidney, gall-bladder and digestive disorders. Of use as syrup for coughs or bronchitis. Distilled water once used for freckles.

Contra-indications POISONOUS in large doses.

Anemone pulsatilla L RANUNCULACEAE
Pasque Flower Windflower

Legend maintains that anemones only open when a wind is blowing, and the Greek word *anemos* means 'wind'. Certainly this very attractive hairy plant waves about in the slightest breeze, a fact reflected in its specific name *pulsatilla* meaning 'to beat'. Gerard called the herb Pasque Flower as it flowers at Easter. It is still respected in traditional medicine, and is grown widely as a decorative plant.

Description Erect, soft, hairy perennial herb 5–40 cm high, with bi- or tri-pinnate leaves appearing as rosette after solitary flower formed; flowers hairy, dark blue-violet, 6 petals, 3–5 cm long, from late spring to mid-summer.

Distribution Wild on dry, sunny, calcareous slopes throughout Europe. Introduced elsewhere. Prefers well-drained chalky soil, in dry, warm situations.

Cultivation Wild plant. Cultivated by division of rhizomes after flowering or seed sown in shallow tray in spring. Other horticultural varieties are *alba* and *rubra*.

Constituents Fresh plant contains glycoside, ranunculin. This is converted via protoanemonine to anemonine on drying. Action due to anemonine.

Uses (dried aerial parts) Sedative; analgesic; nervine; spasmolytic. Used for headaches, some skin eruptions, earache, painful condition of reproductive organs. Employed homeopathically for measles and also for menstrual pain.

Contra-indications POISONOUS when fresh. Dried herb should only be administered by medical personnel. Overdosage causes violent gastroenteritis and convulsions.

Anethum graveolens L UMBELLIFERAE
Dill Dill Weed/Dill Seed

Dill is mentioned in the Bible and has been in use as a medicinal herb from the earliest times; it is still a constituent of gripe water and is often included in children's medicines. The common name is derived from an old Indo-European word meaning 'to blossom'.

Description Aromatic annual; typically umbelliferous plant, to 1 m tall, with spindle-shaped root, bearing usually one stalk; leaves

feathery, leaflets linear; terminal umbels consisting of numerous yellow flowers in mid-summer.

Distribution Origin southern Europe or western Asia. Wild in cornfields of mediterranean countries. Now widespread garden herb. Tolerates most soils.

Cultivation From seed sown in spring; easily cultivated.

Constituents Oil of Dill comprising, d-carvone; d-limonene; some phellandrine.

Uses (dried ripe fruit, fresh or dried leaf). Carminative; stomachic; slightly stimulant. Excellent as Dill water for digestive problems in children, especially flatulence.

Pickled cucumbers, flavouring for soup, fish, sauces, cakes, pastries. Dill vinegar. Most important in Scandinavian and central European cuisine.

Perfumes soap.

Angelica archangelica L UMBELLIFERAE
Angelica European or Garden Angelica
Now best known as a decorative confectionery made from the candied green stems, Angelica is also an important ingredient of liqueurs and aperitifs. It does not appear to have been used until the fifteenth century, soon after which it acquired a reputation as a plant which gave protection against evil and the plague. The plant's north European origins and its Christianized names hints at its deep association with early Nordic magic.
Description Biennial or perennial; if latter lasting up to 4 years; from 1–2.5 m high, stem hollow, to 6 cm thick, bearing few triangular deeply dentate leaves to 90 cm long. Large spherical umbels of numerous greenish-white flowers, mid-summer to early autumn.
Distribution Native to northern Europe or Asia. Introduced and cultivated elsewhere. Common garden herb; prefers damp meadows, river banks, waste-grounds.
Cultivation Seed rapidly loses viability; sow as soon as ripe in mid-autumn in deep moist soil. Transplant following autumn to 1 m apart, or transplant offshoots from 2 year old plants to

60 cm apart.
Constituents Volatile oil and derivatives of coumarin which stimulate digestive secretions, control peristalsis and increase appetite. Also bitter principles; sugar; valeric and angelic acids.
Uses (dried rhizome and roots, seeds, fresh leaf and stems) Aromatic; stimulant; carminative. Stimulates appetite; of benefit in bronchitis, anorexia nervosa, bronchial catarrh.
Wide culinary and confectionery use. Important constituent of liqueurs such as Benedictine.
Contra-indications Large doses first stimulate and then paralyze the central nervous system.

Antennaria dioica (L) Gaertn. COMPOSITAE
Cat's Foot Life Everlasting/Cudweed
The downy leaves and woolly involucre led to this plant being known as Cotton Weed; its

botanical name Antennaria comes from the fact that the pappus resembles antennae. This species was not important even in folk medicine, but much use is made of it in dried flower arrangements. Various related species, however, have been used more than the species *dioica* – for example, an American relative, *Gnaphalium polycephalum* (*A. dioica* previously classified as *Gnaphalium dioicum*) was a favourite Indian remedy for mouth ulcers, and the Chinese herbalists use *G. multiceps* (Wall.) to treat coughs.
Description Stoloniferous, dioecious perennial, 5–20 cm high, on single unbranched erect or decumbent stem. Spatulate basal leaves in a rosette to 2.5 cm long, white and tomentose beneath, green and glabrous above. Linear-lanceolate stem leaves. Flowers 5 mm long in dense terminal involucre, which is woolly at base. White male flowers and pink female appear early summer to early autumn.
Distribution Native to central and western Europe, United States and the North Pacific Aleutian islands; to 2500 m altitude, on semi-dry pasture, light dry woodland and thickets; prefers poor, porous, sandy dry soils.
Cultivation Wild plant.
Constituents Tannin; essential oil; resin; a bitter principle. The combined action promotes the flow of bile.
Uses (dried flowering plant) Astringent; choleretic; weak diuretic.
Once used in mixtures for the treatment of bronchitis and bilious conditions. May be used in diarrhoea, and as a throat gargle.

Anthriscus cerefolium (L) Hoffm. UMBELLIFERAE
Chervil Garden Chervil
Although this is an important culinary herb in France it is not widely grown or used outside that country. It is however one of the best herbs for growing in boxes, and will supply fresh leaf throughout the winter if it is sown

regularly in a warm greenhouse.
Description Annual sweet-smelling herb reaching 70 cm high, with pale green delicate leaves, deeply segmented. Stem slightly hairy; flowers white, 2 mm in diameter, in flat umbels, produced mid-summer.
Distribution Native to Middle East, south Russia, the Caucasus. Cultivated in warm and temperate climates. Prefers light soil with degree of moisture.
Cultivation Easily cultivated from seed, lightly pressed into soil at permanent site, early to mid-spring or autumn. Rapid germination and soon runs to seed. May be sown in boxes for winter supply.
Constituents Volatile oil; stimulates the metabolism.
Uses (fresh leaf before flowering) Stomachic. Warm poultice applied to painful joints. Mainly used for culinary purposes; will complement most dishes.

Aphanes arvensis agg. ROSACEAE
Parsley Piert Breakstone Parsley
The common name is derived both from a superficial resemblance to Parsley and from the old French *perce-pierre* signifying a plant which grows through stony ground. The Flemish botanist De L'Obel suggested in 1570 that although the herb was not widely used by herbalists, it was commonly employed by the poor to 'break' stones in the kidney or bladder. Today it is one of the most highly respected plants used in the treatment of kidney stones.
Description Annual; thin branched stem up to 20 cm tall; leaves, 3–5 lobes, wedge shaped; insignificant flowers 1.5–2 mm in diameter borne in axillary clusters; appearing from late spring until late autumn.
Distribution Native British herb, common in parts of Europe on bare soil in dry places, cornfields, wasteland, walls, gravel pits. Calcifugous.

winter. Strong smelling.
Distribution Southern European native. Wild in marshy and salty soils in Africa, Europe, South and North America.
Cultivation Wild plant.
Constituents Volatile oils; apiol.
Uses (fresh or dried plant, seeds) Tonic; appetizer; carminative. Strong diuretic if fresh juice used. Once recommended in treatment of rheumatism, excess weight, loss of appetite. Decoction of seed beneficial in nervousness. Dried leaf may replace celery for soups, sauces, and stocks, although it has a stronger taste than Celery.

Apocynum cannabinum L APOCYNACEAE
Canadian Hemp Hemp Dogbane/Black Indian Hemp
This was one of many North American plants introduced to settlers by native Indians. No longer used in medicine.
Description Perennial to 2 m high, stems erect, branched only at top, bearing ovoid leaves

with hairy lower surface, to 7.5 cm long; flowers small, whitish-green in terminal clusters, followed by thin double pods 10–15 cm long. Flowers late summer. Root up to 2 m long.
Distribution North America, near streams, open ground, forest borders, in gravel or sandy soil.
Cultivation Wild plant.
Constituents Apocynamarin, a cynotoxin; symarin; apocynin and derivatives; phytosterols. Action of a heart stimulant, dilates renal arteries.
Uses (dried rhizome, roots, bark) Diuretic; powerful emetic; laxative. Used in folk medicine in North America to treat worms and fever. Powerful heart stimulant. The fibrous bark employed as substitute for hemp in manufacture of nets and twine.
Contra-indications POISONOUS; greatest caution needed in usage.

Cultivation Wild plant.
Constituents An astringent principle.
Uses (dried leaf and flowers) Diuretic; demulcent. Considered most effective when freshly collected and dried in the treatment of kidney stones, bladder stones or painful urination.

Apium graveolens L UMBELLIFERAE
Celery Wild Celery/Smallage
Until the seventeenth century all celery flavour was provided by this wild herb, which although somewhat bitter to present day palates, was a favourite of the Romans. The Celery we eat today was developed initially by Italian gardeners on the plain of the Po.
Description Biennial with bulbous fleshy root, producing branched angular stem 30 cm – 1 m high in second year. Leaves opposite, 10–15 cm long, dark green, dentate with fan-shaped leaflets; small grey-white flowers in sparse compound umbels from late summer to early

Aquilegia vulgaris L RANUNCULACEAE
Columbine European Crowfoot
Columbine is from the Latin *columba* meaning dove. In the Middle Ages it was referred to as aquilinae and ackeley after the Latin *aquila* meaning eagle – both terms referring to the

flower shape.
The herb's antiscorbutic effect was recorded in the Württemberg Pharmacopoeia of 1741, but in the nineteenth century *A. vulgaris* fell from official use.
Description Stout perennial with pubescent stems branched at the top; 60–80 cm tall. Basal leaves long-petioled, biternate, upper leaves sessile. Leaflets 3-lobed, crenate. Flowers few to many, nodding on long peduncles, violet-blue or white, 5 cm diameter; appearing early summer.
Distribution Native to Europe. Naturalized in eastern North America, and introduced elsewhere. In mixed woodland, mountain forest on rich calcareous soils to 2000 m altitude.
Cultivation Wild. Frequently grown as a garden ornamental, especially the double-flowered cultivars *Alba Plena* and *Flore Pleno*. Propagate by seed or by division in spring.
Constituents Cyanogenic glycoside; vitamin C; lipid; an uncharacterized alkaloid.
Uses (Root, flowers and leaves) Antiseptic; astringent; weakly sedative.
No longer employed internally; once used in homeopathy to treat nervous conditions. Only the root may be used, externally, for the treatment of ulcers.
Contra-indications POISONOUS. Seeds may be fatal to children. Most parts have a similarly poisonous effect as Monkshood (*Aconitum napellus* L). Medical use only.

Arachis hypogaea L LEGUMINOSAE
Peanut Ground-nut
Although the Peanut is now one of the best known and universally grown edible nuts, it was not until 1840 that Jaubert, a French colonist of Cape Verde, suggested its importation into Marseilles as an oil seed. The first to mention the plant was Fernandez de Oviedo y Valdes who lived in Haiti from 1513 to 1525

and reported that Indians widely cultivated the *mani* – a name for *Arachis* still used in South America and Cuba.

Description Annual herbaceous legume, 25–50 cm tall; stems slightly hairy; leaves consist of 2 pairs of leaflets, oval, 5 cm long. Yellow

flowers possess long calyx tube; after flowering the stem bearing the ovary elongates, bends towards the ground and forces the young pod beneath the soil. Pod oblong, 2.5 cm long, containing 1–4 irregularly ovoid seeds.

Distribution South American native. Widely cultivated, especially Africa, India, China, and America.

Cultivation Unknown in the wild state; grown on a large scale commercially and horticulturally in tropical and subtropical countries.

Constituents Peanut or arachide oil, consisting of the glycerides of 4 fatty acids.

Uses (seed, oil expressed from seeds) Nutritive: the seed is an important foodstuff. Used as a substitute for olive oil. Employed in the manufacture of soap.

Arbutus unedo L ERICACEAE
Strawberry Tree Cane Apples
Known to Dioscorides and early Arabian physicians, but never widely employed; it deserves modern investigation, however.
Arbutus is an ancient name, while *unedo* is from the Latin phrase *unum edo* or I eat only one, after the supposed unpleasantness of the fruit.

Description Erect evergreen shrub or tree 3–10 m tall. Young bark reddish. Leaves alternate, petiolate, serrate, oblong to obovate, shiny above, 5–10 cm long. Flowers creamy-white or pinkish, urceolate, in nodding panicles 5 cm long, appearing late autumn to mid-winter, followed by scarlet, warty berry.

Distribution Native to south Europe, eastern France and Ireland. Introduced elsewhere. In damp situations often in woodland.

Cultivation Wild, locally abundant. Grown horticulturally in warm regions on well-drained soils; requires wind protection. Propagate by seeds and cuttings of half-ripened wood in autumn under glass; also by layering.

Constituents Tannins; arbutoside; ethyl gallate,

the latter possessing strong antibiotic activity against the Mycobacterium bacteria.

Uses (bark, root, leaves, fruit) Antiseptic; anti-inflammatory; astringent; diuretic.

May be used to treat diarrhoea and biliousness, and possibly of use in arteriosclerosis. A decoction provides an excellent antiseptic wash, gargle or poultice. Formerly employed in certain kidney and liver complaints. The flower has weak diaphoretic properties.

Fruit can be used with discretion in alcoholic drinks or preserves such as marmalade. The bark was once used in leather tanning. The wood provides good quality charcoal, and is suitable for turning and marquetry.

Arctium lappa L COMPOSITAE
Greater Burdock Beggar's Buttons/Lappa
A herb with dock-shaped leaves, and fruiting heads covered with hooked spines or burrs, from which characteristics the name is derived. It also resembles Rhubarb, and several com-

mon names such as Gypsy's Rhubarb, Pig's Rhubarb and Snake's Rhubarb refer to this. Still widely employed in folk medicine for skin problems, and cultivated commercially in Japan for use as a vegetable.

Description Biennial or short-lived perennial to 2 m; 5 cm thick hairy stems. Vertical roots 1 m long. Large leaves, ovate and petiolate with undulate margins. Small tubular flowers red to purple, consisting of disc florets only, in spherical capitula of 3–5 cm diameter. Fruit surrounded by hooked bracts (burr). Appearing late summer to mid-autumn.

Distribution European native. North America. Prefers weedy sites and roadsides, on loamy, nitrogen-rich soil.

Cultivation Wild plant; cultivated commercially from seed in Japan.

Constituents Inulin; bitter principle; volatile oil; resin; several antibiotic substances.

Uses (root, fresh or dried – from first year plants; fruits, rarely the leaves) Diuretic. Increases resistance to infection. Of use in various skin diseases, especially psoriasis and eczema.

Stalks, before flowering, may be eaten as salad or boiled as vegetable.

Stalks are candied in the same way as angelica. Chopped root cooked and eaten.

Arctostaphylos uva-ursi (L) Spreng.
ERICACEAE
Bearberry Uva-ursi/Mountain box
This herb's common name comes from the Greek *arkton staphyle* signifying 'bear's grapes'. It was used in the thirteenth century by the Welsh physicians of Myddvai, described in detail by Clusius in 1601, and officially recognized to be of medical importance in 1763 by several German physicians working in Berlin. Although use of the herb declined, recent research has shown that it possesses effective antiseptic properties.

Description Trailing or creeping evergreen shrub; to 15 cm high, forming mats of dark green, leathery, ovoid leaves 1–2 cm long. Small flowers, white or pink in terminal clusters of 3–12, followed by red fruit of 5 mm diameter. Appearing early spring to mid-summer.

Distribution Cool regions of northern hemisphere. In coniferous woodland, moors, alpine mats, on porous acid humus-rich soils.
Cultivation Wild plant.
Constituents Arbutin and methylarbutin, which produce antiseptic substances related to phenol. Also flavonoids; tannins; gallic and egallic acids.
Uses (dried leaves) Diuretic; antiseptic. Specifically used in kidney and bladder infections. Once used for bronchitis and urinary incontinence.
Used for leather tanning. Ash coloured dye. Grouse feed.
Added to smoking mixtures.
Contra-indications Prolonged use results in constipation.

Areca catechu L ARECACEAE
Areca Nut Betel Nut

Areca is also known as Betel Nut since it is a constituent of the 'betel' chewing mixture which is a widespread habit in the East. The mixture consists of Areca, a little lime and leaves of the Betel plant (*Piper betle*). As early as 140 B.C. Chinese conquerors of the Malayan archipelago returned with samples of the Areca palm and nuts, which became known as pin-lang after the Malay word, *pinang*, for them. Asians chew small pieces of the nut to sweeten the breath, strengthen gums and improve digestion.
Description Elegant palm; straight smooth trunk 12–30 m high, 50 cm circumference. Numerous feathery leaflets 30–60 cm long, upper confluent and glabrous. Flowers on branching spadix, male above and numerous; female usually solitary and below. Fruit ovoid 5 cm long, orange or scarlet, in bunches of up to 100.
Distribution Maritime Malaysian native; cultivated in India, Ceylon, Malaya, Burma, East Africa. Introduced into American tropics as an ornamental. Prefers coastal sites.
Cultivation Collected from wild, and cultivated in coastal areas.
Constituents Tannin; gallic acid; oil; gum; four

alkaloids, one of which resembles pilocarpine; also areca red
Uses (fruit – ripe or unripe) Astringent; stimulant; taenicide. Once used in human urinary tract disorders, and for the expulsion of tapeworms. Use now restricted to veterinary medicine.
Dentifrice, using the charcoal made from the nut. Chewed as a masticatory in combination with a little lime and a *Piper Betle* leaf. Stains lips and teeth red.
Contra-indications Toxic in large doses; medical use restricted to veterinary.

Aristolochia clematitis L ARISTOLOCHIACEAE
Birthwort Birchwort

The fact that the herb was at one time considered important in childbirth is emphasized by its common and Latin names. *Aristolochia* is derived from the Greek *aristos* meaning best and *locheia* meaning childbirth. William Turner, the father of English botany, gave the herb its common name in the sixteenth century. The herb has not been subjected to modern investigation and is rarely employed.
Description Perennial on long rhizome; stem erect or slightly twining to 50 cm high; heart-shaped dark green leaves with long petioles. Flowers axillary, 3 cm long, yellowish-green appearing from early summer to mid-autumn.
Distribution Europe and temperate North America, Japan. In thickets, vineyards, weedy edges of fields, in warmer situations on calcareous soil.
Cultivation Wild plant.
Constituents Aristolochine, which is similar to colchicine.
Uses (dried root-stock, entire fresh flowering plant) Diaphoretic; emmenagogue; oxytocic; stimulant. Once used in rheumatism and gout. Juice from stems once used to induce childbirth.

Aristolochia serpentaria L ARISTOLOCHIACEAE
Virginia Snakeroot Birthwort/Serpentary

The earliest belief concerning this herb was that it would give protection from poisoning. Specimens from Virginia were growing in London in 1632, and were described by

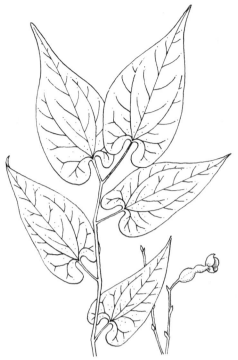

Thomas Johnson. Serpentary was introduced into European medical usage via the London Pharmacopoeia of 1650, and as late as 1741 Geoffroy was praising its effectiveness as a remedy for rattlesnake and rabid dog bites. A century after this it was only being used as a diaphoretic, and then often in combination with Cinchona bark. It is now seldom used even in folk medicine.
Description Perennial herb 25–40 cm high, with erect, slightly branched stems bearing heart-shaped pointed leaves 7.5 cm long; roots fibrous. Dull purple to brown flowers arising singly on short stalk coming from the stem base.
Distribution East Central and southern United States; in shady woods.
Cultivation Wild plant.
Constituents Essential oil; resin; aristolochine.
Uses (dried root-stock) Stimulating tonic; diaphoretic; anodyne; nervine; once used for treating snake bites. Used in early stages of infectious diseases. Small doses stimulate appetite.
Contra-indications Large doses act as irritant, and cause vomiting and vertigo. Respiratory paralysis may also occur.

Armeria maritima (Mill.) Willd.
PLUMBAGINACEAE
Thrift Sea Pink

Sea Pink now belongs to the genus Armeria which consists of at least 100 closely related species and many more subspecies and varieties which are often exceedingly difficult to differentiate. This genus was formerly called *Statice* (*A. maritima* was known as *Statice armeria* L) and is closely related to the Sea Lavender genus – also once called *Statice* but now known as *Limonium*. The American Sea Lavender (*Limonium vulgare* Mill.) has similar antiseptic properties, but like Thrift it is now very rarely used for medicinal purposes.

Thrift has most widely been used as an edging

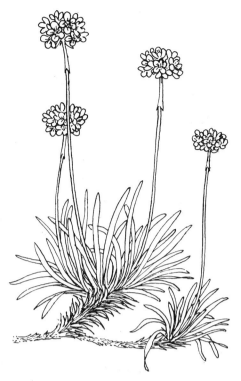

plant in formal gardens, and from the sixteenth to the eighteenth centuries few species were as popular for this purpose.

Description Grass-like perennial on branched woody root-stock forming basal rosette of narrow (3 mm) linear, 1-nerved (occasionally 3-nerved), acute or obtuse, fleshy and glandular leaves, 2–15 cm long, ciliate at the edges. Flowers stalked, rose-pink (or occasionally white), corolla 8 mm diameter, in dense globular heads, 1.5–3 cm diameter, on leafless, downy scape 20–55 cm tall. Appearing mid-spring to mid-autumn. Variable in form.

Distribution Native to Europe, Asia and North America; on dry sandy somewhat acidic soils in sandy turf, coastal salt-marshes, cliffs and mountain pastures to 1400 m altitude.

Cultivation Wild; frequently found growing in dense evergreen masses. Propagate from seed sown in spring on light, dry, well-drained soil, in full sun or partial shade; or by division of clumps, replanting every 2 years, 25 cm apart.

Constituents A napthaquinone, plumbagone; mineral salts comprising mainly iodine, bromine, and fluorine; mucilage. Antibiotic action due to plumbagone.

Uses (dried flowering plant) Antibiotic; anti-obesic. Once used in the treatment of obesity, certain nervous disorders, and urinary infections. Cannot be employed as an antiseptic poultice as it may cause dermatitis or local irritation. Rarely used, even in folk medicine. May be employed horticulturally as an excellent, low, evergreen edging plant for formal arrangements.

Armoracia rusticana Gaertn, Mey et Scherb.
CRUCIFERAE

Horseradish

Linnaeus gave Horseradish the botanical name, *Cochlearia armoracia*, after *cochleare*, an obsolete name for a spoon which its leaves were thought to resemble, and *armoracia*, the Roman name for a wild Radish which cannot be identified with certainty as Horseradish. Gerard gave the herb its present common name, but before him it was known in English as Red Cole or Redcol. Certainly the plant appears to have been more popular in Scandinavia and Germany and otherwise did not find much use in western Europe until the middle of the seventeenth century. The French called it *moutarde des allemands*, and druggists knew it as *Raphanus rusticanus*.

Description Perennial to 1.5 m high on stout, tapering, fleshy taproot to 60 cm long and 5 cm thick; large basal leaves, 30–100 cm long, coarse, lanceolate with dentate margins and long petioles. Erect flowering racemes 50 cm–1 m high bearing clusters of white flowers and, beneath, stem leaves with short petioles. Appears mid-summer to mid-autumn.

Distribution South-east European native; introduced and cultivated elsewhere; tolerates most dampish soils.

Cultivation Wild plant. Cultivated commercially and horticulturally. Propagate by root division in spring or autumn, planting at 50-cm intervals, or sow seed in early spring and thin later. Grows vigorously.

Constituents Fresh root contains a glycoside, sinigrin, which is decomposed in the presence of water by the enzyme myrosin, producing mustard oil – allyl isothiocyanate; vitamin C; antibiotic substances.

Uses (fresh root) Stimulant; rubefacient; weak diuretic.

May be taken internally as a syrup for bronchitis, bronchial catarrh, coughs, and to stimulate digestive organs. Applied externally as sliced root on boils or as a rubefacient poultice in rheumatism.

Most widely used for culinary purposes, especially in sauces and vinegars; complements fish, poultry, and beef.

Contra-indications May be vesicant to some skins; large internal doses produce inflammation of the gastro-intestinal mucosae.

Arnica montana L COMPOSITAE
Arnica Mountain Tobacco

When grown at high latitudes such as in Arctic Asia or America, a form of this herb is produced which is characterized by narrow leaves; although this was once renamed by Vahl as *Arnica angustifolia*, it is really a variant form of *Arnica montana*. The herb is known by Matthiolus and other botanists, and was widely used in sixteenth-century German folk medicine. Largely as the result of exaggerated claims by a Viennese physician, it enjoyed short-lived popularity among the medical profession in the late eighteenth century.

Description Aromatic perennial with creeping rhizome, producing a basal rosette of 4–8 downy leaves 4–7 cm long in the first year. Flowering stem usually unbranched, hairy, 30–60 cm high, with only 1–2 pairs of opposite leaves. Flowers golden-yellow, daisy-like, appearing mid-summer to early autumn.

Distribution Central and northern regions of the northern hemisphere. Prefers sandy acid soils, rich in humus, in a sunny position.

Cultivation Root division in spring; or seed sown in spring in cold frame and transplanted in early summer. Seed may be slow to germinate, occasionally as long as 2 years. Wild plant, but protected in parts of Europe.

Constituents Polyacetylenic compounds in volatile oil; flavones; arnicin; phulin; inulin; unknown substances acting on the circulatory system which initially lower the blood pressure, and later raise it. Also substances which increase biliary secretion.

Uses (dried flower-heads, dried rhizome) Stimulant; diuretic; rubefacient. It is an irritant to the digestive tract and kidneys, and hence only of use externally – in bruising, sprains and dislocations. Homeopathic doses are effective in epilepsy, seasickness and possibly as hair growth stimulants. Used as a gargle for treating inflammations of the throat.

Contra-indications POISONOUS: can be toxic if taken internally. Repeated external use may cause skin irritation.

Artemisia abrotanum L COMPOSITAE
Southernwood Lad's Love/Old Man
In common with other members of the Artemisia family this is a strong-smelling herb which has the ability to repel insects. For this reason it was called *garde robe* by the French

who used it to protect clothes from attack by moths. It was also considered effective against infection and employed in nosegays by court-room and jail officials. The name Southern-wood is derived from the Old English *sutherne-wudu* meaning a woody plant from the south, since it is a native of southern Europe. At one time herbalists considered the herb an aphro-disiac, which led to the common name Lad's Love.
Description Perennial subshrub to 90 cm high; with branched feathery grey-green leaves 6 cm long, finely divided and somewhat downy. Flowers very small, inconspicuous, yellowish-white, in loose panicles, appearing late summer to early autumn.
Distribution Southern European native; intro-duced and widespread in temperate zones as garden plant. Naturalized in North America.
Cultivation Easily propagated from young, green cuttings in summer, or heeled cuttings from old wood in autumn. Prefers full sun and light to medium soil with added compost. Needs hard clipping in mid-spring to prevent straggling growth. May not flower.
Constituents Essential oil, mainly absinthol.
Uses (dried whole plant) Stimulant; emmen-agogue; antiseptic; antihelmintic. Once used as a powder mixed with treacle to treat worms in children. Used in aromatic baths and poultices for skin conditions.
Leaves discourage moths.
Stems yield yellow dye. Foliage used in floral decorations.

Artemisia absinthium L COMPOSITAE
Wormwood Absinthe/Green Ginger
Several species of *absinthium* are mentioned by Dioscorides, and many of them were employed for the removal of intestinal worms. Although one of the most bitter herbs known, it has for centuries been a major ingredient of aperitifs

and herb wines. Both absinthe and vermouth obtain their names from the plant, the latter being an eighteenth-century French variation of the German *Wermut* which was also the origin of the English name Wormwood. The herb contains several substances which may adversely affect the body if taken in excess (including the hallucinogen, santonin) and for this reason it produces some of the strongest, and most dangerous, alcoholic drinks.
Description Perennial undershrub 0.75–1 m high; hairy stems bearing highly aromatic bipinnate and tripinnate leaves covered in down. Flower-heads 3–4 mm diameter, with grey-green bracts and numerous minute yellow florets, appearing late summer to late autumn.
Distribution Central Europe, North America, Asia. Widely introduced garden plant. Found on waste-ground, especially near the sea, in warm regions.
Cultivation Wild plant. Propagated by seed sown outside in late spring, thinned to 30–60 cm apart. Often slow to germinate. Cuttings taken in summer; root division in spring or autumn. Prefers medium soil in full sun or slight shade.
Constituents Bitter principle and volatile oil which stimulate secretions and promote appe-tite; also a glucoside; resins and starch; antihelmintic action due to santonin.
Uses (whole flowering plant, leaves) Anthel-mintic; antipyretic; antiseptic; stomachic. Used to aid digestion, stimulate digestion or for abdominal colic. The tincture was formerly used in nervous diseases. Used in liniments. Used in vermouth, in absinthe, as a tea, and for stuffing geese. Some countries ban its use in wine.
Contra-indications Habitual use causes convul-sions, restlessness and vomiting. Overdose causes vertigo, cramps, intoxication, and delirium.

Artemisia dracunculoides L COMPOSITAE
Tarragon Russian Tarragon
Unlike French Tarragon the flavour of this variety improves as the plant ages, although never achieving the delicacy of *Artemisia dracunculus*. The Latin name is derived from *dracunculus* meaning 'little dragon' after a herbalist's description of the coiled serpent-like root. Artemisia was the Greek name for Diana who was regarded as the discoverer of the *Artemisia* group of herbs. Russian Tarragon is also called *Artemisia redowskii*.
Description Perennial 1.5 m high with erect, branched stems bearing smooth, pale green entire leaves 3–6 cm long, and clusters of greyish-white woolly flowers in late summer.
Distribution Asia and Siberia. Introduced else-where.
Cultivation Wild, and cultivated as garden plant. Seed sown under glass in mid-spring or in the open in early summer. Root division in spring or autumn; cuttings in spring. Hardy during winter and tolerates any soil.
Constituents Essential oil identical to Anise, largely lost during drying.
Uses (dried or fresh herb) Fresh herb promotes appetite.

Similar uses to French Tarragon (*Artemisia dracunculus*) but of inferior flavour.

Artemisia dracunculus L COMPOSITAE
Tarragon French Tarragon
An essential component of French cuisine, plants of the 'true' French Tarragon are difficult to obtain and almost as difficult to maintain. Even under ideal circumstances the delicate flavour of this variety tends to revert

to the coarser flavour of Russian Tarragon. Similarly unless it is dried carefully an inferior product results. The common name is derived from the Arabic *tarkhun*, via the Spanish *taragoncia*.

Description Perennial 90 cm high with slim, erect, branched stems, bearing smooth, dark shiny entire leaves 3–5 cm long, and clusters of greyish-green or white woolly flowers, appearing mid-summer to late summer.

Distribution Southern Europe. Introduced elsewhere as garden plant or for commercial cultivation.

Cultivation Cultivated commercially in Europe and the United States. Cannot be propagated from seed. Divide roots in spring or autumn or take cuttings in spring. Renew every 3 years from young cuttings. Protect in warm situation during winter, especially when young. Prefers a richer soil than Russian Tarragon, and may require the addition of peat. Can be grown indoors as a pot herb. Will not tolerate wet soil.

Constituents Essential oil.

Uses (dried or fresh herb) No modern medicinal use – formerly used in toothache. The herb promotes appetite.

Widely used as flavouring for salads, steak,

fish, preserves, pickles, shellfish, lobster, herb butter, vinegars, and is best known for its use with chicken.
Used in some perfumes and liqueurs.

Artemisia vulgaris L COMPOSITAE
Mugwort Felon Herb/St John's Herb
An ancient magical plant, deeply respected throughout Europe, China and Asia, and once known as the Mother of Herbs (*Mater Herbarum*). It was one of the nine herbs employed to repel demons and venoms in pre-Christian times. Although used to flavour drinks, and especially beer, the common name is derived from the Old Saxon *muggia wort* meaning 'midge plant' after its ability to repel insects.

Description Erect sparsely pubescent perennial; stems grooved with reddish-purple colouring, angular, reaching 1.75 m. Leaves 2.5–5 cm long, dark green above, whitish and downy on the underside; pinnate or bipinnate with

toothed leaflets. Flowers brownish-yellow to red, numerous, small, arranged on panicles and appearing late summer to mid-autumn.

Distribution Asia, Europe. Naturalized in North America. Common on various soils, especially if they are nitrogen-rich. In wastelands, hedgerows and near rivers and streams.

Cultivation Wild and cultivated. Seed sown in spring. Root division spring and autumn. Grows quickly and needs restricting in gardens. A variegated form also exists.

Constituents Volatile oil; resin; tannin; a bitter principle, absinthin, which stimulates digestion.

Uses (dried flowering shoots, leaves, roots) Diuretic; emmenagogue. Used as an aid in irregular menstruation, for lack of appetite, and weak digestion. Chinese employ the cones of the leaves (moxas) for rheumatism, in the therapeutic method known as moxibustion. Used as a tea. A culinary herb for stuffing geese, duck or other fatty fish or meat.

Repels flies and moths. Leaves may be used in tobaccos.

Formerly used for flavouring and the clarification of beer.

Contra-indications Large prolonged dosage injures the nervous system.

Arum maculatum L ARACEAE
Cuckoopint Lords and Ladies/Arum
Because of the obvious sexual symbolism of the erect spadix of this attractive plant, almost all its European common names have some sexual connotation. Even Dioscorides suggested that the herb was an aphrodisiac. It may have been for this reason that large quantities of the tubers were processed and sold as a foodstuff in the eighteenth and nineteenth centuries. The herb was also called Starchwort, and root starch obtained from it was employed to starch ruffs in the sixteenth century, even though the practice often caused blisters on the hands of those who used it.

Description Perennial plant arising from ovoid tuber 2 cm diameter; arrow-shaped leaves to 25 cm long, plain dark green or with dark brown-purplish spots. Flowers occur at base of purplish club-shaped spadix which is enclosed in characteristic 15-cm long leafy greenish-

white bract (spathe). Flowers appear late spring to early summer, followed by scarlet fruits.

Distribution Central and western Europe, north Africa, introduced elsewhere. Found in porous loamy soils, in warm damp sites, hedgerows, woods.

Cultivation Wild plant.

Constituents Aroine, an unstable skin and mucosa irritant, which is largely broken down on drying; starch; gums; saponin; sugar.

Uses (fresh or dried leaves, dried tubers) Diuretic; strong purgative; no longer employed internally. Bruised fresh plant applied externally in rheumatic pain. Used homeopathically for sore throats.

Well-baked tubers are edible, nutritious and harmless.

Root starch, after roasting or boiling, and then drying and powdering, produces an arrowroot substitute used for starching.

Contra-indications All parts of fresh plant are POISONOUS.

Asarum canadense L ARISTOLOCHIACEAE
Wild Ginger Canadian Snakeroot
As the name suggests the root-stock may be used as a substitute for root Ginger. American colonists found the herb was an effective stimulant when taken as a tea, and American Indians believed a decoction of the root-stock to be an effective contraceptive.

Description Stemless ginger-smelling perennial, with round, fleshy root and branched, hairy, root stalks each bearing 2 kidney-shaped leaves, dark green above, pale green beneath, 10–20 cm wide. Flowers single, bell-shaped, dull brownish-purple, appearing close to the ground in summer.

Distribution Canada and northern United

States, Russia, Far East. In rich woodland on moist shaded sites.
Cultivation Wild plant.
Constituents Volatile oil; resin; a bitter principle; asarin; sugars; alkaloid.
Uses (root-stock) Stimulant; tonic; diuretic; diaphoretic; carminative. Tea used in flatulence and indigestion. Thought to exert direct influence on the uterus.
May be used as a substitute for root Ginger.
Oil used in perfumery.
Dried root used as snuff to relieve headaches.
Contra-indications Large doses cause nausea.

Asarum europaeum L ARISTOLOCHIACEAE
Asarabacca Hazelwort/Wild Nard
An inconspicuous herb with nut-shaped flowers and cyclamen-shaped leaves, it was called *asaron* and introduced into medicine by Dioscorides. Herbalists of the Middle Ages incorrectly called the plant *baccharis*, a name given by Dioscorides to another herb which was probably a true cyclamen. Sixteenth-century apothecaries joined the names and described the Hazelwort as Asarabacca. Most members of the family Aristolochiaceae are climbing woody plants from South America.
Description Herbaceous perennial bearing 2 kidney-shaped, leathery, long-stalked leaves on short pubescent stems. Inflorescence arises from thick root-stock and flowers on soil surface or leaf mould. Single purplish flower appears early summer to early autumn.
Distribution Europe, Siberia, Caucasus; in woods and shady sites. Introduced elsewhere in temperate zones as a garden plant.
Cultivation Wild plant. May be propagated by root division in autumn; prefers moist, calcareous soil, rich in humus and shaded.
Constituents Volatile oil; bitter principle; alkaloid; sugars; resin.
Uses (dried root and leaves) Emetic; purgative; sternutatory; stimulant in small doses.
Produces copious mucus flow if taken as snuff. Once an ingredient of tobacconists' 'head-clearin' snuff'.

Asclepias tuberosa L ASCLEPIADACEAE
Pleurisy Root Butterfly Milk Weed
Once officially recognized and included in the United States Pharmacopoeia and long used as an important medicinal herb, it is still employed in European and American folk medicine. Appalachian Indians made a tea from the leaves to induce vomiting during certain religious ceremonies. Several species of Asclepias are grown in warm climates as attractive garden plants.
Description Attractive perennial to 1 m; fleshy white root-stock supporting few stout hairy stems, bearing hairy alternate, lanceolate leaves 5–15 cm long and darker green above. Numerous erect, beautiful orange-yellow flowers in terminal umbels appearing mid-summer to mid-autumn, followed by long, narrow seed pods.
Distribution North American native; common in dry, sandy or gravelly soils on roadsides.
Cultivation Wild plant – propagate by division of root-stock in spring.
Constituents Glycosides, including asclepiadin; resins; volatile oil.
Uses (dried root-stock) Diaphoretic; anti-spasmodic; carminative; expectorant. Specially of use in infections of the respiratory tract such as pleurisy. Powdered roots used as a poultice on open sores.
Young seed pods and root-stock may be boiled and eaten.
Contra-indications Very large doses cause diarrhoea and vomiting. Fresh leaf tea causes vomiting.

Aspalathus linearis (Burm. fil.) R. Dahlgr.
LEGUMINOSAE
Rooibosch Red Bush Tea
Rooibosch was traditionally used by South African Bushmen and Hottentots and its popularity was noted by the botanist Carl Thunberg when he visited the Cape in 1772. The common name derives from the red colour of the leaves and shoots which develops, together with a distinctive aroma, during the fermentation process necessary to obtain the tea.
Commercial exploitation of the tea, which is now gaining in popularity in Europe, began in the early twentieth century after successful experiments to improve seed germination and cropping techniques.
Description Shrub or shrublet, decumbent or erect to 2 m. Branches bearing thin (0.4–1 mm wide), glabrous leaves, 1.5–6 cm long, and short, leafy shoots in the leaf axils. Small, bright yellow flowers, often with violet tinge; followed by 1.5 cm long pod.

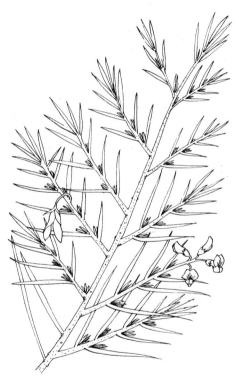

Distribution South African native; especially in western Cape, on well-drained, sandy but moisture-retaining, non-acidic soils.
Cultivation Wild. Cultivated commercially in South Africa from seed sown 10 mm deep in late winter or early spring in seed-beds; seedlings transplanted in mid or late summer when 10–20 cm tall. Later trimmed to promote branching. Plantations replaced every 6 or 7 years.
Constituents Vitamin C; tannin (1–3%); mineral salts; quercitin; unknown substances.
Uses (dried fermented young leaves and branches) Anti-spasmodic; tonic.
Of benefit in vomiting, diarrhoea, and other mild gastric complaints. Clinically untested but traditionally is considered of use in certain allergic disorders – especially milk allergy.

Mostly employed as a hot or cold beverage; also used as a culinary herb, and as a flavouring in baking.

Asparagus officinalis L LILIACEAE
Asparagus Garden Asparagus/Sparrow Grass

Known as Sperage or Sparrow Grass in the sixteenth century, the Garden Asparagus (*Asparagus officinalis* subsp. *officinalis*) has been cultivated as a delicacy for over 2000 years. It became an 'official' medicinal herb due to its laxative and diuretic properties, and some herbalists claimed it also increased the libido. In parts of eastern Europe Asparagus grows wild and is eaten by cattle. The name is from the Greek word meaning 'to sprout'.
Description Perennial with short root-stock 5 cm long, producing in spring the young fleshy shoots which are eaten as a vegetable. If they are left, they mature into many branched stems 1–3 m high which bear insignificant leaves in the axils of which are clusters of needle-like modified branches (cladodes) 1 cm long. Small bell-shaped whitish-green flowers appear in cladode axils early summer to mid-

summer. Bears fruit of red or orange berries 1 cm in diameter.
Distribution Coasts and sandy areas; woods and hedges; Great Britain to Central Asia.
Cultivation Wild plant; cultivated commercially and horticulturally on a wide scale. Production of the vegetable requires 3-year-old plants. Beds last 12 years. Seed sown in late spring, 7.5 cm deep, 2–3 seeds per hole on deep rich sandy loam in open position. A subspecies *A. officinalis* subsp. *prostratus* is also found wild.
Constituents Volatile oil; glucoside; gum; resin; tannic acid.
Uses (root, young fresh stem) Diuretic; diaphoretic; laxative, due to high fibre content. Once recommended for treatment of dropsy, gout and rheumatism.
Wide culinary use as a vegetable.

Asperula odorata L RUBIACEAE
Woodruff Sweet Woodruff/Waldmeister Tea
This attractive low-growing herb which is frequently found carpeting beech woods makes useful ground cover in shady places or beneath

roses in formal beds. It was widely used as a fragrant herb in earlier times as it develops, when dried, a strong scent of new mown hay; for this reason it was one of the main strewing herbs for home and church floors. The Latin name *asperula* refers to the roughness of the wheel or ruff-like leaves.
Description Perennial with creeping root-stock from which many quadrangular smooth, slender stems arise, 15–30 cm high. Leaves in whorls of 6, dark green, lanceolate, 3 cm long, rough-edged. Small white funnel-shaped flowers appear on long stalks early summer to midsummer. Plant has a strong characteristic smell.
Distribution Asia, Europe, North Africa. Introduced elsewhere; cultivated in United States. Prefers porous loamy soil, rich in nutrients, especially in mixed woodland.
Cultivation Wild plant; may be propagated from ripe seed sown in late summer to early autumn, or root division after flowering. Ideal herb for underplanting in borders.
Constituents Coumarinic compounds which release coumarin as the plant dies down; also tannin.
Uses (dried herb) Carminative; diuretic; tonic. Once used for biliary obstructions. Source of coumarin for anticoagulant drugs. Tea relieves stomach pains.
Flowers and leaves make a delicious tea.
Used in certain wines as a flavouring.
In perfumery and pot-pourris, and for scenting linen. Repels insects.
Contra-indications Large quantities can produce dizziness and symptoms of poisoning.

Atropa belladonna L SOLANACEAE
Deadly Nightshade Dwale
Although a plant with such powerful sedative and poisonous properties was undoubtedly widely used for sinister purposes, it cannot be identified with certainty in classical writings,

and the first definite report of its use is found in the *Grand Herbier* (1504) printed in Paris. The herb was known by various names during the sixteenth and seventeenth centuries including *Strygium*, *Strychnon*, *Solanum somniferum*, and *Solatrum mortale*, the latter – the apothecaries' name for it – being translated as 'deadly nightshade'. Matthiolus stated it was the Venetians who first called the plant *Herba bella donna* after the practice of ladies who used a distilled water of it to dilate the pupils.
Description Perennial with leafy, smooth, branched stem 50–200 cm tall on thick creeping root-stock. Leaves dull green, unequal sized pairs to 20 cm long, bearing solitary bell-shaped purplish-brown drooping flowers 3 cm in diameter in the axils. Appearing midsummer to early autumn, followed by shiny black berries.
Distribution Native to Europe, Asia; naturalized and introduced elsewhere. Found especially in woods and wasteland on calcareous soils.
Cultivation Wild plant. Widespread commercial cultivation from seed or by root division.
Constituents Hyoscyamine; atropine; traces of other alkaloids mainly in root-stock. Action due to these affecting the autonomic nervous system.
Uses (root-stock and leaf) Narcotic; mydriatic; sedative. Reduces salivary and sudorific gland secretions. Employed in treatment of biliary and intestinal colic. Formerly used in nervous diarrhoea and enuresis. Used in heart arrythmia. Externally as a liniment in gout or rheumatic inflammation.
Contra-indications All parts extremely POISONOUS; only to be used under medical supervision.

Avena sativa L GRAMINEAE
Oats Groats
One of the dozen members of the grass family which together provide the staple diet for most of the world's population. *Avena* is the old Latin name for the plant.
Description Annual tufted erect grass, 1–1.25 m high, with broad leaves 4 mm – 1 cm wide,

15–30 cm long, flat and scabrous. Short ligules. Terminal panicle 15–25 cm long, open and spreading; lemma without hairs.

Distribution Avena sativa is a cultigen possibly derived from *A. fatua*, *A. sterilis* or *A. barbata*, which originate from southern Europe and east Asia.

Cultivation Widespread commercial cultivation; often found growing wild, having escaped from cultivation.

Constituents Starch; protein; gluten; albumen; salts; gum oil; tocopherol.

Uses (dehusked seed, starchy seed endosperm) Nutritive; antidepressant; thymoleptic. Of use in depressive states and in general debility; highly nutritious.

Ballota nigra L LABIATAE
Black Horehound Stinking Horehound

This generally unattractive herb is distinguished only by its strong and objectionable odour, which caused Turner in 1548 to describe it as the 'stynkyng horehound'. Dioscorides gave the plant the name *ballote* which is probably derived from the Greek

word meaning 'to reject' since it is normally rejected by cattle. Although the plant is of some medicinal value, it is now grown in herb gardens only because it is regarded as one of the traditional herbs.

Description Strong smelling perennial with angular branched hairy stems, 40–100 cm high, bearing heart-shaped leaves, crenulated, 2–5 cm long, opposite and often turning black after flowering. Whorls of typical labiate purple flowers borne in axils. Appearing mid-summer to late autumn.

Distribution Natives of temperate Europe and much of the eastern hemisphere. Found on wasteland, hedgerows and on walls; prefers nitrogen-rich, moist, rather loose soil.

Cultivation Wild plant. Propagate by root division in mid-spring or sow seed in late spring, later thinning to 40 cm apart.

Constituents Flavonoids.

Uses (dried flowering herb) sedative; anti-emetic; especially used to counteract vomiting during pregnancy.

Berberis vulgaris L BERBERIDACEAE
Barberry European Barberry/Sowberry

A useful shrub cultivated in medieval times near monasteries and churches. It was used in dyeing, and as a medicine, and its delicious berries were used for jam, jelly and candied sweets. Now relegated to hedgerows, it is becoming scarce. Barberry is a host plant of the wheat rust and long before plant diseases were understood farmers accused the plant of 'blighting' wheat.

Description Erect deciduous shrub to 2.5 m tall, bearing rod-shaped branches tinged yellowish-red. Leaves obovate 2.5–4 cm long in clusters, greyish beneath with 3 sharp spines at the base. Flowers small, yellow, in clusters appearing late spring to mid-summer, and followed by oblong scarlet to purple fruit.

Distribution Native from Europe to East Asia; naturalized in eastern North America. Prefers light deciduous woodland on chalky soils. Once common in hedgerows but becoming scarcer due to infection by black rust fungus disease.

Cultivation Wild plant. Propagated by layering

of suckers in early autumn; seed sown in late spring or early autumn; or cuttings taken in early autumn and planted in sandy soil. Horticultural varieties include *var. atropurpurea*.

Constituents Alkaloids comprising berberine, oxyacanthine and chelidonic acid. Fruit rich in vitamin C.

Uses (root bark, stem bark, ripe fruit) Cholagogue; specifically used in the treatment of gall-stones and other liver diseases.

Wood used in the manufacture of tooth-picks and bark as a yellow dye for wool, linen and leather. Fruit made into jelly and eaten with mutton, candied and pickled for use in curries.

Betula pendula Roth. BETULACEAE
Silver Birch

Although birch timber is poor, the tree has nevertheless been of use to man for a considerable time; Birch bark rolls have been found in Mesolithic excavations and North American Indians still use the bark for domestic purposes. The tree has also long been considered magical and reputedly has the ability to repel enchantment and evil. Its employment as a form of whip or 'birch' predates the Roman lictors who used *Betula* species in the *fascis* they carried. Now widely grown horticulturally as an attractive garden tree.

Description Deciduous tree to 20 m high; white bark, smooth and peeling in horizontal strips. Pendulous slender branches bearing resinous, rough and scaly glands. Leaves bright green 4–7 cm long, irregularly serrate, heart-shaped to triangular. Flowers consist of male and female catkins.

Distribution Common throughout central and northern Europe, the mountainous parts of southern Europe and Asia Minor. Also found in Canada and the northern United States. Tolerates all soil types and situations.

Cultivation Wild plant. Grown horticulturally.

Constituents Volatile oil; a saponin; a flavonoid; resin.

Uses (dried young leaves) Diuretic, with mild antiseptic action, thus used in urinary tract infections. Formerly used for gout and rheumatism.

A beer can be made from the bark. The tree sap is made into birch wine and vinegar. Birch wood seldom used commercially as timber; but employed for broom handles. Bark once used as candles and the oil extracted from it was used to cure leather, and also in medicated soaps for skin conditions.

Bidens tripartita L COMPOSITAE
Bur-Marigold Water Agrimony

The herb is unrelated botanically to the common Agrimony and it scarcely deserves the name marigold with its inconspicuous brown-yellow flowers. Flies and insects are repelled when the herb is burned.

Description Erect annual 15–60 cm high, with smooth or downy branched stems; leaves 5–15 cm long, opposite, dark green, mostly with 3 or sometimes 5 leaflets. Flowers brownish-yellow, inconspicuous, somewhat drooping. Late summer to mid-autumn.

Distribution European native. Common on river banks, in ditches, near ponds. Prefers muddy soil.

Cultivation Wild plant. Propagate from seed sown in spring.

Constituents Volatile oil.

Uses (dried flowering herb) Astringent; dia-

phoretic; antihaemorrhagic. Formerly used in a variety of conditions, but now rarely used except for antihaemorrhagic purposes.

A weak yellow dye is obtained from the flowers.

Borago officinalis L BORAGINACEAE
Borage Burrage

Almost all the historical descriptions of Borage refer to the herb's abilities to bring happiness and comfort and drive away melancholia. Even Pliny called the plant *euphrosinum* because it made men joyful and merry. Certainly it was widely used in a variety of alcoholic drinks, and it is still a vital ingredient of summer wine cups. As Borage is very attractive to bees, its bright blue star-shaped flowers are always covered with the insects.

Description Annual or sometimes biennial herb, with erect hairy stems to 60 cm, bearing ovate,

alternate, rough leaves, hairy on both surfaces, 3–11 cm long and up to 2.5 cm wide, usually without petioles. Bright blue, drooping star-shaped flowers 2 cm wide appear from early summer to mid-autumn on sparsely flowered racemes.

Distribution Native to mediterranean region; naturalized and introduced elsewhere; found especially as garden escape.

Cultivation Wild plant and prolifically self-seeding. Thrives on ordinary well-drained soil in full sun. Sow seed in shallow drills in late spring or late summer.

Constituents Mucilage; tannin; volatile oil; various mineral acids. Active principles not fully understood, but they act as a mild diuretic and sudorific.

Uses (dried flowering plant, fresh leaves) Mild diuretic; once used for kidney and bladder inflammations. Used externally as a poultice on inflammations. Taken as a tisane for rheumatism and for respiratory infections. Said to stimulate the flow of milk in nursing mothers.

Candied flowers used for cake decoration. Fresh leaves and flowers added to salads, and fresh flowers used to decorate wine cups. Roots flavour wine.

Brassica nigra (L) Koch CRUCIFERAE
Mustard Black Mustard

The powerful flavour of old-fashioned Mustard was due largely to its content of Black Mustard. The plant, however, does not lend itself well to mechanical harvesting as it is often 2–3 m in height, and readily sheds its seed when ripe. As a result it has almost completely been replaced with the shorter Juncea or Brown Mustard (*Brassica juncea*) which is much less pungent. The word 'mustard' is thought to derive from the Latin – *mustum ardens*, or 'burning must' since the French originally ground the seed with grape must.

Description Much branched annual 1–3 m high, smooth above and slightly hairy below; grass-green leaves of varying shapes, generally

narrow or lobed with serrate margins. Flowers small, bright yellow, in twig-like racemes, appearing mid-summer to early autumn. Seed dark reddish-brown in colour, in smooth pods.

Distribution Whole of Europe except far north; northern Africa, Asia Minor, China, western India, North and South America.

Cultivation Wild plant; formerly cultivated commercially on a wide scale – this now restricted to southern Italy, Sicily, Ethiopia. Seed sown in drills in spring preferably on rich soil.

Constituents Glycoside (comprising sinigrin) and an enzyme (myrosin) which react in the presence of water to form allyl isothiocyanate (or essential oil of mustard) which is responsible for the smell, taste and inflammatory action of mustard. Also contains proteins; mucilage; and non-volatile oil.

Uses (seed, leaves) Stimulant; irritant; emetic. Mainly used as a rubefacient poultice for rheumatism, local pain and chilblains. Added to hot water as a foot bath. Used as an ingredient of the condiment Flour of Mustard. Young leaves occasionally used in salads.

Contra-indications May blister tender skins. Should be used sparingly when taken internally.

Bryonia dioica Jacq. CUCURBITACEAE
White or Red Bryony/English Mandrake

The common name is derived from the Greek word *bruein* – meaning to grow luxuriantly; another name, the wild vine, emphasizes the vigorous growth of the annual stems which rapidly cover hedgerow shrubs. The herb is also called English Mandrake since the enormous root-stock is similar in appearance to the legendary Mandrake (*Mandragora officinarum*) and was once used as a substitute for it. Bryony roots carved into human form were often used as shop signs by English herbalists in the eighteenth century.

Description Climbing perennial arising from large white tuberous root 75 cm long, 7.5 cm thick. Long stem, branching near the base reaching 4 m tall, and supported by coiled tendrils. Leaves palmate, 5-lobed and rough. Male plants bear pale green flowers on long

stalks; female plants bear greenish flowers in umbels of 2–5 on short stalks and single red berries; both plants appear early summer to early autumn.

Distribution Mediterranean native; widely distributed in Europe and Western Asia; introduced elsewhere. Prefers a well-drained and chalky or loamy soil.

Cultivation Wild plant.

Constituents Resin comprising the glycoside bryonin; tannin; volatile oil; other glycosides and alkaloids. Purgative action due to resin.

Uses (fresh or dried root) Irritant; once employed to allay coughs in pleurisy, now rarely used due to its violent purgative action. Berries of use as a dye.

Contra-indications All parts POISONOUS.

Buxus sempervirens L BUXACEAE
Box Box Tree
Although once used for medicinal purposes the slow growing and somewhat peculiarly smelling Box Tree is now mainly sought after for its timber which is used in the manufacture of chess pieces and turned boxes. At one time

Box woods were widespread in Europe but the demand for the wood – which is twice as hard as oak – led to extensive felling. Close clipped Box hedges make excellent edgings to formal herb gardens.

Description Slow growing evergreen tree or shrub, 2–7 m tall; bark greyish, leaves dark green above and shiny, pale beneath, oblong 1–3 cm long. Flowers minute, yellow-green in axillary clusters appearing mid-spring to early summer.

Distribution Native to Europe, North Africa, western Asia. Cultivated widely; prefers chalk or limestone.

Cultivation Wild plant. Cultivated from cuttings in sandy soil taken in spring.

Constituents Alkaloids (buxine, parabuxine, parabuxonidine); oil; tannin.

Uses (leaves, wood) Not used medicinally; but formerly used for syphilis and as a sedative. A volatile oil from the wood was once used in the treatment of epilepsy, piles and toothache. Perfume once made from the bark. Leaves and sawdust were formerly used to dye hair auburn. Box wood is as durable as brass and is therefore used in instrument manufacture. Leaves once used as a substitute for Hops.

Contra-indications Animals have died from eating the leaves.

Calamintha ascendens Jord. LABIATAE
Common Calamint Mountain Balm/
Mountain Mint
An ancient medicinal herb which once had such a good reputation as a heart tonic that it was named after the Greek for excellence – *kalos*. Although an 'official' herb of the Middle Ages it now has no place in either orthodox or folk medicine.

Description Hairy perennial; stems square, arising from creeping root-stock, to 30 cm high; leaves stalked, toothed and broadly

ovate, 2–3 cm long. Typically labiate flowers, pale purple, in dense whorls of 10–20, appearing late summer to early autumn.

Distribution European native; prefers dry woodland and waste places on chalky soil.

Cultivation Wild plant. Propagated by cuttings of side-shoots taken in spring; seed sown in early spring; root division late autumn and late spring.

Constituents Volatile oils.

Uses (dried flowering herb) Diaphoretic; expectorant. An infusion is a useful tonic. The leaves may be used as a poultice for bruises. A peppermint flavoured tisane can be made from the leaves.

Calendula officinalis L COMPOSITAE
Marigold Garden Marigold
This well-known garden plant is probably one of the most useful of all herbs. It has valuable medicinal properties, yields a yellow dye, and can be used as a culinary herb and for cosmetic purposes. It has been used in the Mediterranean region since the ancient Greeks, and it was known to Indian and Arabic cultures before the Greeks. The botanical name comes from the Latin *calendulae* or *calends* meaning 'throughout the months', which was intended to emphasize the very long flowering period of the Marigold.

Description Annual; biennial rarely; branching, angular stem to 50 cm; leaves oblong or lanceolate, hairy on both surfaces, 5–15 cm long; flower-heads large, yellow or orange, double-flowered (tubular florets absent), appearing mid-summer to late autumn.

Distribution Mediterranean native; distributed throughout the world as a garden plant.

Cultivation Not found wild. Tolerates any soil in full sun, although prefers loam. Seed sown mid-spring, but once established is generally self-sown.

Constituents Volatile oil; a yellow resin; calendulin; saponins; a bitter principle; all of which aid bile secretion and promote wound healing.

Uses (entire flower-heads, individual florets, rarely the entire flowering plant) Cholagogue;

styptic; anti-inflammatory; vulnerary; anti-septic; possibly emmenagogue.

Specifically of use in inflamed lymphatic nodes, duodenal ulcers, and some inflammatory skin lesions. Used externally for treatment of leg ulcers, and in conjunctivitis as an eye lotion.

Petals are substitutes for Saffron, and may be added to salads and omelettes or used to colour cheese and butter.

Young leaves added to salads.

Petals are also used as tea.

Used in skin and cosmetic preparations, and as a hair rinse.

Yellow dye obtained by boiling flowers.

Calluna vulgaris (L) Hull ERICACEAE
Heather Ling

A common herb long used in European folk

medicine whose generic name is from the Greek meaning to sweep, after the use of its branches in brooms.

Description Evergreen subshrub from 15 cm–1 m tall. Leaves grey-green, later reddish, very small, sessile, overlapping in 4 rows. Flowers 3 mm long, pink in terminal one-sided racemes, appearing late summer to late autumn.

Distribution Native to Europe, Asia Minor. Introduced to eastern North America. On acidic sandy soils, or peat bogs. In woodland, dry hillsides, mountainous districts, to 2500 m altitude.

Cultivation Wild. Numerous horticultural cultivars exist for rock-garden use. Dislikes limestone soils. Propagate by young wood cuttings under glass.

Constituents Citric and fumaric acids; arbutin; tannins; an oil, ericinol; a resin, ericoline; flavonoid glycosides, quercitrin and myricitrin; carotene. The combined action is predominantly antibacterial.

Uses (fresh flowering tops) Antiseptic; diuretic; astringent.

Of use in the treatment of kidney and urinary tract infections, diarrhoea. Frequently included in cleansing mixtures such as acne remedies. May possess a weak sedative action. Can be used as a tea substitute.

Cannabis sativa L CANNABACEAE
Hemp Cannabis

Recorded in the fifth century B.C. in the Chinese herbal Rh-ya but now subject to considerable medical and legal reappraisal. Hemp has long been of economic importance to man. John Gerard described it in the sixteenth century as the Indian Dreamer. *C. sativa* L is considered now to be synonymous with *C. indica* L, although the herb is variable

both in constituents and appearance depending upon region and method of cultivation.

Description Coarse strong-smelling dioecious annual, 90 cm–5 m tall. Leaves long-petioled thin, alternate, palmate; 3–11 leaflets, narrowly lanceolate, toothed, 7.5–12.5 cm long. Male flowers in panicles 23–40 cm long; female sessile leafy spikes 2 cm long. Variable.

Distribution Native to central and western Asia; introduced to many temperate and tropical countries. To 3000 m altitude.

Cultivation Wild and cultivated commercially, in temperate regions for oily seed and fibre (Soviet Union and central Europe, for example) and in tropical regions for the drug (Africa, India, Far East). In many countries it can be cultivated only with a government permit.

Constituents A resin, cannabinone, comprising various compounds; pharmacological action probably due to isomers of tetrahydrocannabinol.

Uses (fibre, seed, oil, female and male dried flowering tops – the latter only rarely) Cerebral sedative; narcotic; analgesic; antispasmodic.

Medicinal use and attitude to the drug varies according to country. Considered of benefit in glaucoma, spasmodic cough, neuralgia, asthma and migraine.

Stem fibre provides 'hemp' for rope, sail-cloth etc. Seed is a bird-feed, and source of a drying oil, 'hemp-seed oil'. Dried flowering tops illegally smoked as a narcotic (marijuana).

Contra-indications Possession is illegal. Physical and psychological effects, ranging from change in blood pressure and impotence to hallucination, vary enormously depending on personality. Medical use only.

Capparis spinosa L CAPPARACEAE
Caper Caper Bush

The unopened flower buds of the Caper Bush, pickled in wine vinegar, have been used as a condiment for at least 2000 years, and have always been known as either *capparis* or *kapparis*. Dioscorides suggested a medical use for them, but they have never widely been used for anything except culinary purposes. The best known substitute for capers is pickled, green nasturtium seeds.

Description Straggling spiny shrub 1 m high; leaves tough, roundish or oval 2–5 cm long, with short petiole and 2 spines at the base. White or pink single flowers 2.5 cm long with 4 petals, and numerous purple stamens hanging below them, appearing from early summer to early autumn and lasting only 24 hours.

Distribution Mediterranean region and North Africa to the Sahara.

Cultivation Wild plant; cultivated in warmer climates (when the bush is often spineless). May be grown in greenhouses in temperate zones.

Cuttings in summer most successfully rooted with the help of mist propagation (requiring very high humidity).

Constituents Capric acid, which develops on pickling the buds, and which is responsible for the characteristic flavour.

Uses (unopened flower buds) Numerous culinary uses: caper sauce, tartare sauce, vinaigrette, butter, in Liptauer cheese, and as a garnish with hors d'oeuvres, fish, meat and salads.

Capsella bursa-pastoris (L) Medic. CRUCIFERAE
Shepherd's Purse Shovelweed
In almost all European languages the common names of this herb allude to the strange shape of the fruit, which are very similar to the purses or pouches which were once commonly hung from belts. The Latin name also simply means the 'little case of the shepherd'.
Shepherd's Purse can be found growing in Greenland at sites where it was introduced by Norsemen 1000 years ago. It was, and in some places is still, extensively eaten as a spring vegetable.

Description Annual, or generally biennial; smooth or slightly hairy stem, branched, to 50 cm; arising from basal rosette of dentate or variable leaves. Upper leaves entire and narrow. White flowers 2.5–4 mm diameter, in loose racemes appearing throughout the year, and followed by triangular shaped fruit called siliculae.
Distribution Widespread in temperate zones; common weed on gravelly, sandy or loamy soils, especially those which are nitrogen-rich.
Cultivation Wild plant.
Constituents Choline; acetylcholine; and other amines – acting as vasoconstrictors and haemostatics.
Uses (dried flowering plant; fresh plant) Anti-haemorrhagic; the herb acts as a vaso-constrictor and is therefore of use in certain haemorrhages especially profuse menstruation. Thought to assist contraction of the uterus during childbirth. Spring leaves eaten as cabbage in many countries.

Capsicum annuum L SOLANACEAE
Chili Peppers Capsicum/Sweet Peppers
All species of Capsicum are of American origin and were unknown before 1494 when Chanca, the physician to the fleet of Columbus in his second voyage to the West Indies, briefly described their use by the natives. Today there are scores of varieties in cultivation, ranging in shape, size, colour, flavour, and degree of

pungency, and the plants are grown commercially in all tropical and subtropical countries. Some varieties grow in the cooler parts of Europe and America. Chili is dried and ground to form Cayenne Pepper; it is also blended with several varieties of Capsicums, herbs and spices to make Chili powder.
Although the origin of the cultivated varieties is uncertain, experts believe all come from one original species. For this reason the botanical classification of these plants is somewhat muddled, and *C. annuum* is often described as *C. frutescens*.
Description Herbaceous annual or biennial; 30–90 cm high; leaves 2.5–12 cm long, acuminate, often narrowing towards the petiole; white flowers, solitary, 5 mm–1 cm wide, or much larger. Fruit from 1.5–30 cm long, varied in colour (yellow, brown, purple, often bright red), in shape and degree of fleshiness.
Distribution Grown in all tropical and subtropical countries; Europe and America.
Cultivation Not found in wild state, but closely related to the Bird Pepper (*Capsicum microcarpum* (*D.C.*). Seed sown under glass in early spring; later transplanted. Best sown in pots or under glass in cool climates to ensure ripening of fruit.
Constituents Capsicin; capsaicin; alkaloids; vitamin C; palmitic acid.
Uses (fresh or dried fruit) Spasmolytic; nutritive and stimulant. Aids digestion; of use in diarrhoea.
Mainly employed as a condiment and a vegetable.

Capsicum frutescens L SOLANACEAE
Tabasco Pepper Cayenne Pepper
Cayenne was classified as *C. minimum* by Roxburgh, but is generally known as *C. frutescens*. It is the species which is used medicinally, and it is still included in many national pharmacopoeias. Traditionally it came from Cayenne in French Guiana.
Description Perennial shrub to 2 m; trunk becoming woody, 7.5 cm diameter. Leaves various, usually elliptical, 2 cm long; flowers white in groups of 2 or 3, 5 mm–1 cm wide. Fruit small and oblong.
Distribution Tropical and subtropical countries.

Cultivation Wild in parts of South America and southern India; cultivated elsewhere.
Constituents Capsicin; capsicain; alkaloids; vitamin C; palmitic acid.
Uses (dried ground fruit) Stimulant; spasmolytic; antiseptic; rubefacient. Used in flatulence, colic and to improve both the peripheral circulation and digestion. Occas-

ionally employed as a liniment in neuralgia or rheumatism. Weak infusion of benefit as throat gargle.
Contra-indications Large doses are an extreme irritant to the gastro-intestinal system.

Cardamine pratensis L CRUCIFERAE
Lady's Smock Cuckoo-flower/Bittercress
Lady's Smock is one of the first wild flowers to appear in spring, and is characteristic of moist meadows in Europe and America. It is rich in vitamins and minerals and was formerly cultivated and used as a common salad herb, often being found on market stalls. It has, unfortunately, now fallen into disuse. Cardamine is an ancient Greek name for Cress, and refers to its supposed heart-benefitting properties.
Description Slender erect perennial on short root-stock, to 25–50 cm. Leaves pinnately subdivided, consisting of 3–7 segments, oblong or rounded, 1 cm long. Basal leaves broader and form a rosette. Pale lilac or white flowers, 4 attractive petals 1 cm long, in terminal racemes appearing spring to early summer, and followed by 2.5 cm long fruit pod. Double flowers occasionally occur.
Distribution Native in temperate zones of northern Europe and America; prefers loamy soil saturated with water, beside streams, in damp meadows and moist woodland.
Cultivation Wild plant; once cultivated. May be raised from seed sown, when ripe, on damp

loamy soil.
Constituents Vitamins, especially C; minerals; mustard oil.
Uses (fresh leaves, flowering tops) Stomachic; nutritive. Infusion may be taken to promote the appetite, or in indigestion.
Eaten raw in salads, or cooked as vegetable; added to soups. Flavour similar to Watercress.

Carlina acaulis L COMPOSITAE
Carline Thistle Dwarf Thistle
Carlina is possibly derived from the name Charles (a king who traditionally protected his army from the plague with this plant); more certainly *acaulis* means 'stemless'.

Known in France as Baromètre because it closes at the approach of rain.
Description Stemless or short-stemmed perennial to 5 cm on taproot. Bearing oblong 30 cm-long pinnate leaves, divided into numerous spiny segments. Flower-head large (to 12.5 cm) solitary, creamy-white, composed entirely of disc florets; appearing late summer to mid-autumn.
Distribution Native to south and central Europe. In heathland, meadowland, on poor, dry, stony calcareous soils in warm positions to 2800 m.
Cultivation Wild plant.
Constituents Essential oil; resin; tannins; inulin; antibiotic substances, carlinoxide and carlinene.
Uses (dried root) Cholagogue; diuretic; antibacterial; vulnerary; stomachic.
Of benefit in dropsy and urine retention; in skin complaints such as acne and eczema; in some liver disorders, or as a stomachic tonic. The decoction may be used to clean wounds or as an antiseptic gargle. Used in veterinary medicine to stimulate appetite of cattle.
Contra-indications Purgative and emetic in large doses.

Carum carvi L UMBELLIFERAE
Caraway Caraway Seed
Both the common and Latin names of this herb stem directly from the ancient Arabic word for its seed *karawiya*, which are known to have been used by man as medicine and as a flavouring since the early Egyptians. Caraway cultivation is mentioned in the Bible, and the seed has been found among the remains of food at Mesolithic sites – it has thus been widely used for 5000 years, and it is still extensively cultivated for use as a flavouring and as a carminative.
Description Typical umbelliferous biennial; rosette of bipinnate or tripinnate feathery leaves in first year followed by erect slender branched stem 20–100 cm bearing few pinnate leaves and umbels of numerous minute white flowers. Appearing mid to late summer. Fruit when ripe (late summer to late autumn) 3–5 mm long, oblong, strongly ribbed.
Distribution Native to mid-East, Asia, Central

Europe; very widely distributed and naturalized. Prefers waste-grounds.
Cultivation Wild plant. Commercially and horticulturally cultivated on a wide scale, especially in Germany and Holland. Tolerates most soils; sow late summer for seed harvesting the following summer.
Constituents Volatile oils, which prevent flatulence and promote secretion of gastric juices.
Uses (ripe fruit, young fresh leaf, fresh roots) Carminative; aromatic. Of much benefit in flatulent indigestion, lack of appetite, diarrhoea. Safe to use with children.
Seed has wide culinary use as flavouring.
Young leaves added to salads; root boiled as vegetable.
Used to flavour liqueurs such as Kümmel.

Cassia angustifolia Vahl. LEGUMINOSAE
Senna Tinnevelly Senna
Senna is well-known for its effectiveness in cases of constipation, and the herb is still officially recognized by inclusion in most national pharmacopoeias. It was first brought into medical usage by Arabian physicians of the ninth century when the best sort was considered to come from Mecca. Another species, *Cassia acutifolia*, provides the slightly inferior 'Alexandrian senna'.
Description Perennial shrub or undershrub to 75 cm with pale erect angled branches. Leaves subdivided into 4–8 leaflets, oval-lanceolate, smooth, 2.5–6 cm long, 7–8 mm wide; flowers on erect racemes, small, yellow, numerous. Followed by fruit, 15–17 mm broad.
Distribution Native to Arabia and Somaliland; introduced in southern India, especially Madura, Mysore and Tinnevelly.
Cultivation Wild plant. Cultivated commercially in India, and to a lesser extent in Arabia and Somaliland.
Constituents Anthraquinone derivatives, especially rhein, aloe-emodin, kaempferin, isorhamnetin; also beta-sitosterol; kaempferol; myricyl

alcohol and resin. Purgative action due to anthraquinone substances acting on lower bowel wall and nerves (Auerbach's plexus) in the wall.

Uses (dried fruit, dried leaflets) Cathartic. Widely used alone or more commonly in combination with aromatics to treat constipation. May be taken as a tea with slices of Ginger or Coriander Seed.

Contra-indications Not to be used in spastic constipation or colitis. Large doses of the leaf cause nausea, griping pain and red coloration of the urine.

Castanea sativa Mill. FAGACEAE
Sweet Chestnut Spanish or Eurasian Chestnut

Kastanea was the classical name for this attractive tree which produces the largest and best nuts only when grown in a mediterranean climate. These nuts, once known as *kastana*, are now called *marones* and traditionally make the best stuffing for turkey.

Description Tree to 30 m; thick dark brown corrugated bark with spiral fissures; large buds 4–5 mm wide, ovoid; leaves oblong-lanceolate 10–25 cm long, coarsely serrated, dark green above, light green and glabrous beneath. Flowers (catkins) 12–20 cm long, appearing late spring to early summer, followed by a burr enclosing 1–3 nuts, 2.5 cm wide.

Distribution Native to western Asia, south Europe and North Africa. Introduced into America and Europe. Tolerates most soils, prefers deep sandy loam.

Cultivation Wild plant; widely grown and hundreds of varieties now exist, some of which are cultivated for food. Best propagated by grafting.

Constituents Tannin; albumin; gum; resin; alkaloids.

Uses (nuts) Nutritive. The fresh leaf was once taken as a decoction in whooping-cough, and the bark was formerly employed as an antipyretic.

Nuts boiled, roasted, ground into flour, and used in pâtés, tarts, bread and soups.

Good quality timber obtained from the tree.

Caulophyllum thalictroides (L) Michx.
BERBERIDACEAE
Blue Cohosh Papoose Root

Eighty years ago this herb was included in the United States Pharmacopoeia and was considered worthy of detailed study and use in obstetric and gynaecological conditions. American Indian women drank an infusion of the root for two weeks prior to childbirth, which was usually comparatively painless. The herb is also called Blue or Yellow Ginseng. Its use is now restricted to herbal medicine.

Description Erect perennial to 1 m on contorted branched root-stock; stem terminated in large sessile tripinnate leaf. Other leaves 2 or 3 pinnate; leaflets being oval, usually 2–3 lobed, 2.5–10 cm long. Flowers 6-petalled, yellowish-green (occasionally purplish) appearing late spring to mid-summer on peduncle arising

from base of upper leaf. Fruit 1 cm diameter, blue-black.

Distribution United States and Canada; especially in moist woodland and mountain glades.

Cultivation Wild plant.

Constituents Saponin; green-yellow colouring matter; resins; starch; salts; unknown substances acting on voluntary and involuntary muscle – especially the uterus.

Uses (dried rhizome and root) Oxytocic. Once used to facilitate childbirth and treat chronic rheumatism. Also used in fevers but only weak diaphoretic action has been shown.

Contra-indications Powder is irritant, especially to mucous membranes. May cause pain to fingers and toes.

Celastrus scandens L CELASTRACEAE
False Bittersweet American or Climbing Bittersweet

A member of the spindle-tree family and a

common plant found growing beside roads in the American Appalachians. This and related species such as *C. orbiculatus* are useful plants to grow as trellis or wall covers. Now rarely used even in folk medicine.

Description Twining shrub to 8 m. Leaves 5–12.5 cm long, ovate to ovate-lanceolate, serrated. Flowers very small, numerous, greenish, on terminal racemes 10 cm long, followed by orange-yellow seed capsules, 1 cm diameter.

Distribution Canada and United States from Quebec to New Mexico. Prefers dense moist thickets and roadsides.

Cultivation Wild plant.

Constituents Active principles unknown.

Uses (dried root bark) Emetic; diuretic; cholagogue; diaphoretic.

Used formerly in biliary obstruction, to promote menstruation and to treat skin cancer. Attractive orange fruits used in flower arrangements.

Centaurea cyanus L COMPOSITAE
Cornflower Bluebottle/Bachelor's Button

Once common in cornfields but in parts of Europe now becoming much rarer because of changing agricultural methods; the Cornflower gained its name by the translation of the apothecaries' term for the drug – 'flos frumenti'. Before the sixteenth century it was called Blue Bothem or Bluebottle. Both this and another species (*C. montana* L), growing in the mountainous areas of Europe, are considered excellent eyewashes for tired eyes. Tradition maintains they are most effective for blue eyes while a completely different plant – *Plantago major* (the Greater Plantain) – is believed to be best for brown eyes.

Description Annual herb on erect wiry stem 20–90 cm high; leaves grey, downy, alternate, linear-lanceolate, usually less than 5 mm wide, 7.5–15 cm long. Bract fringes silvery. Flowers on large solitary capitulae 2.5–4 cm wide, bright blue (occasionally white, pink or purple). Only disc florets present. Appearing midsummer to early autumn.

Distribution Native to south and east Europe, naturalized in parts of North America. Intro-

duced elsewhere. Found especially on waste-grounds on porous nutrient-rich soil.
Cultivation Wild plant (becoming rare or less common). Widely cultivated horticulturally from seed sown in spring on sunny site.
Constituents Sterols; cyanin; cyanin chloride; fragasin.
Uses (dried flower-head) Diuretic; tonic; mild astringent. A decoction may be used as an eyewash in eye inflammation and fatigue. A blue ink was formerly made from the flower juice.
Flowers used in pot-pourris.

Centaurium erythraea Rafn. GENTIANACEAE
Centaury Lesser or Common Centaury/Century
Common Centaury is named after the centaur Chiron who treated himself with the herb after suffering an arrow wound. The plant is also called Gentian since it has similar properties to the true Gentian (*Gentiana lutea*) and is used for the same purposes. It was considered a lucky plant by some of the Celtic peoples of Europe. Centaury was widely grown in the Middle Ages, and it is still used today as an ingredient of vermouth.
Description Biennial or annual 2–50 cm high; stems erect, glabrous, branching to form inflorescence. Basal rosette of elliptic leaves 1–5 cm long, 8–20 mm wide; stem leaves shorter, linear, oval, glabrous with 5 veins. Flowers sessile, pale red, 1 cm long, borne on apical corymbs of 6–10 flowers. Appearing late summer to mid-autumn.
Distribution Central European native; distributed from western Europe to western Siberia; introduced elsewhere. Prefers dry slopes, woodland and roadsides.
Cultivation Wild plant. Cultivated commercially on a small scale in North Africa and central Europe. Seed sown in spring or autumn.
Constituents Glycosidic bitter principles and related compounds which stimulate gastric and salivary secretions.
Uses (dried flowering plant) Aromatic; bitter; stomachic. Stimulates appetite and bile secretion; of benefit in weak digestion. Widely used as a tonic. Has an insignificant antipyretic effect.
Important constituent of gastric herbal teas; used in bitter herb liqueurs.

Centranthus ruber (L) DC VALERIANACEAE
Red Valerian Red-spurred Valerian/Fox's Brush
The Red-spurred Valerian has none of the medicinal properties of the closely related 'official' Valerian (*Valeriana officinalis*). Both Gesner and Linnaeus classified the herb botanically as *Valeriana ruber*, and Gerard called it Red Valerian or Red Cow Basil.
Description Perennial on woody based stems to 1 m; leaves ovate to lanceolate 10 cm long, sessile, entire, occasionally toothed at base. Flowers 5 mm wide, red or pink, the corolla is tubular and spurred at the base. Appears late spring.
Distribution Europe to south-west Asia; prefers old walls, cliffs, chalky sites.
Cultivation Wild plant; limited horticultural use. A white variety, *C. ruber* var. *albus*, exists. Propagated by root division in spring or autumn.

Constituents Unknown.
Uses (fresh leaves and root-stock) No medical use.
Used in salads (bitter), cooked as a vegetable. Root-stock used in soups.
Attractive garden plant.

Cephaelis ipecacuanha (Brot.) A. Rich.
RUBIACEAE
Ipecacuanha
Ipecacuanha – known as *poaya* in its native Brazil and long used there for medical purposes – did not reach Europe until 1672 and was not botanically identified until 1800. Its use for dysentery was proven and promoted by a Parisian physician called Helvetius who in 1688 sold the secret of his success to the court of Louis XIV.
The drug's effectiveness is emphasized by its current inclusion in all national pharmacopoeias except the Chinese.
Description Small straggling shrub on creeping fibrous roots initially smooth becoming en-

larged and annulated (banded). Stem continuous with root-stock, smooth, green, angular to 30 cm, bearing few opposite, ovate, entire leaves. Flowers white in heads on terminal solitary peduncles, appearing late winter to early spring. Bears clusters of dark purple berries.
Distribution Indigenous to Brazil; introduced elsewhere. Grows in clumps in moist and shady forests.
Cultivation Wild plant; cultivated in Brazil, India (Bengal), Malaysia, Burma.
Constituents Alkaloids comprising mainly emetine and cephaeline, together with psychotrine, methyl-psychotrine and emetamine. Also a glycoside; ipecacuanhin; starch, ipecacuanhic acid.
Uses (dried root) Emetic; powerful expectorant. Used in acute and chronic bronchitis. Prevents cyst formation in amoebic dysentery. Useful in acute dysentery and as a diaphoretic.

Contra-indications Dangerous in large doses as it irritates the whole gastro-intestinal tract, causing serious vomiting and diarrhoea. Powder irritates skin and mucous membranes causing violent sneezing and coughing. To be used by medical personnel only.

Cereus grandiflorus Mill. CACTACEAE
Night Flowering Cereus
Although many cacti provide food and drink, comparatively few are proven effective medicinally. One exception is the Night Flowering Cereus which is characterized by its exceedingly large and beautiful scented flowers. The plant is commonly grown as a house plant.
Description Perennial succulent shrub; stem 5 or 6 ribbed, simple or rarely branched, 1–4 cm diameter, dark green, prickly. Flowers white, terminal or lateral, very large 20–30 cm in diameter. They bloom in the evening, last 6 hours, and die. Fruit ovate, scaly, orange-red.
Distribution West Indian native; tropical America, Mexico.
Cultivation Wild plant; grown horticulturally as a house plant in sharp, sandy soil.
Constituents Resins; alkaloids; unknown substances. The method of action is not fully understood.
Uses (fresh or dried flowers, young stems)

Cardiac stimulant; increasing the force of myocardial contractions. Used in cardiac arrhythmias and heart failure. Once used in cases of dropsy.

Cetraria islandica (L) Ach. PARMELIACEAE
Iceland Moss
This is not a moss but a lichen and it has long been used as a foodstuff in the cold northern countries where it flourishes. It is still employed in folk medicine largely because of its nutritive properties, although Linnaeus recommended its general use in medicine for pulmonary diseases. It was once called 'muscus catharticus' which suggests wrongly that it possesses purgative properties.
Description Lichen, consisting of erect dichotomously branched, curling thallus 3–12 cm high; upper surface olive-brown or grey, paler lower surface with depressed white spots;

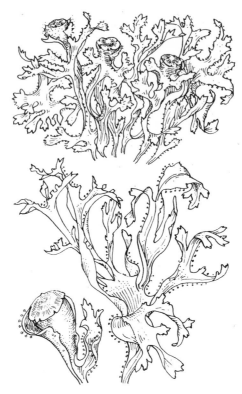

fruits rare, apical, rounded, rust coloured to 1 cm diameter.
Distribution Abundant in high northern latitudes, especially coniferous forests, mountainous parts of central Europe, North America. Also in Antarctica.
Cultivation Wild plant.
Constituents 70% mucilage, comprising lichenin and isolichenin, which acts as a demulcent; also bitter organic acids, including fumaroprotocetraric acid, which stimulate gastric secretions.
Uses (entire dried plant) Demulcent; mild tonic; nutritive; weak antituberculous agent. Stimulates appetite. Specifically of benefit in debilitating diseases associated with vomiting. May be ground and made into flour for baking bread or boiled in milk. Edible jelly made by boiling soaked plant to remove bitterness.

Chamaemelum nobile (L) All. COMPOSITAE
Chamomile Roman, Common or Double Chamomile
This is one of the best known of all herbs and has been in continuous use from the time of the Egyptians (who dedicated it to their Gods), until today when it is widely available prepacked in tea bags. Its name derives from the Greek *chamaimelon* meaning 'apple on the ground' since all parts of the herb are strongly apple-scented.
Description Aromatic perennial to 30 cm with creeping root-stock, low growing, hairy stems, branched and supporting leaflets divided into many segments. Flowers consist almost entirely of yellow-white ligulate florets, 15 mm–3 cm wide, born singly on long erect stems. From mid-summer to mid-autumn.
Distribution Indigenous to southern Europe; introduced and widespread elsewhere; prefers

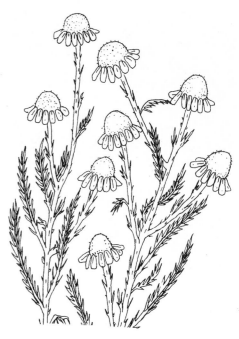

dry, sandy soil in full sun.
Cultivation Commercially grown in central Europe. To ensure double flower-heads, propagate vegetatively by root-stock division in early spring. The non-flowering clone 'treneague' ideal for lawns; 100 plantlets cover 2.5 sq.m., planted at 15 cm spacings. Succeeds on any free-draining soil even in part shade.
Constituents Volatile oil, comprising azulene, esters of angelic and tiglic acids, anthemal, anthemene. Action antiseptic; anti-inflammatory; anti-spasmodic. Improves appetite. Also inositol, and a bitter glycoside, anthemic acid.
Uses (dried flower-heads) Spasmolytic; sedative; carminative. Relieves painful menstruation, dyspepsia, vomiting and nausea. Excellent in flatulent dyspepsia taken as tisane. Whole herb used in beer manufacture.
Used to lighten hair.
Contra-indications Excessive dosage produces vomiting and vertigo.

Chelidonium majus L PAPAVERACEAE
Greater Celandine
The fact that Greater Celandine is commonly found on waste-ground near to habitation indicates that this is yet another herb once cultivated and now forgotten. It is still used in herbal medicine however, chiefly for liver problems, but no longer for its traditional ability to improve poor sight. Dioscorides called the herb *chelidonion* (from *khelidon* – a swallow) since it was supposed to flower when swallows were migrating.
Description Perennial 30–90 cm high; stem branched, slightly hairy, leaves pinnate, finely hairy or glabrous, with 5–7 ovate or oblong leaflets crenated or toothed, blue-green underneath; flowers yellow, 4-petalled, 2–2.5 cm diameter, appearing early to mid-summer. Followed by erect thin green capsules 3–5 cm long.
Distribution Native to Europe, naturalized in eastern North America, introduced elsewhere.

Found on waste-ground, wood edges, paths and walls primarily near habitation.
Cultivation Wild plant. Propagate by root division in spring.
Constituents Acrid orange coloured latex containing several alkaloids, especially chelidonine and chelerythrin; a bitter principle, chelidoxanthin; citric, malic and chelidonic acids; saponin. Acts as an antispasmodic on smooth muscle, such as gall bladder and bladder.
Uses (fresh or dried flowering plant, fresh latex) Cholagogue; narcotic; purgative; antimitotic. Principally used in inflammations of biliary duct and gall bladder, such as gall stones and cholecystitis. Fresh juice formerly used externally on warts.
Contra-indications Large doses POISONOUS; side-effects include sleepiness, skin irritation, respiratory tract irritation causing violent coughing and dyspnoea. Urine stained bright yellow. May cause ulcers.

Chelone glabra L ŚCROPHULARIACEAE
Turtle-head Balmony
This beautiful swamp plant possesses odourless flowers whose shape resembles that of a turtle's head (*chelone* is Greek for tortoise). It has long been a favourite tonic in North American folk medicine, but has not been scientifically examined.
Description Perennial to 1.5 m; stem erect smooth, square, bearing opposite, sessile or shortly petiolate dark green shiny leaves, 7–15 cm long, narrow and pointed, somewhat serrate. Flowers white or rose-tinged, 2.5 cm long, in terminal or axillary spikes. Appearing late summer to mid-autumn.
Distribution North America from Newfoundland to Florida and Texas. Found on low wet ground, stream margins, wet forests and thickets.
Cultivation Wild plant.
Constituents No analysis available.
Uses (dried flowering plant) Cholagogue;

laxative; anthelmintic. Used in general intestinal disorders as a tonic. Of benefit in anorexia, indigestion, constipation and cholecystitis. Once used as an ointment to relieve irritation of piles.

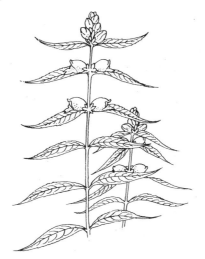

Chenopodium album L CHENOPODIACEAE
Fat Hen White Goosefoot/Common Pigweed
The Chenopodiaceae or Goosefoot family (from the Greek *khenopodion* meaning goose foot which is the shape of the leaves of some species) includes 1500 species of rather unattractive plants, many of which are important edible plants, for example, spinach and beet. Fat Hen and the closely related Good King Henry (*Chenopodium bonus-henricus*) were eaten from neolithic times until the nineteenth century, and the fatty seed from *C. album* was included in the ritualistic last meal of Tollmund Man, sacrificed in Denmark in 100 B.C.
Description Annual to 1 m consisting of short, often reddish, branched stem, bearing bluish-green lanceolate toothed variable-sized leaves, and mealy white inflorescence. Flowers small, greenish-white, in clusters, appearing mid-summer to mid-autumn.
Distribution European native; found in nitrogenous weedy places, often one of the first plants to appear on disturbed soil.
Cultivation Wild plant.

Constituents Rich in iron, calcium, vitamins B₁ and C.
Uses (fresh young leaf, seed) Nutritive. No common medicinal use, although mildly laxative.
Seed can be ground and used as flour.
Leaf eaten as cooked green vegetable or raw. It is more nutritious than spinach or cabbage.
Produces a red to golden-red dye.
Can be used as animal fodder.

Chenopodium ambrosioides var. *anthelmintium* L CHENOPODIACEAE
American Wormseed Mexican Tea
Although indigenous to Mexico this herb has become thoroughly naturalized as far north as New England, and it was introduced into Europe in 1732. Mexican Tea was once included in the United States Pharmacopoeia, but is now restricted to American folk medicine.
Description Strong smelling annual reaching 1.25 m, branching profusely from ground level; leaves alternate, oblong-lanceolate, 12.5 cm long; flowers greenish, small, arranged on leafless spikes appearing late summer to late autumn.
Distribution America, especially tropical central America; widely naturalized. On dry waste

places and previously cultivated land.
Cultivation Wild plant.
Constituents Volatile chenopodium oil.
Uses (fruit, entire flowering plant) Anthelmintic, especially for roundworm and hookworm, and used in both humans and animals. Tea from leaf reported to stimulate milk flow and to relieve pain after childbirth. Main use as the source of chenopodium oil for incorporation into anthelmintic preparations.
Contra-indications POISONOUS. Large doses cause vertigo, deafness, paralysis, incontinence, sweating, jaundice, and death.

Chionanthus virginicus L OLEACEAE
Fringe Tree Snowdrop Tree/Old Man's Beard
All the common names of this beautiful tree refer to its spectacular appearance when in flower, for which reason it has of course been

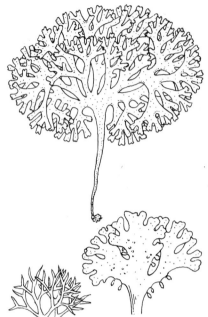

widely cultivated. From a distance the flowering tree appears to be covered with snow, and the name *chionanthus* is from the Greek meaning snow flower. The Fringe Tree belongs to the same family as the olive, lilac, jasmine and forsythia.

Description Deciduous shrub or tree to 8 m; leaves smooth or downy, oblong or oval, 7.5–20 cm long, opposite. Flowers delicate, fringe-like, numerous, white, 2.5 cm long, on long stems, in panicles 10–20 cm long. Appearing late spring to mid-summer and followed by fleshy, purple, ovoid drupes (berries).

Distribution Native to North America from Pennsylvania to Florida and Texas. Found in woods and thickets, on rich moist soils.

Cultivation Wild plant; cultivated as ornamental tree.

Constituents Saponins; phyllyrin; a lignan glycoside.

Uses (dried root bark, fresh trunk bark) Antipyretic; diuretic; cholagogue; hepatic stimulant. An infusion once used as a general tonic after debilitating disease, especially of hepatic origin. Of benefit in skin inflammations, cuts, ulcers and bruises when applied as a poultice.

Chondrus crispus (**L**) Stackh. GIGARTINACEAE
Carrageen Irish Moss
Irish Moss is unimportant medically and is not mentioned at all in classical writings. It was briefly promoted in 1831 by Dr Todhunter in Ireland, but it attracted little attention and is now largely of use in the food and cosmetic industries.

Description Cartilaginous seaweed, yellow-green to purplish-brown when fresh, white to yellow and translucent after drying. Thallus (fronds) 10–30 cm long, arising from subcylindrical stem, becoming flattened, curled and sometimes bifid. Fruiting bodies (cystocarps) small, oval, appearing on the branches of the thallus.

Distribution Coasts of north Atlantic Ocean on mainly rocky shores.

Cultivation Wild plant; collected in Ireland, Brittany and Massachussetts.

Constituents Mainly mucilage; proteins; iodine. When Irish moss is boiled, the soluble substances extracted are called carrageenin.

Uses (dried plant) Demulcent; nutritive. Formerly used to treat coughs.

Used mostly as a gelatin substitute in jelly manufacture; as an emulsifying agent for cod-liver and other oils; in the food industry as a suspending and gelling agent.

Once used for dressing cotton, stuffing mattresses, fining beer, feeding cattle, and as a colour thickener in cloth printing.

Chrysanthemum balsamita L COMPOSITAE
Alecost Costmary/Bible-leaf Mace
The most obvious characteristic of this ancient herb is its pleasant balsam-like scent from which it is known in several languages as the Balsam Herb. The common English names also refer to this aroma by their incorporation of the Greek word *kostos*; *kostos* was an old Asian herb used in perfumery which had a similar odour to *C. balsamita*. Alecost is famous as the pre-eminent Middle Ages agent for flavouring and preparing ale.

Description Hardy aromatic perennial to 1 m; leaves ovate 5–15 cm long, finely serrate, often with pair of small lobes at the base; greyish-green. Flowers 1 cm broad, yellow, button-like, appearing late summer to early autumn.

Distribution Western Asian native; naturalized in North America, Europe. Tolerates any soil; prefers sunny position.

Cultivation Wild plant; once widely cultivated as a garden plant. Propagate by root division spring or autumn, or by seed sown in spring. It cannot be raised from seed in cool climates. If grown in the shade it will not flower.

Constituents Volatile oil.

Uses (fresh and dried leaf) Stomachic. Rarely used medicinally; an ointment once used as a salve in burns and stings.

Wide culinary uses; including spring salad, flavouring home-made beer, soups, cakes, poultry.

Formerly a cosmetic water was made from the leaf.

Chrysanthemum cinerariifolium (Trevir) Vis.
COMPOSITAE
Pyrethrum Flower Dalmatian Pyrethrum
C. cinerariifolium is the source of the best-known natural insecticide, pyrethrum, which is renowned for its possession of an extremely rapid paralyzing effect and toxicity to a wide range of insects. It is non-toxic to mammals, however. For this reason it is used as a spray to kill the vectors of certain insect-transmitted diseases in aircraft. Recent work has shown that the flower-heads possess weak antibiotic activity, although the herb is not used medicinally.

Description Herbaceous perennial 30–75 cm tall with slender, hairy stems; leaves 15–30 cm long, petiolate, oblong or oval, subdivided into linear segments. Flowers solitary on long slender peduncles, white, appearing early summer to early autumn.

Distribution Indigenous to parts of Yugoslavia

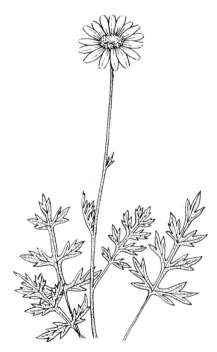

and adjacent coastal islands; prefers littoral zones but also found inland including mountainous areas.

Cultivation Wild plant. Cultivated commercially in Japan, Kenya, South Africa, parts of central Europe. Propagation by seed sown in autumn, thinning out in the following mid-spring.

Constituents Pyrethrins, comprising the keto-esters cinerin I and II, pyrethrin I and II; also chrysanthine and chrysanthene; all possess insecticidal properties.

Uses (dried and powdered flower-heads) No medicinal action; used only as a non-toxic insecticide for control of the bedbug, mosquito, cockroach, domestic fly and other pests.

Contra-indications Prolonged human contact may lead to allergic dermatitis, allergic rhinitis and asthma.

Chrysanthemum parthenium (L) Bernh.
COMPOSITAE

Feverfew Featherfew

There is evidence that Feverfew was used as a general purpose tonic in previous ages, its common name being derived from the Latin *febrifugia* meaning a substance which drives out fevers. The old herbalists' term 'febrifuge' – from the same stem – has now been replaced with the medical description, antipyretic, but strangely the herb is rarely employed in folk medicine to treat fevers. It is an attractive, robust and vigorously growing garden plant.

Description Perennial, sometimes biennial, to 90 cm; much branched with yellow-green, strongly scented pinnate leaves, the 1–2 leaflets not exceeding 7.5 cm long. Many flowers, 1–2 cm wide consisting of yellow disc florets, white ray florets, in tight clusters, appear mid-summer to mid-autumn.

Distribution South-east European native; introduced elsewhere. Prefers dry sites on any well-drained soil.

Cultivation Wild plant, propagated by root division, cuttings and seed sown in early to mid-spring. Double-flowered variety grown horticulturally.

Constituents Volatile oils.

Uses (dried leaf, dried flowering plant) Bitter; aperient; tonic.

An infusion is of benefit in indigestion, as a general tonic and to promote menstruation. Once used as a mild sedative.

Small quantities added to food 'cuts' the grease.

Employed as a moth repellent.

Cichorium intybus L COMPOSITAE

Chicory Succory/Wild Succory

The use of Chicory can be traced back to the Egyptians, who – like the Arabians – used the blanched leaves as a salad, a custom continued to this day on a commercial scale in Belgium and horticulturally throughout Europe. Sometimes the blanched winter salad leaves are known as Endive, which is derived from the Arabic word *hendibeh*: the specific botanical name comes from the same source. Dickens in his *Household Words* described the extensive cultivation of 'chiccory' in England for the root which was ground and roasted to be used

as a coffee substitute.

Description Deep rooted perennial reaching 1.5 m; stem bristly or hairy bearing rigid branches. Upper parts practically leafless with small bract-like leaves; lower leaves entire, broadly oblong or lanceolate, partly clasping and bristly beneath. Flowers in large capitula of 4 cm diameter, azure blue and consisting only of ray florets. Appearing from late summer to mid-autumn. Flower-heads close by midday.

Distribution European native; introduced elsewhere; naturalized in the United States. On roadsides, field edges, on nitrogenous, calcareous and alluvial soils.

Cultivation Wild plant; widely cultivated horticulturally and commercially. Seed sown in well-manured soil from late spring to mid-summer, thinned to 15–20 cm apart in mid-summer to late summer. Forced blanched salad heads best obtained from the variety *Witloof*: lift the root in late autumn, shorten to

20 cm, remove all side-shoots and leaves and stack in dry sand in the dark. For coffee substitute, use roots of the varieties *Magdeburg* and *Brunswick* or *Witloof*. White and pink horticultural races also exist.

Constituents Inulin; sugar; mineral salts; lipids; vitamins B, C, K and P; bitter principles (sesquiterpenoid lactones) chiefly lactucine and lactupicrine.

Uses (fresh leaf, root) Diuretic; weak tonic; laxative. Of little medical use; formerly employed as an aid in jaundice, and may protect the liver from the effects of excessive coffee drinking. Increases glandular secretions slightly.

Root roasted and ground as a coffee substitute or additive; can be boiled or baked, or used as flour. Forced leaves used as a winter salad; young leaves added to summer salads.

Leaves produce a blue dye.

Contra-indications Excessive and continued use may impair function of the retina.

Cimicifuga racemosa (L) Nutt.
RANUNCULACEAE

Black Cohosh Black Snakeroot/Bugbane

Linnaeus described this herb in his *Materia Medica* of the eighteenth century as *Actaea racemis longissimus*, but it was first called *Christophoriana canadensis racemosa* by Plukenet in 1696. It is an American herb, introduced into medical practice in America in 1828 by Garden, and used briefly in Europe from 1860. Now only employed by Anglo-American herbalists of the Physiomedical school.

Description Graceful perennial 1–2.5 m high on thick, gnarled, blackish root-stock bearing smooth, furrowed stem with alternate leaves subdivided into 2-, 3- or 5-ovate, toothed leaflets, 4–7.5 cm long. Inflorescence 30–100 cm long, consisting of foetid, creamy-white flowers with numerous long stamens, on a terminal raceme; appears early summer to early autumn.

Distribution Indigenous to Canada and the eastern United States, especially Massachusetts, Ohio, Indiana and Georgia. Prefers rich open woodland and cleared hillsides.

Cultivation Wild plant.

Constituents Resins and salicylic acid, both acting as anti-rheumatic agents; isoferulic acid; phytosterols; alkaloids; tannic acid; 3 unidenfied crystalline alcohols. (A resinoid impure mixture, cimicifugin, is produced by adding tincture of cimicifuga to water.)

Uses (dried root-stock) Anti-rheumatic; a bitter; mild expectorant; emmenagogue; sedative. Particularly effective in acute stage of rheumatoid arthritis, sciatica, and chorea. Apparently most successfully used in females, and acts specifically on the uterus, easing uterine cramps.

Contra-indications Large doses irritate nerve centres, and may cause abortion.

Cinchona officinalis L RUBIACEAE
Cinchona Quinine Tree/Peruvian Bark

The Spanish conquerors learned of the antipyretic properties of Cinchona Bark from the inhabitants of Peru in the sixteenth century; it is not certain, however, that they used the material themselves, considering it extremely powerful. It was introduced into Spain in 1639, and promoted throughout Europe by the Jesuits who gave the powder to those suffering from fever. Medical opinion varied as to its safety, but by 1677 it was introduced into the London Pharmacopoeia. About 12 species of Cinchona are now used as sources of the bark, which is mainly employed for the isolation of quinine, once used as an antimalarial agent.

Description The Cinchonas are evergreen trees from 6–25 m tall; reduced to shrubs at the limits of their habitat. Leaves extremely vari-

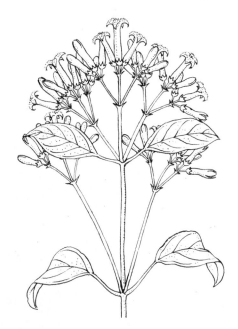

able but often bright green, obovate or lanceolate from 7.5–50 cm long, finely veined with crimson, traversed by prominent midrib, and borne on a brown petiole. Flowers very fragrant, small, deep rose-crimson, clustered on panicles. The useful species are differentiated from others by presence of curly hairs bordering the corolla, by its mode of capsule dehiscence from below upwards and by

presence of small pits (scrobiculi) at the vein axils on underside of leaf.

Distribution South American natives, occurring exclusively on the western side of the subcontinent. Also Java, Ceylon, Burma, India, East Africa. Grows only in mountainous regions, most valuable species being found and cultivated from 1500–2500 m.

Cultivation Wild plant; mostly cultivated commercially in Java.

Constituents 20 alkaloids including quinine, cinchonine, cinchonidine, and quinidine; a glycoside; cinchona red; starch; wax; fat; cinchotannic acid; quinic, quinoic and oxalic acids.

Uses (dried stem bark) Antipyretic; bitter tonic; stomachic.

More slowly absorbed and more irritant to the gastro-intestinal tract than quinine in its pure form. Useful astringent throat gargle. Tincture employed for preventative treatment of the common cold; orthodox medicine still employs quinine for the relief of muscle cramps.

Powdered bark used in astringent toothpowders.

May be used as a red dye for fabrics.

Contra-indications May cause vomiting; prolonged usage can cause cinchonism, symptoms of which include deafness and blindness.

Cinnamomum camphora Nees et Eberm.
LAURACEAE
Camphor Tree Laurel Camphor

The Camphor Tree was mentioned in the sixteenth-century Chinese herbal *Pun-tsao-kang-muh* and earlier by Marco Polo at the end of the thirteenth century.

The camphor product was certainly known before this and was regarded as one of the most rare and valuable perfumes; it is, however, not certain whether this camphor was derived from *C. camphora* or from *Dryobalanops aromatica*, a Sumatran tree. In 1563 Garcia de Orta wrote that Sumatran Camphor was so superior and costly that none found its way to Europe. Certainly Camphor was known in European medicine by the twelfth century since the German abbess Hildegarde used it – as *ganphora*.

Description Dense topped evergreen tree reaching 12 m, and occasionally even taller; trunk enlarged at base. Leaves camphor scented, alternate, acuminate, smooth and shiny above, whitish beneath, 5–12 cm long. Yellow flowers in axillary panicles appearing early summer.

Distribution Indigenous to China and Japan; introduced elsewhere. Flourishing in tropical and subtropical countries up to an altitude of 750 m.

Cultivation Wild plant; introduced horticulturally.

Constituents Obtained by distillation of 24–40-year-old wood. Camphor, white oil of Camphor, both comprising safrole, acetaldehyde, terpineol, eugenol, cineole, d-pinene, phellandrene.

Uses (Camphor; oil of Camphor) Weakly antiseptic; stimulant; carminative; mild expectorant; mild analgesic; rubefacient; parasiticide.

Used internally (rarely) for sedation in hysteria. Commonly employed externally as a counter-irritant in inflamed rheumatic joints, fibrositis, and neuralgia. Small doses stimulate respiration. Often used in combination with other substances.

Contra-indications Large internal doses toxic to children, causing respiratory failure.

Cinnamomum cassia Blume LAURACEAE
Cassia Bark Tree Chinese Cinnamon

Cassia and Cinnamon are confused in early

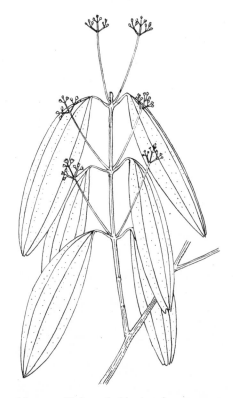

writings, and it is probable that the terms were sometimes used to describe different grades of the same or closely related plants. The spice is called *kwei* in the earliest Chinese herbal by

Shen-nung (2700 B.C.). It reached Europe in classical times via Arabian and Phoenician traders, and is frequently still used as an inferior substitute for Cinnamon.

Description Attractive evergreen tree to 7 m, white aromatic bark and angular branches; leaves oblong-lanceolate 7.5–10 cm long, on slender 6–8 mm long petiole. Flowers small on slender panicles, 7–12 cm long, appearing early summer.

Distribution Native of China; cultivated in China and Burma.

Cultivation Wild plant; also cultivated commercially.

Constituents Volatile oil; resin; tannin; lignin; bassorin; colouring matter. Oil of Cassia comprises largely cinnamaldehyde.

Uses (dried bark) Aromatic; carminative; astringent; stimulant.

Used as a powder or infusion in flatulence and nausea in a similar manner to Cinnamon, which it sometimes replaces. May be used alone or in combination to treat diarrhoea.

Cinnamomum zeylanicum Nees LAURACEAE

Cinnamon Tree Ceylon Cinnamon

Cinnamon was considered by the ancients as one of the most important aromatic spices available and is mentioned in the Old Testament in the same context as Myrrh, Olibanum, gold and silver. It is doubtful, however, whether the species *C. zeylanicum* was known before the thirteenth century, since the spice is not mentioned as a product of Ceylon – to which it was indigenous – until 1275, when it was documented by an Arab writer, Kazwini. The Portuguese occupied Ceylon in 1536 mainly to obtain supplies of Cinnamon, and the Dutch began its cultivation there in 1770 with such success that the total European demand was far exceeded, and for years large quantities had to be burned.

Description Medium-sized evergreen tree 6.5–10 m tall, with thick, smooth and pale bark; leaves opposite or rarely alternate, hard, 7.5–20 cm long and 4–7.5 cm wide, ovate or ovate-lanceolate, shiny above and paler beneath. Numerous yellowish-white flowers, disagreeable odour, in silky loose panicles longer than leaves on long peduncles.

Distribution Native of Ceylon, wild in southern India and Malaya; cultivated in Ceylon, India, Jamaica, Brazil, the Seychelles, and other tropical countries. In forests to 1000 m.

Cultivation Wild plant; cultivated commercially in coppices.

Constituents Volatile oil, whose action is carminative and antiseptic; also tannin and mucilage.

Uses (dried bark; volatile oil) Aromatic; astringent; stimulant; carminative.

Used as an intestinal stimulant and astringent to treat vomiting and nausea.

Widely employed as a spice; oil used in flavouring and in cordials. Limited use in perfumery.

Citrus aurantium var. *amara* (L) Link RUTACEAE

Bitter Orange Seville Orange/Bigarade

Known to the early Greeks, this was probably also the first orange grown in Europe in about the twelfth century. The Sweet Orange was not known until the mid-fifteenth century. The

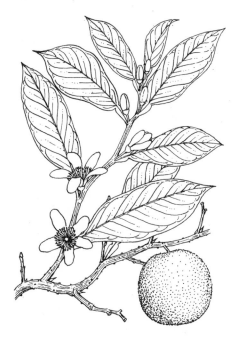

Bitter Orange is usually only employed in the food and perfume industry.

Description Glabrous evergreen tree to 8 m; branches spiny. Leaves alternate, ovate-oblong to 8 cm long, sinuate or crenate, petiole broad-winged. Flowers fragrant, white or pink, axillary, single or few; followed by 7.5 cm diameter globose orange to reddish fruit.

Distribution Asian native. Introduced and naturalized in south Europe, Florida, United States and elsewhere.

Cultivation Wild and cultivated commercially. Used as stock for the Sweet Orange. Easily raised from seed.

Constituents (flowers) Oil of neroli. a complex volatile oil. (fruit and rind) Volatile oil comprising limonene (to 90%); vitamin C; flavonoids; bitter compounds including naringine.

Uses (flowers, leaves, fruit, fruit rind) Aperitif; antispasmodic; sedative; cholagogue; tonic; vermifuge.

Neroli oil in vaseline is used in India as a preventive against leeches. Leaves and flowers in infusion act as sedative stomachics. Orange-flower water is used to flavour medicines. Employed in perfumery.

Used in conserves, and for flavouring.

Citrus limon Burm. RUTACEAE

Lemon

The Lemon is a household fruit today, but it was unknown in ancient Greece and Rome. The wild Lemon is probably a native of northern India, and is known in Hindustani as *limu* or *ninbu*, which passed into the Arabic *limun*.

European cultivation of the Lemon was carried out with Arabian knowledge and plants, and probably started in the thirteenth century in Spain or Sicily. Numerous varieties now exist.

Description Small glabrous tree 3–6 m high, with stout stiff thorns; leaves pale green, oblong to elliptic-ovate, 5–10 cm long, on short petioles with very narrow margins. Flowers 8–16 mm long, white inside and pink outside, clustered in the axils. Sour fruit 7.5–12.5 cm long, light yellow, oblong to ovoid terminating in a nipple.

Distribution Native to Asia; wild in India. Cultivated commercially especially in Mediterranean countries.

Cultivation Wild plant; extensive horticultural and commercial cultivation.

Constituents Citric acid; pectin; hesperidin; vitamins A, B and C; citral; citronellol; d-limonene; phellandrene; sesquiterpene.

Uses (fresh fruit, dried peel, juice, oil) Antiscorbutic; tonic; refrigerant; carminative; stimulant; aromatic.

Fresh juice employed as a household remedy

for the common cold; Lemon oil was once used as a carminative, and the peel is still employed as a bitter.

The widest use is for culinary purposes as a flavouring agent and as an antioxidant.

Used for cosmetic purposes as astringent, skin tonic, in scents.

Claviceps purpurea (Fried.) Tulasne
ASCOMYCETES
Ergot Ergot of Rye

Ergot is best known as the cause of a serious and spectacular human disease characterized by symptoms of hallucination and madness. It is now known as ergotism and arose in epidemic proportions throughout Europe from at least as early as the sixth century and lasted until 1816. The disease was called by a variety of names the most common being *Ignis sancti Antonii* or St Anthony's Fire, and was eventually discovered to be caused by eating flour or bread containing a high proportion of the Ergot fungus.

It was found to be of obstetric value in the 1550s by Lonitzer of Frankfurt and is retained to this day in many pharmacopoeias, including the British, French and German.

Description Ergot is the dried sclerotium, or resting stage, of a fungus which develops in the ovary of the rye plant (*Secale cereale* (L)), and other grasses belonging to the genera Agropyrum, Alopecurus, Anthoxanthum, Avena, Brachypodium, Calamagrostis, Dactylis, Hordeum and Triticum.

The sclerotium externally is dark violet to black, usually 1–3 cm long and 1–5 mm broad, fusiform, often tapering towards both ends, brittle. Internally whitish-pinkish to white with a faint odour. Appears in the autumn.

Distribution In all the cereal producing countries in areas or years of high humidity and then often at edges of rye fields.

Cultivation Wild; cultivated commercially by artificial inoculation of rye plant heads with the fungal spores.

Constituents Extremely complex, containing a number of alkaloids; carbohydrates; lipids; quaternary ammonium bases; sterols; dyes; amino-acids and amines. Six isomeric pairs of alkaloids have been isolated, including ergo-cistine, ergotamine, ergocryptine, ergocornine, ergosine and ergometrine. Most are derivatives of lysergic acid or iso-lysergic acid; action on the uterus is largely due to these alkaloids.

Uses (dried fungus) Uterine stimulant, haemostatic; circulatory stimulant; emmenagogue. Most effectively employed as a preventative against post-partum haemorrhage and as a stimulant to arrest bleeding in menorrhagia and metrorrhagia. Also used in neurology.

Contra-indications Large doses may induce abortion in pregnant women. Increases blood pressure. To be used by medical personnel only.

Cnicus benedictus L COMPOSITAE
Blessed Thistle

Carduus sanctus or *carduus benedictus* (the Sacred or Blessed Thistle) is still cultivated as a medicinal herb in certain European countries and has long enjoyed a reputation as an effective remedial plant. At one time considered a

cure-all its use now is generally restricted to inclusion in herbal tonics. *Cnicus* is the Latin name for Safflower which was once the name given to the thistle family.

Description Thistle-like branched annual to 70 cm; leaves lanceolate, dentate, with spines on each tooth, dark green, white-veined, 5–15 cm long. Flowers partially concealed within spiny bracts, yellow 3–4 cm wide, and appearing mid-summer to early autumn.

Distribution Mediterranean native; naturalized in United States; introduced elsewhere. Tolerates most soils.

Cultivation Wild plant; cultivated commercially. Easily raised from seed sown in spring or autumn, preferably on well-manured soil.

Constituents Volatile oil; a bitter principle, cnicin, which aids digestion.

Uses (dried flowering plant) Tonic; emetic; diaphoretic. Used as a weak infusion it stimulates the appetite and is said to act as a galactagogue. The flowering tops were once used to treat worms.

Mixed with wine to make an aperitif.

Young leaves used to be eaten in salads, flowerheads eaten in the manner of Artichokes, and root boiled as a pot herb.

Contra-indications Large doses strongly emetic.

Cocos nucifera L PALMAE
Coconut Palm

A well-known tree of enormous economic and nutritional importance in many tropical countries. Many parts of the palm are exploited, but the fruit or coconut is most useful; for this reason cultivated varieties have been bred which produce 100 to 200 coconuts each year. The generic name *Cocos* is from the Portuguese for monkey, as the nut looks like a monkey's face; *nucifera* means nut-bearing.

Description Palm tree to 25 m; trunk usually curving to one side and regularly ringed with leaf scars. Leaves in a terminal crown, very long (5 m) on a yellowish petiole which is deeply embedded in loose fibre surrounding the trunk; deeply pinnate and pendulous. Flowers followed by ovoid nuts 20 cm long, usually in bunches of 10 to 20.

Distribution Native to Malaysia and Polynesia; widely distributed throughout tropical zones. In coastal situations or occasionally inland.

Cultivation Wild. Widely cultivated commercially.

Constituents Oil, comprising the glycerides, trimyristin, trilaurin, triolein, tristearin and tripalmitin; also the glycerides of caprylic, capric and caproic acids.

Uses (oil, kernels, seed, leaves, sap) Nutritive;

anthelmintic. The seed is sometimes used as an anthelmintic in tropical countries. Fractionated coconut oil (containing medium chain triglycerides) is used in certain diets for conditions such as cystic fibrosis and steatorrhoea where patients are unable to absorb normal fats completely.

The oil is used as an ointment base, and in massage creams and certain medicated shampoos. Also used in sea-water soaps, and formerly in margarine.

Wide culinary use of the kernel as a food and flavouring, particularly in Indonesian cuisine; and the apical bud or 'cabbage' of the tree is eaten as a delicacy. The fermented sap is employed in palm wine and spirit manufacture.

Leaves are extensively used in basket, mat and rope manufacture; the husk fibre from the nut is similarly used in coconut matting and rope.

Coffea arabica L RUBIACEAE
Coffee Common or Arabian Coffee

The Coffee plant forms wild forests in parts of the Sudan and Abyssinia and for centuries the berry has been eaten raw by natives as a stimulant.

The habit of drinking Coffee probably originated with the Abyssinians, from whom the use

of Coffee spread into Arabia.

Rauwolf, the botanist, mentioned Coffee for the first time in 1573 when travelling in the Levant, and Prosper Alpinus described it more fully in 1591. European Coffee drinking began in Venice at the beginning of the seventeenth century, and was fashionable in England by 1652 and France by 1669.

It is thought that all the Coffee now exported from Brazil and the West Indies stems from the propagation of a single plant introduced to the Celebes in 1822.

Description Evergreen shrub 3–5 m high, initially with a single main trunk, later developing others from this; leaves dark green and glossy, thin, opposite, 7–12 cm long; 2.5–4 cm wide, abruptly acuminate with a point 15 mm long. White star-like flowers, fragrant, followed by 2-seeded deep red berry (beans) 15 mm long.

Distribution Native to tropical Africa; early introduction to Arabia. Introduced to tropical countries, especially abundant in the Americas. Prefers jungle conditions and partial shade.

Cultivation Wild and extensively cultivated commercially in plantations, often under artificial shading. Horticultural variegated

forms exist; grown indoors as a house plant.

Constituents Caffeine (1–2%), acting as a stimulant upon the central nervous system; volatile oils; colouring matter; tannin; traces of theobromine and its isomer, theophylline.

Uses (freshly roasted ground kernel) Stimulant; diuretic.

Taken as a general tonic stimulant, especially useful in narcotic poisoning. Decoction employed as a flavouring agent in pharmaceutical preparations.

Very wide use as a beverage, for colouring and flavouring purposes, and in liqueur and confectionery manufacture.

Contra-indications Excessive intake may cause insomnia, muscle tremor, restlessness, palpitations and tachycardia.

Cola acuminata (Beauv.) Schott et Endl.
STERCULIACEAE
Cola Nut Kola/Goora Nut

The Cola Nuts commercially available consist of the cotyledons, fleshy and white before drying, obtained from the 5 to 15 seeds of the large fruit of the Cola tree.

Fresh Nuts are seldom found outside Africa, where they are consumed raw before meals to promote digestion. They are also considered to improve the flavour of food.

Cola Nuts, described as *colla* were first seen in the Congo by Father Carli in 1667. The dried product does not contain the same properties as the fresh Nut, and most of it is used in soft drinks. It is still used in folk medicine as a stimulant.

Description Evergreen tree to 15 m high; leaves leathery, acute, entire, obovate, 10–20 cm long; yellow flowers of 15 mm diameter, in panicles, calyx tube green. Fruit 10–15 cm

long, containing red or white seeds 4–5 cm long, and consisting of cotyledons 2–5 cm long.

Distribution Native to north-west African coast, especially Sierra Leone and the Cameroons. Introduced elsewhere. Prefers coastal and estuary sites in forests.

Cultivation Wild plant; cultivated in West Africa, Java, Brazil and the West Indies.

Constituents Caffeine (1.5%), combined with kolatin in the fresh state, and unbound when dried; also theobromine; kola red; fat; sugar; starch.

Uses (dried cotyledons) Stimulant; anti-depressive.

Particularly employed in debilitated, exhausted and depressive conditions; in melancholia, anorexia and migraine.

A flavouring for soft drinks, cordials, ice creams and wines. Used in the manufacture of cola-type beverages.

A red dye is obtained from the Cola Nut.

Colchicum autumnale L LILIACEAE
Autumn Crocus Colchicum/Meadow Saffron

The Autumn Crocus is a rare example of a plant known since the early Greeks which was not introduced into medical practice until quite recently. Most of the ancient and medieval writers, except the Arabic physicians, considered Colchicum too poisonous to use, although it did appear briefly in the London Pharmacopoeia from 1618 to 1639.

Its modern use derives from the research of Wedel (1718) and Storck (1763) on the treatment of gout, for which purpose it is retained to this day in many countries.

Description Perennial; solitary pale purple flower, 6 petals on 20-cm long white 'stalk' which is actually an elongated corolla tube, appearing in the autumn from a corm 15 cm

below ground; 6 stamens, 3 styles; fleshy, lanceolate leaves 30 cm long first appear in the following spring, and enclose the seed-filled brown capsular fruit by mid-summer.

Distribution European native; prefers deep clay and nutrient rich loam in damp meadows and fen woodland.

Cultivation Wild plant; cultivated from seed collected in late summer, or from corms.

Constituents Several toxic alkaloids, largely

colchicine to which its action is due; also starch; gum; sugar; fat; tannin.

Uses (dried corms, seeds) Anti-rheumatic. Used to relieve the pain and inflammation of acute gout and rheumatism.

Contra-indications All parts highly POISONOUS, causing diarrhoea and sometimes death. Only to be used by medical personnel.

Commiphora molmol Engler BURSERACEAE
Myrrh Gum Myrrh/Myrrha

Used from the earliest times as a constituent of perfumes, unguents and incense, the modern name is directly derived from the old Hebrew and Arabic word *mur*, meaning bitter.

The ancient Greeks knew of Myrrh and a liquid form called *stacte* which is no longer found, but is thought to be a natural exudation of the Myrrh tree or a closely related species. Myrrh was highly prized in the Middle Ages and is still used as a mouthwash and in folk medicine.

Description Low stunted bush or small tree to 2.75 m high; trunk thick and bearing numerous irregular, knotted branches and smaller stout clustered branchlets, the latter spreading at right angles and terminating in a sharp spine. Few leaves, 1–1.5 cm long, at ends of short wart-like branchlets; trifoliate, the lateral leaflets minute, the terminal 1 cm long, obovate-oval, narrowed at the base, entire, glabrous.

Gum discharged through the bark naturally or after wounding.

Distribution Arabia; Somaliland. On basaltic soil in very hot areas.

Cultivation Wild plant.

Constituents Oleo-gum-resin, comprising 25–35% resin, 2.5–6.5% volatile oil, 50–60% gum.

Uses (dried oleo-gum-resin) Carminative; antiseptic; mildly expectorant; diuretic; diaphoretic.

Astringent to mucous membranes, and used as a gargle and mouthwash in inflammations of the mouth and pharynx. Tincture is applied to ulcers. Stimulates natural resistance of the body in septicaemia. Small doses effective in dyspepsia.

A constituent of some tooth-powders.

Used in veterinary medicine for wound treatment.

Employed in incense, and when burned repels mosquitos.

Conium maculatum L UMBELLIFERAE
Hemlock Poison Hemlock/Mother Die

Hemlock is best known historically as the principal, if not the only, ingredient of the Athenian State poison used as a method of execution for, among others, Thermanes, Phocion and Socrates. Dioscorides introduced it as a medicine mostly for the external treatment of herpes and erysipelas, and both Pliny and Avicenna considered it effective in the treatment of tumours. The old Roman name

for the herb was *cicuta*, a term found in tenth-century Anglo-Saxon works.

The poisonous nature of the plant varies considerably. Carpenter in 1850 claimed that Hemlock growing in London was harmless, and others maintain that it is less poisonous in colder climates than warmer ones. It must, however, always be treated as a dangerously poisonous plant.

Description Erect biennial herb, smelling of mice, arising from a forked root, and reaching 1.5 m; much branched, stems speckled and purple towards the base. Foliage dark and finely cut, 2–4 pinnate, glabrous; umbels of small white flowers appearing mid-summer to mid-autumn.

Distribution European native; extensively distributed in temperate zones. Found in weedy places especially in moist, warm sites by streams or field edges in loamy soil.

Cultivation Wild plant.

Constituents Several alkaloids, chiefly coniine, to which the intense toxicity of all parts of this plant is attributed; also methylconiine; conydrine; paraconine; oil of conium; conic acid.

Uses (unripe seed, fruit) Anodyne; sedative; antispasmodic.

Once used in neurological conditions such as epilepsy, mania and chorea, and in ancient times externally to treat breast tumours. Never employed today, not even in folk medicine. Although cooking is said to destroy the toxic constituents, this herb should never be eaten.

Contra-indications All parts, and especially the seed, are intensely POISONOUS.

Convallaria majalis L LILIACEAE
Lily-of-the-Valley May Lily

A flower which is frequently found in country gardens and which was shown as early as the sixteenth century to possess strong therapeutic action. It was known as *lilium convallium* to sixteenth-century apothecaries. Like the Foxglove, with which it shares similar heart-assisting properties, the herb did not previously enjoy wide medicinal use. Today, however, it is an important drug in some national pharmacopoeias.

Description Perennial fragrant plant 10–20 cm high producing annually a pair of oblong-oval petiolate leaves 10–20 cm long, 3–7.5 cm wide, deeply ribbed longitudinally; 5–10 bell-shaped white flowers 10 mm wide, borne on leafless peduncle, appearing early summer, and followed by round, red berries containing 2–6 seeds.

Distribution Native to Europe, East Asia, North America; introduced elsewhere. Prefers damp, calcareous, porous soil in woods, in some alpine locations, often forming dense areas of growth.

Cultivation Wild; introduced horticulturally, cultivated races bearing larger flowers. Propagated by root division in the autumn; prefers some shade may spread rapidly.

Constituents Cardio-active glycosides (cardenolides) similar to foxglove glycoside, especially convallatoxine, also convalloside, convallotoxole and convallotoxoside; a saponoside, convallamarine.

Uses (dried flowers) Cardiac tonic; emetic; diuretic.

Regulates heart action in a similar manner to the Foxglove and is considered to be safer and as effective. Seldom used outside eastern European countries.

Flowers provide a perfume base.

Dried ground roots were formerly an ingredient of snuff.

Contra-indications POISONOUS. To be used by medical personnel only.

Coriandrum sativum L UMBELLIFERAE
Coriander

Cultivated for over 3000 years Coriander is mentioned in all the medieval medical texts, by the Greeks, in the scriptures, by early Sanskrit authors – who called it *kustumburu* – and even in the Egyptian Ebers papyrus. Its

name is derived from *koris*, the Greek for bed-bug, since the plant smells strongly of the insects.

Description Small glabrous solid-stemmed hardy annual plant from 30–60 cm tall on a thin, pointed root, lower leaves pinnate, cleft and lobed, the upper bipinnate and finely dissected. Small, flat, compound umbels of white and reddish flowers appear from mid-summer to early autumn, followed by brownish orbicular fruit with an unpleasant smell before they ripen, then becoming spicy and aromatic.

Distribution Indigenous to mediterranean and Caucasian regions; now widespread weed in many temperate zones. Prefers dry soil and full sun.

Cultivation Unknown in the wild state, cultivated commercially and horticulturally throughout the world. Seed sown in late spring or early summer in drills 2 cm deep; need thinning later. Germination may be slow.

Constituents Volatile oil, comprising borneol, coriandrol, d-pinene, β-pinene, terpinene, geraniol, and decyl aldehyde.

Uses (dried ripe fruits, leaf and root) Aromatic; carminative; stimulant.

Mostly used to prevent griping caused by other medication, such as Senna or Rhubarb. Chewing the seed stimulates secretion of gastric juices. Bruised seed is applied externally as a poultice to relieve painful joints in rheumatism. Root can be cooked and eaten as a vegetable. The fresh leaf is probably the most widely used of all flavouring herbs throughout the world.

The seed is employed in baking, as a spice or condiment, in liqueur manufacture, and in confectionery.

May be added to pot-pourris.

Crataegus monogyna Jacq. ROSACEAE
Hawthorn May/Whitethorn

The botanical name of Hawthorn, *Crataegus*, comes from the Greek meaning strength which describes the strength of the wood, while the plant's common names in several European languages refer to the fact that this is a thorny bush producing fruit, the haw.

Much of the Hawthorn's previously considered powerful magical properties are now forgotten, although as with lilac and peacock's feathers, some people still refuse to bring the flowers indoors.

Medicinally the herb is very important and is widely used in orthodox Eastern and unorthodox Western medicine for the treatment of hypertension.

Description Shrub or small tree to 9 m; spreading branches with thorns 1.5 cm long; leaves glabrous, broad-ovate or obovate, deeply lobed, 15 mm–5 cm long; flowers white 1–1.5 cm across, in clusters of 5–12; 20 stamens with red anthers; appearing early summer to mid-summer followed by ovoid scarlet false fruits of 8–10 mm diameter, sub-globose, which each contain 1 stony fruit.

Distribution Europe, North Africa, western Asia; introduced in other temperate zones. In hedges and open deciduous woods.

Cultivation Wild plant. Often planted as hedge.

Constituents Flavone glycosides; catechins; saponins; vitamin C; several unidentified constituents. Combined action improves blood flow in coronary arteries. It appears to act as an adaptogenic agent.

Uses (fresh or dried fruits) Hypotensive. Of specific use in hypertension associated with myocardial weakness, arteriosclerosis, paroxysmal tachycardia, and angina pectoris. Prolonged treatment is necessary.

Liqueur once manufactured from the berries. Timber formerly used for small boxes.

Crithmum maritimum L UMBELLIFERAE
Samphire Peter's Cress/Rock Samphire/Sea Fennel

Samphire has long been collected from the rocks of its natural habitat for shipment in barrels of brine to urban areas or for local use. Surprisingly it was also grown as a kitchen herb. Gerard described its cultivation in 1598 in England, and Quintyne described it in France in 1690. The English particularly

favoured the seed pods for inclusion in sauces and pickles. It was cultivated in American gardens from 1821, but is now rarely seen anywhere.

Description Bushy, aromatic, perennial, umbelliferous plant reaching 30 cm; smooth, bright green and much branched on woody base, fleshy and somewhat spiky leaf segments, and greenish-yellow flowers appearing mid-summer to mid-autumn. Numerous bracts and bracteoles.

Distribution Growing upon rocks on the southern European Atlantic seaboard and on the shores of several mediterranean countries.

Cultivation Wild plant, may be grown horticulturally on well-drained soils.

Constituents Mineral salts; oils; volatile oil; iodine; vitamin C.

Uses (fresh young leaves) Used for culinary purposes as a boiled spiced pickle, as a salad, a buttered vegetable or as a condiment. Said to stimulate the appetite.

Crocus sativus L IRIDACEAE
Saffron Crocus Saffron

The Saffron Crocus has been considered an important trade item from the earliest times, and has long been employed as a medicine, dye, perfume and condiment. Its earliest name was probably the Hebrew *carcom*.

It was cultivated in many countries and exported from Persia and India to China as

early as the Yuen dynasty (A.D. 1280–1368); the Chinese called it *Sa-fa-lang*.

Records suggest the Saffron Crocus was cultivated in Spain in the ninth century, in France, Italy and Germany in the twelfth, and in England by the fourteenth. Such was the standing of the drug that severe penalties were suffered by those who adulterated Saffron: Hans Kölbele, for example, was buried alive in Nuremberg in 1456 with his impure drug.

Description Typical crocus, producing blue, lilac or purple fragrant flowers in the autumn arising from a corm 3 cm in diameter. Numerous narrow, linear leaves to 45 cm long, greygreen. Yellow anthers longer than filaments, blood-red style branches.

Distribution Originally from Asia Minor, now widespread in temperate zones. Prefers sunny, well-drained sites.

Cultivation Now unknown in the wild. Cultivated in the mediterranean, Middle East, Persia, India and China. Propagation by corms planted in rows 10–15 cm apart in late summer.

Constituents Oil 8–13%; essential oil; a bitter glycoside, picrocrocin; crocin, the glycoside of the colouring matter crocetin.

Uses (dried stigma) Stomachic; antispasmodic; sedative.

No longer used medicinally except to colour medicines. Formerly considered an aphrodisiac.

Employed in many culinary dishes both for taste and colour and in some liqueurs.

Cannot be used to dye fabrics as it is readily water-soluble.

Croton tiglium L EUPHORBIACEAE
Croton Croton Seed
Oil from Croton Seeds is one of the most violent purgatives known, and should never be used by non-medical personnel. The seeds were described first by Christoval Acosta in 1578 and called *pinones de Maluco*. They were regarded as 'official' in the seventeenth century but fell into disuse from then until 1812 when English medical officers in India reintroduced the oil into medicine.

Description Small tree or shrub to 6 m with few branches bearing alternate, smooth ovate or acuminate leaves, dark green above, paler beneath and with a strong, disagreeable odour. Inconspicuous flowers in erect terminal racemes 7.5 cm long, appearing early summer. Brown, capsular, 3-celled fruit, each containing a single seed 1.5 cm long.

Distribution Indigenous to the Malabar coast, south-west India, and Tavoy in Burma.

Cultivation Wild and cultivated as a garden plant in many parts of the East. Commercial cultivation in China and south Asia.

Constituents Fatty oil 60%; croton oil comprising the following acids: palmitic, stearic, myristic, lauric, acetic, butyric, formic, oleic, tiglic, linoleic and valeric. The active constituent is croton-resin, a lactone, which is also responsible for the vesicant activity.

Uses (oil expressed from seed) Powerful cathartic; counter-irritant; vesicant; rubefacient. Formerly administered as a purgative to violent mental patients; now rarely used internally and only for extremely obstinate constipation. May be used externally with great care, in diluted form, as a counterirritant in gout and neuralgia.

Contra-indications Powerful gastro-intestinal irritant; capable of causing death. May induce severe external blistering.

Cuminum cyminum L UMBELLIFERAE
Cumin
Although indigenous to the upper regions of the Nile, the seeds of this herb ripen as far north as Norway. The *fructus cumini* or Cumin seeds were known as early as the prophet Isaiah, and, later, Dioscorides. They found wide use in Europe from the Middle Ages. The Romans used ground Cumin seed in the same way that we use Pepper. In the last 300 years, however, it has been discarded from European cooking and is now chiefly used in Indian cooking.

Description Slender, glabrous, annual herb 15 cm high; stems branched above; leaves with few filiform divisions 15 mm–5 cm long; sparsely flowered umbels, white or rosecoloured with simple involucral bracts, appearing late spring. Fruit 7 mm long, bristly.

Distribution Indigenous to Egypt and the mediterranean. Widespread distribution. Tolerates most well-drained soils in sunny situations.

Cultivation Wild plant. Cultivated on North African coast, Middle East, India, Malta and China. Seed sown in late spring in sandy soil in a warm situation, or in the greenhouse. Thin out, harden off and plant 20 cm apart. Keep free of weeds.

Constituents Essential oil, 2.5–4%, which comprises cumaldehyde, terpenes, cuminic alcohol, pinenes; also fatty oil and pentosan.

Uses (dried ripe fruit) Stimulant, carminative. Useful in diarrhoea and dyspepsia.

Commonly used in curries, for pickling, and also for flavouring liqueurs and cordials.

The oil is used in perfumery.

Oil chiefly employed in veterinary medicine.

Curcuma longa L ZINGIBERACEAE
Turmeric Turmeric root or rhizome
Turmeric was once much more highly esteemed than it is today; it fell into disuse in the Middle Ages having previously held a position at least equal to that of Ginger to which it is closely related. Dioscorides called it *cyperus*, and in the sixteenth century it was known as *crocus indicus*, *turmeracke* and *curcuma*. Several types exist of which Bengal Turmeric is considered the best for dyeing. The yellow robes of Buddhist

monks were often dyed with it.

It is similar to another ancient spice, Zedoary (*C. zedoaria Roscoe*), which is today even less well-known in the West.

Description Tall perennial herb arising from large ovoid rhizome with sessile cylindrical tubers, orange coloured within. Leaves very large, lily-like, in tufts to 1.2 m long; oblong-lanceolate blades tapering towards the base, long petiole. Pale yellow flowers, clustered in dense spikes 10–15 cm long; peduncle 15 cm long and enclosed in a sheathing petiole. Pale green bracts. Appears late spring to mid-summer.

Distribution Native to south-east Asia; distributed and introduced elsewhere. Prefers humid conditions and rich loamy soils.

Cultivation Wild and cultivated in many tropical countries; propagation by root division in autumn.

Constituents Volatile oil 5–6%; a terpene, curcumen; starch 24%; albumen 30%; colouring due to curcumin or diferuloyl methane.

Uses (dried rhizome) Aromatic, stimulant. Employed in eastern medicine externally for bruising and internally in certain blood disorders, to relieve catarrh, and in purulent opthalmia. A pharmaceutical colouring agent. Main use is as a condiment and culinary colouring agent in curries and Piccalilli.

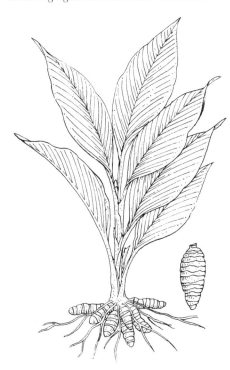

Cynara scolymus L COMPOSITAE
Artichoke Globe Artichoke

The Globe Artichoke is not only a delicacy, but an important medicinal herb which was known to the medieval Arabic physicians as *al-kharsuf*. Its name *Cynara*, from the Latin *canina* or canine, is derived from the similarity of the involucral spines to the dog's tooth. It has proven remedial effects on the liver. The plant was one of the Greek cultivated garden herbs, and still enjoys wide horticultural use.

Description Thistle-like perennial usually 1–1.75 m tall, leaves large and deeply pinnatifid, greyish, green above, whitish beneath; very rarely spiny. Large capitula with enlarged fleshy receptacle, broad involucral bracts and numerous purple flowers, appearing mid to late summer.

Distribution Native to North Africa; in most temperate and subtropical zones. Preferring well-manured, moisture-retaining soil, rich in humus.

Cultivation Wild only as an escape; a close relative of the Cardoon (*C. cardunculus*). Cultivated commercially and horticulturally either from seed or preferably from suckers arising from the root-stock, retaining a portion of the parent plant. The 'heels' are planted in rich moist soil 75 cm apart in late spring or early summer. Give plenty of water, some protection in cold weather may be required. Optimal cropping is reached in the third year, and plants should be replaced in the fifth season.

Constituents Cynarine, a bitter aromatic substance; polyphenolic acidic substances; flavonoids; tannins; several enzymes including catalases, peroxydases, cynarase, oxydases, and ascorbinase; also provitamin A. The combined action is diuretic and stimulant to liver cell regeneration and action.

Uses (fresh receptacle, leaves, root) Cholagogue; diuretic.

Of proven value in jaundice, liver insufficiency; anaemia and liver damage caused by poisons. Stimulates and aids digestion; anti-dyspeptic. Considered to be prophylactic against arterio-sclerosis. A major constituent of proprietary

digestive tonics.

Fleshy receptacle eaten as a delicacy; the blanched central leaf stalks may be cooked as a vegetable.

Flower-heads employed in floral decorations.

Cynoglossum officinale L BORAGINACEAE
Hound's Tongue Gipsy Flower

All the usual names of this herb refer to the fact that its leaves look like a dog's tongue; it smells, however, more of mice, and is called Rats and Mice in some parts of western England. The medieval name was *lingua canis* and the Greek, *kunoglosson*. It is rarely used in folk medicine today, but is still occasionally employed homeopathically.

Description Annual or biennial herb with unpleasant smell, reaching 30–90 cm; bearing grey leaves covered with silky hairs, the lower to 30 cm long, lanceolate to ovate, stalked, the upper generally without stalks. Flowers dull red-purple, occasionally white, 1 cm diameter, arranged on branched cymes 10–25 cm long, appearing mid-summer.

Distribution European native; on light dry grassy soils, wood fringes, walls and ruins, in particular near to the sea.

Cultivation Wild plant.

Constituents Two alkaloids, cynoglossine and consolidine; essential oil; resin; tannin; gum.

Uses (dried root, dried whole herb, fresh leaves) Anodyne; demulcent.

Effective soothing sedative in coughs and diarrhoea. Administered internally and as a poultice for haemorrhoids. Formerly considered a narcotic and prescribed in combination with Opium, Henbane, and aromatic herbs.

The bruised leaf may be rubbed on insect bites. Used in homeopathic medicine as a tincture.

Contra-indications Incompletely studied therapeutically and therefore to be used with caution; may cause dermatitis.

Cypripedium pubescens Willd. ORCHIDACEAE
Lady's Slipper Yellow Lady's Slipper/ Nerve Root

Cypripedium was included in the United States Pharmacopoeia a century ago, and was considered at that time worthy of further investigation. It has continued to be used to the present day in folk medicine for the same purpose that American Indians have always used it, as a sedative. It has been called the American Valerian, and was introduced to European medicine by Rafinesque in the eighteenth century.

Description Perennial orchid on fleshy root-

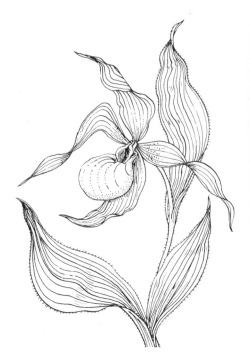

stock producing several 5–20 cm long, many-nerved, acuminate, alternate leaves; on glandular hairy stems 10 cm–1 m high. Flowers distinctive, dull cream to golden yellow, spotted magenta-purple, with lower lip forming the shape of an inflated sac; appearing early to late summer. The plant is variable in shape and degree of fragrance.

Distribution Native to eastern United States, especially the north; prefers shady areas, moist meadows, bogs, woods, rich soils.

Cultivation Wild plant; cultivated in parts of eastern Europe. Very closely related to, and often confused with, *C. calceolus* (L). *C. pubescens* (Willd.) is also named *C. calceolus* var. *pubescens* (Correll), and both orchids are known commercially as Lady's Slipper.

Constituents Volatile oil; glucosides; 2 resins; tannin; gallic acid. The combination of these root constituents, which are not water-soluble, form a resinous complex known as cypripedin.

Uses (root-stock) Sedative: spasmolytic.

Effective in and specifically used for anxiety neurosis associated with insomnia, hysteria or nervous headaches. Formerly taken in sugar water to promote sleep.

Contra-indications Large doses may cause hallucinations. Fresh plant may cause dermatitis.

Daphne mezereum L THYMELAEACEAE
Mezereon Spurge Olive

An attractive winter-flowering shrub of great decorative use in herb gardens. It was known to Arabian physicians as *mazariyun* and considered of similar use as the substance, *euphorbium*, from *Euphorbia resinifera*. It is uncertain if the Greeks used the plant, but it was known as *daphnoides* and *thymelaea* to medieval botanists and herbalists. Tragus (1546) called it *mezereum germanicum*.

Description Perennial deciduous shrub; to 1.25 m; bearing on erect branched stem, alternate, oblong or oblanceolate leaves, 5–7.5 cm long; leaves thin and glabrous. Flowers rose-pink or

rose-violet, 10–15 mm long; strongly fragrant and appearing in sessile clusters of 2–5 along previous year's branches before leaves develop. Appearing late winter to early spring; followed by red berries.

Distribution Native to Europe and Western Asia; introduced elsewhere. Found in deciduous mixed woodland and on rich calcareous soil.

Cultivation Wild. Cultivated as garden plant. Propagate from cuttings taken in early summer. A white variety, *D. mezereum* var. *alba* (West.) is in existence.

Constituents An acrid resinous poisonous substance, mezerine; a glucoside, daphnin; also coccognin.

Uses (root bark, bark) Alterative; stimulant; sudorific; vesicant; rubefacient.

Formerly used internally as an alterative in the treatment of venereal, scrofulous and rheumatic conditions, or as a purgative. Bark applied externally as poultice as a counter-irritant or vesicant in certain ulcerative skin conditions. Now only employed homeopathically for some skin complaints.

An excellent horticultural herb.

Contra-indications POISONOUS and fatal; not to be taken internally.

Datura stramonium L SOLANACEAE
Thorn Apple Jimsonweed

The Thorn Apple is indigenous to the shores of the Caspian Sea, and was distributed throughout Europe by the end of the first century A.D. It is doubtful whether the Greeks or Romans used the herb, but it was traditionally smoked by Nubians for chest complaints. Gerard the herbalist cultivated the plant in London in 1598, and Störck (1762) introduced stramonium into wide medicinal use. It is now little used in folk medicine.

Description Strongly and unpleasantly scented annual, from 30 cm–1.5 m high; erect and straggly, bearing glabrous or pubescent, ovate and petiolate leaves 7.5–20 cm long, broad and with irregular acute lobes. Flowers 5–8 cm long, erect, funnel shaped, terminal and white or pale blue. Appearing late summer to late

autumn; followed by prickly capsules, 5 cm long.

Distribution Native to the Near East; naturalized in North America, and throughout Europe; on waste-ground, roadsides, forest edges, walls, preferring porous nitrogen-rich soil in sunny situations.

Cultivation Wild; cultivated commercially in Europe by seed sown in late spring.

Constituents Alkaloids, comprising mainly hyoscyamine, hyoscine, atropine, whose action relieves spasms of the bronchioles during asthma.

Uses (dried leaves) Antispasmodic; narcotic; anodyne.

Of benefit in bronchial asthma, either as a tincture or smoked in the form of a cigarette. Also controls muscular spasm and salivation in postencephalitic parkinsonism. May be applied externally as a poultice to reduce local pain.

Contra-indications POISONOUS, hallucinogenic.

Daucus carota L UMBELLIFERAE
Wild Carrot

Daucus is the old Greek name for a wild plant still to be found in the hedgerows of Europe,

and which has long been of service as food and medicine. *Carota* is the Latin name for the same plant.

Several subspecies exist, the root crop being developed by German horticulturalists in the sixteenth century from *D. carota* ssp. *sativus*. Both this and *D. carota* ssp. *carota* are used medicinally.

Description Erect biennial on solid, striate or ridged stem 30 to 100 cm tall; leaves pinnately compound; segments pinnatifid, lobes 5 mm long. White flowers in compound umbels 3–7 cm diameter, flat or convex, with usually one blackish-purple flower in the centre, appear mid-summer.

Distribution Native to Europe, west Asia, North Africa; prefers semi-dry, sandy, or stony soil near to the sea.

Cultivation Wild plant. Wild relative of the common carrot.

Constituents Volatile oils; carotene; B vitamins; an alkaloid daucine; vitamin C; potassium salts.

Uses (dried herb) Diuretic; antilithic. Specifically employed in the treatment of urinary stones; often in combination with other antilithic remedies. Weakly anthelmintic. Decoction of the seed may be employed in flatulence and stomach acidity, as may Carrot juice.

Contra-indications Do not drink excessive quantities of Carrot juice, as it induces hypervitaminosis A.

Delphinium consolida L RANUNCULACEAE
Larkspur Field or Forking Larkspur

A member of the Buttercup family and the Northern European equivalent of the historically much more well-known *Delphinium Staphisagria* (L), or Stavesacre, which was known to the Romans as *Staphisagria* or *herba pedicularia*. There is no evidence that the specific name of Larkspur refers to any power of consolidating wounds, which it does not. It is probably a pre-Linnaean name referring to the consolidated petals. Like Stavesacre, it is effective against skin parasites.

Description Annual herb reaching 1 m, arising from slender taproot. Stem glabrous, forking and diffuse, bearing petiolate and sessile, finely divided, simple leaves 3–4 cm long. Flowers

few or scattered, blue or purple, growing in sparse terminal racemes and distinguished by an upward curving spur behind the corolla. Appearing mid-summer.

Distribution European native; introduced in other temperate zones especially on chalky, loamy soil in weedy places, compost sites, and cornfields.

Cultivation Wild plant. The common garden Larkspur is *D. ajacis*. Propagated from seed sown 1 cm deep in early summer.

Constituents Delphinine; unknown substances.

Uses (seed, flowering plant) Purgative, anthelmintic, anti-parasitic.

Formerly used internally for a variety of conditions, its only certain effect being violently purgative.

A strong tincture of fresh seeds may be applied externally to head and pubic hair to destroy human parasites.

Blue ink may be prepared from the fresh petals.

Useful garden ornamental.

Contra-indications POISONOUS.

Dianthus caryophyllus L CARYOPHYLLACEAE
Clove Pink Gillyflower/Carnation

The true Gillyflower (*gilly* was the Old English

for July and was so named probably because of its appearance in July), is rarely seen in gardens today, having been replaced by the more showy but far less aromatic Carnations. Its specific name reflects the old term for Cloves, *caryophyllon*.

Description Much branched glabrous perennial 30 cm to 1 m high; stems hard with conspicuous nodes, bearing thick linear leaves 7.5–12.5 cm long, obtuse and keeled. Flowers 3 cm in diameter, 2–5 per stem, very fragrant especially at night, rose-purple or white; appear late summer to early autumn.

Distribution Native to southern Europe and India. In open sunny position on old walls, ruins. Calcareous.

Cultivation Wild plant and widely cultivated commercially. All modern horticultural Carnations derive from *D. caryophyllus*; the modern

Pink derives from *D. plumarius*.

Constituents Volatile oils comprising eugenol, which are responsible for the clove-like scent.

Uses (fresh flower) No medicinal use, although tonic cordials were made from a conserve of the flowers.

Mainly used as a flavouring agent for beverages, liqueurs, wine cups, cordials, and vinegars.

The fresh flowers decorate soups, stews, sauces, salads, and open sandwiches. A syrup, prepared by steeping petals in a hot sugar solution has culinary applications.

Dried petals added to pot-pourris, scented sachets, cosmetic products.

Digitalis purpurea L SCROPHULARIACEAE
Foxglove Common Foxglove

For all its fame and importance in medicine in the last two centuries, the Foxglove does not seem to have been described by Greek and Roman physicians, nor did it have a classical name. Fuchs in 1542 first called it *digitalis* after the finger-like shape of its flowers, but he considered it a violent medicine, and it was not until William Withering investigated (1776–9) the use of Foxglove tea in Shropshire for

dropsy that the herb entered wide medical use. The common name probably derives from the Anglo-Saxon 'foxes-glew' or 'fox-music' after the shape of an ancient musical instrument.

Description Biennial, occasionally perennial; reaching 2 m. Leaves rugose and downy arising in a rosette; radical leaves long, stalked and ovate to ovate-lanceolate, stem leaves short-stalked or sessile. Stem rarely branched and bearing a one-sided raceme 30–40 cm long. Attractive purple flowers, often spotted internally; appearing mid-summer to mid-autumn.

Distribution Western European native, preferring acid soil in sunny situations on rough land. Now cultivated widely.

Cultivation Wild; very widely cultivated both commercially and horticulturally. Many garden variants exist; var. *campanulata*, var. *alba*, var. *maculata*. Propagated from seed which should be sown in late spring.

Constituents Several glycosides including digitoxin, gitoxin, and gitaloxin, which act directly on heart muscle increasing the output in patients with congestive heart failure.

Uses (dried leaves) Cardiac tonic.

Acts as a cardio-active diuretic in conditions of oedema due to heart failure.

May be used externally as a poultice to aid healing of wounds.

Contra-indications POISONOUS. Only to be used by medical personnel.

Dryopteris filix-mas (L) Schott
POLYPODIACEAE
Male Fern

The Male Fern is an effective remedy for tapeworms which it kills and expels from the intestines. It is, however, an irritant in large doses and must be used only by those medically trained.

It was well known to the ancients, and was also a constituent of secret 'worm remedies' of the eighteenth century, particularly those made by German apothecaries. Frederick the Great purchased the secret of one such mixture for his personal use.

Other ferns, however, seem to be equally or more effective as taenicides; *Dryopteris spinulosa* O. Kuntze, for example, is twice as effective as *Dryopteris filix-mas*.

Description Perennial fern on dark-brown rhizome 20–50 cm long, 10 cm diameter; foliage growing in a crown, fronds arranged spirally, 60 cm to 1.5 m high, 2-pinnate, oblong-lanceolate in outline, leaflets alternate, subdivided, and with rounded segments. Spore-bearing sori, greenish white, later brown, appear from summer to autumn.

Distribution Widespread in temperate zones, to 1600 m altitude.

Cultivation Wild plant; extensively collected.

Constituents Oleoresin; filicin and related taenicidal substances; desaspidin; albaspidin; flav-

aspidic acid; volatile oil.

Uses (dried rhizome, frond bases, apical buds) An effective agent for removing tapeworms. Poultice may be applied externally to aid tissue healing.

Contra-indications To be used under medical supervision only: large doses may cause blindness or death.

Ecballium elaterium (L) A. Rich CUCURBITACEAE
Squirting Cucumber Elaterium Fruit

An appropriately named herb both from the point of view of its action, as a strong purgative, and from its violent method of seed dispersal which involves ejaculation of the contents of the ripe fruit to a distance of 10 m. The generic name derives from the Greek meaning expel. It was certainly well-known to Theophrastus and Dioscorides who described the manufacture of Elaterium, and it was cultivated throughout Europe in the sixteenth century. Constituents of Elaterium are now mostly

employed for scientific research into cytotoxicity.

Description A coarse, fleshy, trailing perennial, lacking tendrils and borne on a thick white root. Leaves triangular-ovate, downy, 7.5–10 cm long, with sinuate margins. Flowers 3 cm diameter, followed by an ovoid-oblong fruit, 4–5 cm long, rough-haired due to a covering of numerous short, fleshy prickles, green becoming yellowish when mature. Contains a mass of oblong seeds and bitter succulent pulp, which is forcibly ejected up to 10 m.

Distribution Mediterranean native; preferring dry, sandy soil in sunny situations.

Cultivation Wild and cultivated commercially to a limited extent.

Constituents Cucurbitacins B, D, E, and I. The action of cucurbitacin B is that of a powerful hydragogue – purgative; also cytotoxic.

Uses (dried sediment, *elaterium*, deposited in the juice) Purgative.

Once administered to patients suffering from dropsy as a purgative, especially those with kidney complaints. The preparation is very variable from season to season.

Echinacea angustifolia DC COMPOSITAE
Purple Coneflower Black Sampson

This stark and attractive herb is one of several outstanding examples of plants deserving modern examination. The United States Dispensatory stated a century ago that the tincture increased resistance to infection, and the experience of folk medicine supports this claim.

It was formerly classified as *Brauneria angustifolia*, but the present generic name reflects the shape of the sharp-pointed bracts of the receptacle, after the Greek *echinacea*, meaning hedgehog.

Description Coarse perennial reaching 45 cm. Leaves sparse, lanceolate to linear; 7.5–20 cm long, entire with slender petioles. Flower-head solitary on stout terminal peduncle, consisting of spreading ray florets 3 cm long, purple or rarely white, and 3 cm long conical erect disc florets, also purple. Appearing mid-summer to early autumn.

Distribution Native to central and southwestern United States; on dry open woodland and roadsides.

Cultivation Wild plant. Propagated by root division in spring and autumn.

Constituents Resins, sugars, mineral salts, fatty acids and inulin which act in combination.

Uses (dried root-stock) Antiseptic, digestive. Particularly effective remedy for boils, acne, pharyngitis, tonsilitis, abscesses and septicaemia; useful externally and internally. Dilates peripheral blood vessels.

Echium vulgare L BORAGINACEAE
Viper's Bugloss Blue Weed

This is not a true Bugloss, that term being reserved for *Lycopsis arvensis*, nor is it the plant known to Dioscorides as the Viper Plant – *echion*. Nevertheless, medieval proponents of the Doctrine of Signatures noticed that the brown stem pustules looked rather like a snake's skin, and that the seed is shaped like a viper's head. It is regarded as a weed in some parts of America, and is of doubtful medical use.

Description Rough hairy biennial, 30–90 cm tall. Stem erect and branched with stiff hairs arising from white or brown pustules. Leaves oblong to linear-lanceolate, 5–15 cm long, sessile, or with short petioles only. Inflorescence loose, flower buds pink, flowers blue to violet-purple, 15 mm long, with longer stamens. Appears mid-summer.

Distribution Native to Europe and Asia; on light porous or stony soils, or semi-dry grass-land.

Cultivation Wild plant. Traditionally cultivated in herb gardens.

Constituents Tannins; an alkaloid.

Uses (dried herb) Weak diuretic; weak diaphoretic.

A simple mild tonic infusion is useful in treating nervous headaches or the common cold.

Formerly one of the most respected plants employed for the treatment of vipers' venom.

Elettaria cardamomum var. *miniscula* Maton
ZINGIBERACEAE

Cardamom Lesser Cardamom

As Cardamoms thrive in shady mountain forests ideally with a mean rainfall of 3.5 m and mean temperature of 23°C (73°F), they are not easy to cultivate or harvest, and for this reason are expensive. The best type is the Malabar Cardamom, and others of good quality are Mysore, Ceylon, Aleppi and Madras. Seed pods from related members of the Ginger family are frequently offered as Cardamom, especially *Amomum cardamon* L, but they are inferior.

Elettari was the Malabar name for the plant.

Description Perennial arising from fleshy thick rhizome bearing from 8–20 smooth erect green stems to 2.7 m. Leaves alternate, oblong-lanceolate, sheathed, 30–60 cm long, 7.5 cm wide. Flowers arising from near the stem base on a long peduncle, arranged in a panicle 30–60 cm long, and are followed by an ovoid 3-celled capsule.

Distribution Indigenous to south and west India; in rich moist forests and in wooded hillsides. Wild in Burma. Introduced in other tropical countries.

Cultivation Wild plant. Commercial cultivation in many tropical countries in Asia and the Americas.

Constituents Volatile oil (3–8%), comprising terpinene and terpineol; also cineol; starch; gum; yellow colouring matter.

Uses (dried fruit and seed) Carminative. Employed in flatulent dyspepsia, to allay griping caused by purgatives, and to flavour other medications.

A flavouring agent in some mixed spices, curries and pickles. Also used in mulled wine and in Coffee, especially Persian.

Limited use in scented domestic articles, and for cosmetic purposes.

Ephedra gerardiana (Wall.) Stapf.
EPHEDRACEAE

Ephedra Ma-Huang

Ephedra is a Gymnosperm and hence, like the

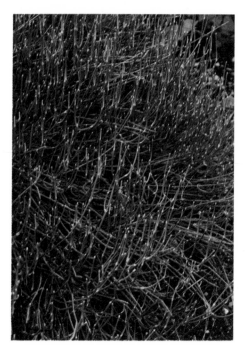

Horsetail, primitive in evolutionary terms. It has been used for thousands of years in the East in the treatment of bronchial asthma, and yet today the herb is included in only the British, Indian, Japanese and Chinese pharmacopoeias.

Other species used for the same purpose include *E. sinica*, *E. equisetina* and *E. nebrodensis*. It is rarely available commercially.

Description Tufted, rigid shrub 15 cm–1.2 m high on woody gnarled stem. Green ascending branchlets smooth and striate, with leaves reduced to small sheaths at branch nodes, 2 mm long. Bearing 2–3 male spikes of 4–8 flowers, and solitary female spikes of 1–2 flowers; latter followed by ovoid, edible red fruit, 10 mm long.

Distribution Native to the dry temperate regions of the alpine Himalayas at altitudes 2250–4500 m; also China.

Cultivation Wild plant.

Constituents Alkaloids comprising mainly ephedrine, to which the hypertensive and bronchodilatory action is due; pseudoephedrine, benzyl methylamine; ephidine.

Uses (dried stem) Anti-asthmatic; stimulant. Primarily of use in bronchial asthma and hay fever; also employed in enuresis, urticaria, serum sickness, and in the treatment of myasthenia gravis.

A commercial source of the ephedrine alkaloids.

Contra-indications Not to be used in patients suffering from hypertension, coronary thrombosis or thyrotoxicosis.

Epigaea repens L ERICACEAE

Trailing Arbutus May Flower/Gravel Plant

The botanical name reflects the fact that this aromatic plant clings very closely to the damp mossy banks of its natural habitat: *epigaea* from the Greek meaning upon earth and *repens* meaning creeping. Also known as Moss Beauty because of the attractiveness of its rust leaves and small, pink, scented flowers.

Description Fragrant prostrate evergreen branching shrub, spreading to 50 cm diameter on the ground; with hairy, rounded stems of rust colour, arising from tangled red-brown fibrous roots. Leaves alternate, oval to orbicular 3–7.5 cm long, 1–3 cm wide, entire, and hairy beneath. The apical or axillary inflorescence consists of pink, deep rose and occasionally, white flowers 15 mm long, appearing mid-spring to early summer.

Distribution Native to central and eastern North America, on rich, damp, acid soils in shady protected sites.

Cultivation Wild plant; may be propagated easily by layering any part of the stem.

Constituents The glucosides urson, ericolin, and arbutin; formic acid; gallic acid; tannic acid and an aromatic oil, ericinol; the combined action being antilithic and antiseptic.

Uses (whole dried plant, fresh leaf) Urinary antiseptic; diuretic; antilithic.

Although rarely used, even in folk medicine, this is one of the most effective remedies for cystitis, urethritis, prostatitis, bladder stones and particularly acute catarrhal cystitis.

Horticulturally the herb offers useful fragrant ground cover in shady situations thriving with some protection and little light.

Equisetum arvense L EQUISETACEAE
Horsetail Bottlebrush/Shave Grass

Horsetails have an almost prehistoric appearance, and indeed have hardly evolved since the coal seams were laid down. They were known to medieval apothecaries as *cauda equina*, and were an article of trade from the Middle Ages until the eighteenth century, being used to polish pewterware and woodwork. The herb has continued in cultivation in some eastern European countries and plays a useful role in folk medicine.

Description Perennial on thin creeping rhizome, producing 20 cm long grey-brown, simple, fertile shoots with 4–6 sheaths in the spring; the shoots die after the spores are shed, and are then followed by green sterile shoots 20–80 cm long, erect, or decumbent, bearing whorls of segmented solid lateral branches at each node.

Distribution European native; abundant on moist waste-ground.

Cultivation Wild plant: limited cultivation in eastern Europe.

Constituents Silicic acid and water-soluble silicic compounds; saponins; phytosterol; flavonoids; aconitic acid; traces of the alkaloids, nicotine, palustrine and palustrinine.

Uses (dried sterile stem, fresh juice) Diuretic; vulnerary; genito-urinary astringent; weak anti-haemorrhagic.

A poultice may be applied externally to aid the healing of wounds, sores or ulcers; the tisane is effective as a mouthwash in aphthous ulcers or gingivitis, and can be used as a douche in leucorrhoea or menorrhagia. Also employed in prostatic disease, enuresis and incontinence.

Dried stems may be used to polish pewter or fine woodwork.

Employed in cosmetic preparations to strengthen finger nails.

Erigeron canadensis L COMPOSITAE
Canadian Fleabane

The Canadian Fleabane has received almost universal abuse as an unwanted weed with little to commend it beside extraordinary powers of survival and distribution. Originally from eastern and central North America, it was introduced into Central France in 1653, became naturalized in that country within 30 years, and rapidly spread through Europe, Asia, Australia and several of the Pacific Islands.

The Latin name indicates not only its original home, but also its hoary appearance; from the Greek *erigeron* signifying 'old man in spring'.

Description Annual with stiff, erect stem from 8–100 cm tall depending on soil type. Very leafy and varying from sparsely hairy to glabrous; all leaves sessile; basal leaves obovate-lanceolate, stem leaves linear-lanceolate, 1–4 cm long, entire. Inflorescence in terminal panicle, capitula small, cylindrical, 3–5 mm diameter. Ray florets whitish, disc florets pale yellow; appearing late summer to early autumn.

Distribution North American native; intro-

duced and naturalized elsewhere. Common on dry, weed-covered roadsides, walls, dunes, waste-ground; preferring warm, light, sandy soil, but tolerating most conditions.

Cultivation Wild plant.

Constituents Volatile oil, comprizing mainly a terpene, acting as a styptic; also gallic and tannic acids, acting as astringents.

Uses (whole dried herb, oil) Astringent; tonic; diuretic; styptic.

The tisane or tincture was formerly employed in the treatment of a range of urinary and renal disorders; it appears effective in diarrhoea. The oil soothes sore throats and relieves associated swollen glands, and has been employed in haemoptysis, haematemesis, and haematuria.

Eruca vesicaria ssp. *sativa* (Mill.) Thell
CRUCIFERAE
Rocket-salad Rocket

Although described as a 'good salat-herbe' by

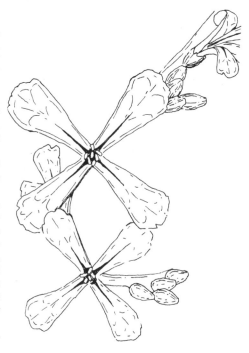

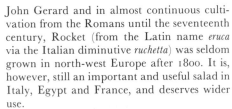

John Gerard and in almost continuous cultivation from the Romans until the seventeenth century, Rocket (from the Latin name *eruca* via the Italian diminutive *ruchetta*) was seldom grown in north-west Europe after 1800. It is, however, still an important and useful salad in Italy, Egypt and France, and deserves wider use.

Description Half-hardy annual, 30–70 cm tall; much branched. Upper leaves sessile, lower long petioled, large-toothed or pinnatifid. Flowers to 3 cm long, creamy-yellow or whitish, with purplish veins; appearing mid to late summer.

Distribution Native to mediterranean region and western Asia. Introduced horticulturally elsewhere. In waste areas or on cultivated land in warm positions.

Cultivation Wild. Grown as a salad herb, especially in south-east mediterranean, southern France and Italy. Propagated from seed

sown in spring or autumn on rich, moist soil; may run to seed in summer. Harvest leaf within 8 weeks and keep cutting. Cultivated herb is milder flavoured than the wild plant *E. vesicaria* L.
Constituents Essential oil; heterosides.
Uses (fresh young leaf and stalk) Tonic; mild stimulant; stomachic.
Only used as a constituent of mixed salads.

Eryngium maritimum L UMBELLIFERAE
Sea Holly Eryngo
The striking prickly nature and coastal habitat of this herb led to it being named, quite obviously, as Sea Holly. In fact, unlike most herbs, it has few other names, and Eryngo is a popularization of the old generic term *eryngium* which signifies a thistle-like herb.
The plant's virtues and uses centre mostly on the sexual organs; even the extremely long roots have been given aphrodisiacal qualities, a fact explaining why they enjoyed widespread

sale in Europe for 250 years.
Description Attractive bluish and glaucous biennial or perennial, much branched plant, on 1.5 m long root, forming hemi-spherical bushes 30 cm high. Leaves fleshy, very stiff and deeply veined, ovate, 3-lobed, 5–10 cm long, broad, spiny and long-petiolate. Flowers in spherical umbels, 3 cm diameter, pale blue, appearing mid to late summer.
Distribution European native; introduced elsewhere. On sand dunes and ideally requiring a sandy saline soil.
Cultivation Wild plant; sometimes cultivated on light soils horticulturally, and propagated by root division in the autumn, or from seed sown in the autumn.
Constituents Saponins; unknown substances.
Uses (fresh or dried root) Aromatic; tonic; diuretic.
The herb was formerly considered of use in genito-urinary irritation and infection, especially local inflammations of mucous membranes and painful urination. The powdered root applied externally as a poultice aids tissue regeneration.
Once an important culinary flavouring, the roots being parboiled and candied prior to incorporation in sweet dishes. Young flowering

shoots can be boiled and eaten in the same way as Asparagus.

Erythroxylum coca Lam.
ERYTHROXYLACEAE
Coca Leaf
Coca was well-known in pre-Columban days and revered as a magical plant; small bags of the leaves have been found in the graves of Incas. It is still widely employed as a means of maintaining endurance by South American peoples, and is cultivated commercially for cocaine extraction. The generic name refers to the bright red colour of the fruit.
Description Small hardy shrubby tree to 5 m; but pruned to 2 m in cultivation; leaves oval 4–8 cm long, 2.5–4 cm wide, glabrous and entire, with prominent reddish-brown midrib projecting as a small apex (apiculus). Fruits red or reddish-brown.
Distribution Peru and Bolivia. Introduced to Taiwan and Indonesia. On steep valley sides in

well-drained, light, humus-rich soil.
Cultivation No longer known in wild state; cultivated commercially in South America, Taiwan, and Indonesia. Propagated from fresh seed sown in shaded humus-rich seed-beds and planted out 2 m apart.
The cultivation of this herb is subject to worldwide constraint.
Constituents Several alkaloids, the most important being cocaine; also cinnamyl-cocaine, α- and β-truxilline; cocatannic acid; vitamins; proteins; mineral salts.
Uses (fresh or dried leaf) Stimulant tonic.
The leaf is chewed in combination with a little lime or the ash of certain *Chenopodium* species as a general stimulant, to reduce fatigue, allay feelings of hunger, to relieve gastric pain, nausea, and vomiting, and as a cerebral and muscular stimulant.
Contra-indications Dangerous; hence not obtainable.

Eucalyptus globulus Labill. MYRTACEAE
Tasmanian Blue Gum Eucalyptus
The genus *Eucalyptus* consists of 300 species of trees indigenous to Australasia of which the most successful in terms of economic importance and distribution is *E. globulus*. In the last

century the tree has become well established as a source of timber, oil, shade, and as a means of soil drainage in Africa, the Americas, Southern Europe, and India. The name is derived from the Greek *eucalyptus* meaning a well and a lid, since the sepals and petals fuse forming a cap, which resembles a well with a lid. 'Globulus' or 'little globe' signifies the shape of the fruit.
Description Tree reaching 70 m. Trunk smooth and grey or bluish following natural loss of bark; leaves leathery, lanceolate, glaucous, whitish, sessile and usually opposite; covered with oil-bearing glands. Flowers, 4 cm wide, either single or 2–3 on short flat peduncles, followed by 3-cm wide fruit, surrounded by woody receptacle.
Distribution Native to Australasia; introduced in semi-tropical countries.
Cultivation Wild; extensively cultivated and grows rapidly.
Constituents Eucalyptus oil, chiefly comprising cineol; also pinenes; sesquiterpene alcohols; aromadendrene; cuminaldehyde.
Uses (oil, occasionally leaf) Antiseptic; deodorant; stimulant; counter-irritant.
Widely used in proprietary medicines for external application in burns, colds, and for antiseptic purposes. Vapour inhaled to relieve cough in catarrhal colds and chronic bronchitis. Occasionally taken internally in small doses on sugar for catarrhal inflammation of the respiratory tract.
Limited use in perfumery; leaves included in dry pot-pourris.
Employed in veterinary medicines.
Contra-indications Large doses toxic, leading to delirium, convulsions and death.

Euonymus europaeus L CELASTRACEAE
Spindle Tree European Spindle Tree
This herb is also described as *Evonymus europaeus*, *Evonymus europaea* and *Euonymus europaea*. Its common name is derived from the Dutch practice of spindle (and peg) manufacture from the strong wood.
Description Deciduous shrub or small tree 2–6

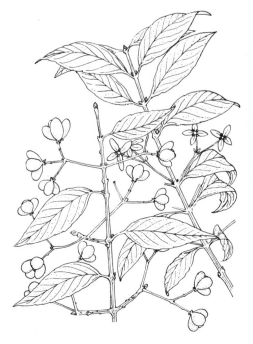

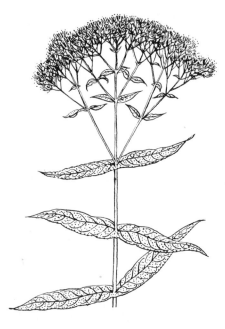

Cultivation Wild plant.
Constituents A glucoside, eupatorine; also tannin; volatile oils; resin; gum; sugar; gallic acid. Diaphoretic action probably due to the glucoside and volatile oil.
Uses (dried flowering plant) Diaphoretic. Although the cold decoction is tonic and stimulant in small doses and emetic in large, the widest use is for the common cold or similar feverishness, taken as a hot infusion it is practically unequalled in its effectiveness.

Eupatorium purpureum L COMPOSITAE
Gravel Root Joe-pye Weed
This enormously tall North American herb with its mass of purplish-white flowers makes such a splendid sight when in flower that it has been given the name Queen of the Meadow. Indians used the plant for dyeing and to induce perspiration to break a fever, uses which were quickly adopted by European settlers. Still used by British and American herbalists.
Description Perennial of a variable nature, reaching from 75 cm–3 m high, but typically

m tall; somewhat bushy. Young twigs square-stemmed. Leaves blue-green, opposite, decussate, dentate, ovate or oblong-lanceolate, 3–8 cm long, yellow-red in autumn. Pale green flowers, up to 6 in axillary panicles, appearing early to mid-summer followed by attractive, deeply 4-lobed, red-orange or pink capsule of 15 mm diameter.
Distribution Native to Europe and western Asia. In open woodland, clearings, hedgerows, close to water, on deep moist loam.
Cultivation Wild. Several cultivars including *Aldenhamensis* and *Burtonii* are used as garden ornamentals. Tolerates most positions and soils. Raise from seed in spring and from hardwood cuttings or layering in summer.
Constituents Vitamin C; lipids; tannins; cardiotonic heterosides including euonoside, to which the toxicity is due; organic acids and esters; several pigments including physaline and phyllorhodine.
Uses (dried seed and fruit, fresh leaves) Emetic; purgative; insecticide; cholagogue.
Effective when used externally against scabies, pediculoses (head, body or pubic), ticks and other skin parasites.
Contra-indications POISONOUS; not to be used internally.

Eupatorium cannabinum L COMPOSITAE
Hemp Agrimony Water Hemp
An attractive plant which in some parts of England is called Raspberries and Cream because of the appearance of its flowers.
Its leaves are similar to those of Hemp (*Cannabis sativa* L) hence its common, Latin, and old botanical (*Cannabina aquatica*) names. It has not, however, been employed in the manufacture of rope or cloth, and no longer enjoys wide use.
Description Perennial on woody base, reaching 30–120 cm. Stems erect, downy, bearing petiolate, oblanceolate, basal leaves and ovate or lanceolate branch leaves. Most leaves sub-

divided into 3 leaflets. Flowers in cymose capitula, each with 5–6 mauve or whitish florets and 10 purple involucral bracts, appearing mid to late summer.
Distribution European native, found on damp calcareous soil which is rich in nutrients. In marshes and fens or less frequently in mixed deciduous woodland.
Cultivation Wild plant. May be cultivated by root division in the autumn, but only on moist soils.
Constituents Tannin; resins; volatile oil; inulin; iron; bitter principle.
Uses (dried herb) Cholagogue; diaphoretic; emetic; expectorant.
In small doses the herb acts as a bitter tonic or aperitif suitable for those disposed to biliousness or constipation. Often combined with other remedies as a tonic.
In large doses it is laxative and emetic.

Eupatorium perfoliatum L COMPOSITAE
Boneset Thoroughwort
Although it is a less imposing herb, Boneset is closely related to Gravel Root as it possesses similar chemical constituents.
This herb played a role in the American domestic economy during the nineteenth century at least equal to that now enjoyed by hot lemon tea in the treatment of coughs and colds. It is certainly more effective. It was first introduced into Europe in 1699.
Description Perennial herb reaching from 50 cm to 1.5 m; pubescent stem which is stout and cylindrical, branched above, bearing 10–20 cm long lanceolate leaves united at the base around the stem; dark and shiny green above, cotton-like beneath and fine-toothed. Inflorescence of 10–16, small white or, rarely, blue flowers, on a dense corymbose cyme. Appearing late summer to mid-autumn.
Distribution Indigenous to North America from Dakota to Florida and Texas; prefers open marshy regions.

tall and graceful. Stem rigid, generally hollow, tinged with purple above the nodes, bearing oblong-lanceolate vanilla-scented, roughish leaves, in whorls of 2–5 leaves, 30 cm long. Flowers creamy white, often tinged with purple, arranged in clusters of 5 or 10 on very numerous dense terminal compound corymbs. Appearing late summer to mid-autumn.

Distribution North American native; preferring rich calcareous woodland soils, either dry or moist.

Cultivation Wild plant; may be propagated by root division in late spring or autumn.

Constituents Resin; volatile oil; a flavonoid, euparin; an oleoresin, eupurpurin, is produced by pouring the tincture into cold water – it has the same action as that of the whole root.

Uses (dried root-stock) Astringent tonic; diuretic; stimulant; antilithic; anti-rheumatic.

Specifically of use in the treatment of renal or urinary calculi (stones), caused by excess uric acid. Hence also useful in gout and rheumatism.

The fruit yields a pink or red textile dye.

Euphorbia hirta L EUPHORBIACEAE
Euphorbia Asthma Weed

The Spurge family consists of several thousand species distributed worldwide; most of the 1000 species of the genus *Euphorbia* exude an acrid milky latex which ranges from irritant in its action to extremely poisonous. *E. heptagona* (L), for example, is used in Ethiopian arrow poisons. The common name for the family indicates the widest use for Euphorbias, that of purgatives – from the Latin *purgatoria*, the purging herb. The dried latex of *E. resinifera* (Berg.), known as *euphorbium* in honour of Euphorbus, physician to Juba II (died A.D. 18), was used continuously from ancient times until the last century. Asthma Weed, however, is one of the few species still considered safe to use.

Description Annual, 15–50 cm high; stems erect covered with stiff yellow hairs, considerably branched. Leaves dark green above, paler beneath, obovate-lanceolate, acute, and dentate; opposite, 1–4 cm long, 5 mm–1.5 cm

wide. Flowers small, numerous, crowded on 1 cm diameter globose cymes; followed by 3 celled capsular fruit.

Distribution Native to tropical India; introduced and naturalized in most tropical and subtropical countries.

Cultivation Wild plant.

Constituents An ill-defined glycoside and alkaloid; phytosterol; melissic acid; euphosterol; tannin; a phenolic substance; quercetin; gallic acid; sugar.

Uses (dried flowering plant) Expectorant; antasthmatic; anti-amoebic.

Chiefly employed in the treatment of intestinal amoebiasis; also effective in bronchitic asthma and laryngeal spasm since it causes relaxation of the bronchi by central depressant action. The fresh latex is applied externally in the treatment of warts.

Contra-indications Large doses cause gastrointestinal irritation, nausea and vomiting.

Euphrasia rostkoviana Hayne
SCROPHULARIACEAE
Eyebright Meadow Eyebright

Eyebright is the best known of all herbs used to treat eye conditions. Although its name is

derived from the Greek meaning gladness, it appears unknown to ancient physicians prior to the Middle Ages – when it was introduced by Hildegarde.

The flower certainly gives the appearance of a bloodshot eye. Apothecaries knew the plant as *ocularia* and *ophthalmica*, and its use has been retained to this day in folk medicine. Linnaeus classified it as *Euphrasia officinalis*, but his type species consists of a mixture of a number of species. *E. officinalis* is, therefore, an ambiguous name which has no standing. Only Eyebright species possessing glandular hairs on the calyx have medicinal value.

Description Small attractive annual on erect, usually branched, stems from 5–30 cm high, bearing opposite, ovoid, downy and crenate-serrate leaves 0.5–1 cm long, and spikes of 1 cm long white flowers in the axils of upper leaves. Calyx and leaves close to the inflorescence bear glandular hairs; flower also has

purple stripes and yellow flecks. Appears from mid-summer to late autumn.

Distribution European native, on poor meadow land and turf. Calcifugous, and found to 3000 m altitude.

Cultivation Wild plant; cannot be cultivated easily as it is a semiparasite on certain grass species requiring a close physical association with the grass roots, from which it obtains nutrients.

Constituents Tannin; resin; saponin; volatile oils; a glycoside, aucubine. The combined action is anti-inflammatory for mucosae.

Uses (dried flowering plant) Anti-inflammatory; weakly astringent; weak vulnery.

Almost exclusively employed as a mild eye lotion for use in conjunctivitis. Also as a nasal douche in nasal catarrh, head colds and sinusitis. Externally in poultices to aid wound healing.

A constituent of herbal smoking mixtures.

Ferula foetida Regel UMBELLIFERAE
Asafetida

Asafetida is a strongly foetid brownish gum, hence its name. In small quantities, however, it gives food a particular flavour and has long been used as a condiment by Indians in vegetable dishes.

In the second century A.D., a tax was levied on the drug in Alexandria, and it was used by the Arabian physicians of the Middle Ages who called it *hiltit*. The thirteenth-century Welsh Physicians of Myddvai considered it an important medicinal substance; it is now rarely used in Europe.

Description Herbaceous monoecious perennial, 1.5–2 m high, bearing large bipinnate radical leaves, and developing a massive fleshy rootstock 14 cm thick at the crown, which is covered by coarse fibres. The inflorescence is usually produced in the fifth year of growth on

a 2.5–3 m high, to 10 cm thick, naked, flowering stem. Flowers yellow in umbels appearing mid-spring.

Distribution Native to eastern Persia and western Afghanistan, on rocky hillsides.

Cultivation Wild plant; the resin is collected commercially from plants which must be at least 5 years old.

Constituents Volatile oil (10%); resin (50%); gum (25%); ferulic acid. The volatile oil contains terpenes, disulphides and pinene, and is responsible for the therapeutic action.

Uses (dried oleo-resin-gum, obtained by incision of living root-stock) Nervine stimulant; powerful antispasmodic; expectorant; carminative.

Very effective in hysteria and some nervous conditions, and in bronchitis, asthma and whooping-cough. Once employed in infantile pneumonia and in the treatment of flatulent colic.

A condiment commonly used as an ingredient of Indian sauces, pickles, Worcestershire Sauce, and vegetable dishes; also with fish.

Ferula galbaniflua Boiss. et Buhse
UMBELLIFERAE
Galbanum

Galbanum was an important ingredient of the incense used by the Israelites who called this plant product *Chelbenah*. It is obtained from this and other species of *Ferula*, notably *F. rubricaulis* (Boiss.), either by collecting the milky-white tears of gum-resin which naturally exude from the stem, or by severing the plant's root crown. *Ferula* is from the Latin, to strike. Both Hippocrates and Theophrastus mentioned its medicinal properties, and Pliny called it *bubonion*. It was known by the Arabic term, *kinnah*, to the physicians of the School of Salerno. Previously imported from Persia, but now only from the Near East.

Description Umbelliferous perennial on solid stem reaching 1.5–1.75 m high, bearing greyish tomentose leaves, yellowish-white flowers in flat umbels appearing in mid-spring, and thin flat fruits.

Distribution Indigenous to Persia.

Cultivation Wild plant.

Constituents Volatile oil (10%), resin (60%); gum (20%).

Uses (semi-hard gum-resin obtained from stem or root crown) Stimulant; expectorant.

Once used in chronic bronchitis as a stimulating expectorant, often in combination with other remedies. May be incorporated in plasters for application on ulcers.

A constituent of incense.

Ficus carica L MORACEAE
Fig Common Fig

Known to the Romans as *ficus*, figs were valued as a food by the ancient Hebrews, and, with the vine, signified peace and plenty in the writings of the scriptures. The plant was so extensively cultivated that even in Pliny's time several different varieties existed, of which the best was considered to be that flourishing in Caria in Asia Minor; hence the modern botanical classification *F. carica*.

Charlemagne promoted its cultivation in central Europe in the ninth century, and today it is still an official plant in the British Pharmacopoeia.

Description Deciduous tree to 9 m, much branched, soft-wooded, with large rough leaves, 10–20 cm long, broad-ovate to orbicular, 3–5 deep lobes and pubescent beneath; forming mass of attractive foliage. Leaves entire in some cultivated forms. Flowers uniquely hidden within a hollow fleshy receptacle (syconus) and therefore never visible. Receptacle 3–7.5 cm long, single, axillary and often pear-shaped, or variable. Appearing early summer to mid-autumn.

Distribution Indigenous to Mediterranean region, widely distributed.

Cultivation Wild; several forms grown for fruit, shade and ornament, of which the best is the variety Brown Turkey. Easily cultivated in full sun; to ensure good harvest, root growth must be severely restricted by planting in 50 cm diameter pot, sunk in the soil. Propagate from cuttings.

Constituents Grape (invert) sugar, gum, sucrose.

Uses (fresh and dried fruit) Mild laxative; nutritive.

Most widely known medicinally as a folk remedy for constipation: taken as syrup of figs. Also used in combination with stronger purgatives like Senna. Once used externally as a demulcent poultice for boils and ulcers.

Wide culinary use in confectionery, in jams, and used to flavour some coffees. May be used in home wine manufacture.

Filipendula ulmaria (L) Maxim ROSACEAE
Meadowsweet Queen of the Meadow

Queen of the Meadow is this herb's most modern common name, and it seems to have been the more popular in several European languages. It is certainly apt, for when the plant is fully established, it may completely dominate a low-lying damp meadow.

Meadowsweet is simply derived from the earlier 'meadwort', since it was once used to flavour mead. Botanically, the herb was classified by Linnaeus as *Spiraea ulmaria* since the fruit consists of small spiral achenes

twisted together. This generic name has been immortalized in the word Aspirin (meaning, from Spiraea), because it was from the flower-buds of Meadowsweet that salicylic acid was first discovered in 1839 – and from which Aspirin was later synthesized.

Description Stout perennial herb 60–120 cm tall on thick, pink aromatic root-stock. Stems erect, reddish, bearing alternate, acute, ovate leaves, irregularly pinnate with 2–5 pairs of leaflets, 2–8 cm long, glabrous above and whitish and tomentose beneath. Faintly aromatic flowers white or cream, small (2–5 mm), 5-petalled, with numerous long stamens, in dense but irregular paniculate cymes on glabrous stems; appearing mid-summer to early autumn.

Distribution European and Asian native. Introduced and naturalized in North America. On wet, nutrient-rich, but not too acidic, sandy or loamy soils near streams and rivers in fens, marshland or wet woodlands, to 1000 m altitude.

Cultivation Wild, often growing in profusion in suitable habitat. Propagate from seed sown in spring or from root division in spring; thin or plant to 40 cm apart. A damp, rich soil in partial shade is required; water well in dry weather.

Constituents Tannins (10%); volatile oil comprising, salicylaldehyde (to 10%) also methyl salicylate; vanillin, heliotropin, ethyl benzoate; also flavonoid glycosides including spiraeoside; salicyclic glycosides, comprising gaultherin and spiraein; vitamin C; sugars; mineral salts.

Uses (dried flowers, dried root-stock) Antipyretic; anti-rheumatic; astringent; weak antispasmodic; diuretic; antiseptic.

The root is employed specifically in the treatment of diarrhoea, while the flowers are of benefit in influenza, fluid retention, rheumatism and arthritis. They are probably the most effective of all plant remedies for the treatment of hyperacidity and heartburn. Useful therefore in the control of peptic ulcers and gastritis. The infusion also has an effect in certain urinary tract infections.

Formerly used in mead and wine cups.

A black dyestuff has been obtained from the plant, using a copper mordant.

May be used in scented articles.

Foeniculum vulgare Mill. UMBELLIFERAE
Fennel Sweet Fennel

The appearance of dried Fennel leaf, which is rather like coarse, crumpled hair, gave rise to both the common and botanical names being derived from the Latin *faeniculum*, meaning little hay.

It has been used for culinary purposes for at least 2000 years, and was formerly prized more for its succulent stems than for its seed, which is the part now commonly employed. Special varieties have been developed supplying swollen bulbous stalk bases (Finnocchio or Florence Fennel), large stalks (Carosella), and foliage for decorative purposes (Bronze Fennel). The seed flavour also varies considerably from the Bitter or Wild Fennel and the less bitter Saxon or German Fennel to the Sweet Roman or Sweet Fennel. It is traditionally considered one of the best herbs to use with fish dishes.

Description Hardy biennial or perennial, often cultivated as an annual; erect blue-green stem, 70 cm to 2 m high, bearing fine, 3–4 pinnately compound leaves, often almost filiform, to 4 cm long, on broad and clasping petioles. Small yellow flowers, on large umbels of 15–20 rays, succeeded by fruit, bluish turning grey-brown. Appearing mid-summer to mid-autumn.

Distribution Native to mediterranean region, introduced and naturalized in other places; prefers wasteland on well-drained soil in sunny locations.

Cultivation Wild, and extensively grown horticulturally and commercially in all temperate

zones. Propagated in any soil except heavy clay, from seed sown in autumn. Remove flower-heads if seed is not required. Different races produce seeds of varying flavour.

Constituents Volatile oil, comprising mainly anethole and also fenchone, d-pinene, limonene, dipentene, phellandrene and anisic acid. Carminative action due to the oil.

Uses (fresh and dried leaf, oil, dried ripe fruit, rarely roots) Carminative; aromatic; weak diuretic; mild stimulant.

The oil is added to purgative medication to prevent griping and intestinal colic; aids flatulence and allays hunger. Once used to promote lactation. Thought to aid in slimming. All parts of culinary use; leaves traditionally garnish fish, and are added to salads, soups, sauces and pork dishes. Root and stalks may be boiled and eaten as a vegetable; seed used in liqueur manufacture and as a condiment.

Contra-indications Very large doses disturb the nervous system.

Fomes officinalis (Vittadini) Bresadola
POLYPORACEAE
Agaricus Purging Agaric

This fungus has also been known as *Polyporus officinalis* Fries., *Boletus laricis* Jacq. and *Ungulina officinalis*. Owing to the difficulty of classification of the fungus group, it cannot be identified with certainty in ancient writings and probably the related species *Fomes fomentarius* (L) Fries. was used more frequently and as a styptic agent in fresh wounds. *F. fomentarius* is only occasionally available, known as Amadou, and is used as a cigar lighter.

Because of its bitter taste *F. officinalis* was once used to flavour confectionery and it was also used as an ingredient of the *Tinctura antiperiodica* or Warburg's Fever Tincture, a compound medication whose composition was published in 1875 by Dr Warburg after years of secrecy. The fungus is not an edible mushroom, and it is now very rarely used.

Description A variably shaped, soft, fleshy, whitish fungus with yellowish spots and pores; to 50 cm long and 30 cm wide. The surface is dry and marked by irregular furrows; it has an aroma of flour.

Distribution Southern Tyrol and French Alps to Russia, in larch forests.

Cultivation Wild plant. Growing on various species of Larch (*Larix* spp.) especially *Larix sibirica* Led., *L. europaea* DC, (*Larix decidua* Mill.). Formerly collected in early autumn.

Constituents Riconoleic acid; phytosterol; agaric acid; agaricol; resins.

Uses (dried whole fungus) Astringent; bitter; purgative.

Formerly used in compound antipyretic medicines, and either alone or in combination with other remedies to treat diarrhoea, excess lactation and fevers.

Also once used as the source of crystalline agaricin which was used for similar medical purposes.

Formerly employed as a bitter flavouring in confectionery.

Contra-indications Large doses cause vomiting and purgation.

Fragearia vesca L ROSACEAE
Wild Strawberry Wood Strawberry

Numerous varieties have been developed since cultivation of the Strawberry began in the early sixteenth century, but it was this species which was gathered wild from the woods of Europe for centuries. *Fraga* was the Latin name, and probably refers to the fruit's fragrance.

Description Perennial 5–25 cm tall, on stout, woody root-stock, producing long, rooting runners. Leaflets ovate, bright green above, pale beneath, silky, toothed, 1–6 cm long. Lateral leaflets sessile, terminal, short-stalked. Flowers white, 15 mm diameter, erect, 3–10 per peduncle; appearing early to mid-summer, followed by red (or white) ovoid, false fruit.

Distribution Native to Europe, western Asia, North America. In woods, scrubland, preferably on moist, somewhat calcareous soils; to 800 m altitude.

Cultivation Wild plant. Propagate by transplantation of daughter plants produced on runners.

Constituents (leaves) Tannins; flavonoids. (fruit) Organic acids; vitamin C; mucilage; sugars.

Uses (fresh fruit, leaves, root-stock rarely) Astringent; diuretic; antiscorbutic; tonic; laxative.

The root decoction was formerly used to treat gonorrhoea, and as a diuretic; it also acts as a weak, bitter tonic. Leaf and root-stock can be used to treat diarrhoea, while the fruit is laxative.

The dried leaf can be used as a tea substitute.

Contra-indications Strawberries may produce an allergic response.

Frangula alnus Mill. RHAMNACEAE
Alder Buckthorn

This medicinal plant is so named because it bears a superficial foliage similarity to the Alder (*Alnus glutinosa* (L) Gaertn.), with which it shares a predilection for wet environments and because it has the same purgative qualities as *Rhamnus catharticus*, which was known as *cervi spina* (buck's thorn) to the early apothecaries.

The quite thornless Alder Buckthorn does not appear to have been used until the beginning of the fourteenth century when the Italian Pierre Crescenzi introduced it. German physicians were to make most use of it in subsequent years.

Since it has similar properties to Cascara sagrada (*Rhamnus purshiana* D.C.), but can be collected locally, it is retained in several European pharmacopoeias.

Description Small tree or deciduous shrub to 6 m; usually 1–4 m. Branches supple, smooth, erect towards the base, young branchlets red-brown at the tips, later darkening to grey-black. Leaves alternate, acute, entire, or sometimes undulate, obovate to oblong, 3–4 cm long, dark green and shiny above. Flowers small, bisexual, greenish, borne in umbelliform cymes. Appearing late spring to mid-summer; followed by globose fruit 7.5 mm diameter, red then black or blue-black.

Distribution Native to Europe, Central Asia, North Africa; introduced and naturalized in eastern United States. On acidic, often heavy soils, in open, damp, deciduous or coniferous woodland, especially near streams, to 1000 m altitude.

Cultivation Wild. Commercial plantations are being established in Eastern Europe. Collected commercially in Russia, Holland, Poland and Czechoslovakia.

Constituents Anthraquinone glycosides, comprising frangulin (produced during drying and storage), frangula-emodin, frangularoside, chrysophanic acid, an iso-emodin; also tannic acid; bitter principles; mucilage.

Purgative action due to the presence of emodins, which act on the large intestine causing peristalsis.

Uses (12-month old stem and inner branch bark) Purgative; choleretic.

Almost exclusively used in the treatment of constipation, often in combination with other remedies. Very small doses may be used to stimulate bile secretion. Once applied externally to aid the healing of wounds.

Contra-indications Fresh bark contains anthrone glycosides which cause severe catharsis, emesis and cramps.

The fruit is POISONOUS.

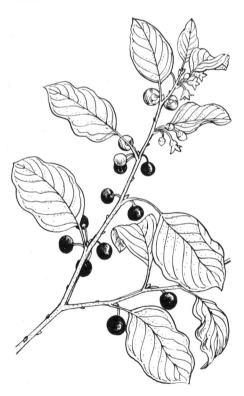

Fraxinus ornus L OLEACEAE
Manna Flowering Ash

According to the Bible, Manna was the substance miraculously supplied to the Israelites during their progress through the wilderness to the Holy Land, and the name has been applied to several substances both real and imaginary, thought to provide spiritual nourishment. Prior to the fifteenth century, Manna was imported from the East and its provenance is uncertain, but from the middle of the sixteenth century most Manna was the dried sugary juice obtained by incisions in the bark of the Flowering Ash grown for the purpose in Sicily and Calabria in southern Italy. Now rarely obtainable in Europe.

Description Deciduous tree 10–20 m. Rounded in shape, and with great variation in leaflet and fruit shape. Leaves 20–25 cm long with 7–11

leaflets, usually ovate or oblong, somewhat pubescent. Flowers dull white, on numerous dense feathery panicles, 7.5–12.5 cm long appearing early to mid-summer, and followed by linear or lanceolate fruit 3 cm long.

Distribution Native to southern Europe and western Asia. Introduced into central Europe, North America and elsewhere.

Cultivation Wild, and cultivated as an ornamental tree and for commercial purposes.

Constituents Various sugars, chiefly comprising mannitol, mannotriose, mannotetrose and dextrose; also mucilage; aesculin and fraxin. Laxative action due to fraxin.

Uses (the yellow-white saccharine exudation obtained by bark incisions during the flowering season) Mild laxative. Exclusively of service as a gentle laxative for children and pregnant women, taken in quite large dosage either alone or in combination with Rhubarb. Nutritive and therefore useful during convalescence.

Contra-indications May cause flatulence.

Fucus vesiculosus L FUCACEAE
Bladderwrack Kelp

Although commonly called Kelp, this is a term usually applied to species of *Laminaria*, which are somewhat larger algae. It is one of several seaweeds long used both as food and medicine,

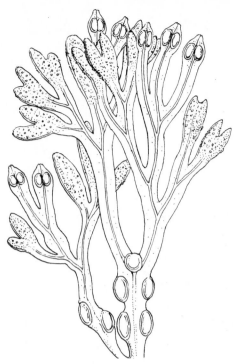

and sometimes as a cheap manure. Iodine was first discovered by distillation of *Fucus* in the early nineteenth century, and for about 50 years most commercial supplies of Iodine were obtained in this way. Its common name is derived both from the typical bladder-like air vesicles on the thallus, and from an ancient word signifying something which is driven ashore.

Description Perennial seaweed consisting of a thin, leathery, branching, brownish-green or yellowish thallus, 18 mm wide and 1 m long. Woody stipe attached to rocks by discoid holdfast; margins entire, midrib broad and distinct, running the length of the plant, along which air vesicles are borne in pairs. Terminating in strong globose fructifications consisting of ovoid receptacles 3 cm in length.

Distribution Common on north-west Atlantic coastlines, especially west Scotland, Norway, and North America; attached to rocks.

Cultivation Wild plant; collected commercially.

Constituents A gelatinous substance, algin; mannitol; iodine; a volatile oil; β-carotene; zeaxanthin; various inorganic substances.

Uses (dried whole plant) Anti-obesic; anti-hypothyroid.

Specifically of use in obesity which is associated with hypothyroidism. A decoction of the whole fresh plant may be applied externally in rheumatism and rheumatoid arthritis.

An excellent source of manure for horticultural purposes; one of the commercial sources of alginates.

Fumaria officinalis L FUMARIACEAE
Fumitory

Much legend surrounds this herb, including the belief that it arose not from seed but from emanations in the ground, and that its smoke when burned repelled evil spirits. Both its common and botanical names derive from the Latin word for smoke, probably because at a

distance the wispy grey-green leaflets look smoky.

From the earliest times Fumitory was considered effective in conditions of intestinal obstruction leading to skin diseases, but today it is rarely used.

Description Annual; variable in form, the stem being erect, bushy or trailing, from 15–70 cm long; leaves grey-green 1 cm long, pinnate, petiolate, with lanceolate leaf segments. Flowers 8 mm–1.2 cm long, pinkish-purple, dark red at the tips, borne in racemes 5–7 cm long, appearing mid-summer to late autumn.

Distribution European native; naturalized in America and parts of Asia. Common in weedy areas of gardens, fields, vineyards, rarely cornfields. Prefers loamy soils.

Cultivation Wild plant.

Constituents 7 alkaloids, chiefly fumarine; tannic acid; fumaric acid; potassium salts.

Uses (dried flowering plant) Laxative; stomachic; tonic; weak diuretic.

Formerly chiefly employed in the treatment of various skin complaints including eczema, exanthema and dermatitis. Also once considered of benefit in arteriosclerosis.

The flowers produce a yellow wool dye.

Dried leaves may be added to smoking mixtures.

Contra-indications POISONOUS.

Galanthus nivalis L AMARYLLIDACEAE
Snowdrop Bulbous Violet

The Snowdrop is well known as the first flower of the year, and its name *galanthus* is derived from the Greek meaning milk flower after its snow-white appearance.

It is very rarely mentioned in the herbals and has never attracted attention as being of medicinal use except for a poultice of the crushed bulbs which may be applied externally in cases of frostbite. Recent research in Europe, however, suggests that the plant may possess

the ability to stimulate the regeneration of some nerve cells.

Description Perennial reaching 10–20 cm tall; leaves linear and glaucous, 7 mm wide, fleshy, basal, ridged, on bulbs growing in compact masses. Pedicel slender, usually less than 25 cm long, bearing single flower; outer segments white, 15 mm–3 cm long, inner segments white and green. Appearing early spring.

Distribution Native to central and south Europe, to the Caucasus; introduced elsewhere. Prefers soils rich in humus and nutrients in mixed deciduous woodland.

Cultivation Wild plant; cultivated as a garden plant and found as an escape. Propagate by division in the autumn. A giant form, *G. Elwesii* (Hook) exists.

Constituents Alkaloids, chiefly in the bulb, comprising tazettine, lycorine, galanthamines.

Uses (bulb) Emetic.

The plant is rarely used medicinally, but in eastern Europe a preparation known as 'nivaline' has been promoted as being of benefit in a range of conditions characterized by nervous tissue degeneration, for example, poliomyelitis.

Contra-indications POISONOUS.

Galega officinalis L PAPILIONACEAE
Goat's Rue French Lilac

The ability of Goat's Rue to promote the flow of milk, by as much as 50% in some animals, is reflected in its name *galega* from the Greek for milk. The most effective galactogenic preparation is an infusion of the fresh plant.

Description Attractive bushy perennial to 1 m on hollow stem bearing leaves consisting of 11–17 oblong or oblong-ovate glabrous, mucronate, leaflets 1–4 cm long. Purplish-blue flowers 1 cm long in racemes slightly longer than the leaves; appear mid-summer to mid-autumn and are followed by 3–4 cm long red-brown pods.

Distribution Native to Europe and western Asia; introduced elsewhere. Prefers slightly moist positions in fields.

Cultivation Wild and occurs as an escape from garden cultivation. *G. officinalis* var. *albiflora* (Boiss.) has white flowers, and *G. officinalis* var.

Hartlandii (Hort.) has lilac flowers and variegated leaves. Propagate by division of roots in spring or autumn, planting in deep soil.

Constituents Alkaloids, chiefly galegine and especially in the seed; a glucoside, galuteoline; tannic acid; saponin; vitamin C; bitter principles.

Uses (dried flowering plant, seeds) Galactogogue; hypoglycaemic; diuretic; diaphoretic.

A tea of Goat's Rue has supportive antidiabetic action and is used to promote milk flow in both women and animals.

The fresh juice clots milk and may be used in cheese-making.

Galipea cusparia St Hilaire RUTACEAE
Angostura Cusparia Bark

First used in 1759 in Madrid by Mutis, Angostura was introduced into England by Brande in 1788 who was the apothecary to Queen Charlotte. Until the end of the nineteenth century Angostura was considered an effective tonic, and it was originally introduced by Dr Siegert as a medical recipe for the treatment of fever. 'Angostura bitters' no longer contains extract of angostura bark, this having been replaced by Gentian root.

Angostura is the former name for Ciudad Bolivar, a town in Venezuela.

Description Small tree 4–5 m tall, 7.5–12.5 cm in diameter, the trunk being straight, irregularly branched and with a smooth bark, covered externally with a yellowish-grey corky layer.

Leaves smooth and glossy, alternate and petiolate, divided into 3 leaflets which are oblong, pointed, 4 cm long. Flowers strongly scented, arranged in terminal peduncled racemes.

Distribution Tropical South America, especially Venezuela. Mostly abundant in mountainous districts.

Cultivation Wild plant.

Constituents Volatile oil; glucoside; alkaloids, chiefly angosturine; a bitter substance, cusparine.

Uses (stem bark) Stimulant tonic.

Employed locally in South America for dyspepsia, chronic diarrhoea and dysentery. Once considered a valuable tonic, and used in fevers in preference to Cinchona Bark. In combination with sliced Lemon and sugar, Angostura bitters was used for hiccups.

Formerly an ingredient of some commercial bitter liqueurs.

The bark acts as a fish poison.

Contra-indications Large doses cause diarrhoea.

Galium aparine L RUBIACEAE
Goosegrass Cleavers/Clivers

Many of the common names refer to the clinging nature of the stems of this common weed of roadsides and hedgerows, a character shared also by the globular seed capsules which assist in the distribution of the plant via animal coats. The Greeks called it *philanthropon* meaning love man because the leaves and fruit cling to the clothes. It has been widely used in folk medicine for centuries, generally being considered of most benefit in the treatment of various skin conditions.

Description Annual herb with straggling habit, the trailing, quadrangular, rough, stem attaining 120 cm in length. Leaves prickly, cuneate, in whorls of 6 or 8, coarse-haired on the leaf margins. Flowers very small, white, or greenish-white on 2–3 cm long inflorescences borne on leaf axils and extending longer than the leaves.

Distribution European native; prefers moist nutrient-rich loamy soils, in weedy sites, particularly field and garden edges and hedgerows.

Cultivation Wild plant.

Constituents A glycoside, asperuloside.

Uses (dried flowering plant, freshly expressed juice) Vulnerary; weak diuretic.

Used externally to treat wounds and ulcers, and internally in painful urination associated with cystitis; in enlarged lymph glands, and in psoriasis. The herb reduces body temperature and blood pressure slightly. Also employed homeopathically.

The dried plant may be drunk as a tea, and the roasted seeds provide an excellent coffee substitute.

Galium verum L RUBIACEAE
Ladies' Bedstraw Cheese Rennet/Yellow Bedstraw

The pleasant honey scent of the flowers and hay-like aroma of the dried leaves and stems made this an admirable herb for stuffing mattresses in medieval times. It was commonly mixed with bracken or some aromatic or flea-repelling herb for this purpose. Dioscorides knew it as *galion* or the milk plant, and it was used throughout Europe from the time of the Greeks until the 1800s as a means of curdling

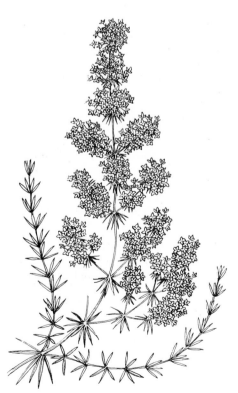

milk in cheese manufacture.

Description A perennial herb with erect or decumbent somewhat woody stems, round with 4 prominent edges or almost square, glabrous, slightly branched and from 20–80 cm tall. Leaves white and slightly hairy on the underside, recurved, bristle-tipped, in whorls of 8–12, linear, 1.5–2.5 cm long, 1–2 mm wide. Flowers 2–3 mm wide, smelling of honey, on terminal panicles, golden-yellow, appearing early summer to mid-autumn.

Distribution European native; now a weed in the eastern United States. On semi-dry or dry grassland.

Cultivation Wild plant.

Constituents Silicic acid; saponin; an enzyme, rennin.

Uses (dried flowering plant) Weak diuretic; styptic.

Formerly employed as a diuretic for dropsy and in epilepsy. Applied externally to wounds and some skin eruptions.

Strong decoctions curdle milk when boiled, and may be used in cheese manufacture; the herb also colours cheese a greenish-yellow.

A red dye can be obtained from the lower stem.

Gaultheria procumbens L ERICACEAE
Wintergreen Checkerberry/Mountain Tea
Most commercial oil of Wintergreen now consists of synthetically produced methyl salicylate. It was formerly obtained largely from young birch trees (*Betula lenta*), and before that it was isolated from the Wintergreen plant. Wintergreen was once mentioned in the United States Pharmacopoeia but has never attracted much medical attention, nor is it widely used in folk traditions. It is named after Dr Gaultier, a physician practising in Quebec in about 1750.

Description Evergreen shrub with creeping stems and erect stiff branches to 15 cm tall, bearing at the top oval leaves, 3–5 cm long, glabrous and shiny above, paler beneath, petiolate and apiculate; white flowers 7.5 mm long, solitary and drooping, appearing from the leaf base in mid and late summer, and followed by scarlet berries 7 mm in diameter.

Distribution North American native, from Newfoundland to Georgia. On poor soils.

Cultivation Wild plant.

Constituents Arbutin: ericolin; urson; tannin; a volatile oil (oil of gaultheria or oil of wintergreen) is obtained by distillation of the leaves and comprises chiefly methyl salicylate, and an alcohol, a ketone and an ester.

Uses (leaves, oil) Stimulant; astringent; tonic; aromatic; counter-irritant.

An infusion of the leaves may be used as a throat gargle, as a douche and for headaches. The oil is readily absorbed by the skin and is employed in various aches and pains, including rheumatism. It is occasionally used internally as an emulsion against hookworm.

Leaves may be used as a tea substitute.

The oil is a flavouring agent in various dental preparations.

Contra-indications The pure oil may irritate skin; it must not be used internally without medical advice.

Gelidium spp. RHODOPHYCEAE
Agar-Agar Japanese Isinglass
The use of Agar as a semi-solid medium for the cultivation of bacteria and fungi by Robert Koch in the 1880s revolutionized bacteriological research and made it possible to cultivate and identify many of the bacteria responsible for human and animal disease. Today most of the Agar produced is employed for this purpose, and although Japanese Agar made from various species of *Gelidium* is considered the finest and has the greatest gel strength, other seaweeds also provide Agar; British Agar is from either *Chondrus crispus* or *Gigartina stellata* or a combination of the two, the New Zealand variety from *Pterocladia lucida*, and Australian from *Gracilaria confervoides*.

Description Perennial seaweed to 25 cm long; the thallus develops from a persistent basal portion each growing season, is cylindrical or flattened, pinnately subdivided and of a tough consistency. The spherical fruit appear in the late autumn and winter months.

Distribution Gelidium amansii Kutz., *G. elegans* Kutz. and *G. polycladum* Sond. are found in the maritime zones of Japan and *G. cartilagineum* (Gaill.) in the maritime zones of South Africa and United States.

Cultivation Wild marine plant; collected commercially and sometimes encouraged to grow on poles driven into the sea bed.

Constituents Chiefly composed of a calcium salt, of a sulphuric ester of a carbohydrate complex; also a trace of protein, and mineral salts.

Uses (dried Agar; greyish-white translucent strips obtained by drying the liquor resulting from boiling the seaweed for 6 hours in the presence of dilute sulphuric acid) Bulk laxative; emulsion stabilizer.

Unlike gelatine Agar-Agar has no nutritive or

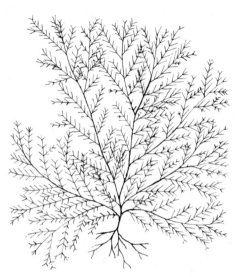

therapeutic value, but it is used medically as a mild evacuant since it absorbs water in the intestine, increases the faeces bulk, and thus promotes peristalsis. Also used to stabilize emulsions of other laxatives. Mostly employed as the basis of bacteriological culture media, and as a thickening agent in some foodstuffs, both commercially and domestically.

Employed as the physical base for certain air purifiers.

Gelsemium sempervirens Ait. LOGANIACEAE
Yellow Jessamine Yellow Jasmine Root
Gelsemium is derived from the Italian *Gelsomino* the name of the true Jessamine or Jasmine. It was introduced to medicine accidentally in the early nineteenth century after a Mississippi planter mistakenly took a tea made from the plant to cure bilious fever. The first tests were made in 1852, and it eventually entered the United States Pharmacopoeia, and the British Pharmaceutical Codex. Until quite recently it was used in various mixtures for migraine treatment, but it is toxic even in quite small doses and now seldom used.

Description Perennial evergreen vine to 10 m on woody purplish-brown rhizomes; stem slender, woody, bearing opposite lanceolate to ovate-lanceolate, short-petioled leaves 2.5–10 cm long, entire, shiny dark green above, and paler beneath. Flowers yellow, 2.5–4 cm long, highly fragrant, 1–6 on axillary or terminal cymes, appearing from mid-spring to mid-summer.

Distribution Native to southern United States, Mexico, Guatemala; in moist woodlands.

Cultivation Wild plant; sometimes cultivated horticulturally as cover, or in greenhouses. Propagate from cuttings or from divisions of root-stock in the late spring.

Constituents Alkaloids: gelsemine, sempervirine and gelsemicine; phytosterol; resin; fixed oil; emodin monomethyl ether; β-methylaeculetin. Action largely due to the alkaloids which depress the central nervous system.

Uses (dried rhizome and roots) Sedative; nervine. Formerly employed in the treatment of neuralgia, sick headache, menstrual and rheumatic pains and particularly migraine and trigeminal neuralgia. A perfume can be

made from the flowers.

Contra-indications All parts POISONOUS; toxic effects include double vision, giddiness, respiratory depression and death. Gelsemium is more strongly depressant than Hemlock.

Genista tinctoria L LEGUMINOSAE
Dyer's Greenweed Dyer's Broom

As the common name suggests this herb was an important dyeing plant, and was often combined with Woad to produce a green wool dye. It is closely related to *Sarothamnus scoparius* which in the Middle Ages was itself called Genista, but unlike this plant Dyer's Greenweed does not possess very strong medicinal qualities and is now mainly employed in homecraft dyeing.

Description Perennial herbaceous shrub, prostrate or decumbent, to 1 m, usually 30–50 cm

tall. Bearing glabrous or pubescent forked branches and 1.5–3 cm long, oblong-elliptic or oblong-lanceolate, alternate, nearly sessile, glabrous, simple leaves. Flowers 15 mm long, golden yellow, in racemes 3–7.5 cm long, appearing mid-summer to early autumn, and followed by long narrow pods.

Distribution Native to Europe and western Asia; naturalized in North America. Introduced elsewhere. On dryish loamy or sandy soils in light woodland, pastures, heaths and meadows.

Cultivation Wild plant.

Constituents The alkaloids, sparteine, cytisine and methyl-cytisine; a flavone, genistein; a yellow glycoside, luteolin. The combined action weakly cardio-active and vasoconstrictive.

Uses (flowering plant, seeds, leaves) Emetic; purgative; diuretic; weakly cardio-active.

Formerly used as a diuretic and purgative; in dropsy, rheumatism and as a prophylactic against hydrophobia.

The young buds may be pickled and used as a caper substitute.

The flowering plant furnishes a yellow-green dye.

Contra-indications Not to be used internally during pregnancy or hypertension.

Gentiana lutea L GENTIANACEAE
Gentian Yellow Gentian

Yellow Gentian root is the most bitter plant material known, and has been used for centuries as a bitter tonic. Several other *Gentiana* species native to Europe and North America have been employed for the same purpose, and it is not certain which of the European species was known to the Greeks. The name *gentiana*, however, is derived from Gentius, King of Illyria (180–167 B.C.) who, according to Dioscorides, introduced the herb to medicine. It has been widely employed ever since. Some plants survive as long as 50 years.

Description Herbaceous perennial to 110 cm on thick taproot reaching 60 cm long. Stems simple and erect, glabrous, bearing oval, 5–7 veined, shiny leaves 30 cm long and 15 cm wide; lower leaves on short petioles, upper leaves sessile. Bright yellow flowers, 2.5–3 cm long, on long peduncles in 3–10 flowered axillary clusters, appearing late summer to early autumn on plants at least 10 years old.

Distribution Native to Europe and Asia Minor; introduced elsewhere. Common in mountain pastures, and thinly wooded mountain forests, on calcareous soils which are porous but often moist.

Cultivation Wild and cultivated commercially in Eastern Europe and North America.

Constituents Unsaturated lactones (gentiopicrosides), amarogentine and gentiopicrine, which are partially or totally converted (depending upon the method of drying) to the bitter glycosides, gentiin and gentiamarine; volatile oil; sugars; mucilage; tannin.

The combined action stimulates secretion of bile and its release from the gall bladder.

Uses (dried root, and dried fermented root) Cholagogue; choleretic; stomachic; promotes

salivation.

Acts as a tonic on the gastro-intestinal system; particularly useful in anorexia associated with dyspepsia. In small doses it stimulates the appetite, and should be taken an hour before eating.

Formerly used externally for cleaning wounds, also used as a powder in veterinary medicine to improve appetite.

The fermented root is used as a bitter preparation in alcoholic drinks.

Geranium maculatum L GERANIACEAE
American Cranesbill Wild Geranium

The specific name of American Cranesbill is derived from *macula* meaning spotted, since the leaves become blotched with whitish-green when they age. *Geranium* is from the Greek word for the crane after the beak-like shape of the fruit; hence also the herb's common names. This was a favourite herb of the American Indians, once official in the United States Pharmacopoeia, but now restricted to folk medicine.

Description Erect hairy perennial to 6o cm; stem solitary, but occasionally forking, on stout rhizome. Some leaves arise from root and are long-petioled. Stem leaves opposite, 7.5–15 cm wide, 5-lobed, deeply incised and cut at the end, hairy. Flowers rose-purple, large, 2.5–4 cm wide, on 2.5 cm long peduncles, 2–3 flowers arising in the axils, appear late spring to late summer.

Distribution North American native.

Cultivation Wild plant.

Constituents Tannic and gallic acids, 10–25%, which produce astringent action; oleo-resin.

Uses (dried rhizome) Astringent; styptic. Useful in diarrhoea, in haemorrhage of the upper gastro-intestinal tract, haemorrhoids, peptic ulcers and aphthous ulcers. Formerly recommended in dysentery and cholera. Used as a douche in leucorrhoea, as a gargle for sore throats, and in the powdered form externally to stop wound bleeding.

Geranium robertianum L GERANIACEAE
Herb Robert Red Robin

A common herb in Europe and an old medicinal plant which was once official in the Middle Ages, and ascribed to St Robert or Pope Robert, hence the medieval name *herba sanctii ruperti*. It is probable that the plant was commonly associated with magic and goblins in earlier times, a fact reflected in the range of names it has been given in various European countries. Still used in folk medicine in many parts of the world.

Description Unpleasantly smelling annual or biennial, on erect or decumbent, glandular-

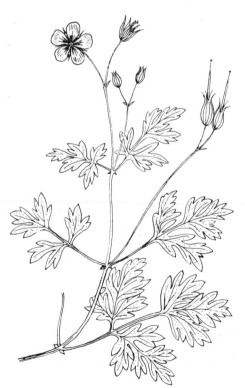

pubescent, reddish stems to 45 cm. Leaves opposite, palmate with 3–5 leaflets with deeply cut divisions, on long petioles, deep green and red tinged. Flowers pink or rose, 5 mm–1 cm wide, in pairs or peduncles arising in terminal axils. Petals have 3 longitudinal white stripes. Appear early summer to late autumn.

Distribution Native to North America, Eurasia and North Africa; common on rocky soils, walls, mixed and deciduous woodland edges, preferring moist and nitrogenous soils.

Cultivation Wild plant.

Constituents Volatile oil; tannin; a bitter substance, geraniine.

Uses (fresh flowering plant, dried plant) Styptic; astringent; weak diuretic; sedative. Of most use externally for treatment of skin eruptions, stomatitis, bruises and erysipelas. The leaves may be chewed or used as a gargle in inflammations of the mouth and throat. Formerly used in diarrhoea and applied externally as a poultice to relieve inflammations; also used as an eyewash.

Geum urbanum L ROSACEAE
Avens Herb Bennet/Wood Avens

Avens is also known as Herb Bennet or Benedict's herb; names which derive directly from the medieval name *herba benedicta* from the Latin meaning the blessed herb, since the strongly aromatic roots were thought to drive away evil spirits.

For this reason amulets of the herb were worn, and it was also kept in homes.

The botanical name also reflects the roots' scent: *geum* is from the Greek meaning to produce an agreeable smell. The fragrance is unfortunately lost on drying. It is rarely used today except in folk medicine.

Description Perennial herb on clove-smelling rhizome 3–7 cm long, 1–2 cm thick, bearing richly branched downy stems to 30 cm. Leaves 3-lobed, the terminal leaflets largest, irregular, crenate or dentate; upper leaves palmate and sessile. Pale yellow flowers, 5-petalled, 5–7 mm diameter, in loose open panicles, appearing early summer to late autumn. Variable in form.

Distribution European native; common in thickets, wasteland, wood edges, hedgerows, mixed and deciduous woodland; prefers moist nitrogenous soil.

Cultivation Wild plant.

Constituents Volatile oil, comprising mainly eugenol, the latter being combined as a glycoside (geoside) in the fresh plant; tannin; bitter principles.

Uses (dried rhizome, fresh flowering plant) Astringent; styptic; bitter; tonic; anti-inflammatory.

Useful in diarrhoea, and as an aromatic bitter tonic to promote appetite following illness. Applied to wounds to reduce inflammation, and employed as a gargle for sore gums or in halitosis.

The dried rhizome was formerly used as a substitute for Cloves; used as a pot herb in broths and soups, and hung with clothes to repel moths.

Also used to flavour ale.

Glechoma hederacea L LABIATAE
Ground Ivy Gill Over The Ground/Field Balm

In the second century A.D. Galen was aware of the use of Ground Ivy for treating inflamed eyes, and it is probable that the herb was a popular folk remedy from the earliest times.

The plant was also employed in clarifying ale to impart flavour to it and to improve its keeping qualities. *Glechoma* was used much earlier than hops were, being widely employed until the early 1600s.

It is also known as Alehoof or Tunhoof from an old English word for the herb, *hofe*, and from the process of mashing and fermenting the brew known as tunning.

Description Pubescent perennial, strong-smelling with long creeping or decumbent stems which form a dense mat. Leaves hairy, long petioled and rotund or reniform to 4 cm wide, coarsely crenate and deeply cordate at the base. Flowers in clusters of 2–3 borne in the terminal leaf axils, bluish or pink, appear mid-spring to early summer.

Distribution Native to Europe, north Asia; naturalized in North America. Common on damp grassland in open woods and fen wood-

land, preferring moist, nitrogenous soil.
Cultivation Wild plant; a variegated variety is grown horticulturally as ground cover. Propagate by division in the autumn.
Constituents Essential oil; tannin; a bitter compound, glechomine.
Uses (fresh flowering plant) Tonic; diuretic; vulnerary.
Formerly mostly used to soothe coughs, and as a gentle stimulant tonic following digestive disorders. Also once applied externally as a poultice for the treatment of bruises, contusions, and sore eyes. Taken as snuff to relieve headache.
Used to clarify beers and ales.
Drunk as a tea known as Gill tea.

Glycyrrhiza glabra L LEGUMINOSAE
Liquorice Licorice
Liquorice has been used medicinally for 3000 years and was recorded on Assyrian tablets and Egyptian papyri. It was known as Scythian root to Theophrastus and the old names *glycyrrhiza* and *radix dulcis* reflected the sweet taste of the roots.
Liquorice is a corruption of the medieval *gliquiricia*, itself from *glycyrrhiza*.
Now grown on a wide scale, it does not appear to have been cultivated in Central or Western Europe until the fifteenth century, and it was first introduced to the Pontefract district of England by the Dominican Black Friars.
Description Herbaceous perennial, 50 cm–1.5 m tall, on primary taproot 15 cm long which subdivides into 3–5 subsidiary roots 1.25 m in length and several horizontal stolons which may reach 8 m. Erect stem bearing 4–7 pairs of leaflets 2.5–5 cm long, ovate, glutinous beneath. Inflorescence of 20–30 lilac-blue flowers 1 cm long in loose racemes 10–15 cm long, arising in leaf axils. Appearing mid to late summer, followed by reddish-brown pod, 1–2.5 cm long.
Distribution Europe to West Pakistan. On deep sandy rich soils, preferably in river valleys.
Cultivation Wild plant, although rarely wild in central and western Europe and more common in eastern Europe. Introduced to temperate

zones, and extensively cultivated in Russia, Persia, Spain and India. Propagated by root division in autumn; roots harvested from 3–4-year-old plants in early winter. Several varieties exist, the commonest are var. *typica* and var. *glandulifera*.
Constituents Glycyrrhizin (5–10%), comprising calcium and potassium salts of glycyrrhizic acid; flavonoid glycosides, liquiritoside and isoliquiritoside; sucrose and dextrose (5–10%); starch (30%); protein; fat; resin; asparagin; volatile oil; saponins.
Uses (dried root-stock, dried extract) Demulcent; expectorant; laxative; spasmolytic; anti-inflammatory.
Of value in coughs and bronchitis, and in the treatment of gastric ulcers; also has a mineralo-corticoid action in treatment of Addison's disease. Once used as an eye lotion for use on inflamed eyelids.
Used as a sweetening agent and flavouring in pharmaceutical preparations, and once in the powdered form as a base in pill manufacture.
Used to flavour some beers such as Guinness.
Large quantities are employed in tobacco flavouring (some tobaccos contain 10% Liquorice), in snuff manufacture, and in confectionery.
Root pulp incorporated in insulating mill board, and mushroom compost.
Contra-indications Large doses may cause sodium retention and potassium loss leading to water retention, hypertension, headache and shortness of breath.

Gnaphalium uliginosum L COMPOSITAE
Marsh Cudweed Everlasting/Low Cudweed
As its name indicates, Marsh Cudweed is an inhabitant of wet situations; the specific name *uliginosum* derives from the Latin *uliginosus* meaning of marshy places. *Gnaphalium* is from the Greek *gnaphalon* meaning a flock of wool, from its woolly appearance.
The herb has never achieved wide use even in folk medicine, and is rarely mentioned in classical writings. Although it possesses useful properties, it is still rarely used.
Description Annual, 5–20 cm tall, with woolly, ascending or decumbent stems, much branched at the base; bearing narrow, spirally arranged, simple, oblong, woolly leaves 1–5 cm long. Small flower-heads in terminal clusters, yellow,

4 mm wide, with brown bracts, and overtopped by the terminal leaves. Appearing late summer to early autumn.
Distribution European native. On damp, acidic, sandy soils – especially wet heathland.
Cultivation Wild plant.
Constituents Volatile oil; resin; tannic acid; the combined action being antiseptic and astringent.
Uses (dried flowering plant) Astringent; antiseptic; antitussive; weak diaphoretic.
Specifically used as a gargle and mouthwash in aphthous ulcers, quinsy and tonsillitis. Also of benefit in diarrhoea, pharyngitis and laryngitis. A poultice may be applied externally to cuts, bruises or ulcers.
Once used in smoking mixtures.

Gossypium herbaceum L MALVACEAE
Cotton Cotton Root
The plant has been cultivated in India since the earliest times as a source of Cotton fibre, and its botanical name *gossypium* is the ancient Latin name for the Cotton-producing plant. The method of cultivation was introduced to China and Egypt from India in about 500 B.C., and in 1774 *G. herbaceum* was taken to the United States.
This species of Cotton is also called Levant Cotton; many other species and varieties are employed today in cotton manufacture including American Upland Cotton (*G. hirsutum* L), Chinese Cotton (*G. arboreum* L) and Sea Island Cotton (*G. barbadense* L).
The species *G. peruvianum* was probably grown in Peru before Cotton was cultivated in Egypt.
Description Herbaceous annual, in warm climates biennial or perennial, forming a subshrub to 1.5 m with branching stems, hairy or occasionally glabrous, bearing reticulate, coriaceous and cordate leaves, with 5–7 acute and lanceolate lobes. Flowers yellow with purple centre, followed by 18 mm long 3–4 celled capsule containing about 36 seeds covered with greyish trichomes, lint.
Distribution Originally native to East Indies, and now to Arabia and Asia Minor; prefers rich sands and loams, especially alluvial soils.
Cultivation Wild plant; widely cultivated in United States, India and Egypt. Seed sown in rows 1–1.5 m apart, later thinning to 30–60 cm apart; manure applied in early stages of growth, and plants are treated as annuals to prevent insect and disease attacks.
Constituents (root bark) acid resin; dihydroxy benzoic acid; salicylic acid; fatty acids; ceryl alcohol; betaine; sugars; phytosterol; phenolic substances.
Uses (root bark, seed oil) Abortifacient; emmenagogue.
Formerly used in the treatment of metrorrhagia. Cotton seed oil is used similarly to olive oil for external applications, but internally as a lubricant cathartic. Emulsions of the oil have been administered intravenously in cases of severe nutritional deficiency, or where nitrogen-free diets are required.
Seed once used as a food.
The oil is employed in soap manufacture.
The seed trichomes are a major source of

cotton fibre.

Contra-indications No part of the plant should be used internally without medical advice.

Gratiola officinalis L SCROPHULARIACEAE
Hedge Hyssop

Hedge Hyssop belongs to the same family as Foxglove and possesses similar cardio-active properties. It was introduced to northern Europe in the Middle Ages and used as a purgative; its employment has been described as 'heroic' since it was so powerful, and, indeed, it was probably responsible for several deaths. Nevertheless it was described as *Gratia* or *Gratia Dei* meaning thanks-be-to-God in appreciation of its effectiveness.

After the sixteenth century its use declined, but it has recently been introduced into homeopathic practice.

Description Perennial, on white, scaly, creeping rhizome, from which arise erect or decumbent, square, simple or occasionally branched stems to 35 cm. Leaves opposite and decussate, sessile, finely serrate, glabrous, and lanceolate.

Flowers 1.5 cm long, white or pink, with yellowish corolla tube on short peduncles; appear singly in leaf axils from late summer to early autumn.

Distribution Native to southern Europe; introduced to north and west Asia and North America. On marshy fields, in ditches, peat bogs, river-banks, beside slow-flowing or stagnant water. Prefers wet calcareous soils, but will stand summer drought.

Cultivation Wild plant.

Constituents Cardio-active glycosides (cardenolides), gratioline and gratiotoxin; a bitter principle.

Uses (dried flowering plant, root) Emetic; cathartic; cardiotonic diuretic.

Formerly used as a violent purgative and emetic, and as a diuretic in dropsical conditions. Also in liver disorders such as jaundice and as a heart tonic. Many other uses have been ascribed to the plant. Still used homeopathically.

Contra-indications Highly toxic and drastically purgative. Large doses may cause death.

Guaiacum officinale L ZYGOPHYLLACEAE
Guaiacum Wood or Resin

Guaiacum Wood was first exported from the island of St Domingo in the Carribean in 1514 after Oviedo had learnt of the drug *guayacan* from the local inhabitants.

The Wood, then known as *lignum vitae*, achieved a considerable reputation in the sixteenth century for the treatment of 'Frenche pockes' or syphilis. Its success was possibly due to the method of administration: patients were given massive doses of the Wood decoction, tightly wrapped up in bed and shut in a hot room. In 1932 it was demonstrated that raising a patient's body temperature to 42°C was a partially effective method of destroying the syphilis bacterium. Guaiacum Resin was introduced to the London Pharmacopoeia in 1677, but the drug was gradually relegated to being merely a constituent of the proprietary blood-purifying mixtures of the eighteenth and nineteenth centuries known as Compound Alterative Mixtures, often combined with sarsaparilla, which had no effect in syphilis treatment.

Description Low to medium sized evergreen tree reaching 18 m; trunk covered with greenish-brown furrowed bark; leaves pinnate with ovate very obtuse leaflets, in pairs. Blue flowers and a 2-celled capsule-shaped fruit.

Distribution Native to Carribean islands, north coast of South America; especially on arid plains.

Cultivation Wild plant. Collected commercially and exported either as the wood or as the resin which is extracted by heating the logs.

Constituents Resin (20–25%), comprising α- and β-guaiaconic acid (20%), guaiaretic acid (10%), guaiac acid; guaiac-β-resin; guaiac yellow; vanillin; guaiacsaponin and guaiacsaponic acid; guaiaguttin.

Uses (heartwood, resin) Local stimulant; irritant; mild laxative; anti-inflammatory.

Formerly frequently prescribed as a preventative in gout and in the treatment of rheumatoid arthritis. Taken as a hot decoction it is mildly diaphoretic; also useful in sore throats when applied as a lozenge.

Guaiacum tincture is used as a colour test to detect the presence of oxidizing agents which will turn it blue.

The hard wood was once used in the manufacture of such articles as rulers, pulleys and bowling alley balls.

The resin is employed as an antioxidant for edible fats and oils.

Hamamelis virginiana L HAMAMELIDACEAE
Witch Hazel

A well-known garden ornamental and source of the distilled commercial preparation also known as witch hazel. Forked Hamamelis branches were employed as divining rods by water diviners in North America, and Indians brought the medicinal virtues of the plant to the notice of European settlers. *Hamamelis* was included in the United States Pharmaco-

poeia of 1882, and the leaves are still included in some national pharmacopoeias today. The name *hamamelis* is from the Greek words for apple and together, since the flowers and fruit are produced at the same time.

Description Small tree or spreading shrub, from 1.5–2.5 m tall, stem usually single and to 10 cm in diameter. Bark smooth and brown. Leaves elliptic to obovate 7.5–12.5 cm long, coarsely crenate-dentate, downy pubescent when young. Flowers bright yellow externally, brownish-yellow inside, 2 cm long, strap-like, appearing in the late autumn when leaves have fallen.

Distribution North American native; common and profuse in damp woods from Nova Scotia to Nebraska and Georgia.

Cultivation Wild plant; cultivated horticulturally as a hardy garden ornamental; prefers lime-free soil and flowers best in the open, although can be grown in semi-shade.

Constituents Tannin, comprising hamamelitannin (bark 6%, leaves 12%); gallic acid; calcium oxalate; and traces of volatile oil, saponin and flavenoid pigments. Leaves also contain phlobatannin. Distilled witch hazel is prepared from witch hazel brush, the young flower-bearing twigs. It consists entirely of a volatile oil, to which 13 to 15% ethyl alcohol is added.

Uses (bark, leaves, flower-bearing twigs) Astringent; haemostatic.

Once employed in haemorrhages from the rectum, nose and uterus; now externally in the treatment of haemorrhoids and varicose veins. Distilled witch hazel is applied to bruises and sprains, as is the diluted tincture. Very dilute distilled witch hazel may be used in eye lotions. A constituent of proprietary haemorrhoid ointments and cosmetic preparations – specifically as an astringent.

Contra-indications Distilled witch hazel must not be confused with the tincture made from bark or leaves; the latter may be extremely astringent and may cause disfigurement to the skin.

Hedera helix L araliaceae
Ivy Common Ivy/English Ivy

The Ivy has never been widely accepted as having great medicinal value, yet it was once much respected as a magical plant protecting against evil spirits and symbolizing fidelity.

It was also dedicated to Bacchus, possibly because an infusion of the leaves in wine was considered an effective preventative and treatment for drunkenness. For the same reason an Ivy bush painted above tavern doors symbolized the good quality of the wine served therein. No modern work has been undertaken to test this ancient belief.

Some Ivy plants may reach more than 500 years of age.

Description Woody evergreen perennial, climbing by means of adventitious roots and often reaching great heights. Young leaves usually 3–5 lobed, margins entire or nearly so, varying from triangular-ovate to reniform, and from 2–18 cm long; veins often light-coloured. Upper leaves and those on fruiting branches unlobed, narrowly ovate. Flowers small, green-

ish, appearing mid to late autumn on 10-year-old plants; followed by black, globose, 6 mm diameter fruit.

Distribution Native to Europe; widely naturalized in temperate zones and very common, although rarer in coniferous woodland.

Cultivation Wild plant; extensively grown horticulturally with approximately 40 foliage forms recognized.

Constituents Saponin, hederacoside; hederegenine.

Uses (young leaves) Antispasmodic.

Once used internally in the treatment of whooping-cough, neuralgia, rheumatic pain, bronchitis. The berries, though toxic, were formerly considered an effective purgative. Leaves may be applied externally as a poultice for some skin complaints, sores and rheumatic pain. For toothache the mouth may be rinsed with a decoction of leaves in vinegar; the decayed teeth were formerly plugged with the black gummy resin produced by the plant. A varnish was made from the gummy resin.

Contra-indications The whole plant is POISONOUS and should only be used externally. The berries may cause blisters and the leaves dermatitis.

Helianthus annuus L compositae
Sunflower Common Sunflower

The aptly named Sunflower is well-known as the source of a fine salad oil, and is cultivated commercially in several countries for this and other purposes. Its origins are uncertain, but the plant is most probably indigenous to Mexico where it is called *chimalati*. American Indians have long cultivated the Sunflower for its seed, often growing the plant in the same field as maize.

It was once believed that growing Sunflower near to one's home gave protection against malaria, which may be explained by the fact that an infusion of the flowers has weak insecticidal properties.

Description Robust annual from 30 cm to 5 m tall; stems erect, sometimes mottled, rounded and rough, bearing opposite leaves below and alternate long-petioled, ovate, acute or acuminate leaves above, 10–30 cm long and 10–20 cm wide.

Peduncles long, thickening towards the involucre. Flower-heads 7.5–15 cm in diameter, and up to 35 cm in diameter in cultivated forms, appearing late summer to early autumn. The central disc is brownish-purple and the ray florets are chrome-yellow.

Distribution Native to Central America and western North America; introduced and widespread in many countries; tolerates most soils in full sun.

Cultivation Wild; often found as a garden escape. Cultivated commercially, particularly Rumania, Bulgaria, Russia, Hungary, United States, Mexico, Argentina and parts of Africa. Grown horticulturally in sunny position from seed sown in late spring to early summer – they should not be transplanted. Several hybrids exist including some with double heads, and with colours ranging from a dull white to

chestnut brown.

Constituents Seed contains an unsaturated fixed oil (30%); albumin; lecithin; betaine; choline; plant contains potassium nitrate; potassium carbonate; tannins; a flavonic glycoside, quercimetrin.

Uses (seed, seed oil, occasionally leaf and flowers) Nutritive; expectorant; diuretic.

Formerly the seeds were considered useful in treating coughs and bronchial infections; and leaves and flowers were used in malaria. Used externally on bruises, and a homeopathically prepared tincture is employed in constipation. Sunflower oil is widely used in foodstuffs as a salad and margarine oil, and pharmaceutically as a substitute for olive or ground-nut oils.

Seed is roasted and eaten, used as a Coffee substitute, ground into meal for cakes and soups. Unopened flower buds are boiled and eaten with butter in the same way as Artichokes.

It has excellent burning qualities and may be used in old-fashioned oil lamps.

Leaves provide animal fodder, and when dried may be used as a substitute for cigar tobacco. Seed receptacles and stalk pith may be used in paper manufacture.

Helleborus niger L RANUNCULACEAE
Black Hellebore Christmas Rose
Helleborus is the classical name for a closely related species *Helleborus orientalis*, and was a term also applied to the White Hellebore and other Hellebores by the Greeks.

Many of the Hellebores have similar actions, and several species such as *H. viridis* L and *H. foetidus* L, the Green and Stinking Hellebores respectively, were employed by herbalists in the Middle Ages – largely for their purgative effect, but also in the treatment of certain skin complaints. Outside homeopathy, their use is now confined to horticulture.

Description Perennial to 30 cm; on slowly creeping, tangled, blackish-brown root-stock. The true stem does not rise above ground; basal leaves have long petioles, are leathery and evergreen, serrate, and deeply divided into 7 or more oblong leaflets. Flowering stem simple or occasionally forked, bearing single white or purplish flowers 3–8 cm wide, appearing mid-winter to mid-spring.

Distribution European native; especially southern and central mountainous regions. In mountain forests, open woodland, on stony, humus-rich, calcareous soils only.

Cultivation Wild. Cultivated as a garden plant. Propagate by division of root-stock, or from seed sown as soon as ripe, in the open or under a cold-frame. Well-drained shady positions on chalky soil are ideal. Horticultural varieties include var. *Altifolius* (Hayne) and Potters Wheel; both have large flowers.

Constituents A cardenolide, hellebrigenine; saponosides, comprising helleboreine and helleborine; also protoanemonine. The combined action of the cardenolide and saponosides is cardio-active and purgative.

Uses (dried root-stock) Powerful hydragogue cathartic; cardio-active; local irritant.

Once used as a purgative; emmenagogue; heart tonic; local anaesthetic; abortive and in many other conditions. Now obsolete except in homeopathy which employs a tincture for treating certain psychoses.

The powdered root-stock was once a constituent of sneezing powders.

Contra-indications All parts POISONOUS; produces violent inflammation of the gastro-intestinal mucous membranes, and of the skin if applied locally.

Heracleum sphondylium L UMBELLIFERAE
Cow Parsnip Hogweed
A common weed, dedicated to Hercules (hence its generic name, *Heracleum*) after its robustness; related species have long been used both as human and animal foodstuffs. Particularly favoured by Scandinavian peoples.

Description Stout, erect biennial or perennial 50–200 cm tall, with ridged, hollow stems bearing hairy, large (15–60 cm), pinnate to palmately lobed leaves. Flowers white in umbels of 5–15 cm diameter, appearing mid-summer to mid-autumn. Variable in form.

Distribution Native to Europe, northern Asia,

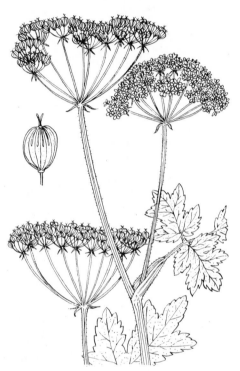

western North America. In woodland, grassland, roadsides, on nutrient-rich, moist soils, to 1800 m altitude.

Cultivation Wild plant.

Constituents Pimpinellin; sphondrin; a complex oil; bergapetene, a furo-coumarin to which the photosensitization is due.

Uses (young shoots, seed, leaves) Stimulant; stomachic; hypotensive; emmenagogue; mild aphrodisiac.

Leaf is of benefit in combination with other remedies in hypertension. Once used to treat epilepsy. Now used homeopathically. The seeds have a substantiated aphrodisiacal action. Young shoots can be cooked and eaten, or used in certain east European beers. Young stems are peeled and eaten raw.

Contra-indications Percutaneous photosensitization (blisters and possibly permanent purple pigmentation) may follow ingestion or handling of juice with subsequent exposure to sunlight.

Hibiscus sabdariffa L MALVACEAE
Roselle Sudanese Tea/Red Tea/Jamaica Tea
Hibiscus is the old Latin name for this plant which was introduced to Jamaica and used as

an acid flavouring at least as early as 1774; the calices being the parts used. It is now being used in other parts of the world, and is especially popular in Switzerland where it is called *karkade* and is used in wines and sauces.

Other parts of the plant are used medicinally, and the stem yields an excellent fibre known as rosella hemp.

Description Bushy annual reaching 2 m, forming a broad growth by branching at the base. Stems reddish and almost glabrous. Basal leaves undivided and ovate; stem leaves 3-lobed, 7.5–10 cm wide, lobes 2.5 cm wide and crenate. Flowers borne in the leaf axils,

solitary, and almost sessile; consisting of red calyx and yellow corolla and followed by 2-cm long ovoid fruit.

Distribution Native to tropical Asia; introduced to Sudan and Mexico. Needs a tropical environment.

Cultivation Wild, and cultivated commercially in Ceylon, Egypt, Asia and Mexico. Can be grown horticulturally from seed sown in the early spring. Red and white forms also exist.

Constituents Organic acids, comprising tartaric, citric, malic and hibiscic acids; red pigment comprising gossipetin and hibiscin; vitamin C; also glucosides and phytosterolin.

Uses (dried young calices) Diuretic; weak laxative; antiscorbutic.

Used in Africa and Asia as a cough remedy, wound dressing and diuretic. Mostly employed as an acid flavouring for sauces, jams, jellies, drinks, wines, curries and chutneys.

A pleasant tea which can also be used as a red colourant for other herb teas.

Hieracium pilosella L COMPOSITAE
Mouse-ear Hawkweed Mouse Bloodwort
The botanical name *Hieracium* is from the Greek for hawk after the tradition that hawks

improved their vision by using the plant's sap. Because of this early belief, herbalists employed it for some eye complaints, but it has now largely fallen into disuse. The common name Mouse-Ear is from the apothecaries' term *auricula muris*, being a description of the shape of the leaves.

Description Perennial on creeping leafy runners, forming a basal rosette of hairy leaves, 4–7 cm long, entire, oblong, white or grey on the underside; leafless stem. Flowers usually solitary, occasionally 2–4, reaching 10–40 cm high on hairy or bristly scape; flower-heads consist of capitula of ray florets only, sulphur yellow, appearing early summer to mid-autumn. Very variable in form.

Distribution European native; introduced to other temperate zones. On dry waste-ground, dry grassland, rocky screes, preferring moderate sunshine and tolerating most soils.

Cultivation Wild plant.

Constituents Volatile oils; tannic acid; flavones; an umbelliferone; antibiotic substances.

Uses (dried flowering plant) Weak diuretic; astringent; cholagogue; antibacterial.

Formerly used in the treatment of liver disorders, enteritis and diarrhoea. Possesses weak antipyretic action and was used in the treatment of intermittent fever. The powdered herb arrests nose bleeds. Various claims have been made for its effect in eye conditions. Possesses antibiotic action, and is an effective gargle.

Hordeum vulgare L GRAMINEAE
Barley Big Barley/Bere/Six-rowed Barley
Barley was the first cereal crop to be cultivated and its use has been traced back to Neolithic times. The Egyptians believed it was introduced by their goddess Isis, while the Greeks

considered it was a sacred grain. Besides its use as food and medicine, many civilizations from the early Egyptians have enjoyed beer obtained from fermented Barley. The Greeks and later generations grew a closely related species, *H. distichon* L, which itself was the parent of many other cultivated forms.

Description Stout erect annual grass, to 90 cm; leaves 7 mm–2 cm wide, short and tapering. The terminal spike is 7.5–10 cm long, erect or occasionally nodding, topped by many long, stout beards.

Distribution Temperate cereal crop.

Cultivation H. vulgare is a cultigen derived from an oriental wild grass, either *H. spontaneum* (Koch) or *H. ischnatherum* (Schulz.). Wide commercial cultivation.

Constituents Starch (75–80%); proteins; fat; vitamins B and E; mucilage.

Uses (seed, germinating seed) Nutritive; demulcent. Barley water is a soothing preparation for inflammations of the gastro-intestinal system, and a nutritive demulcent in convalescence. Cooked Barley is a useful poultice for sores. The germinating grain contains an alkaloid, hordenine, whose action resembles ephedrine and it is thus of use in bronchitis.

A well-known cereal with many culinary uses in soups and stews.

Humulus lupulus L CANNABACEAE
Hops Hop Bine
The use of Hops revolutionized brewing since it enabled beer to be kept for longer, yet although the plant was grown by the Romans Hop gardens were not widespread in France and Germany until the ninth and tenth centuries. Bavarian Hops were famous in the eleventh century, but the English only introduced Hops as a replacement for traditional bitter herbs (such as Alehoof and Alecost) in the sixteenth century. Pliny called the plant *lupus salictarius* or 'willow wolf' after its habit of twining tightly around willows and other trees in its damp natural habitat. *Humulus* is a medieval latinization of the Anglo-Saxon term,

humele.

Hops were once grown as a kitchen herb.

Description Dioecious perennial; rough-stemmed and twining clockwise to 6 m tall. Leaves opposite usually 3-, sometimes 5- or 7-lobed, broad terminal lobe, coarsely serrate and long-petioled.

Flowers indistinct, in greenish-yellow catkins, the female enclosed in a conical inflorescence (strobilus) 2 cm in diameter; appear late summer to mid-autumn.

Distribution Native to northern temperate zones; in hedgerows, thickets, alder, willow and osier groves, on damp humus-rich soils in warm situations.

Cultivation Wild; cultivated commercially, especially in northern Europe, United States and Chile. Propagate from cuttings taken in the early summer.

Constituents Volatile oil (0.3–1%) comprising humulone, cohumulone, adhumulone, lupulone, colupulone, adlupulone and xanthlumol; tannins (5%); bitter principles; resin.

Uses (dried female strobilus) Mild sedative; weak diuretic; weak antibiotic; bitter.

Employed alone or in combination with other herbs as a soporific in insomnia and restlessness. Aids nervous indigestion and may be applied externally to ulcers. Once used in the treatment of certain prostate disorders.

Young shoots and male flowers may be eaten in salads.

The oil is used in some perfumes.

Stems once used in basket and wickerwork.

Most widely employed in brewing.

Hydrastis canadensis L RANUNCULACEAE
Golden Seal Orange Root/Ground Raspberry
Golden Seal was once common in the damp shady forests of North America and was used both as a dye and a medicine by the Indians. It entered the United States and British Pharmacopoeias as a treatment for uterine mucosa inflammation, and was so extensively

collected in America that by the beginning of the twentieth century it was necessary to devise methods of commercial cultivation. Now it is a very expensive herb which still finds considerable use in folk medicine.

The name *hydrastis* is derived from the Greek meaning water-acting after its effect on the secretion of mucous membranes.

Description Low herbaceous perennial from 15–30 cm tall; on knotted, gnarled, tortuous, sub-cylindrical rhizome which grows horizontally or obliquely and is 1–6 cm long and 4–15 mm thick, yellowish-brown outside and bright yellow internally. Flowering stem erect, subcylindrical, hairy, bearing two sessile, rounded, doubly-serrate leaves reaching 20 cm wide, each consisting of 5–9 lobes. Occasionally a single 24-cm wide root-leaf arises on a tall petiole from the root-stock. Single flower, greenish-white, without petals, 7.5 mm wide, appearing late spring to early summer; followed in late summer by raspberry-shaped, inedible berry.

Distribution Native to Canada and eastern United States; in shady woods and the edges of woodland on rich moist soil.

Cultivation Wild, and becoming rarer. Cultivated commercially on damp humus-rich soil under artificial shading from root buds or divided root-stock; planted 20 cm apart in early autumn.

Constituents Alkaloids, hydrastine (1–3%), berberine (2%), canadine (trace); fixed oil; volatile oil; resin; starch; also mineral salts.

Uses (dried root-stock) Bitter tonic; stomachic; laxative; smooth-muscle stimulant; nervine stimulant; anti-haemorrhagic; hypoglycaemic. Used internally in atonic dyspepsia, anorexia or gastritis. Also in dysmenorrhoea and menorrhagia. Its main action (due to the alkaloid hydrastine) is on mucous membranes – especially those of the uterus. Large doses cause over-secretion of these membranes, while therapeutic doses aid in catarrhal conditions. The powdered root-stock was once used topically on mouth ulcers and as a snuff in nasal catarrh. A weak infusion is employed in conjunctivitis, as eardrops, and acts as an antiseptic mouthwash.

The root tea was formerly drunk as a tonic. Produces a yellow or orange cloth dye.

Contra-indications POISONOUS in large doses; not to be used in pregnancy.

Hydrocotyle asiatica L UMBELLIFERAE
Indian Pennywort Centella/Indian Water Navel Wort

Indian Pennywort was employed traditionally in the Indian and African continents as an important treatment of leprosy, and modern research has now shown that the plant does possess some action against the leprosy bacteria. The herb is called *brahmi* in the Indian Ayurvedic medical system which still employs it. In Europe it was last mentioned in the French Pharmacopoeia of 1884.

Hydrocotyle is attributed with many other medicinal properties and one which has recently attracted attention is its supposed general beneficial tonic effect; this, however, remains to be proved.

Description Slender trailing umbelliferous plant with reddish prostrate stems, rooting at the nodes, from which also arise 1–3 petioles to 15 cm tall bearing glabrous, entire, or crenate, cupped, orbicular-reniform leaves, 7–15 cm long. Flower-heads bear 3 or 6 reddish, sessile flowers.

Distribution Indigenous to subtropical zones such as India, Ceylon, southern Africa, southern United States, Malaysia. Also found in eastern Europe. On marshy sites to a 600 m altitude.

Cultivation Wild plant.

Constituents A heteroside (saponoside), asiaticoside, which is antibiotic and also assists in the formation of scar tissue; triterpene acids, including indocentoic acid; a glycoside, indocentelloside; an alkaloid, hydrocotylin; resin; pectic acid; vitamin C; a bitter compound, vellarin; tannin (9%); sugars; volatile oil.

Uses (fresh or dried plant) Diuretic; tonic; purgative.

Used in India and Africa for 'blood-purifying' purposes in venereal conditions and tuberculosis. The active principle, asiaticoside, appears to exert a direct effect on the bacterium (*Mycobacterium leprae*) involved in leprosy (possibly by dissolving the protective waxy coat around the bacterium), and also assists in scar healing – for which purpose it is used in ointments. Also formerly used in fevers, rheumatism and gastric complaints, including dysentery. There is some evidence it may act as a general tonic.

Used in Africa as a snuff.

Contra-indications POISONOUS. Large doses narcotic, producing vertigo and possibly coma.

Hyoscyamus niger L SOLANACEAE
Henbane

Henbane has a long medicinal history which runs from the Assyrians to the present day, and which derives from the sedative, analgesic and spasmolytic properties of the leaf's powerful constituents. At various times it has been considered as a love potion, a magical herb, and an ingredient of witches' brews.

Its name *Hyoscyamus* comes from the Greek meaning hog bean, a term which is still retained in some areas. The herb has had several other names including Symphoniaca, Jusquiamus, Henbell, Belene, Hennibone, and Hennebane.

Description Strongly smelling, erect, coarse annual or biennial; the former less robust and shorter than the biennial form which reaches 30–150 cm on a stem covered with long, jointed hairs. Leaves pale-green, ovate-oblong, coarsely dentate, hairy and slightly sticky, 5–30 cm long. Flowers on short stalks in leaf axils, or sessile in terminal unilateral panicles; funnel-shaped, 3–4 cm long, yellow-brown or cream, usually marked with purple veins, particularly at the petal base. Appearing late summer to early autumn (annual) or early to mid-summer (biennial).

Distribution Indigenous to Europe; widely distributed throughout Eurasia and introduced to North America, Asia, Australia and Brazil. On waste-ground and roadsides, and in well-drained sandy or chalky soils.

Cultivation Wild and cultivated, or collected, on a small scale. Seed sown in sunny position in early summer (annual) or early autumn (biennial), and the soil kept moist until germination.

Constituents Alkaloids, hyoscyamine, atropine and hyoscine – to which the narcotic and sedative actions are due.

Uses (fresh or dried leaves) Sedative; antispasmodic; analgesic.

Formerly used in a wide range of nervous or painful conditions which required sedation

and analgesia, but due to its poisonous nature it is now generally only employed internally in homeopathic dosage; it is retained, however, in several South American and European pharmacopoeias as an aid in spasm of the urinary tract, or to alleviate the griping caused by strong purgatives.

Oil of Henbane or a poultice of the fresh leaves may be applied externally to relieve rheumatic pain.

Contra-indications POISONOUS. To be used only under medical supervision.

Hypericum perforatum L HYPERICACEAE
Common St John's Wort

St John's Wort has been closely associated with supposed magical properties since the Greeks gave it the name *hypericon*. This indicated that the smell was strong enough to drive away evil spirits, and it was believed to purify the air. The oil glands when crushed certainly release a balsamic odour similar to incense. In addition the yellow flowers turn red when crushed due to the release of the red fluorescent pigment hypericine – and this was undoubtedly an important factor in the development of the folklore which surrounds the herb – red signifying, of course, blood. As St John was beheaded, and the herb is in full flower on St John's Day (24 June), it became known as *herba Sancti Ioannis* and, later, as St John's Wort – the herb of St John.

Besides the magical attributes which predate Christianity, *Hypericum* has real and effective medicinal properties and it is still widely used in European folk medicine.

Description Perennial; rapidly spreading from many long runners produced at the base. Stem erect with 2 raised edges along its length, branched at the top, reaching 30–60 cm; bearing oblong or linear leaves 1.5–3 cm long, opposite, entire, glabrous, and marked with numerous translucent oil spots. Flowers 2–3 cm wide, yellow, consisting of 5 petals dotted with small black oil glands, and carried on many flowered terminal cymes, appearing late summer to mid-autumn.

Distribution Native to temperate zones of Europe and western Asia; naturalized in the Americas and Australasia. In open situations, on semi-dry soils of various sorts, but particularly calcareous soils.

Cultivation Wild plant. May be propagated by division in autumn, and efforts are being made to cultivate it commercially.

Constituents Volatile oil, called red oil; resin; a red pigmented glycoside, hypericine; a polyphenolic flavonoid, hyperoside; tannin (8–9% in the whole herb and 16% in the flower); carotene; vitamin C.

Uses (fresh or dried flowering plant, fresh flower, fresh leaves) Vulnerary; weakly diuretic; sedative; anti-inflammatory; anti-diarrhoeic; cholagogue; antidepressant; antiviral; antibiotic; astringent.

Many virtues have been ascribed to this plant ranging from the antipyretic and anthelmintic properties reported by the most ancient writers, to modern suggestions of antiviral activity. Certainly when taken internally the herb stimulates both gastric and bile secretions, and is effective in irregular menstruation. It has been shown to improve the blood circulation and to be of use in some conditions characterized by neurosis and disturbed sleep patterns.

It is one of the most effective agents for assisting in the healing of wounds or burns when applied externally, especially where nervous tissue has been damaged; it is also applied to haemorrhoids and bruises. The plant contains an antibiotic which has been patented as a possible food preservative. Leaves once used as a salad herb.

An alcoholic extract of the flowers dyes silk and wool a violet-red, but does not colour cotton.

Contra-indications If eaten by light-skinned animals, the herb may cause photosensitization, leading to swelling of the face, generalized skin irritation of unpigmented areas, and possible death.

Hyssopus officinalis L LABIATAE
Hyssop

The genus Hyssopus consists of this single species, and the herb's common name is practically identical in all European languages. Hyssop is a very ancient name and can be traced back almost unchanged through the Greek *hussopos* to the Hebrew *esob*.

Whether *Hyssopus officinalis* is in fact the Hyssop frequently referred to in the Old Testament is doubtful, however – this was probably a marjoram – and how it came to be given the biblical name is not known.

The herb was once much respected as a medicinal plant being mentioned by Paulus Aegnita in the seventh century, and was also used both for cosmetic and strewing purposes. Gerard (1597) described 3 varieties and Mawe (1778) 6 varieties.

Hyssop has had a mixed fortune as a culinary herb due to its strong flavour, and is now mostly employed for decorative purposes especially as a low hedge in herb gardens.

Description Aromatic perennial subshrub with erect branched herbaceous stems 20–60 cm long, covered with fine hairs at the tips. Leaves linear to oblong, 2.5 cm long and 4–9 mm wide, sessile or nearly so, opposite and tomentose. Blue flowers 7.5–15 mm long in one-sided whorls in leaf axils, the terminal inflorescence being 10 cm long; appear late summer to early autumn. Violet, red, pink or white forms occasionally occur.

Distribution Native to central and southern Europe, and temperate western Asia; introduced into North America. On rocky, calcareous dry soils in sunny situations.

Cultivation Wild in native habitat; occasionally wild elsewhere as a garden escape. Cultivated commercially in Europe, Russia and India. Wide horticultural employment as an ornamental; propagate by seed sown in spring, root division in spring or autumn, or cuttings taken in late spring or early summer. Plant out 30 cm apart in full sun on well-drained light soil, and clip occasionally. Replace after 4 or 5 years.

Constituents Volatile oil (0.2–1%); a flavonoid glycoside, diosmin; tannin (8%).

Uses (dried flowering tops, fresh leaf) Tonic; stomachic; expectorant; carminative; sedative; weak diaphoretic; weak diuretic; astringent; mild spasmolytic.

Specifically employed in bronchitis and the common cold; to improve appetite and stimulate gastric secretions; and as a gargle to soothe sore throats. The herb also reduces perspiration and may be applied externally to cuts or bruises around the eyes. Once used to treat hysterical conditions, but its action is weak.

A constituent of some herb teas.

Small quantities may be used to flavour meats or soups.

The oil distilled from the flowering tops is employed in the liqueur and perfumery industries.

Ilex aquifolium L AQUIFOLIACEAE
Holly Common Holly/English Holly
Although Holly is no longer considered of any importance medically, it has retained an important role in the traditions associated with Christmas and in northern Europe red Holly berries and branches are symbolic of Christmas-time – perhaps representing drops of blood and a crown of thorns.

The plant was not called Holly until the seventeenth century, previously having been known as Holy Tree and earlier as Holme; the latter being derived from the old English plant name *holen*. Its botanical name *Ilex* was the ancient name for the Holm or Holly Oak (*Quercus ilex*), while *aquifolium* is from the Latin meaning point and leaf after the well-known shape of its leaves.

Description Evergreen shrub or tree usually 2–5 m, occasionally to 12 m tall; with many spreading glabrous branches forming an oblong-shaped plant. Leaves shiny, leathery, ovate or oblong-ovate, 4–7.5 cm long, margins wavy and spiked with 6-mm long spines, short-petioled. Small unisexual or bisexual, dull white, scented flowers produced in axillary clusters on previous year's growth, appearing early to mid-summer.

Distribution Native to Europe and widely distributed from western Asia to China; introduced elsewhere. Common in deciduous woodland, less so in mixed or coniferous woodland; on most soils but preferably humus-rich, acid, moist well-drained types.

Cultivation Wild. Cultivated horticulturally for decorative purposes and as hedging; avoid planting in frost-prone sites.

Constituents Leaves: tannin; a bitter substance, ilicine; theobromine; unknown substances. Bark: tannin; pectin; a yellow pigment, ilixanthine.

Uses (leaves) Antipyretic; weak diuretic; tonic. Once used in the treatment of fevers, bronchitis and rheumatism. Occasionally employed in diarrhoea, and as a tonic tea.
Wood used for engraving.

Contra-indications Berries are purgative and toxic.

Ilex paraguariensis St Hil. AQUIFOLIACEAE
Maté Yerba Maté/Paraguay Tea/Hervea
Maté has been taken as a refreshing stimulant tonic drink by South American inhabitants long before the Jesuits recorded the habit in the sixteenth century. Although in many South American countries it is drunk more frequently than any other beverage, 'Jesuits' tea' as it was first called has only recently become known in Europe as an alternative to Indian or Chinese tea.

Description Evergreen shrub or tree to 6 m, often kept low in cultivation; branches glabrous bearing glossy, obovate, crenate-serrate, short-petioled, alternate leaves, 4–10 cm long; flowers white and axillary, followed by rounded, reddish 7-mm diameter fruit.

Distribution Brazil, Argentina, Chile, Peru, Paraguay; frequently in mountainous areas.

Cultivation Wild, and cultivated commercially in Paraguay.

Constituents Caffeine (0.2–2%); chlorogenic acid (10–16%); neochlorogenic acid; theobromine catechols; the combined action being tonic.

Uses (dried leaves) Tonic; nervine; diuretic; stimulant.
Almost entirely employed as a tonic tea in the manner of Indian or Chinese tea, but devoid of any undesirable stimulant effect.

Ilex verticillata (L) Gray AQUIFOLIACEAE
Black Alder Winterberry/Feverbush
North American Indians were the first to use this attractive plant for medical purposes and it was once included in the United States Pharmacopoeia; it was also used homeopathically. Other remedies have now replaced it, even in folk medicine, and it is rarely found in use as other than a garden ornamental. It was formerly classified as *Prinos verticillatus* L. The specific epithet *verticillatus* means whorled or clustered around the stem, after the arrangement of the flowers and fruit.

Description Upright and spreading deciduous shrub 1.2–3 m tall, with thin obovate, oval or

oblanceolate, acute to acuminate, serrate leaves, 4–7.5 cm long, pubescent on lower veins; petiolate and alternate. Flowers dioecious, white, small, in groups of usually less than 10, on short peduncles in umbels, appearing in leaf axils in late spring and early summer. Followed by bright red globose berry 7.5 mm in diameter.

Distribution North American native, from Canada to Florida and Wisconsin; introduced elsewhere. Usually in woodland thickets on wet, marshy, rich soils or beside rivers and lakes.

Cultivation Wild plant. Cultivated as a garden ornamental for its attractive berries which remain until mid-winter on the bare branches. Requires rich soil in damp, preferably shady, site.

Constituents Tannins (to 5%); bitter principles; resins; unknown substances.

Uses (fresh bark, rarely dried bark, fruit) Astringent; antipyretic; bitter; tonic.

The bark may be employed as an infusion or decoction in the treatment of diarrhoea, or as a tonic following severe diarrhoea or feverish complaints. It acts as a carminative and promotes both the appetite and the digestion. Due to its astringent action it was once used externally as a wash in skin complaints such as herpes and ulcers. The berries possess slight antihelmintic and laxative action, but should not be used as the effective dose is slightly toxic.

Illicium verum Hook. f. MAGNOLIACEAE
Star Anise Chinese Anise

The oil obtained by steam distillation of the fruit of Star Anise is now an important substitute for expensive European aniseed oil, and is widely used in commercial preparations requiring aniseed flavour.

It has long been used as a spice in the East, but was not seen in Europe until 1588 when Candish brought a sample from the Philippines to London. Clusius first described it in

1601, but even in 1694 when the Dutch used it to flavour tea it was rare in Europe.

The Latin name *illicium* means that which entices from the very pleasant scent of the tree and fruit. It is also classified as *I. anisatum* (L). A closely related species *I. religiosum* (Siebold) or Japanese Star Anise, which in the East is sometimes found as an adulterant of the Chinese Star Anise, has poisonous leaves and fruit due to their content of sikimitoxin. This plant is called the 'mad herb' in China, but in Japan it is revered and used at funerals. Fruit of the plant cannot be used, and may be distinguished by their lack of aniseed smell, unlike the Chinese variety.

Description Small tender evergreen tree or shrub to 5 m; leaves aromatic, alternate, entire, shiny, 7.5 cm long, elliptic and acuminate; magnolia-like attractive greenish-yellow solitary, unscented flowers with many petals. Followed by 4-cm wide, 8-rayed star-like fruit consisting of one-seeded follicles which are collected when green, and then sun-dried until they are woody and reddish-brown.

Distribution Indigenous to south and south-west China and north Vietnam; introduced elsewhere. On well-drained soils, frequently above a 2500-m altitude.

Cultivation Wild and cultivated in south China and parts of eastern Asia. Prefers sheltered sunny situations on well-drained, moisture-retaining soils.

Constituents Volatile oil (to 10%), comprising 80–90% anethol; fixed oil; sugar; resin; tannin.

Uses (dried fruit) Carminative; slightly stimulant; mild expectorant.

Chiefly employed as an aniseed flavouring agent, and as a carminative for digestive disorders. Used in cough remedies as an expectorant and considered to benefit the bronchial mucous membranes.

Used in the East as a spice, particularly with duck and pork; added to tea and coffee in China. The oil is of commercial importance as an aniseed flavouring for drinks and liqueurs.

Inula helenium L COMPOSITAE
Elecampane Scabwort

Elecampane is still employed in folk medicine as a favourite constituent of cough remedies and has always been popular both as a medicine and a condiment. Its use as a flavouring in sweets continued until the 1920s, and it was traditionally cultivated in herb gardens.

Much controversy surrounds the origin of the plant's names, but *helenium* is from Helenus, the son of Priam – a somewhat obscure association – while *elecampane* is derived from the ancient Latin name *inula campana* via the French *énule-campane*. It was commonly used both by the early Anglo-Saxons and Celts as well as by the Greeks and Romans; the Welsh called it *marchalan* in the thirteenth century.

Description Tall attractive perennial to 2 m; on thick 15-cm long taproot. Stems hairy, erect, bearing large, alternate, elliptical leaves to 45 cm long and 15 cm wide, velvety beneath, hairy above, dentate-serrate, the lower leaves petiolate, others partly clasping. Flower-heads

large, to 7 cm in diameter, solitary or corymbose, yellow, the ray florets numerous, long, slender, and arranged in a single row, appearing mid-summer to mid-autumn.

Distribution Native to central and southern Europe and north-west Asia, naturalized in United States; introduced elsewhere. On damp

soils near ruins (probably because they were once cultivated near monasteries, etc.), or roadsides and woodland edges.

Cultivation Wild. Limited cultivation in central Europe; on rich moist soil from seed sown in spring or by division of root-stock in autumn. Plant in semi-shaded position at back of the border.

Constituents Inulin (40%); essential oil, comprising a mixture of lactones, chiefly alantolactone; resin; a complex camphor, elecampane camphor; mucilage.

Uses (dried root-stock) Bactericidal; antitussive; expectorant; tonic; weak cholagogue.

Almost exclusively employed in the treatment of respiratory disorders, especially bronchitis, coughs, and catarrh. Also used to promote appetite as it acts as an aromatic tonic. Once used in the treatment of skin diseases and in veterinary medicine for the same purposes – hence its other name, Scabwort. The herb is strongly antibacterial.

Formerly candied and eaten as a sweetmeat; used in the flavouring of certain sweets.

Still employed in some wines and liqueurs in central Europe.

Iris foetidissima L IRIDACEAE
Stinking Iris Gladdon/Scarlet-seeded Iris

Most Iris species possess substances in the fresh root-stock which act as purgatives, and when purging was a popular form of medicinal treatment Stinking Gladdon was commonly used.

The name Gladdon is derived from the Latin *gladiolus* meaning a little sword after the shape of its leaves; while the term stinking is an inaccurate description of the roast-beef smell of its crushed leaves.

Description Slow growing perennial on slender

should be considered a variety, *florentina*, of *I. germanica*; others consider *I. florentina* is a synonym of *I. spuria*, while some feel it is a true species with its own, pure white, variety – *I. florentina* var. *albicans*.

The white Florentine Iris became associated with Florence in the early Middle Ages, and the plant's cultivation there was described by Petrus de Crescentiis in the thirteenth century. It is still represented on the heraldic arms of the city.

Description Perennial on stout rhizome bearing 45 cm tall, 3–4 cm wide, sword-shaped leaves, and flowering stalk reaching 60 cm–1 m. Terminal flower-head usually 2-flowered, sessile; the flowers unscented, white tinged with violet and with a yellow beard, or pure white and beardless. Appearing early to mid-summer. Variable in the form and colour of the flowers.

Distribution Native to southern Europe; naturalized in central Europe, Persia, north India; introduced elsewhere. Tolerates most well-drained soils, but prefers sunny, stony, dry, hilly situations.

Cultivation Wild. Cultivated commercially in Italy, Persia, India and Egypt. Propagate by division of root-stocks in late spring or early autumn, planting in deep, rich, well-drained soil in sunny position.

used as a powerful purgative. It is now rarely used even in folk medicine.

Used as a bitter flavouring in certain liqueurs. Widely employed as a violet scent in the perfume industry, and as a fixative in pot-pourri manufacture. May be used in some tooth powders or dusting powders.

Contra-indications Fresh root-stock may be violently purgative. Large doses of the powdered root-stock cause vomiting. The powder may cause allergic reactions.

Iris versicolor L IRIDACEAE
Blue Flag Flag Lily

Blue Flag is a common American herb which was employed by both the Indians and early settlers as a remedy for gastric complaints. It was once included in the United States Pharmacopoeia and is still believed in folk medicine to be a blood purifier in eruptive skin conditions.

In some places the plant is known as Liver Lily because of its particular effect on that organ.

The herb may be a hybrid between the closely related *I. virginica* (L) and another Iris.

Description Perennial bog plant on thick branched creeping root-stock bearing erect, stout, coarse stem 30 cm–110 cm tall, and sword-shaped leaves 20 cm–1 m long, 15 mm–

horizontal rhizome; producing 60–90-cm tall branched stems which bear glossy dark green, narrow (3 cm) leaves, 30–45 cm long. Leaves remain during winter, and are sometimes variegated. Flowers inconspicuous, purple-grey with purple veins, beardless, appearing early to mid-summer and followed by 4–5-cm long capsule containing scarlet-red globose seeds.

Distribution Native to North Africa, west and south Europe. Prefers rich moist soils by rivers or ponds in a semi-shaded position.

Cultivation Wild. Cultivated horticulturally by root-stock division in late spring or early summer. Requires humus-rich wet soil.

Constituents Acrid resin; unknown substances.

Uses (fresh root-stock) Purgative.

Once used as a purgative by drinking a macerate of the fresh root in ale. No longer employed medically.

Chiefly cultivated for the use of its attractive ripe flower capsules and seeds in dried flower arrangements.

Iris germanica var. *florentina* Dykes IRIDACEAE
Orris Florentine Iris

The Greek word *iris* means the rainbow and is used to describe the variable colouring of the members of this genus.

Orris, derived directly from *iris*, is the descriptive term for the violet-scented, powdered root-stock which has been used in perfumery since the Egyptians and ancient Greeks.

Several species or hybrids are used as the source of Orris of which the most important are *I. germanica* L (especially *I. germanica* var. *florentina* Dykes), *I. pallida* Lamk. and *I. florentina* L. Due to the variation and hybridization of this group, some authorities believe that *I. florentina* L is not a distinct species and

Constituents Essential oil (0.1–0.2%) comprising myristic acid (85%) and methyl myristate; oleic acid; a ketone, irone, which develops on drying and storage; resin; tannic acid; starch; sugars.

Uses (dried root-stock) Stomachic; diuretic; aromatic; weak expectorant.

Formerly used in mixed remedies for the treatment of chest complaints such as bronchitis and asthma. The fresh juice was once

3 cm wide.

Attractive blue or violet flowers, marked with yellow, 2–6 per plant, on short peduncles, appearing early to mid-summer, followed by globose, leathery capsule.

Distribution North-east North America; in wet places on peaty soils.

Cultivation Wild plant.

Constituents An acrid resinous substance, irisin; volatile oil; fixed oil; starch; tannic acid; an unidentified alkaloid.

Uses (dried root-stock; leaves) Purgative; diuretic; sialagogue; emetic.

Chiefly employed in eruptive skin conditions caused by a sluggish gastro-intestinal system and constipation. It stimulates the flow of saliva, bile and gastric secretions, acting particularly on the liver and pancreas. Leaves applied externally on bruises.

Contra-indications Large doses cause nausea, vomiting and facial neuralgias. Handling the plant may cause dermatitis.

Isatis tinctoria L CRUCIFERAE
Woad Dyer's Weed

Woad was cultivated as the source of a blue dyestuff for over 2000 years in Europe and was only superseded 50 years ago by indigo, which was first extracted from subtropical *Indigofera* species.

Isatis is an ancient name for a healing herb, which was described by Dioscorides as being an excellent styptic. Doubtless the habit adopted by ancient Britons of painting their bodies with a paste of the leaves served the dual purpose of frightening their enemies and healing the wounds of battle.

The herb is now mainly of historical interest, although as its blue colour is more permanent than *Indigofera indigo* it is in demand by homecraft dyers.

Description Biennial from 45 cm to 130 cm tall; produces in the first year a rosette of entire or toothed, oblong or obovate leaves from which arises stout, erect stems branching near the top, bearing lanceolate to linear glaucous sessile leaves, 10 cm long at the base and 4 cm long near the flowering top. Small yellow flowers, very numerous, in 45 cm wide panicled racemes, produced in early to mid-summer, and followed by pendulous black seeds that

persist on the stem for weeks.

Distribution European native; introduced elsewhere. On humus-rich, well-drained chalky waste places in sunny situations.

Cultivation Wild. Cultivated in western Europe until the 1930s. Propagate from seed sown in sunny position on well-drained, very rich soil, in late summer. Thin to 40 cm apart by transplanting in early spring.

Seeds itself readily, but acts as a short-lived perennial if the unripe flower-heads are removed.

Constituents Indigo (developed by fermenting leaves).

Uses (fermented leaves, rarely fresh leaves) Vulnerary; styptic.

Once employed externally to stop bleeding and assist in the healing of wounds and ulcers. Too poisonous and astringent to be used internally. Traditionally the source of a blue dye obtained by fermenting, drying and refermenting the crushed leaves, and adding lime-water to the final product.

Contra-indications POISONOUS. Not to be used internally.

Jateorhiza palmata Miers MENISPERMACEAE
Calumba Colombo

Calumba remains a favourite tonic for the treatment of gastric disorders in Africa and India, and retains a place as a bitter in some European pharmacopoeias. In East Africa it is known as kalumb or koamwa and has long been used as a treatment for diarrhoea and as a general tonic, as well as being used as a dye. The Portuguese introduced it to Europe in the seventeenth century when it was considered an antidote to poisons, but it was generally neglected until Percival promoted it in 1773. By 1781 it was valued at $12 a kilo and in 1788 it was included in the London Pharmacopoeia. Lamarck first described the plant in 1797 and called it *Menispermum palmatum*.

Description Tall dioecious twining perennial vine; often reaching the tops of trees. Large fleshy tuberous root. Annual stems herbaceous, hairy and bearing large, membranous, alternate, palmate-lobed, long-petioled leaves, and insignificant greenish-white flowers, which are followed by a moon-shaped stone contained within a globose drupe. Male flowers in panicles 30 cm long.

Distribution Indigenous to East Africa, especially northern Mozambique; introduced elsewhere, for example, Brazil. In forests.

Cultivation Wild. Some small-scale cultivation in East Africa.

Constituents Volatile oil (0.07–1.15%), comprising mainly thymol; 3 yellow alkaloids, columbamine, jatrorrhizine, palmatine; bitter principles, chasmanthin and a lactone, columbin; traces of the sapogenins, diosgenin and kryptogenin; mucilage; starch.

Uses (dried root) Stomachic; bitter tonic. Chiefly employed as an aqueous infusion in vomiting during pregnancy or atonic dyspepsia associated with hypochlorhydria. In Africa it is used as a remedy for diarrhoea and dysentery, and in India as an antipyretic and anthelmintic.

The alkaloids present in the root have been shown to increase the intestinal tone and lower the blood pressure. An excellent bitter tonic. Used as a yellow dye.

Juglans cinerea L JUGLANDACEAE
Butternut White walnut/Oil-nut

The walnut family derive their generic name, *Juglans*, from the Latin *Iovis glans* meaning the nut of Jupiter after the ancient belief that the gods ate walnuts.

Most of the names of this tree, in fact, refer to its nut, for example, butternut, Oil-nut and Lemon nut, indicating both the oily nature and shape of the fruit. This species is described as both white and as *J. cinerea* after the light colour of its bark, the botanical name being derived from the Latin *cinereus* meaning ash-coloured. It is thus distinguished from the closely related black walnut, *J. nigra*.

Oil from the nut was once used as a strongly flavoured seasoning in America.

Description Tree from 12–30 m tall; bark light grey, deeply furrowed with broad ridges; branches pubescent, bearing 11–19 opposite leaflets, 5–12.5 cm long, irregularly serrate, acuminate, short-petioled and oblong lanceolate. Flowers in drooping catkins. Fruit elongated, pointed, 4 cm long in groups of 2–5, externally sticky and strong smelling, containing an edible nut.

Distribution North American native, from New England to Georgia and Maryland. Introduced elsewhere. In rich damp woods or close to rivers, on well-drained soils.

Cultivation Wild.

Constituents Fixed oils; a complex resin, called juglandin, containing nucin.

Uses (inner root bark; ripening fruit, leaves) Cathartic; anthelmintic; weak rubefacient.

The bark was formerly used as a domestic remedy for constipation. The oil from the fruit was employed to remove tapeworms. It is now rarely used even in folk medicine.
Ripening fruit can be pickled.
The sap produces a syrup similar to maple syrup.
Root bark, leaves and fruit provide a brown wool dye.

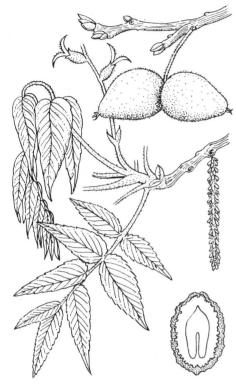

Juglans regia L JUGLANDACEAE
Walnut Persian Walnut
This tree bears the name *regia*, meaning royal, both because of its attractive appearance and its historical importance as a source of timber and food. It was known to Theophrastus as *karuon*, and Pliny – who believed it entered Europe from Persia – first described the use of the shells for dyeing white hair brown. He suggested that the green husks be boiled with lead, ashes, oil and earthworms, and the

mixture applied to the head!
Both the green walnut husks and fresh leaves have been used as a brown hair dye for centuries, remaining as the main constituent of proprietary hair tints until the beginning of the twentieth century.
Description A number of varieties exist, and the form of the tree is variable. Tree to 30 m; bark silvery-grey. Usually 7 or 9 glabrous leaflets, entire, acute, oblong-ovate, 5–12.5 cm long. Male flowers in drooping catkins appear late spring to early summer. Indistinct female flowers followed by almost globular, glabrous fruit singly or in groups of 3.
Distribution Native to western Asia, south-east Europe, China and the Himalayas. Introduced elsewhere. In open woodland.
Cultivation Wild. Widely cultivated for its timber.
Constituents Fruit: Fixed oils; vitamin C. Leaves: A bitter compound, juglone; hydro-juglone; tannic acid; unknown substances.
Uses (dried leaves, fresh fruit) Tonic; astringent; anti-inflammatory; weakly hypoglycaemic.
Leaves considered of benefit in a wide range of eruptive skin conditions, and used both internally and externally. Also employed homeopathically for the same purposes.
Ripening fruit can be pickled. The ripe nuts are of commercial importance. Oil expressed from the nuts provides a cooking oil, and is occasionally employed in non-drying artists' paints.
Timber used in furniture.
Leaves yield a brown dye.

Juniperus communis L CUPRESSACEAE
Juniper Common Juniper
Juniperus is the classical name for this variable and widely distributed plant of the northern temperate zones, which has remained in use from the Greek and Arabic physicians to the present day. Although no longer generally considered as a spice, it is still an important flavouring for certain preserved meats, liqueurs and especially gin. The English word gin is derived from an abbreviation of Hollands Geneva as the spirit was first called – which, in turn, stems from the Dutch *jenever* meaning Juniper. Only 1 kilogram of the berries is used to flavour over 400 litres of gin.
Description Variable, from a dense procumbent shrub to a 12 m tall tree; evergreen. Leaves needle-like, 5–13 mm long, in whorls of 3, spreading from the branchlets, bluish-white on upper surface. Flowers indistinct, axillary, dioecious, greenish-yellow, appear late spring to early summer; followed by 7.5–10 mm diameter blue-black, fleshy, 3-seeded berries.
Distribution Native to Mediterranean region; also Arctic Norway to Soviet Union, north-west Himalayas, North America. On heaths, moorland, open coniferous forests and mountain slopes.
Cultivation Wild. Berries collected commercially. Other forms may be used, for example, *J. communis* ssp. *nana* Syme, *J. communis* ssp. *hibernica* Gard., *J. communis* cv. *prostrata* Beissen.

Constituents Essential oil (0.5–2%), comprising terpene hydrocarbons (α-pinene, β-pinene, limonene) sesquiterpenes (α-caryophyllene, cadinene, elemene), bitter substances, alcohols, and a monocyclic cyclobutane monoterpenoid, junionone; resin (10%); sugar (30–33%); organic acids.
Uses (dried fruit, leafy branchlets) Antiseptic; diuretic; stimulant; carminative; rubefacient. Used internally as a urinary antiseptic, specifically in cystitis; also promotes gastric secretions and improves the appetite. Applied externally to relieve rheumatic pain, to counteract alopecia, as a styptic and to wounds. Used homeopathically and in veterinary medicine.

Berries are used to flavour meats, gin and liqueurs. Once used as a spice and substitute for pepper, and when roasted as a coffee substitute.
Contra-indications Not to be used in pregnancy or when the kidneys are inflamed.

Juniperus sabina L CUPRESSACEAE
Savin Savin Tops
Savin has a long history as a stimulant veterinary drug in Europe, and was applied to the wounds and ulcers of animals. Due to its toxicity, however, it has never been widely used as a medicine for humans.
Description Evergreen shrub, usually low-growing and of spreading habit, to 2 m tall; sometimes a small tree, to 7.5 m. Young leaves opposite, acute and pointed; older leaves scale-like, closely adhering to branchlets, bright green. Flowers indistinct, greenish-yellow, dioecious, appearing late spring followed by 7 mm diameter brownish-purple, 2-seeded berries on pendulous pedicels.
Distribution Native to central and south Europe; distributed from the Caucasus to south Siberia. Also in North America. On sunny mountain slopes.
Cultivation Wild. Grown horticulturally as a hedge-plant, for which purpose *J. sabina* var. *tamariscifolia* Ait. and *J. sabina* var. *variegata* Laws. are also used.

Constituents Volatile oil (1–4%), similar to that of *J. communis*; tannic acid; resin.

Uses (young green shoots) Powerful uterine stimulant; emmenagogue; irritant.

Now only used externally, with care, as a stimulant dressing for blisters, wounds, ulcers, and to remove warts. Employed in veterinary medicine.

Contra-indications POISONOUS and occasionally fatal. Causes severe gastro-intestinal irritation, haematuria and hallucinations. To be used only under medical supervision.

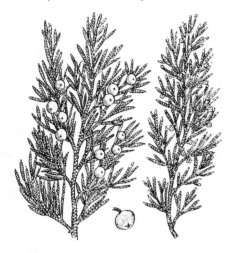

Lactuca virosa L COMPOSITAE
Wild Lettuce Greater Prickly Lettuce

In the nineteenth century this, and a closely related species *L. scariola* L, was cultivated on a small scale in western Europe as the source of lactucarium – the dried latex which exudes from the cut surface of the plant's stem. It was introduced to medical practice in 1771 by Collin and called 'lettuce opium' by Coxe in 1799.

Although its action as a sedative is fairly weak, it was used as an adulterant of true opium and entered the Edinburgh and other European pharmacopoeias as a cough suppressant. The common Garden Lettuce, (*L. sativa* L), was also once used as a source of lactucarium, but by breeding out the bitterness of this salad herb modern cultivars only contain a trace of the complex.

Description Strongly smelling biennial, producing a rosette of obovate, undivided leaves 12–30 cm long in the first year, and an erect stout, cylindrical, pale green branched stem to 1.5 m high in the second. Stem-leaves dark green, clasping, scanty, alternate, ovate-oblong.

Numerous flower-heads, arranged in panicles, short-stalked, pale yellow, appearing late summer to mid-autumn.

Distribution European native. On dry nitrogen-rich soils, in wasteland and hillsides.

Cultivation Wild. Formerly cultivated on a small scale.

Constituents Lactucarium, comprising bitter substances (lactucine, lactucopicrin, lactucic acid); crystalline substances (including lactucerin); sugar; caoutchouc; traces of a mydriatic alkaloid; and other substances.

Uses (dried latex, dried leaves occasionally) Mild sedative; mild hypnotic.

Formerly used as a constituent of remedies employed in the treatment of irritable coughs. May be used in insomnia or restlessness.

Contra-indications The latex is very irritant to the eyes.

Lamium album L LABIATAE
White Dead-Nettle Blind Nettle

This is not a true nettle, nor is it botanically related to the nettle family, but *L. album* does bear a superficial similarity to nettles and is often found growing close to or among them. The common name Dead-Nettle reflects the fact that it does not possess any sting, while its generic name *Lamium* is from the Greek word for throat after the shape of the plant's flower. Not of importance historically, but nevertheless a useful medical plant particularly for menstrual problems.

Description Perennial 20–60 cm tall, spreading by underground stolons; stems rigid, square, bearing opposite, decussate, stalked or sessile, downy, deeply dentate, nettle-shaped leaves, 4–6 cm long. Flowers off-white, usually 5–8 (or occasionally to 16) in axillary whorls, the calyx consisting of 5 long, toothed projections. Appearing early summer to late autumn.

Distribution European native; introduced elsewhere. On rich soils in waste places, preferably in sunny positions.

Cultivation Wild.

Constituents Traces of essential oil; mucilage; tannic acid; flavonic heterosides, (kaempferol, isoquercitin); potassium salts; histamine; tyramine; and unknown substances.

Uses (flowering plant) Astringent; expectorant; diuretic; vulnerary; anti-inflammatory. Useful internally in cystitis, leucorrhoea and particularly metrorrhagia; as a bowel regulator, it can be used to treat either diarrhoea or constipation; in respiratory or nasal catarrh.

Applied externally to wounds it is both styptic and healing. It may also be applied to haemorrhoids and burns.

Young leaves may be boiled and eaten as a green vegetable, or added to soups.

Lapsana communis L COMPOSITAE
Nipplewort

In the sixteenth century this was called *papillaris* by the apothecaries, after the Latin *papilla* meaning nipple, since the herb was traditionally employed to treat cracked nipples – a use which may originally have been

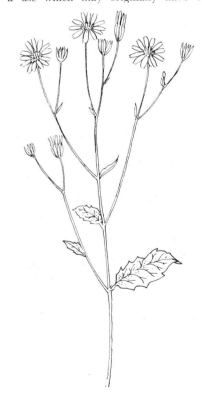

suggested by the nipple-shaped unopened flower buds.

In some parts of Europe ointments made from the fresh juice are still used for this purpose.

Description Annual 20 cm–120 cm; stem hairy, much branched near the top, bearing three types of alternate leaves, the lower lyre-shaped, the middle oval and petiolate, the upper small, sessile and lanceolate. Flowers composed entirely of ray florets, yellow, in small capitula, arranged in panicles, appear early summer to mid-autumn.

Distribution From Europe to northern Asia; naturalized in America. On humus-rich moist soils on wild or cultivated land, wood edges, and in thickets, to an 1800 m altitude.

Cultivation Wild.

Constituents Unknown.

Uses (fresh leaves, fresh juice) Laxative; vulnerary.

Traditionally used externally to treat cracked nipples or to promote the flow of milk from the breast. Considered useful in constipation associated with liver problems. Supposed, but unproven, antidiabetic agent. May be applied to wounds or cuts.

Young radish flavoured leaves eaten in salads, or boiled as a green vegetable.

Laurus nobilis L LAURACEAE
Bay Tree Sweet Bay/Sweet Laurel

This is an ancient aromatic plant, once dedicated to Apollo, and for thousands of years it was considered to be a powerful antiseptic. It is a vital ingredient of the genuine bouquet garni.

Its botanical name emphasizes the respect with which the ancients held the plant; *laurus* from the Latin meaning to praise, and *nobilis* meaning renowned or famous.

This was the leaf used to make the victor's crown of laurels in classical times – and the tree was once called the *baccae lauri* or noble berry tree, from which by direct association with the victor's crown the modern French educational term *baccalauréat* is derived.

Description Evergreen tree to 15 m; with grey shiny bark. Usually grown as a bush to 2 m. Leaves leathery, dark green, shiny above, lanceolate to oblong-lanceolate, 3–7.5 cm long. Flowers small, yellowish, in groups of 3–4 in the leaf axils, appearing late spring to early summer and followed by 15 mm-diameter dark purple berries.

Distribution Native to Asia Minor and Europe; introduced elsewhere; in sheltered sunny mountain valleys on rich soils.

Cultivation Wild plant. Grown horticulturally on a commercial scale as a garden ornamental, especially in Holland and Belgium. Plant bushes in late spring or mid-autumn, in sunny frost-free sites, on rich soil; or in tubs filled with rich soil which should be kept moist and protected in winter. Propagate from cuttings in autumn, or by layering of lower branches in late summer or early autumn.

Constituents (leaves) Volatile oil (1–3%), comprising geraniol, cineol, eugenol, terpenes; tannic acid; bitter principles. (berries) fat (25–30%), comprising glyceryl laurate; volatile oil

(1%), with similar composition to that of the leaf, comprising mainly cineol.

Uses (berries, leaves, oil expressed from berries) Antiseptic; stimulant; stomachic; weak insecticide. Formerly used to stimulate digestion. Once used externally to relieve rheumatic pain and as an antiseptic. Employed in stimulant liniments in veterinary medicine.

A flavouring in some liqueurs.

Most widely used as a culinary herb (the freshly dried leaf). Can be used in both savoury and some sweet dishes and confections.

Lavandula angustifolia Mill. LABIATAE
Lavender English Lavender

One of the most popular and well-known of the traditional herbs. This species has also been classified as *L. vera* DC and *L. officinalis* Chaix., and is closely related to *L. latifolia* Vill. with which it is sometimes confused. The latter, however, (which is also called *L. spica* L) produces an inferior oil, called spike lavender oil.

In classical writings these species are not clearly differentiated and it is probable that French Lavender has been used longer for medicinal purposes, although *L. angustifolia* was a popular strewing and cosmetic herb from at least the twelfth century.

Many horticultural varieties were developed in the eighteenth and nineteenth centuries, but some of these are now difficult to obtain.

Description Aromatic perennial subshrub to 80 cm; on woody stem. Leaves opposite, entire, very narrow, lanceolate or oblong-linear, 2–5 cm long, the smaller often clustered in axils, grey-green and tomentose. Flowers usually grey-blue, 6–15 mm long, in spikes on peduncles from 10–20 cm long; appearing mid-summer to early autumn.

Distribution Native to mediterranean region; widely distributed in southern Europe; introduced elsewhere. Often on poor, well-drained soils.

Cultivation Wild. Cultivated commercially in southern Europe. Very wide horticultural use as garden ornamental. Propagate from seed sown in pans in late spring, later planting out 45 cm apart (germination may be slow). Or use green cutting, 10 cm long taken in spring, or hardwood cuttings taken between early spring and late summer.

Constituents Volatile oil, comprising an alcohol, linalol, and linalyl acetate; a hydroxycoumarin, herniarin eucalyptol; limonene; cineole; geraniol.

Uses (dried flowers; oil of lavender) Carminative; rubefacient; sedative; antispasmodic; antiseptic; stimulant; weak diuretic.

Still used in folk medicine internally as a mild sedative and cough suppressant, or in gastric disturbances characterized by flatulence. Externally the oil is stimulant and is occasionally employed to counteract rheumatic pain, or in tonic embrocations.

Lavender oil vapour is traditionally inhaled to prevent vertigo and fainting.

May also be used as an antiseptic lotion for cuts.

The oil is used as an insect repellent; to mask unpleasant odours in ointments; in perfumery and as a flavouring agent.

Dried flowers are employed in scented pillows, sachets, moth repellents and pot-pourris.

Lavandula dentata L LABIATAE
Fringed Lavender French Lavender

This is one of the least hardy lavenders and is best grown indoors or as a winter flowering pot plant under glass.

Its botanical name *dentata* refers to the attractive fern-like leaves which are quite different from those of English Lavender. The aroma of Fringed Lavender is also different – being a sweet blend of Rosemary and Lavender.

Description Aromatic perennial, usually shrubby from 30–80 cm tall; leaves 3–4 cm long, linear, light green or grey, pubescent, pinnately dentate, truncately toothed. Deep lavender flowers, 6–15 mm long on small, long peduncled spikes, 7.5–20 cm long, appear winter.

Distribution Native to the mediterranean region as far east as Malta; introduced elsewhere.

Cultivation Wild. Grown horticulturally as a garden plant in warm climates, and as a greenhouse or indoor pot plant elsewhere. Propagate from cuttings in sandy, slightly alkaline soil; prune to prevent straggling growth or cut back to produce a bushy plant. Requires full sun and feeding occasionally with liquid manure if grown in pots.

Constituents Volatile oil.

Uses (dried flowering plant, dried leaves) Cultivated as a winter-flowering ornamental. Dried flowers and leaves used in floral arrangements and in scented sachets and pot-pourris.

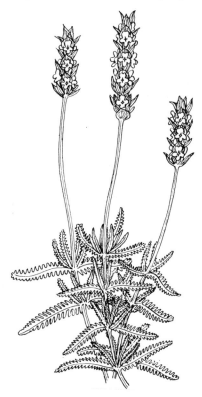

Lavandula stoechas L LABIATAE
French Lavender Spanish Lavender
This is the lavender species which was best known and possibly most widely used by the ancient Greeks, Romans and Arabs – usually as an antiseptic and sweet-smelling herb for inclusion in bath and other washing water.

The generic name *lavandula* is derived from the latin *lavare* meaning to wash. Like *L. dentata*, the scent is somewhat balsam-like and a mixture of Rosemary and Lavender.

It continued to be used medicinally (known as *Flores stoechados*, *sticadore* or *stoechas arabica*) until the eighteenth century, and was even included in the London Pharmacopoeia of 1746. Gradually, however, it was replaced by

the hardier *L. angustifolia* Mill.

Description Perennial subshrub, 30 cm–1 m tall. Leaves linear, narrow, hairy, entire, grey-green, 1.5–4 cm long. Flowers 3 mm long, dark purple, specked with orange, in short wide spikes on 3 cm long peduncle. Flowers surmounted by attractive purple bracts one-third or one-quarter the length of the spike; appearing mid-spring to early summer.

Distribution Native to the mediterranean region; also the Canary Islands, Turkey and Asia Minor; introduced elsewhere. In coastal sites on sandy soils.

Cultivation Wild plant. Grown horticulturally as a garden ornamental in warm countries, and occasionally in cooler temperate zones in very warm protected sites. May be propagated from seed sown under glass in spring or from cuttings taken in spring or summer. Also cultivated indoors as a pot plant; requires a dry, sandy, well-drained soil, full sunlight, and occasional feeding with liquid manure.

Constituents Volatile oil.

Uses (dried flowers, dried leaves, dried flowering plant) Antiseptic; antispasmodic; carminative; vulnerary; stimulant; insect repellent. Formerly used in a wide range of complaints; now only employed in southern Europe as a mild sedative, antiseptic and remedy for nausea and vomiting. The flowers may be used in conserves.

Dried flowers and leaves employed in scented articles such as sachets.

Lawsonia inermis L LYTHRACEAE
Henna Mignonette Tree/Egyptian Privet
Henna, or Al Kenna as it is called in Arabic, has played an important role in religion and mysticism in the East for centuries. The red colouring produced from the leaf was considered to represent the fire and blood of the earth, and to link mankind with nature.

For this reason it has long been used to dye the nails, hands, feet and hair – and the Berbers still colour both corpses and young babies with the dye, as well as using it in marriage ceremonies. The shrub now has a very wide distribution and commercial henna varies greatly in composition and quality – often being adulterated with Lucerne leaves or powdered *Acacia catechu*, Catechu. The variety now considered finest for use as a hair dye comes from Persia. Green Henna gives the deepest red tones and is made from young shoots, while so-called 'compound henna' consists of inferior leaf and synthetic dyes. The botanical name *Lawsonia* is named after the Surveyor-General of North Carolina, who was burned to death by Indians in 1712.

Description Shrub to 6 m with glabrous branches bearing greenish brown, opposite, shortly petiolate, oblong or broadly lanceolate leaves, 1.5–5 cm long, 1–2 cm wide. Small highly scented, white, light red or deep red flowers to 7.5 mm diameter in a corymbose terminal panicle, followed by spherical fruits 7.5 mm diameter.

Variable in form.

Distribution Indigenous to Arabia, Persia, India, Egypt and Australia; naturalized in tropical America; introduced elsewhere.

Cultivation Wild. Grown horticulturally as an ornamental and cultivated commercially for the leaves, mainly in India, Egypt, China, Morocco and Iran.

Constituents Fats; resin; mannitol; volatile oil; fixed oil; a yellow pigment, lawsone (hennotannic acid or oxynaphthochinon).

Uses (dried leaves, dried green shoots, dried twigs) Astringent; stimulant.

Used for the treatment of leprosy in African folk medicine; the powdered leaf has also been used to treat intestinal amoebiasis.

Most widely used as a hair, skin and nail dye.

Ledum groenlandicum Oed. ERICACEAE
Labrador Tea Marsh Tea

This aromatic herb, (synonym *L. latifolium* Jacq.) is named after Greenland where it grows in profusion.

It is rarely used today, perhaps because of its slightly narcotic qualities, but during the American War of Independence it was one of several herbs used as a substitute for tea.

Labrador Tea may be grown horticulturally in cold, wet, exposed sites.

A closely related plant, *L. palustre* L is also called Marsh Tea and has similar properties.

Description Evergreen shrub to 90 cm; bearing aromatic, alternate, entire leaves 3–5 cm long on short petioles. Leaves folded back at the edges, green above and rust-coloured beneath. Flowers small (to 12 mm wide), scented, white, and carried on thin pedicels in terminal clusters; appearing in spring.

Distribution Native to Greenland and Canada. In sphagnum bogs and wet peaty soils in colder parts of the northern hemisphere.

Cultivation Wild. May be cultivated in cold wet situations; propagate by root division in mid-autumn.

Constituents Tannic acid; arbutin; resin; essential oil, comprising ledol; mineral salts.

Uses (leaves, fresh or dried) Astringent. Once used to treat dysentery and diarrhoea.

Now rarely used as a tea.

Formerly added to beer to increase its intoxicant properties.

Contra-indications Evidence suggests excessive use of the tea may cause delirium or poisoning.

Leonurus cardiaca L LABIATAE
Motherwort

Several *Leonurus* species from various parts of the world, which include *L. sibiricus*, *L. glaucescens*, *L. deminutus* and *L. heterophyllus*, have been shown in animal experiments to possess hypotensive and sedative properties. The European species *L. cardiaca* has the same properties and was used since the early Greeks to treat pregnant women for anxiety – hence its name Motherwort.

Its action on the heart led to the specific name *cardiaca*, from the Greek *kardiaca* meaning heart, while the generic term, *Leonurus*, is from the Latin *leo* or lion and the Greek *oura* or tail, since it was thought that the tall, leafy stem resembled a lion's tail.

Once commonly grown in herb gardens but now rare, even in the wild.

Description Strongly smelling erect perennial 90–150 cm tall; on stout stem, square in section, branching below and hairy. Leaves pale green beneath, darker above, long petioled, serrate, the lower leaves deeply palmately lobed, the upper leaves less deeply 3-lobed. Flowers pale pink to purple, very hairy, small,

arranged in whorls of 6–12 in leaf axils; appearing mid-summer to mid-autumn.

Distribution European native; introduced elsewhere. Usually rare or localized on waste-ground and roadsides near ruins. On well-drained, light, calcareous soils in sunny situations.

Cultivation Wild. May be propagated by root division in mid-autumn or late spring. Self-seeds easily.

Constituents Tannic acid; essential oil; an alkaloid, leonurinine; glucosides; a bitter principle, leonurine. The combined action is sedative.

Uses (fresh or dried flowering plant) Sedative; antispasmodic; emmenagogue; cardiotonic; hypotensive; slightly astringent.

Formerly used in the treatment of bronchitis, diarrhoea, asthma, and rheumatism. Now considered of benefit in amenorrhoea and dysmenorrhoea, and specifically useful in tachycardia.

May be of use in anxiety. Employed homeopathically.

Contra-indications May cause contact dermatitis.

Levisticum officinale Koch UMBELLIFERAE
Lovage Love Parsley

With its interesting and unusual flavour Lovage has a wide culinary potential, but it is not widely used except as a soup flavouring.

The Greeks, who called it *ligustikon*, chewed the seed to aid digestion and relieve flatulence – a medicinal use which was promoted in the Middle Ages by Benedictine monks.

The common name is derived from the fact that in many European countries the herb had a traditional reputation as a love charm or aphrodisiac. The botanical name is a corruption of the earlier name *Ligusticum*, after Liguria, Italy, where it once grew in abundance.

Description Glabrous aromatic perennial on stout fleshy root-stock to 2.20 m. Stem stout and hollow, bearing large dark green long-petioled, ovate-cuneate, to 3-pinnate leaves, 70 cm long and 50 cm wide near the base, smaller at the top. Flowers small, greenish yellow, in umbels 5–7.5 cm wide, appearing summer, followed by 7.5 mm long oblong fruit.

Distribution Southern European native; naturalized in Asia Minor and eastern United States; introduced elsewhere. Tolerates most soils except heavy clay.

Cultivation Very rarely wild, and then usually as a garden escape. Cultivated commercially on a small scale in central Europe, and widely as a garden herb. Seed sown as soon as ripe or in spring in well-manured, moist, but well-drained soil; transplanting 60 cm apart. Also propagate by root division in autumn or spring, replanting 5 cm deep. Full size is reached in 3–5 years.

Constituents Essential oil comprising mainly umbelliferone and butyl phthalidine; resin; starch; sugars; tannin; gum; vitamin C; coumarin.

Uses (dried root, fresh or dried plant, seed) Diuretic; stomachic; emmenagogue; expectorant.

Formerly used as a diuretic, in the treatment of rheumatism and migraine, and for bronchial catarrh. Of use in flatulence and to promote the appetite.

Sometimes employed externally to treat some simple skin problems.

The powdered root was once used as a pepper.

The leaf may be used as a flavouring in soups, sauces and salads, and as a vegetable; the seed in biscuits and with meat.

Young stems may be candied like Angelica. Stems and leaf stalks can be blanched and eaten in the same way as celery.

Contra-indications Large quantities should not be taken by pregnant women or by people suffering from kidney disease.

Liatris odoratissima Willd. COMPOSITAE
Deer's Tongue Vanilla Plant

Deer's Tongue, so called because of the shape of its leaves, is one of 40 species in the North American Blazing Star or *Liatris* genus. The group is difficult to classify botanically due to hybridization between species, but is characterized by attractive flower-heads which persist for weeks.

This species possesses coumarin in its leaves which is responsible for its attractive scent.

Description Glabrous perennial on thick tuberous root-stock, to 1.2 m. Leaves alternate, clasping, narrow, entire, spoon-shaped and fleshy to 25 cm long. Flowers bright purple on spikes 35 cm long; appearing early to late autumn.

Distribution North American native. On damp soils in meadows and open woods.

Cultivation Wild. Propagate by root division in early spring.

Constituents Coumarin; unknown substances.

Uses (dried root, fresh or dried leaf) Diuretic.

Once used as a diuretic, but it is rather too strong for this purpose.

Leaves once employed as a tobacco flavouring. Largely cultivated as an attractive late flowering garden herb, and as a source of vanilla-scented leaves for use in pot-pourris.

Liatris spicata Willd. COMPOSITAE
Blazing Star Dense Button Snakeroot

The botanical name, *Liatris*, is of unknown origin, while *spicata* refers to the spikes on which the flowers are carried.

Although now rarely used medicinally it is

still found as a horticultural plant, (sometimes called *L. callilepis*). A related species, *L. chapmannii*, also called Blazing Star, contains a substance (liatrin), which has been shown to possess anti-cancer properties.

Description Nearly glabrous erect perennial on tuberous root; stem 30 cm–2 m, bearing alternate linear, punctate leaves, 30 cm long and 10 mm wide. Flowers dark blue, 4–8 mm diameter, in groups of 5–13, in dense spikes 40 cm long, appearing from early to late autumn.

Distribution North American native from Massachusetts to Florida and Arizona. On rich, damp meadow soils or near marshes.

Cultivation Wild. May be propagated by root division in early spring, planting in well-manured, damp soils. A white variety *alba* exists.

Constituents Coumarin; unknown substances.

Uses (root, fresh plant) Diuretic; antibacterial.

Formerly used in New England as a treatment for venereal diseases, particularly gonorrhoea. The decoction is of use as a gargle for the treatment of sore throats.

Powdered root and leaf may be employed in scented sachets and pot-pourris.

The leaf was once used to flavour tobacco. The powdered root and leaf may also be used as an insect repellent.

The herb may be employed horticulturally as a hardy late flowering plant.

Ligusticum scoticum L UMBELLIFERAE
Lovage Sea Parsley

This herb is so called because it was particularly collected and used as a culinary herb in Scotland, where it is known as *shunis*.

North American Indians also ate it, peeling the stem and eating it raw. Because of its viatmin C content, the plant was also popular with sailors and fishermen suffering from scurvy. It was once cultivated, but has long ceased to be of medicinal or culinary importance.

Description Coarse perennial to 60 cm on branched root-stock. Stem red below, bearing dark green, long stemmed, ternate leaves with

few segments, 3–5 cm wide, toothed on upper half only. Flowers yellowish white, in umbels, appearing late summer to early autumn, followed by fruit with prominent ridges.
Distribution Sub-arctic Atlantic coasts; occasionally inland. Especially on rocky shores and river estuaries.
Cultivation Wild. May be propagated from fresh seed, and grown in damp, slightly shady situations.
Constituents Essential oil, comprising umbelliferone; starch; vitamin C.
Uses (root, fresh plant, seed) Diuretic; aromatic; carminative.
Once used medicinally as an aromatic flavouring and in the treatment of rheumatism.
Young leaves and stems may be eaten raw as a salad, or cooked as a vegetable. Stems can be candied like Angelica, and they may also be eaten in the same way as celery.
The seed may be powdered and used like Pepper.
The root was formerly chewed as a tobacco substitute.
Bath water may be scented by the root.

Linum usitatissimum L LINACEAE
Flax Linseed
Flax has been of exceptional economic importance to man and has been grown since 5000 B.C. It was used by Mesopotamians and and by early Egyptians who wrapped their mummies in cloth made from it.
Unknown in the wild state, it is thought to have been derived from the Pale Flax, *L. bienne*

Mill. by selection and cultivation.
Today several cultivars exist, some with large seeds which are used for oil extraction, and the small seeded types which are used in linen and cloth manufacture.

Flax has been described in detail in all the classical writings of the Egyptians, Hebrews, Greeks and Romans, and was promoted in northern Europe first by the Romans and later by Charlemagne; Irish linen manufacture, however, was not reported until A.D. 500.
Description Thin annual, branching at the base, from 30–130 cm tall; stems erect, usually glabrous with narrow, sessile, linear or lanceolate alternate glaucous green leaves, 3–5 cm long, and marked with 3 veins.
Flowers 5-petalled, blue or occasionally white or red, 3 cm diameter, on erect terminal panicles, appearing mid to late summer and followed by globose capsules somewhat longer than the calices. Variable in form depending upon variety and environment.
Distribution Originally Asian; widely distributed through temperate and subtropical zones, often as escape from cultivation.
Especially on well-drained wasteland in sunny situations.
Cultivation Unknown in the wild state.
Different cultivars are commercially grown for seed (Holland, England, Argentina, North Africa), oil (United States, Morocco, USSR), and fibre (United States, USSR, India, Middle East). Some varieties are biennial. Seed is sown in drills in late spring or early summer, on dryish, well-drained soils.
Constituents (seed) Fixed oil (30–40%) comprising the glycerides of linoleic, linolenic and other fatty acids, and stearic and palmitic acids; mucilage (6%); a cyanogenic glycoside, linamarine; vitamin F; pectin; other nitrogenous substances. The laxative action is due to the oil and mucilage content.
Uses (stem, seed, seed-oil, powdered oil-exhausted seed) Laxative; demulcent; anti-inflammatory. Seed is of value internally as a mild laxative; it is sometimes combined with other anti-inflammatory medicinal plants for the treatment of respiratory and gastrointestinal inflammatory disorders.
Both the seed and powdered seed may be applied externally as a poultice to relieve pain and heal skin wounds, certain skin conditions and suppurations.
Seed may be roasted and eaten, and unripe capsules can be eaten raw. The oil has been used for culinary purposes. It is of importance in paint and varnish manufacture. Fibre from the stems is very widely used in linen and cloth manufacture.
Although linseed oil is rarely used internally as a purgative in humans, it is used in veterinary medicine for this purpose.
Exhausted seed pulp is utilized as cattle fodder.

Lobelia inflata L LOBELIACEAE
Indian Tobacco Lobelia
Indian Tobacco is so called because it was formerly smoked by North American Indians to relieve asthma and related conditions. Early settlers used it for a wide variety of complaints, and some early American herbalists considered it almost a panacea. Samuel Thomson, who was an important figure in the physiomedical school of herbal medicine, particularly promoted Lobelia in the early

nineteenth century, but was charged with murder after poisoning one of his patients with it. Cutler examined its anti-asthmatic properties in 1813, and the herb was introduced to British medicine in 1829. It is now rarely used.
The generic name, *Lobelia*, is after the Flemish botanist Matthias de L'Obel (1538–1616),

while *inflata* refers to the way in which the seed capsule inflates during ripening.
Description Hairy, erect, somewhat angled stem from 20–70 cm, branching near the top, containing an acrid latex, and bearing oval or ovate-lanceolate, alternate, sessile, toothed leaves. Flowers pale blue externally, often violet within, small (4–6 mm long), irregular, on loose terminal spike-like racemes; followed by 2-celled capsule which inflates to a 1 cm long oval, glabrous structure.
Distribution Native to North America from Labrador to Georgia. Introduced elsewhere.
Cultivation Wild. Propagated from seed sown on the surface of rich soil, in the autumn.
Constituents Alkaloids (0.3–0.4%) comprising, lobeline, lobelidine, lobelanine, isolobelanine; also lobelic acid; inflatin; resin; fat; fixed oil; caoutchouc (India rubber). In small doses the combined action dilates bronchioles and relaxes bronchial muscles.
Uses (dried fruiting plant) Expectorant; anti-asthmatic; emetic; diaphoretic.
Of benefit in chronic bronchitis with associated dyspnoea and in bronchial asthma.
Formerly used to induce vomiting and in the treatment of whooping cough, croup and tetanus. May be applied externally to relieve pain and irritation caused by rheumatism, bruises, bites and certain skin conditions.
Contra-indications POISONOUS – may be fatal. Large doses cause purgation, vomiting, convulsions, medullary and respiratory depression.

Lonicera caprifolium L CAPRIFOLIACEAE
Perfoliate Honeysuckle

Honeysuckle receives its common name from an old habit of sucking the sweet honey-tasting nectar from the flowers, while this species – most common in southern Europe – is also called perfoliate because its upper leaves surround the stem.

Now widely used as a climbing or hedge plant.

Description Climbing deciduous shrub. Stems glabrous to 6 m. Leaves opposite simple, oval, 5–10 cm long, green above glaucous beneath; the upper 2 or 3 leaf pairs united at their base forming a cup (connate). Flowers fragrant, pale yellow, 4–5 cm long, corolla not glandular, borne in terminal whorls of 2–3. Bracts large. Appearing early to mid-summer and

followed by orange berries.

Distribution Native to central and southern Europe and western Asia; introduced elsewhere. On well-drained loamy soils. Calcifugous.

Cultivation Wild. Cultivated horticulturally: propagate from woody cuttings taken in early autumn and rooted in peat and sand mix; or by layering in late summer.

Constituents Mucilage; an amorphous glucoside; salicylic acid; sugars; invertin.

Uses (flowering plant) Diuretic; antiseptic; emetic; expectorant.

Similar actions to Honeysuckle (*L. periclymenum* L).

Contra-indications POISONOUS berries. External use only.

Lonicera periclymenum L CAPRIFOLIACEAE
Honeysuckle Woodbine

This is the taller growing of the two common European honeysuckles, and may live for 50 years. It is often found bound tightly around

trees – hence its alternative name Woodbine. The generic name, *Lonicera*, refers to a sixteenth-century German physician, Lonicer (or Lonitzer).

Description Climbing, twining, deciduous shrub; stems to 9 m. Leaves opposite, simple, ovate to oblong-ovate, 4–7.5 cm long; dark green above, often glaucous or pale beneath; upper leaves not united.

Flowers fragrant, yellow, 4–5 cm long, corolla glandular, borne in many-flowered, peduncled, terminal clusters. Bracts small. Appearing mid-summer to mid-autumn and followed by red berries.

Distribution Native to Europe, western Asia and North Africa; introduced elsewhere. Especially on porous sandy or loam soils, in mixed woodland. Calcifugous.

Cultivation Wild. Cultivated horticulturally; propagate from woody cuttings taken in early autumn and rooted in peat and sand mix; or by layering in late summer. The varieties *var. Aurea* and *var. Belgica* are garden plants.

Constituents Mucilage; an amorphous glucoside; salicylic acid; sugars; invertin.

Uses (flowering plant) Diuretic; antiseptic; expectorant; emetic; slightly astringent.

Formerly used internally for several conditions; but now recommended only for external use as an application for skin infections.

Contra-indications POISONOUS berries: external use only.

Lycopodium clavatum L LYCOPODIACEAE
Club Moss Stags-Horn Moss

Club Moss, known to apothecaries as *muscus clavatus*, is so called because of the club-shaped fruiting bodies which it carries.

It has also been called vegetable sulphur, not

only because of the yellow colour of the moss's spores, but also because they burn brightly in a similar manner to powdered sulphur.

The generic name, *Lycopodium*, means fox or wolf foot – another allusion to the shape of the plant.

This and closely related species, such as *L. selago* L (the Fir Club Moss), were once widely used medicinally, especially in North America and continental Europe. The use of the spores in treating wounds, which was introduced by German apothecaries in the seventeenth century, continues to this day in several parts of the world.

Description Procumbent evergreen perennial moss, reaching at least 100 cm long; rooting along the branching stem which is thin and

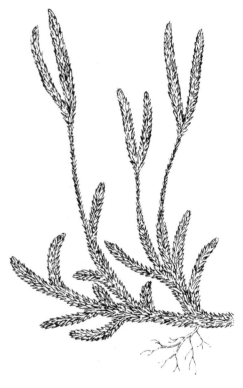

densely covered with bright green, smooth, narrow, pointed, bristled leaves, 3–5 mm long. Spores yellow, minute, carried in large numbers in yellow-green cones, usually 1 or 2 (rarely 3), which are borne at the ends of stalks extending from aerial branches, to 15 cm long. Spores ripe from early to mid-autumn.

Distribution World-wide distribution on acidic or silica-containing soils; on moorland, coniferous woodland and grassland, especially in mountainous districts.

Cultivation Wild plant.

Constituents (spores) Fixed oil (50%) comprising glycerides of palmitic, stearic, arachitic and lycopodium oleic acids; phytosterin; sporonine; lycopodic acid (2%); hydrocaffeic acid; a carbohydrate, pollenin (45%).

(whole plant) in addition to the above, contains alkaloids (0.12%) comprising clavatoxine, clavatine and lycopodine.

Uses (spores) Vulnerary; haemostatic; aperient; weak antispasmodic.

Formerly used internally in the treatment of kidney, liver and bladder inflammatory disorders, and in urinary incontinence. Use now is confined to its external application as a soothing dusting powder for wounds and in skin irritations such as in eczema. Also employed homeopathically. Hypoglycaemic action has been demonstrated experimentally.

It was also used to coat pills to prevent their adhesion when stored.

Once used as a basis for medicinal snuffs and as a vehicle for the application of powdered herbs to the nose and ears.

Still employed in firework manufacture.

Contra-indications The whole plant is toxic; only the spores may be used internally. The powder may ignite explosively if introduced to a flame.

Lycopus europaeus L LABIATAE
Gipsywort Gipsyweed
Called Gipsywort because it was supposed gypsies stained their skin with the herb. More certainly the plant has been of use as a cloth dye for centuries.

Although quite closely related to the mints this herb lacks aroma almost entirely.

Description Perennial on creeping rhizome. Stems erect, simple or branched from 30–100 cm tall; bearing opposite, shortly petiolate, ovate-lanceolate to elliptic leaves up to 10 cm long. Lower leaves pinnate, upper leaves crenate. Flowers, 3 mm diameter, white and dotted with purple, numerous, in dense whorls in upper leaf axils. Appearing late summer to mid-autumn.

Distribution Native to Europe, western Asia; introduced to North America. On many soil types, but especially those which are flooded; river margins, marshland and ditches.

Cultivation Wild.

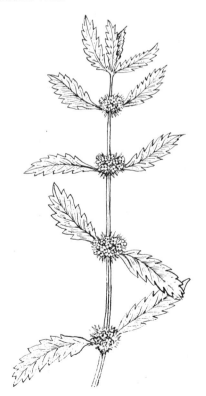

Constituents Tannic acid; essential oil; a bitter, lycopine; flavone glycosides.

Uses (fresh or dried flowering plant) Sedative; anti-haemorrhagic; cardioactive; antithyroidic.

Many uses have been ascribed to this herb; it has been used in the treatment of tuberculosis, haemoptysis and other forms of haemorrhage including menorrhagia.

It is a sedative, as it reduces the pulse rate in conditions involving an overactive thyroid gland.

The fresh juice provides a black dye, which is permanent on wool and linen.

Lycopus virginicus L LABIATAE
Bugle Weed Virginia Bugle Weed
Virginia Bugle Weed is very similar to the European Gipsywort (also known as Gipsyweed), and is itself sometimes called Gipsyweed. Its action was investigated originally in the latter half of the nineteenth century and its effectiveness in the treatment of internal haemorrhages and other conditions led to its inclusion in the United States Pharmacopoeia. It is now rarely used outside folk medicine.

This species is slightly more active than Gipsywort (*L. europaeus*) when used medicinally.

Description Perennial from 15–60 cm tall. Stem erect, glabrous or nearly so, producing stolons at the base, and bearing ovate or oblong-lanceolate, shortly petiolate, coarsely serrate leaves. Flowers whitish, sometimes heavily marked with purple, small, in loose axillary whorls; appearing late summer to mid-autumn.

Distribution North American native; from Labrador to Florida and British Colombia. On rich, damp soils, in shady situations, especially marshy land and moist forests.

Cultivation Wild.

Constituents Tannic acid; essential oil; a bitter, lycopine; flavone glycosides.

Uses (fresh or dried flowering plant) Sedative; anti-haemorrhagic; cardio-active; antithyroidic; hypoglycaemic.

Action the same as that of *L. europaeus*. It has also been employed in the treatment of diabetes.

Lythrum salicaria L LYTHRACEAE
Purple Loosestrife Spiked Loosestrife
This is still popular in European folk medicine, and was once used in tanning leather. Pliny described a purple-red *Lysimachia* which Matthiolus thought was this species. The generic name, *Lythrum*, is derived from the Greek for blood after its haemostatic properties. *Salicaria* refers to the Willow-like (*Salix* means willow) appearance of the leaves.

Description Erect, somewhat downy perennial 50–175 cm tall, on creeping rhizome; stem square and branched at the top. Leaves mostly

opposite, cordate below, lanceolate above to 10 cm. Flowers purple in whorled clusters on tall, leafy terminal spikes; appearing mid-summer to mid-autumn.

Distribution Native to Europe and western Asia, Russia. Introduced and naturalized in other temperate zones. In reed-beds, ditches, fenland, beside stagnant or flowing water; to 1500 m altitude.

Cultivation Wild. Horticultural cultivars exist; may be propagated by seed or by division in spring.

Constituents Tannins; pectin; essential oil; provitamin A; calcium oxalate; a glycoside, vitexin. The combined action is antibacterial and haemostatic.

Uses (fresh or dried, whole flowering plant) Astringent; haemostatic; antibacterial; tonic. An excellent gargle, douche and wound cleanser, and of benefit in diarrhoea or gastro-intestinal disorders such as mild food poisoning. Rapidly stops bleeding. Once used in diluted form as an eye-wash.

Mahonia aquifolium (Pursh.) Nutt.
BERBERIDACEAE
Mountain Grape Barberry
This is known as *Mahonia aquifolium* after the American horticulturalist Bernard McMahon. The herb was introduced into Europe in 1823, and is now often grown because of its attractive foliage and fruit.
Description Fast growing evergreen shrub to 2 m; leaves consisting of 5–9 ovate leaflets 2–7 cm long, dark green and glossy, lighter beneath. Flowers yellowish-green, heavily scented, in terminal racemes. Bears purple-blue smooth berries.
Distribution Indigenous to mountainous regions of British Columbia. Distribution from British Columbia to Oregon. Introduced elsewhere.

Description Usually perennial, occasionally biennial. Stem hairy, erect or decumbent, branched, 30–150 cm tall; bearing tomentose, reniform or round-cordate, long-petioled leaves, 4 cm diameter, with 5–7 crenate lobes. Few pinkish-violet flowers, 4 cm diameter, 5-petalled, in clusters in leaf axils; appearing early summer to mid-autumn.
Distribution Native to Europe, western Asia, North America; on porous nutrient-rich soils, especially hedge banks, field edges, and wasteland; in sunny situations.
Cultivation Wild. Once grown as a garden plant; propagate from seed sown in late spring, later thinning to 75 cm apart.
Constituents Mucilage; volatile oil; tannin; vitamins A, B_1, B_2, C.

pulled it out of the ground.
Certainly Mandrake, like Henbane and Belladonna, was an ingredient of witches' brews and poisons, but it was also used by the Greek and Roman physicians as an anaesthetic and employed in early surgery.
It continued to be included in many European pharmacopoeias until the nineteenth century, and an official homeopathic preparation was introduced in 1877.
Description Perennial on thick, branching, tuberous root; practically stemless. Leaves reaching 30 cm long, ovate and undulate, basal or nearly so, dark green. Flowers greenish-yellow or purplish, 3 cm long, single or clustered within the leaves; appearing mid to late spring and followed by orange, globose, fleshy, many-seeded fruit.
Distribution Native to Himalayas and south-eastern mediterranean region. On poor thin, sandy soils in full sun.
Cultivation Wild plant. Rarely cultivated horticulturally in historical gardens or in botanic drug collections. Requires warm situation and winter protection in north Europe. Propagated from seed sown as soon as ripe, or by division.
Constituents Alkaloids, including atropine, scopolamine and hyoscyamine, to which the action is due.
Uses (dried root, fresh leaves rarely) Sedative; hallucinogenic; purgative; emetic; anodyne. No longer used medicinally owing to its high

Cultivation Wild plant. Cultivated as garden plant and now naturalized in temperate zones.
Constituents Alkaloids comprising mainly berberine, berbamine and oxyacanthine.
Uses (dried rhizome and root) Used in digestive complaints and for skin diseases – especially psoriasis. Combined with *Cascara sagrada* for use in constipation.

Malva sylvestris L MALVACEAE
Common Mallow
The Common Mallow was once highly respected as a medicinal plant and foodstuff, and from the days of the Romans was cultivated as a garden herb. In the sixteenth century it was given the name *omnimorbia*, meaning a cure-all – probably because of its gently purgative action; a practice which in itself was thought to rid the body of disease.
The common name Mallow is from the Latin *malva* for soft and emollient, after the feel, and properties respectively, of the leaves.
For medicinal purposes it has largely been replaced by the more effective Marshmallow.

Uses (dried leaves and flowers, occasionally roots) Demulcent; anti-inflammatory; laxative; slightly astringent.
Useful in irritation of the gastro-intestinal system. Taken for the treatment of coughs and bronchitis.
Large doses are gently purgative.
Externally may be used as a soothing poultice. Its supposed sedative effect is unproven. Leaves were once cooked as a vegetable; and seeds and capsules (known as cheeses) may be eaten raw in salads.

Mandragora officinarum L SOLANACEAE
Mandrake
Mandrake is the most commonly cited example of the former abuse of medicinal plants by those obsessed with magical rites and orgiastic ritual with which some hallucinogenic and narcotic herbs became closely associated in the dark ages.
It was protected by the early Greek collectors who invested the root with such fictitious harmful attributes as the ability to kill a man who

toxicity. The leaves were once applied externally to ulcers, while the root formerly had wide application in the relief of pain, in the treatment of nervous disorders and as an aphrodisiac.

Contra-indications POISONOUS and dangerous; not to be used internally or externally.

Maranta arundinacea L MARANTACEAE
Arrowroot Maranta Starch

Arrowroot was first noticed on the West Indian island of Dominica at the end of the seventeenth century, and it was subsequently grown in Jamaica where it was employed both as a source of starch and as a poison antidote.

The common name is thought to be derived from the fact that a poultice of it was applied to arrow wounds. Its Brazilian name, however, is *araruta*, which may indicate a different etymological origin.

Supplies of Arrowroot first reached Europe from Jamaica at the beginning of the nineteenth century, but by 1840 it was being grown in India, and by 1858 *Maranta* was a commercial crop in Georgia, in the United States. The generic name is after B. Maranta, sixteenth-century Venetian botanist and physician; *arundinacea* refers to the reed-like shape of the plant.

Although it is still used, it was much more popular before the 1914–1918 war.

Description Herbaceous perennial on creeping rhizome and fleshy tubers; stems 60 cm–2 m tall, thin, reed-like, branched, bearing ovate-oblong, petiolate, glabrous, 15–30 cm long and 4–10 cm wide leaves; the petioles sheathing around the stem. Few small, white flowers on long thin peduncles.

Distribution Native to tropical America, from Brazil to Mexico. Introduced to Africa, India and south-east Asia.

Cultivation Wild. Cultivated commercially by lifting it at harvest time and replanting a portion of the rhizome that has buds on it.

Constituents Starch; small quantities of gum and fibre.

Uses (starch, occasionally rhizome) Nutritive; demulcent.

The powdered rhizome was applied to poisonous bites and wounds in some tropical countries.

Of benefit as a soothing food-stuff following diarrhoea or illness. Once employed in pill manufacture, and in barium meals for X-ray of the gastro-intestinal system.

It may be candied as a sweet. It can also be used in cooking as a thickener.

Marrubium vulgare L LABIATAE
White Horehound

White Horehound has been used as a cough remedy from the time of the Egyptians to the present day. The herb is still included in the Austrian and Hungarian pharmacopoeias as an expectorant, and it remains a popular domestic and folk medicine. Wherever European emigrants have travelled they have taken this plant and grown it in herb and cottage gardens, thus widely distributing it. The generic name, *Marrubium*, was first used by Pliny and refers to the bitter taste; the common name is derived from the Old English *har hune* meaning a downy plant.

Description Faintly aromatic woody perennial, almost entire plant is woolly. Branched near the base; stems erect, nearly square, 30–60 cm tall, bearing wrinkled, dentate, ovate, opposite leaves 1.5–5 cm long; tomentose beneath and long-petioled. Flowers whitish, 5–8 mm long, numerous in axillary whorls; followed by nutlets. Appearing mid-summer to mid-autumn.

Distribution Native to southern and central Europe, North Africa, Asia; introduced elsewhere, often widespread. On dry grassland or pastures, field edges and wasteland, in warm situations.

Cultivation Wild. Cultivated commercially on a small scale by root division in mid-spring. May also be grown from seed sown in late spring, thinning to 30 cm apart, or from cuttings taken in summer.

Constituents Tannins; volatile oil, comprising marrubiol; mucilage; resin; sterols; a bitter principle, marrubin; vitamin C.

Uses (dried flowering plant, dried leaves) Expectorant; emmenagogue; weak diuretic; spasmolytic; weak diaphoretic.

Useful in many respiratory disorders, but specifically in bronchitis and coughs. Promotes bile flow and stimulates the appetite. Considered of benefit in disorders of the gall bladder and stomach, and acts as a stomach tonic. Formerly used to treat menstrual pain. Possesses some weak sedative action, suitable for use in conjunction with other herbs in nervous tachycardia.

May be applied externally to minor cuts and certain skin conditions. Laxative in large doses. Leaves may be used powdered as a bitter condiment, or whole as a tisane and in the manufacture of the confection, Horehound candy.

Matricaria recutita L COMPOSITAE
German Chamomile Wild Chamomile
German or Wild Chamomile was previously called *M. Chamomilla*, but in botanical terms it is not a true chamomile and it is also sometimes called Sweet False Chamomile. Although now considered slightly inferior to Roman Chamomile (*Chamaemelum nobile*) – even its aroma being somewhat less pronounced – there is no certainty which of the chamomiles was meant by the *chamaimelon* of Dioscorides. Today both *C. nobile* and *M. recutita* are used for similar purposes. The name, *Matricaria*, is either from the root word *mater* meaning mother or from *matrix*, the Latin for womb, after its use for treating female complaints.
Description Aromatic glabrous annual to 60 cm; stems erect, much-branched, bearing 2–3 pinnate leaves with almost filiform segments. Flower-heads pedunculate, single at branchlet apices. Flowers to 2 cm wide, ray florets (10–20) white; disc florets yellow; receptacle hollow and conical. Appearing early summer

to mid-autumn or sometimes later.
Distribution Indigenous to Europe, northern Asia, naturalized in North America; widespread on wasteland, farmland and in gardens.
Cultivation Wild. Cultivated and collected commercially in central Europe. Propagate from seed sown thinly in the autumn, or with less success in the spring.
Constituents Volatile oil (0.3–0.75%) comprising azulene (chamazulene), farnesene, α-bisabolol, sesquiterpenes, palustrine, quercetol, methoxycoumarin, furfural; also apigenin; salicylic acid; choline; phytosterol; triacontane; fatty acids and flavonic heterosides. The anti-inflammatory action is due mainly to α-bisabolol, but also to chamazulene; spasmolytic action due to dicyclic ether; antiseptic action due to several components.
Uses (dried flower-heads) Anti-inflammatory; antiseptic; antispasmodic; carminative. Of great benefit as an aromatic bitter for gastric

disorders, promoting bile and gastric secretions and increasing the appetite. In large doses it is emetic.
Promotes sweating and is used to treat the common cold; a weak infusion acts as a tonic. Although formerly used to treat painful menstruation, it is not very effective.
May be applied as an antiseptic douche; used as a gargle for aphthous ulcers; applied to haemorrhoids; or used as a poultice or compress for cuts, bruises, ulcers and skin disorders.
A flavouring in certain alcoholic drinks. Employed as a tisane.
Widely employed as an anti-allergic agent in cosmetic preparations.
A constituent of some liquid and dry hair shampoos, and lotions. Highlights and lightens fair hair.

Medicago sativa L LEGUMINOSAE
Lucerne Alfalfa
The name, *Medicago*, is derived from Medea in North Africa where this important plant was thought to have originated.
Certainly the Arabs have used Lucerne fodder for centuries to feed their horses, and it has been in cultivation for so long that, like Flax, it exists in many different forms.
The plant was not known in north-west Europe until the seventeenth century however, when it was given the name *lucerna* meaning lamp, after the bright shiny appearance of the seeds. The specific name *sativa* means cultivated.
Lucerne has few traditional medicinal uses outside the veterinary field, but recent investigation has shown that it is of great nutritional importance and contains, for example, four times as much vitamin C as citrus juice, measured weight for weight.
Description Glabrous perennial 30 cm–1 m; on deep, thick taproot; much-branched stem often forming dense bushy growth. Leaves pinnate, with 3 denticulate leaflets to 3 cm long, obovate-oblong. Flowers 1.5–3 cm long, violet-blue, on axillary racemes, appearing late summer to mid-autumn; followed by pubescent spiralled seed pod.
Distribution Originally native to mediterranean region and western Asia; naturalized in North America. Now worldwide in distribution, especially on dry, light or chalky soils.
Cultivation Wild as an escape. Many strains exist and the form of the plant depends on the variety grown. Very widely cultivated as fodder and for commercial purposes. Seed sown in late spring after risk of frost has passed, preferably on calcareous loam, which is free of weeds and prepared to a fine tilth. When grown commercially, seed is usually inoculated with a specific nitrogen-fixing root nodule bacterium to ensure growth. Replace after 5–7 years. Very drought resistant.
Constituents Protein (16%); fat (3%); vitamins C, B_1, B_2, D, E, K_1; provitamin A; several mineral salts, including potassium, calcium and phosphorus; choline; trimethylamine; betaine; alfafa saponin; an alkaloid, stachydrine; a bitter principle; a hormonal

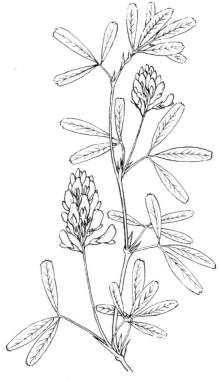

substance, coumestrol.
Uses (fresh or dried leaf, occasionally seed) Nutritive; diuretic; anti-haemorrhagic.
The seed was once used by Indians as an abortifacient. Of benefit as a tonic and nutritive herb; an infusion taken regularly promotes appetite and leads to weight increase. A very rich source of vitamin C, when used fresh.
May be applied externally to aid wound healing.
Used as a beverage.
The leaf is employed as a salad herb, or cooked as a vegetable.
The seed is sprouted indoors and eaten as a rich source of vitamins and amino-acids.
Of considerable veterinary importance as a food-stuff; in cows it increases milk yield. One of the major commercial sources of chlorophyll; also a source of vitamin K_1.
The seed provides a yellow dye. Formerly used as a diluent to adjust the strength of powdered medicinal plants such as *Digitalis*.

Melaleuca leucadendron L MYRTACEAE
Cajuput Tree Punk Tree
Cajuput oil is extracted by steam distillation from the leaves of a number of related Australasian trees or shrubs, all of which are members of the Bottle Brush group. *Melaleuca leucadendron* is the most important commercial source. The characteristic flowering spike with its numerous long creamy-white stamens led to the specific name *leucadendron* meaning white tree, while *melaleuca* is from the Greek for black and white, after the trunk and bark colours of one of the species.
The word Cajuput is derived directly from the local Malaysian name *kayu-puti* which means white wood – another reference to the colour. The oil was first noticed by Rumphius in the

late seventeenth century who described the use of the plant by Malaysians.

Lochner, a physician to the German Emperor, and von Wittneben, promoted its use in the early eighteenth century particularly in Germany, where it was called *Oleum Wittnebianum*.

Description Large tree with spongy, shiny and peeling bark; branches usually pendulous, bearing oblong tapering strongly-veined leaves, 1.5–2 cm wide and 5–10 cm long. Flowers creamy white, small, with numerous stamens extending 15 mm, borne on terminal spikes to 15 cm long, which themselves terminate in a tuft of leaves; followed by brown capsules.

Distribution Native to Australasia and Malaysia; introduced elsewhere in tropical situations, especially swamps.

Cultivation Wild. Limited cultivation; propagate from cuttings.

Constituents Oil comprising cineole (60%), terpineol, l-pinene, aldehydes, including those of benzoic, valeric and butyric acids.

Uses (oil, occasionally leaves and twigs) Carminative; antispasmodic; antiseptic; stimulant; rubefacient; antihelmintic; expectorant.

Formerly used internally in the treatment of chronic bronchitis and tuberculosis (the oil is excreted via the lungs), as a gastro-intestinal antiseptic, and for the removal of roundworms. Of benefit internally in some digestive disorders. Used externally in stimulant-rubbing oils for rheumatic pain; in various liniments; to treat scabies; and in tooth cavities to relieve pain.

A tea is made from the leaves.

Oil and leaves repel insects.

Contra-indications All essential oils should be used only in very small quantities.

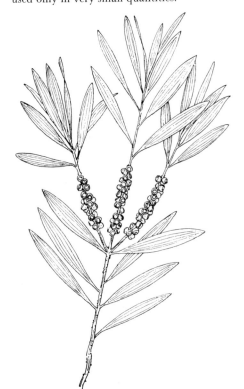

Melilotus alba Medic. LEGUMINOSAE

White Melilot White Sweet Clover/ Bokhara Clover

This is the taller of the common melilots and although of little benefit to man directly it is of great importance as an agricultural fodder crop, honey plant and cover crop for green manuring. Spoiled White Sweet Clover may sometimes cause cattle poisoning due to the presence of large quantities of dicoumarol, which delays blood coagulation and leads to severe, often internal, haemorrhage. Evidence suggests the cultivated races of the herb have lower concentrations of dicoumarol.

Description Sweet smelling erect, branched, annual or biennial from 1–2.5 m tall. Stems ribbed longitudinally, glabrous, bearing pinnate leaves with oblong, denticulate leaflets 1.8–4 cm long. Flowers white, honey-scented, small (4 mm long), numerous, on long thin, erect, terminal racemes; appearing midsummer to early autumn and followed by small pods.

Distribution Native to Asia and Europe. Naturalized in North America, especially the eastern states; varieties introduced elsewhere. In weedy wastelands, especially on stony and nitrogenous soils in sunny situations.

Cultivation Wild. An annual variety of this herb, *M. alba* var. *annua* Coe, also called Hubam Clover, developed as a drought-resistant, high weight yielding fodder and honey yielding crop, is grown worldwide – from seed sown in spring.

Constituents Coumarin and related substances; occasionally dicoumarol (melitoxin); fixed oil. Dicoumarol acts as a vitamin K antagonist, thus reducing prothrombin synthesis which delays blood coagulation.

Uses (cured fresh plant, occasionally flowering plant) Nutritive; aromatic; stimulant; vulnerary.

Rarely used medicinally, but used in Central America as a stimulant. May be employed in ointments to promote the healing of skin complaints. Possesses weak antibacterial activity. Formerly used homeopathically.

Of greatest importance as cattle fodder, and honey plant.

Melilotus officinalis (L) Pall. LEGUMINOSAE

Common Melilot Yellow Sweet Clover

This member of the Laburnum family (which is also called Wild Laburnum) is a very old medicinal plant from which an antithrombotic preparation is now made commercially. It is also of commercial importance as a flavouring for cheese and tobacco and was once used in beer manufacture. Its botanical name, *Melilotus*, means honey-lotus or honey clover, and reflects the sweetness of its nectar. The hay-like smell of the substance coumarin develops only when the plant is dried, and it was for this aromatic property that Common Melilot was once used as a strewing herb.

Known to the apothecaries as *corona regis*, or the kings crown, it is not now used very widely.

Description Straggly biennial to 130 cm; stems glabrous or pubescent, ribbed, erect or decumbent, branched. Bearing trifoliate leaves, and obovate or oblanceolate, 1–2 cm long, denticulate leaflets. Flowers yellow, honey-scented, small (4–6 mm long) borne on long, narrow axillary racemes, appearing midsummer to early autumn.

Distribution Eurasian native; naturalized in North America. Especially on nitrogenous wasteland, embankments and fields.

Cultivation Wild plant. Collected commercially.

Constituents Coumarin and related substances, released on drying; a glycoside, melilotoside; fixed oil; melilotic acid.

Uses (dried flowering plant) Aromatic; carminative; expectorant; antithrombotic; antispasmodic; antibiotic.

Formerly used in a wide range of conditions.

May be taken regularly to help prevent thrombosis; also to treat bronchial catarrh and flatulence. Externally applied to wounds and skin inflammations and can be used with care on inflamed eyes. The seeds possess antibiotic activity.

Formerly used in herb beer; flowers and seeds used to flavour Gruyère cheese, snuff and smoking tobacco.

May be employed in some meat dishes, for example, rabbit.

Limited cosmetic use where hay-like aroma is required. Repels moths and is used to protect clothes.

Contra-indications Large doses are emetic.

Melissa officinalis L LABIATAE
Balm Lemon Balm/Common Balm

Although Balm has been cultivated in the mediterranean region for over 2000 years, it was for almost half this period considered important only as a bee plant, and until the fifteenth century was known as either *melissophyllon*, Greek for bee leaf, or *apiastrum*, Latin for bee plant. Its modern botanical name, *Melissa*, reflects this early association.

The Arabs introduced it as a medicinal herb specifically of benefit in anxiety or depression, and it has been used as a sedative or tonic tea ever since. Balm has frequently been incorporated in proprietary cordials or liqueurs, and its popularity in France led to its name *Thé de France*. Balm is an abbreviation for balsam after its sweet aroma, but this aroma is rapidly lost, together with much of its therapeutic value, on drying and storing.

Description Sweet-smelling perennial, on slightly hairy square stem, branching near the top, from 30–80 cm. Leaves opposite, petiolate, ovate, greenish-yellow, dentate or crenate-dentate, to 7.5 cm long; lemon scented. Flowers whitish, occasionally pinkish or yellow; small (0.75–1.5 cm long) in scanty axillary clusters; appearing late summer to mid-autumn.

Distribution Native to southern Europe; mediterranean region; central Europe; introduced and widespread in northern temperate zones, often as a garden escape. Especially common on nutrient-rich soils in sunny position.

Cultivation Wild. Cultivated commercially and horticulturally; from seed sown in mid to late spring (slow germination) or by root division in spring or autumn. Prefers rich, moist soil in sunny position with some shade; some shelter required in cooler climates, as it is susceptible to frost. A variegated form exists.

Constituents (fresh plant) Essential oil (0.1%) comprising citral, linalol, citronellal and geraniol; tannins (5%); a bitter principle; resin; succinic acid.

Uses (fresh or dried leaves, occasionally flowering tops, oil) Carminative; diaphoretic; antispasmodic; sedative.

Of use in aromatic waters or as a tea for the treatment of minor gastric disturbances, nausea and headaches. Also used in conjunction with other remedies to treat nervous tachycardia and restlessness. Some hypotensive action. Fresh leaf is soothing when rubbed on insect bites.

Oil once used alone as a diaphoretic, but is slightly toxic.

Wide culinary potential where delicate lemon flavour is required.

An important constituent of several liqueurs, including Benedictine and Chartreuse. Useful in wine cups and cold drinks. Taken alone as a tisane.

A useful bee plant.

May be used in pot-pourris, herb pillows, and in herb mixtures for aromatic baths.

Mentha aquatica L LABIATAE
Water Mint

A very variable plant which is sometimes considered to exist in distinct varieties. This species hybridizes readily with other mints, producing a large array of varieties.

It is strong-smelling and not as pleasant as most

common mints, although in the Middle Ages Water Mint (then called *menastrum*) was used as a strewing herb. The related *Mentha spicata* L is used as a commercial source of oil of Spearmint.

Description Strong-smelling perennial; variable in form. Angular, glabrous or pubescent, much-branched stem to 1 m, on stolons. Leaves opposite, serrate, decussate, ovate, petiolate, and rather crisp; 2–6 cm long. Flowers lilac or red, in rounded terminal inflorescence, 4 cm diameter, with usually only 1 (rarely 2) axillary whorls of flowers beneath this. Appearing late summer to late autumn.

Distribution Native to Europe and naturalized in many northern temperate zones. On wet soils, beside streams, in ditches and on regularly flooded land.

Cultivation Wild. May be propagated by stolon division in spring. Plant in water or keep very wet.

Constituents Volatile oil (poco oil, to 0.85%) comprising menthofuran, linalol acetate, limonene, L-carvol; also betaine; choline; succinic acid; glucose; menthyl pentose; dotricontane; aquaticol; tannins.

Uses (fresh herb, occasionally root bark and oil) Carminative; antispasmodic; cholagogue; slightly astringent.

Of benefit as a warm infusion in disturbances of the gastro-intestinal system, particularly diarrhoea, and intestinal spasms. Also useful in the treatment of the common cold and in painful menstruation. In Africa the root bark is employed in the treatment of diarrhoea and colds.

May be taken as a tisane.

May be employed with discretion in scented articles.

Once used as a strewing herb.

Contra-indications Large doses may be emetic.

Mentha x *piperita* L LABIATAE
Peppermint

Peppermint is now one of the best known of all herbs, but it was not definitely recorded until 1696 when the botanist, Ray, published a brief description of a pepper-tasting mint which had, near to that date, first been observed by Dr Eales in Hertfordshire, England.

In his *Historia plantarum* (1704) Ray called the mint Peper-mint or *Mentha palustris*, and although the latter correctly refers to the marsh-loving nature of the plant, no satisfactory explanation can be given for his erroneous description of the plant's taste; the common name has nevertheless been retained. Peppermint's medicinal value was soon recognized and within 25 years of its description the herb was included in the London Pharmacopoeia – it is still retained in many national pharmacopoeias.

Botanically the herb represents a hybrid between *M. spicata* and *M. aquatica* and by some authorities is thought to exist as two main varietal forms called Black (*forma rubescens*), and White (*forma pallescens*) Peppermints.

Description Aromatic perennial on root-stock producing runners. Stem square, erect, somewhat branched above, slightly hairy, either purple (Black Peppermint) or much less so (White Peppermint), from 30 cm–1 m tall; variable. Bearing petiolate green or purple-green, lanceolate, or ovate-lanceolate, acute, deeply dentate leaves, 4–8 cm long and 1–2.5 cm wide. Flowers mauve (occasionally white) irregularly arranged on a conical terminal spike 3–7.5 cm long; appearing late summer to mid-autumn.

Distribution European native; widely distributed and often naturalized. In sunny or partially shady conditions on rich damp soils; hedgerows, ditches and it is also found near habitation.

Cultivation Wild only as an escape, and seldom established permanently. Cultivated commercially and horticulturally in many parts of the world. Divide stolons in autumn and replant 30 cm apart, 5 cm deep. Water well in ordinary garden situations; replace after 5 years. Does not breed true if raised from seed.

Constituents Volatile oil (to 2%) comprising menthol (50%), menthone, menthyl isovalerate, cineole, jasmone, phellandrene, amyl alcohol, acetaldehyde, cadinene; tannins; bitter compounds.

Uses (fresh or dried plant, oil) Aromatic stimulant; carminative; antiseptic; antispasmodic; anti-inflammatory; cholagogue.

May be employed in a variety of gastro-intestinal disorders where its antispasmodic, anti-flatulent and appetite-promoting actions are required. Particularly useful in nervous headaches and agitation. Used in conjunction with other remedies for the common cold. Both the herb and the oil may be used externally in baths to treat cuts and skin rashes.

Wide cosmetic, dental and confectionery use of the oil where a mint flavouring or cold-taste is required.

Well-known culinary uses.

Also employed to flavour some liqueurs.

Contra-indications The oil may cause allergic reactions.

Mentha x *piperita* var. *citrata* (Ehr.) Briq.
LABIATAE
Bergamot Mint Eau de Cologne Mint/ Orange Mint

This mint is one of the most attractively scented of all herbs and should occupy a place in every herb garden. The aroma is, however, somewhat intangible and it is variously described as lemon, orange, bergamot, lavender and eau de Cologne mint – the latter being the most widely used. Its former botanical name, *M. odorata*, is therefore rather more accurate than the present one, which suggests only a lemon scent.

Description Very aromatic decumbent, glabrous perennial from 30–60 cm tall, on overground leafy stolons. Stems branched, bearing dark green, purple-tinged, smooth, ovate or elliptic, petiolate leaves 1.5–4 cm long. Mauve flowers in rounded dense terminal spikes or in upper leaf axils, appearing from mid to late autumn.

Distribution European native, naturalized elsewhere. On rich, moist soils in conditions of partial shade.

Cultivation Wild. Cultivated horticulturally by division of stolons in spring; planting 5 cm deep.

Constituents Volatile oil.

Uses (fresh or dried leaves) Not used medicinally. Used sparingly in tisanes, jellies, cold drinks, or salads.

May be employed in a range of scented and cosmetic articles.

Mentha pulegium L LABIATAE
Pennyroyal Pudding Grass

Pennyroyal was held in very high repute for many centuries throughout Europe and was the most popular of all the members of the mint family, being used both for a wide range of medicinal purposes and in various ancient ceremonies.

Pliny is regarded as the originator of its name *pulegium* which is derived from *pulex* meaning flea, since both the fresh plant and the smoke from the burning leaves were used to eradicate the insects.

This association with fleas has been retained in the botanical name given to the plant by Linnaeus. Before his scientific classification the superficial appearance and unusual aroma of the herb led to it being considered as a thyme. *Puliol* was an old French name for thyme and this plant was designated the royal thyme – hence *puliol royale* and thus the corruption, Pennyroyal. The modern French name is *la menthe Pouliot* – from *puliol*. Although long considered an abortifacient, it has been found that this effect is usually only possible with a dose of the oil which is highly toxic and leads to irreversible kidney damage.

The plant can therefore be used as a flavouring agent, but only when the concentration of pulegone does not exceed 20 mg in 1 kg of the final product being flavoured.

The American Pennyroyal (*Hedeoma pulegioides* (L) Pers.) has similar properties and uses.

Description Aromatic perennial with much branched prostrate or erect stems to 30 cm tall; on overground runners. Leaves dark green, slightly hairy, petiolate, oblong or oval crenate or serrate, 0.8–2 cm long. Flowers mauve-blue, in rounded dense axillary whorls, along upper half of the stem. Appearing late summer to early autumn.

Distribution Native to Europe, North Africa and western Asia; introduced elsewhere. On nutrient-rich, moist but sandy soils. Prefers sunny situations.

Cultivation Wild. Commercial cultivation

limited. Grown horticulturally; the prostrate form as a lawn (var. *decumbens*) or for aromatic ground cover. Sow seed in late spring under glass in cool zones, planting out in early summer on open, friable, loamy soil 15–20 cm apart. Keep well watered in dry weather, and protect from hard frosts. Propagate also by root division in autumn or spring, or from cuttings taken in the summer.

Constituents Volatile oil (0.5–1%) comprising a ketone, pulegone (80–90%), to which the action is largely due; also menthone; β-caryophyllene; methylcyclohexanol; iso-menthone; tannins.

Uses (fresh or dried flowering plant) Emmenagogue; antispasmodic; carminative.

May be used in minor gastric disturbances, flatulence, nausea, headache, and menstrual

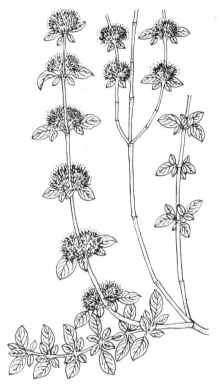

pain. In combination with other remedies it is of benefit at the onset of the common cold. Fresh leaves may be applied externally to skin irritations and insect bites, as it acts as a rubefacient.

May be taken, weak, as a tea (Organy tea). Formerly used as a flavouring in puddings.

Useful in scented articles, particularly clothes drawer sachets.

The oil may be used in cosmetics as an insect repellent.

In the eastern mediterranean region it has been used as a dye plant.

Contra-indications Somewhat irritant to the genito-urinary tract possibly causing reflex uterine movements; not to be used in pregnancy, or in kidney disease.

May cause contact dermatitis.

Mentha rotundifolia (L) Huds. LABIATAE
Apple Mint Round-leaved Mint

Apple Mint is so-called simply because its aroma is a combination of mint and apples. It

is more subtle than most mints and may therefore be employed far more widely in the kitchen.

Bowles Mint (also sometimes incorrectly called Apple Mint) is a hybrid between this species and *M. spicata*, but is usually known as *M. rotundifolia* 'Bowles Variety.' An attractive variegated form of Apple Mint is commonly grown as a garden ornamental.

Description Aromatic pubescent perennial on

leafy stolons, bearing erect, somewhat branched, thin stems to 90 cm. Leaves green, white and velvety beneath, sessile, oblong to round, crenate-serrate, 3–10 cm long. Flowers white, cream to pink, on dense irregularly flowered, somewhat pointed terminal spikes, from 3–6 cm long; appearing early to mid-autumn.

Distribution European native; widely naturalized; on damp soils in ditches and waste places.

Cultivation Wild. Widely cultivated horticulturally. Propagate by stolon division in autumn.

Constituents Volatile oil; tannins.

Uses (fresh leaf) Not used medicinally.

Many culinary uses, including meat and fish, egg dishes, fruit dishes, jellies, hot and cold beverages, sauces and vinegars.

Once used in confectionery manufacture.

Mentha spicata L LABIATAE
Spearmint Garden Mint/Pea Mint

Spearmint was formerly known as *Mentha viridis* L; the specific name *viridis* meaning green emphasized the bright green colour of the herb. The modern botanical name, and the common name, reflect the spear or spike-like shape of both the inflorescence and the leaves. In the sixteenth century the plant was called Spere mynte and even then, as today, it was the most commonly used of all mints.

The Romans were responsible for its distribution throughout north and west Europe.

Besides important culinary and flavouring uses it is still retained in the Hungarian Pharmacopoeia for its medical use.

Description Aromatic nearly glabrous perennial on leafy underground stolons. Stems erect, square, somewhat branched, from 30–60 cm tall. Leaves smooth and green, opposite, almost sessile, lanceolate or ovate-lanceolate and

curled, margin deeply serrate, to 6 cm long. Flowers pale lilac, on cylindrical, irregularly flowered terminal spikes 5–10 cm long, appearing early autumn.

Distribution Native to southern Europe. Widely naturalized, especially in damp, shady sites near habitation.

Cultivation Wild. Very widely cultivated commercially and as a garden plant. Propagate from stolon division in the autumn; plant 5 cm

deep and water well. Replace after 4 years. Rarely grown from seed since it does not breed true.

Constituents Volatile oil comprising menthol, carvone, limonene; vitamin A; tannins.

Uses (fresh or dried leaf, oil) Carminative; aromatic; antispasmodic; weak emmenagogue.

Similar uses to Peppermint.

Wide culinary use in sauces, jellies, hot and cold beverages, and for garnishing and general flavouring.

The oil is used as a flavouring agent in toiletries and confectionery.

Menyanthes trifoliata L MENYANTHACEAE
Buckbean Marsh Trefoil/Bog Bean

Menyanthes is the old Greek name for an attractive and distinctive herb, common locally and sometimes extensive in shallow water in many cooler parts of the northern hemisphere. Its Greek name means flower of the month, which reflects not only the duration of its beautiful shaggy flowers, but also its beneficial effects on menstrual pain. At one time Buckbean was considered in Germany to be a panacea and was used to treat many ailments from gout to scurvy and rheumatism. The Swedes, Norwegians, Icelanders and Scots also particularly favoured this bitter tasting plant. It is now generally considered to be a useful substitute for Gentian Root.

The common name, Bog Bean, is less than 200 years old and is derived from the German *Bocksbohnen* meaning goat's beans, which in English became Buckbean.

Description Glabrous, aquatic perennial on black, creeping, thick horizontal root-stock; bearing alternate, basal, trifoliate leaves with pale prominent midribs, sheathing at the base, on petioles to 25 cm high. Petioles thicker at the base and surrounded by bracts. Leaflets obovate or oblong, entire, sessile, terminal, 4–7.5 cm long, dark green. Flowers white; pinkish or purplish externally with shaggy petals, 15 mm long, 10–15 per terminal raceme on long scapes; appearing early to mid-summer.

Distribution Native to northern temperate zones, from North America to Siberia including Iceland and Greenland. In ditches, fresh-water marsh and bog, reed-beds and meadows which are always wet and consist of acidic, peaty soils.

Cultivation Wild plant. May be grown as a pond or bog plant by division of root-stock in spring or autumn.

Constituents A glycoside, menyanthin; bitter principles, loganine, sweroside, meliatine; flavone heterosides; inulin; vitamin C; choline; resin; malic acid.

Uses (dried leaves, occasionally dried whole plant) Bitter tonic; emmenagogue; stomachic. The fresh plant was formerly used as a cathartic. Now of greatest benefit as a gastro-intestinal tonic; stimulates gastric and biliary secretions, and hence promotes appetite. It has a direct beneficial effect on the liver; it is of

value in amenorrhoea, and possesses some anti-helmintic activity. The root has been used externally to treat obstinate skin complaints. Leaves once used in brewing and baking and may be taken as a tonic tea.

Leaves used as a tobacco substitute.

Contra-indications Not to be used in the treatment of diarrhoea. Large doses of the whole plant may cause vomiting and diarrhoea.

Monarda didyma L LABIATAE
Red Bergamot Bee Balm/Oswego Tea
Red Bergamot has become widely cultivated

as a garden ornamental for its combination of orange scent and attractive flowers. It is called Bergamot because of its scent which resembles that of a Bergamot orange. Several varieties now exist of which the best-known is Cambridge Scarlet; other types are salmon, rose, purple, or white in colour – but the wild, red *M. didyma* is the most aromatic.

Red Bergamot belongs to the *Monarda* or Horsemint genus, named after the sixteenth-century Spanish medical botanist Nicholas de Monardes, and is closely related to Wild or Purple Bergamot (*M. fistulosa* L) which is also called Oswego Tea – and which has long been used by American Indians for medicinal purposes. Oswego derives its name from the Oswego River district near Lake Ontario in the United States where the herb grew in abundance and from where most supplies originally came. After the Boston Tea Party, 1773, a protest at the tea duty imposed on the colonies, Oswego Tea replaced Indian tea in many American households.

Description Aromatic, usually glabrous perennial from 40–100 cm tall; stems erect, acutely quadrangular, bearing opposite, serrate, ovate to ovate-lanceolate dark green, often red-tinged, leaves to 15 cm long. Flowers scarlet-red, 4–5 cm long, usually in solitary terminal whorls, with slightly hairy calyx. Appearing late summer to mid-autumn.

Distribution North American native, from Ontario to Georgia; naturalized in South America. On moist nutrient-rich soils preferring shade but tolerating full sun; especially deciduous woodland.

Cultivation Wild. Cultivated throughout the world as a horticultural plant; occasionally wild as an escape. Many horticultural forms exist. Propagate from seed sown in spring or by root division in spring; succeeds best on light soils and may be a vigorous grower. Cut back each autumn and replace after 3 years.

Constituents Volatile oil comprising compounds related to thymol; tannic acid.

Uses (fresh or dried flowering plant; some-

times root and oil) Carminative; stimulant; rubefacient; weak diaphoretic; weak emmenagogue; expectorant.

May be used as a tea to relieve nausea, flatulence, menstrual pain, vomiting and, with less success, headaches and colds. It is also taken internally and by inhalation of the water vapour (pouring on boiling water) for bronchial catarrh and sore throats.

Formerly used externally as an ointment for skin problems.

May be taken as a tea, and used sparingly in salads.

Useful in a very wide range of scented articles.

Once an ingredient of hair preparations. The oil is sometimes used in perfumery.

Morus nigra L MORACEAE
Mulberry Black or Common Mulberry
Morus and *morarius* were the classical Latin names for the Mulberry and come from the Latin verb meaning to delay after the tree's habit of delaying spring bud formation until the cold weather had passed. The Greeks knew it as both *moron* and *sukamnos* – from its sweetness; the fruit being only slightly less sweet than the sweetest fruits known to them, namely

the fig, grape and cherry. Until the fifteenth century *M. nigra* was important as a medicinal plant, and its leaves were used for silkworm rearing, but after this date it was mostly replaced by the oriental species *M. alba* L. The tree is now becoming quite scarce in parts of Europe.

Description Bushy tree to 10 m; branches dark coloured, bearing thick, alternate, cordate-ovate, pointed leaves, 5–20 cm long; margins serrate, somewhat variable. Flowers unisexual catkins; the female, numerous, consisting of green perianths and 2 stigmas. Fruit to 3 cm long, purplish red.

Distribution Native to western Asia, Persia and the Caucasus; introduced to other temperate zones.

Cultivation Wild. Cultivated as a fruit-tree in areas that are protected from cold winds and frost. Propagate from cuttings taken in early spring or by layering in autumn. Slow growing. Requires a loamy soil in warm position.

Constituents (fruit) Sugar (10%); malic acid

(2%); pectin; gum; vitamin C.

Uses (fresh fruit, root bark and occasionally leaves) Nutritive; laxative; antipyretic; anti-helmintic.

Until recently the leaves were employed in the Balkans as an hypoglycaemic agent for use in diabetes. The root bark was formerly used as a cathartic and to remove tapeworms.

Once used to colour medicines.

Now usually employed as a food, and in the home manufacture of wines, jams, and conserves.

May be used as a dyestuff.

Myrica cerifera L MYRICACEAE
Wax Myrtle Bayberry/Candleberry

Both the specific and common names of this fragrant North American plant indicate the fine yellow or light green wax (strictly an edible fat) which is produced on the berries as they ripen. This substance, called bayberry tallow or myrica wax, was once widely collected on the East Coast of the United States and was used in soap and candle manufacture. Related members of the *Myrica* genus are used throughout the world for various domestic and medicinal purposes; in South Africa, for example, *M. cordifolia* L is both a source of berry wax and a valuable anti-diarrhoeic remedy. *M. cerifera* is now unused outside folk medicine except as a constituent of some proprietary domestic cold cures such as Composition Powders.

Description Fragrant perennial evergreen (occasionally semi-deciduous or deciduous) dioecious shrub (1–3 m) or evergreen tree (to 10 m), much branched with pubescent, somewhat rough branchlets bearing glandular, entire or occasionally serrulate oblong-lanceolate to lanceolate, acute leaves 3–7.5 cm long. Flowers consist of short, conical or globular scaly catkins, either sterile or fertile; followed

by grey, waxy, spherical, 1-seeded berries. Appearing late spring to mid-summer.

Distribution North American native, especially on the East Coast from New Jersey to Florida. On poor, sandy, well-drained soils, but frequently near swamps or marshland. In coniferous woodland and thickets near the sea.

Cultivation Wild.

Constituents (berries) Myrica wax, comprising glycerides of palmitic, stearic and myristic acids; lauric acid; unsaturated fatty acids.

(root bark) Volatile oil; tannic acid; gallic acid; an acrid resin, myricinic acid; an astringent resin; gum; starch. Action largely due to the resin content.

Uses (root bark, berries' wax, occasionally fresh leaves) Astringent; weak diaphoretic; tonic; sialogogue. Principally employed as a gargle, douche and poultice in the treatment of sore throats, leucorrhoea and ulcers respectively. May be used internally for mucous colitis, diarrhoea, the common cold and feverish conditions. Powdered bark formerly taken as a snuff in the treatment of nasal catarrh. Small pieces of bark may be chewed to promote salivation, aid gingivitis, and reduce toothache.

Once taken as a tonic tea.

Wax used in candle and soap manufacture.

Contra-indications Large doses emetic; may cause flatulence.

Myrica gale L MYRICACEAE
Bog Myrtle Sweet Gale

Bog Myrtle was once one of the many important herbs used in northern Europe to flavour beer, and was both widely collected and protected by law.

The herb's ability to repel and destroy insects, such as fleas, led to the now obsolete common name Flea Wood, and the plants' domestic employment in mattresses and linen drawers. Small quantities can be used as a flavouring in meat dishes.

Description Deciduous shrub to 1.5 m tall; branchlets reddish and growing almost vertically, bearing grey-green oblanceolate, glandular-pubescent, aromatic, obtuse leaves 3–6 cm long. Brown and yellowish-green unisexual flowers borne in dense apical catkins to 15 mm long; appearing late spring to early summer, and followed by numerous small

flattened berries.

Distribution Native to north-west Europe; north America as far south as Virginia; Asia. Introduced elsewhere. Especially in thickets on wet heathland or fens. To 600 m altitude.

Cultivation Wild. May be propagated from suckers, by division or from cuttings. Requires a damp, acidic soil in a shady position.

Constituents (berries) Myrtle or Myrica wax; similar to *M. cerifera* (Wax Myrtle). (leaves) Aromatic volatile oil.

Uses (berries' wax, occasionally leaves and bark) Aromatic; insecticide.

Formerly used externally to treat scabies.

Dried leaves may be employed with discretion as a spice in soups and stews. Berries can be similarly used.

Leaves formerly flavoured beer (Gale beer), and may also be used as a tea.

Wax may be used in the manufacture of aromatic candles. Roots and stem bark dye wool yellow.

Repels fleas and may thus be used in scented sachets.

Myristica fragrans Houtt. MYRISTICACEAE
Mace Nutmeg

The early history of the use of Mace (the outer covering of the seed of the plant) and Nutmeg (the seed itself) is not known with certainty, but it is improbable that these spices were used by the Greeks and Romans. By the sixth century, however, both Indians and Arabs were obtaining them from the Far East, and they were known in Europe by 1191. In that year they were one of several fumigant strewing aromatics used in the streets of Rome during the coronation of Emperor Henry VI.

Around 1300 an Arabian writer, Kazwini, had named the Molucca Islands as the source of both materials, but it was not until 1506 to 1512 that the Portugese took possession of the Islands and began a spice monopoly which was to be continued by the Dutch and English until the beginning of the nineteenth century.

It has been recognized for centuries that moderate doses of Nutmeg cause a feeling of unreality and visual illusions. These effects have now been shown to be caused by a proto-alkaloidal constituent, myristicin, which is a psychotropic with structural similarities to mescaline – found in the Peyote Cactus.

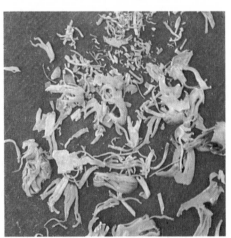

Description Tall, dioecious, bushy, glabrous, evergreen tree to 12 m. Leaves yellowish, coriaceous, petiolate elliptic – or oblong-lanceolate, 5–12 cm long. Flowers 6 mm long, in axillary umbels; followed by nearly globular or pear-shaped, red or yellow, pedunculous fruit which splits on maturing to release the ovoid seed (Nutmeg) surrounded by a scarlet aril (Mace).

Distribution Indigenous to the Molucca Islands; introduced and widespread in the tropics. Frequently on volcanic soils in shade and high humidity.

Cultivation Wild; now cultivated in East and West Indies, Zanzibar, Brazil, Ceylon and India. Trees first produce seed in ninth or tenth year of growth and may last 80 years. Outside the tropics may be grown as an ornamental hothouse plant, in humus-enriched soil with high ambient temperature and humidity.

Propagate from woody cuttings in a peat and sand mix.

Constituents (kernel) Volatile oil (5–15%) comprising eugenol and iso-eugenol; fixed oil (25–40%) yielding nutmeg butter and comprising myristic acid (60%), oleic, palmitic, lauric and linoleic acids; also terpineol, borneol and terpenes.

Action mainly due to volatile oil, acting as a carminative.

Uses (seed, aril, occasionally oil) Carminative; aromatic; stimulant.

Used in small doses to reduce flatulence, aid digestion, improve the appetite and to treat diarrhoea, vomiting and nausea.

Both Mace and Nutmeg may be used in a range of sweet and savoury food-stuffs. Mace is less strongly aromatic, and Nutmeg particularly complements milk and cheese dishes.

The oil is employed as a flavouring agent and in some rubefacient liniments and hair lotions.

Contra-indications POISONOUS. Use very sparingly. Even moderate doses overstimulate the motor cortex causing disorientation, double vision, hallucination, tachycardia, and possibly epileptiform convulsions.

Myrrhis odorata (L) Scop. UMBELLIFERAE
Sweet Cicely British Myrrh

Sweet Cicely was once cultivated as a pot shrub in Europe. It is among the first garden herbs to emerge after winter and is almost the last to die down, and it was therefore considered a useful plant. Its aniseed-like aroma is responsible for the botanical name – *myrrhis* meaning perfume, and *odorata* meaning fragrant, while many of its common names are prefixed 'sweet' because of the taste of the leaf. Until the sixteenth century it was known as Seseli, a name first used by Dioscorides although not necessarily for this particular species.

Description Strongly smelling hirsute-pubescent perennial on grooved, hollow, branching stems 60–100 cm tall. Leaves bright green, pale beneath, soft, thin, 2 or 3-pinnate to 30 cm long, with oblong-ovate, narrow-toothed segments. Stem-leaf petioles sheathing. Flowers small, white, in umbels 1–5 cm diameter,

appearing early to mid-spring; followed by large (2–2.5 cm long) ridged brown fruit.

Distribution European native. Introduced to some temperate regions, locally naturalized. On grassy soils, in hedgerows, often in mountainous regions; prefers shady sites, but tolerates full sun.

Cultivation Wild. Cultivated commercially on a small scale in Western Europe, and elsewhere as a garden herb. Propagate from seed sown in mid or late spring on well-drained, but humus-rich, soil in partial shade; transplant to 45 cm

apart. Taproots may be lifted, cut into sections each having a bud, and replanted 5 cm deep in either spring or autumn. Often self-sown and may become rampant when established.

Constituents Essential oil, comprising anethole.

Uses (fresh or dried leaf, occasionally seed and root) Weak diuretic; tonic; hypotensive; weak antiseptic. Rarely used medicinally. Once an ingredient of wound-healing ointments. May be used as a sugar substitute by diabetics.

Fresh leaf and chopped green seed may be used in salads; leaves may be boiled as a vegetable or added to soups. They may also be used as a sugar substitute in sweet conserves and tart fruit dishes.

Roots were once boiled, cooled, and eaten in salads.

A useful honey plant.

An anise flavouring used in certain liqueurs.

Myrtus communis (L) Herm. MYRTACEAE
Myrtle Common Myrtle

Myrtle is frequently mentioned in the Old Testament, the writings of ancient poets and in the works of the Greeks and the Romans, to whom it was known as *myrtos*. *Myrtus* is directly derived from this old name, while *communis* means common.

It was almost certainly because the aromatic leaves bear a resemblance to the female pudenda that Myrtle has been dedicated to Venus, that it has been considered as an aphrodisiac, and carried by Israeli brides, for example, at their weddings.

Every part of the shrub is highly scented and in southern Europe it is used in a number of home-made cosmetic recipes.

Description Aromatic evergreen shrub 1–3 m high; occasionally taller. Highly branched, bearing glossy dark green, opposite, entire, acute, ovate to lanceolate leaves, 3–5 cm long and dotted with transparent oil glands. Petioles short. Flowers pure white, but often rose coloured, very fragrant, 5-petalled to 2 cm wide, numerous golden stamens; on long thin pedicels in pairs in leaf axils; appearing mid to late summer and followed by 12-mm diameter bluish berries.

Distribution Native to mediterranean region and western Asia, growing to 800 m altitude; introduced elsewhere.

Cultivation Wild. Cultivated as a garden plant against south-facing walls in all except the warmest south European sites. Requires full sun and well-drained, medium rich soil. Propagate from woody cuttings, taken in summer, under glass in a sand and peat mix. Usually slow growing in cool regions.

Constituents Volatile oil; malic acid; citric acid; resin; tannic acid; vitamin C.

Uses (fresh or dried leaves, dried fruit, dried flower-buds, fresh flowers, occasionally oil) Astringent; antiseptic. Rarely used medicinally, but a leaf decoction may be applied externally to bruises and haemorrhoids. An infusion was once used as a douche in leucorrhoea, and it was formerly employed internally for psoriasis and sinusitis. The fresh fruit juice has been used as a drink to stimulate the mucous membranes of the stomach.

Dried flower-buds and fruit may be crushed and used as a spice in the same way as peppercorns.

The leaves can be added to roast pork for the final 10 minutes of cooking.

Fresh flowers once added to salads. Formerly used in the manufacture of toilet water called *Eau d'ange*.

Nasturtium officinale R.Br CRUCIFERAE
Watercress

Watercress is so common that its valuable medical and dietic values are often forgotten, even though for centuries it was an official medicine. *Nasturtium* is from the Latin *nasi tortium* or distortion of the nose, after its pungent taste.

Description Aquatic perennial, either floating or creeping with freely rooting, succulent stems; leaves dark green to bronze, entire, ovate, or cordate; pinnate when older, the terminal leaflet largest. Flowers small, white, in pedicelled racemes, appearing early summer to mid-autumn.

Distribution European native; world-wide introduction and widespread naturalization. In ditches, streams to 2500 m altitude.

Cultivation Wild, and world-wide commercial cultivation as a salad herb. Easily propagated by stem or root cuttings, taken at any time and rooted in water. May be cultivated in rich, moist garden soil with frequent watering, but the pungency then increases.

Constituents Vitamins A, B_2, C, D, E; nicotinamide; a glucoside, gluconasturtin; volatile oil comprising phenylethylisothiocyanate; minerals including manganese, iron, phosphorus, iodine and calcium.

Uses (leafy stems) Stimulant; diuretic; antipyretic; stomachic; irritant.

Numerous medicinal attributes from many countries including use as a contraceptive, aphrodisiac, purgative and asthma remedy. It is an excellent cough remedy when mixed with honey.

May be eaten raw or cooked and as a delicious summer soup.

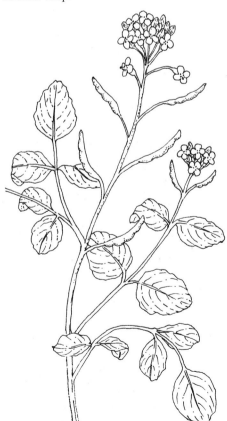

Nepeta cataria L LABIATAE
Catnip Catmint/Catnep

Although this herb possesses what many consider to be a disagreeable mint-like aroma, it is relished by cats and for this reason commonly used to stuff toy mice. Cats frequently damage the plant in gardens, which is unfortunate since their attractive light grey foliage and long persistant flowers are suitable for formal displays.

Catmint is now very rarely used for medicinal purposes even in folk medicine.

It was once used by hippies as a mild hallucinogen.

Description Strongly smelling, branching, pubescent, erect perennial 40–100 cm tall. Leaves 3–7 cm long, coarsely serrate, whitish beneath, grey-green above, ovate or oblong-ovate, petiolate. Flowers white, dotted with purple, or purple, 6 mm long, in crowded terminal whorls and spiked axillary whorls. Appearing mid-summer to mid-autumn.

Distribution Native to Europe, East and West Asia. Introduced and often naturalized in other temperate zones. On moist calcareous soils, especially road or railway sides, hedgerows, in open situations.

Cultivation Wild. May be propagated from cuttings taken in summer and rooted in a peat and sand mix under glass or by root division in spring or autumn.

Constituents Volatile oil comprising thymol, carvacrol, nepetol, nepetalactone and nepetalic acid; also tannic acid. Antispasmodic action due to the oil content.

Uses (dried – or occasionally fresh – flowering plant) Antispasmodic; anti-diarrhoeic; carminative; stomachic; weak emmenagogue. The tea is of benefit in the treatment of a number of gastro-intestinal complaints but particularly infantile colic and diarrhoea. It is also of value in the common cold, irritability and delayed menstruation. Externally it may be applied to cuts, abrasions and bruising. Combined with ground Cloves and Sassafras bark it was formerly applied to aching teeth.

Leaves may be used with discretion as a flavouring (mint-like) in sauces, and as a mildly stimulant tea.

Once smoked to relieve chronic bronchitis – but this may cause hallucinogenic effects.

Contra-indications A mild hallucinogen when smoked.

Nymphaea alba L NYMPHAEACEAE
White Water Lily

Although controversy surrounded the supposed anaphrodisiac qualities of this attractive aquatic herb, it is now considered that *N. alba* and some related plants may depress sexual activity. The Chinese have coincidentally used two other members of the family Nymphaeaceae – *Nelumbium nucifera* Gaertn. and *Euryale ferox* Salisb. – for precisely similar purposes indicating their possession of similar chemical constituents.

Nymphaea is from the Greek *nymphae* meaning water nymphs, while the pre-sixteenth century name Nenuphar (still retained as the modern French common name) was derived from the Arabic *niloufar* and Sanskrit *nilotpala* – terms first used for the Indian Blue Lotus.

N. odorata Aix is the similar, but more fragrant, American White Pond Lily; it has similar properties and uses.

Description Perennial aquatic herb with stipulate, round or heart-shaped, floating leaves 10–30 cm in diameter; on horizontal, black, branched, rhizome. Leaves reddish when young, later dark green, smooth and shining. Flowers white, 20-petalled, 5–20 cm diameter, stamens numerous and golden. Appearing mid-summer to early autumn, followed by 15–40 mm diameter obovoid fruit which opens under water.

Distribution Native to Europe and North America; introduced elsewhere. On rivers, lakes, ponds to 800 m altitude.

Cultivation Wild. Cultivated as an ornamental aquatic. Propagate in spring from rhizomes planted under water not deeper than 50 cm. In cold situations the flowers and leaves are much reduced in size.

A red variety, *N. alba* var. *rubra* Lönnr. is the parent of most water lily hybrids in cultivation.

Constituents Alkaloids, especially nupharine; tannins as nymphaea-tannic acid; a cardenolide, nymphaline; mucilage.

Uses (rhizome, occasionally seeds) Weak astringent; antiseptic; antispasmodic; anaphrodisiac.

A decoction may be used as a gargle for sore throats, a douche in leucorrhoea, and externally for ulcers or, much diluted, as an eyewash. Rarely used internally but acts as a sedative cardiac tonic, and is considered of benefit in spermatorrhoea. Once taken to reduce libido.

Well-cooked leaves once eaten as a vegetable. Fresh root once used as a soap substitute. Provides a dark brown dyestuff.

Ocimum basilicum L LABIATAE
Basil Sweet Basil

Basil was introduced to Europe from the East in the sixteenth century as a culinary herb and

is still popular with cooks who utilize its sweet, pungent flavour. Unfortunately the dried herb is not comparable with the flavour of leaves freshly picked from the garden. Several forms are in cultivation, including a lettuce-leaved variety, and the flavour varies with the volatile oil content; one type has a peppermint-like taste.

Both this species and the smaller Bush Basil originally from Chile (*Ocimum minimum* L), make excellent pot or window-box herbs, and can only be grown indoors in cooler, temperate climates in winter.

The common name is an abbreviation of *basilikon phuton*, Greek for kingly herb. A related plant, *Ocimum sanctum* L, is still considered kingly or holy by the Hindus.

Description Much-branched aromatic annual 30–60 cm tall, with glabrous entire or slightly serrate ovate leaves 3–5 cm long; often slightly reddish in colour. Flowers small, white, or purplish, in whorls of 6 flowers on open terminal racemes. Appearing mid-summer to mid-autumn.

Distribution Native to southern Asia, Iran, Middle East. Naturalized in parts of Africa and some Pacific Islands. Introduced elsewhere in subtropical zones.

Cultivation Rarely wild. Cultivated commercially in central and southern Europe, North Africa, Asia, and in subtropical America. Wide

horticultural cultivation as a culinary herb. Propagate from seed sown in early summer, or after frost danger, on moist, well-drained, medium-rich soil in full sun. Varieties exist with somewhat different aromas.

Constituents Essential oil comprising mainly estragol (present also in French and Russian Tarragons); also eugenol, lineol and linalol; sometimes thymol; tannins; basil camphor. Antispasmodic and other actions due to the oil content.

Uses (fresh leaf) Antispasmodic; galactagogue; stomachic; carminative; mild sedative.

May be employed in a wide range of simple gastro-intestinal complaints; particularly for stomach cramps and vomiting. Its weak sedative action may be used in the treatment of nervous headaches or anxiety.

Mainly used for culinary purposes in soups, salads, fish and meat dishes; particularly compatible with tomatoes.

Dried powdered leaf once taken as snuff. Basil oil, obtained by steam distillation, is used as a commercial flavouring and in perfumery as a substitute for mignonette scent.

Oenothera biennis L ONAGRACEAE
Evening Primrose Evening Star

Evening Primrose has recently received attention from pharmaceutical concerns who discovered that it possesses a compound capable of reducing the rate of blood clotting or thrombus formation, and hence possibly acting as a prophylactic against some forms of heart attack.

This is an American native introduced to Europe in 1619 via the Padua Botanic Garden, and is now well established in parts of Europe. It has never been extensively used even in folk medicine.

The name *Oenothera* is of uncertain provenance but it may come from an older Greek plant name which signified that its roots were eaten to promote the appetite for wine. As late as the nineteenth century in Germany, pickled *O. biennis* roots were still eaten as an aperitif.

The less well-known common name Evening Star is derived from the fact that the petals emit phosphorescent light at night.

Description Biennial, or occasionally annual, producing, on thick yellowish conical root, compressed rosette of obtuse basal leaves to 60 cm diameter, from which arise much-branched reddish, rough stems to 1.25 m bearing alternate, lanceolate to ovate, entire, shortly petiolate leaves 4 cm long. Flowers very fragrant, 3–5 cm diameter, yellow, erect on spikes, 4-petalled, opening in the evening. Appearing mid-summer to mid-autumn.

Distribution North American native. Introduced and naturalized in Europe. In wastelands especially on dry, sandy or stony soils such as railway embankments.

Cultivation Wild. May be propagated from seed sown as soon as ripe, usually in late summer, in a permanent position. Tolerates most soils in a sunny position. Readily self-sown. Several varieties exist including large-flowered and hairy forms.

Constituents (seed) Unsaturated fatty acids;

unknown anticoagulant substances.
(whole plant) Tannins; mucilage; resin; bitter principle; potassium salts.

Uses (fresh whole plant, fresh root, seeds) Antispasmodic; nutritive; demulcent; weak astringent; vulnerary; anticoagulent. May be applied externally as a poultice or in ointments in the treatment of minor wounds or skin eruptions, and used internally for coughs, colds, gastric irritation and intestinal spasm. A direct effect on the liver is suspected but not proven.

Young roots can be boiled or pickled, and can be eaten hot or cold; all parts of the plant are edible.

Olea europaea L OLEACEAE
Olive

The Olive is well known from frequent references in the Bible and in the writings of the Greeks and Romans, to whom it symbolized peace.

It has been in cultivation for more than 3000 years and for this reason many different varieties now exist; some providing oil and others the large fruit so frequently used in salads and with drinks.

The ancient Egyptians called the plant *bak*, while the Romans knew it as *olea* from *oleum* meaning oil, after the large quantity of this important commodity which may be extracted from the fruit.

Description Evergreen tree usually to 8 m, and occasionally to 12 m. Branches pale grey, thin, thornless, bearing opposite, entire, lanceolate or oblong leaves, dark green above and lighter beneath; 3–7.5 cm long. Flowers fragrant, numerous, off-white, borne on short panicles in leaf axils, followed by dark purple fruit (drupe) 1.5–4 cm long.

Distribution Native to mediterranean region; introduced elsewhere.

Cultivation Wild only as an escape. The wild parent of the Olive is considered to be *Olea europaea* var. *oleaster* DC, which may be differentiated by its thorny branches, wider leaves and smaller fruit. Cultivated commercially and domestically on a wide scale in the Iberian Peninsula, North Africa, southern France, Greece, Italy and the Middle East. Propagated by grafting or from suckers; fruiting begins in the second year of growth.

Constituents (fruit) Oil (to 70%) comprising mainly glycerides of oleic acid, also glycerides of palmitic, stearic, myristic and linoleic acids; protein; mineral salts, particularly calcium; organic acids; vitamins A B_1 B_2 and PP (nicotinamide or B_3).

Uses (oil, fruit, occasionally fresh leaves) Nutritive; demulcent; mildly purgative; antiseptic; weakly astringent.

The oil is used internally as a physical laxative in chronic constipation, and as it reduces the flow of gastric secretions it has been used to

treat peptic ulcers. Externally it may be applied as a liniment or embrocation for a variety of purposes, particularly as the vehicle for more active substances.

The leaves possess antiseptic activity and have been used in a decoction for wound treatment. They may also have some antipyretic and hypotensive activity.

For medicinal purposes the oil should be extracted by the 'cold press' method to retain its active ingredients.

The fruit is of considerable commercial importance in the food industry.

The oil is of culinary importance and is also used in soap manufacture.

Ophioglossum vulgatum L OPHIOGLOSSACEAE
Adder's Tongue

Both the common and botanical names refer to the distinctive shape of this small fern's leaves from the Greek *ophis* meaning snake and *glossa* meaning tongue. Once famous as a wound-healing herb it is now only of historical interest.

Description Fern, on small, yellow, fibrous root-stock; to 20 cm tall. Stem solitary, arising from root-stock crown, round, hollow and succulent, expanding at 5–10 cm above ground level into broad, leathery, concave,

oval leaf blade which sheaths the stalk of the fertile spike; the latter usually 2–5 cm long and rising above the leaf blade. Spores ripen early to mid-summer.

Distribution Europe, North Africa, Asia and America. On grassland, pastures, scrub and fens.

Cultivation Wild plant.

Constituents Unknown.

Uses (fresh leaf, fresh juice) Vulnerary.

Formerly an ingredient of wound healing ointments, and once used internally for the same purpose. Not used today.

Origanum majorana L LABIATAE
Sweet Marjoram Knotted Marjoram/ Annual Marjoram

Also classified botanically as *Majorana hortensis* Moench. it has been cultivated in Europe for many centuries for its culinary and medicinal value. *Majorana* or *maiorana* is a very old name of unknown derivation by which the plant was known when first introduced to Europe in the Middle Ages. The common name Knotted Marjoram refers to the unusual knot-like shape of the spherical, clustered flower spikes. This plant is one of the most important of all western culinary herbs and its use in meat flavouring is emphasized by the German name *Wurstkraut* or sausage herb.

Description Spicy aromatic perennial (usually grown as an annual or biennial), 30–60 cm tall, with square, branched, tomentose stems; sometimes occurring as a subshrub. Leaves elliptic, entire or toothed, petiolate, opposite, greyish-pubescent, 0.75–3 cm long. Flowers small and insignificant, white to pink, in spherical clustered spikes, 3–5 per cluster. Appearing late summer to mid-autumn.

Distribution Native to North Africa, Middle East, parts of India. Introduced and naturalized in south-west Africa, mediterranean region, central Europe and North America. On dryish or well-drained, nutrient-rich soils, in sunny positions.

Cultivation Wild. Impermanently established in parts of central Europe. Cultivated commercially in Asia, America, central Europe and the mediterranean region. Grown horticulturally

as a perennial in warm regions or as a half-hardy annual in cooler temperate zones; sensitive to frost. In north-west Europe and North America sow seed in late spring or early summer, on medium-rich, finely prepared soil, later thinning to 25 cm apart; or raise under glass and plant out when hardened off.

Constituents Essential oil (to 2%) comprising terpineol, borneol and other terpenes (to 40%); mucilage; bitter substances; tannic acid.

Uses (fresh or dried flowering plant) Weak expectorant; antispasmodic; carminative; choleretic; aromatic; weak hypotensive; antiseptic.

Useful in most simple gastro-intestinal disorders, and an excellent digestive aid. Similar external uses to Oregano (*Origanum vulgare*).

Very wide culinary use; particularly in meat dishes, but must be added only in the last 10 minutes of cooking.

Employed as a tisane.

May be used in domestic cosmetic waters, and scented articles.

Origanum onites L LABIATAE
Pot Marjoram

This is also known as *Majorana onites* Benth. from the classical name *onitin* used by Pliny in the first century. This species was not cultivated very widely in north-west Europe or America, and was only introduced to Great Britain in the eighteenth century. Pot Marjoram is inferior to Sweet Marjoram and is now only cultivated as an alternative in areas too cold for *O. majorana*, or where the decorative perennial variegated variety is required for ornamental purposes.

Description Aromatic perennial on erect tomentose or hirsute stems to 30 cm tall; leaves serrate, sessile, tomentose and usually ovate, 0.75–2.5 cm long. Flowers small, white to pink, in numerous ovoid spikelets arranged in a

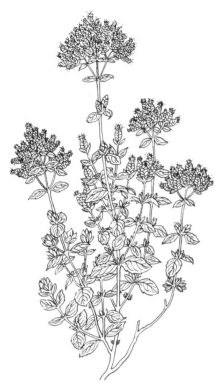

cluster. Appearing late summer to mid-autumn.

Distribution Native to Sicily, south-east Europe, Syria and Asia Minor. Prefers full sun and light well-drained soils in open positions and hillsides. Tolerates most conditions.

Cultivation Wild. Cultivated in cooler climates as a semi-hardy alternative to *O. majorana*; from cuttings in early summer, root division in spring or autumn, or from seed sown 1 cm deep in light, dry soil in late spring (germination may be slow or poor). Variegated forms exist. In very cold positions grow in pots and keep in a cool greenhouse during winter.

Constituents Essential oil (to 1%), comprising terpenes; also bitter substances; tannic acid.

Uses (fresh or dried flowering plant) Not used for medicinal purposes.

Employed in cooking as a substitute for Sweet Marjoram, although its flavour is inferior. Variegated forms may be used as garden ornamentals.

Origanum vulgare L LABIATAE

Oregano Wild Marjoram

Although Wild Marjoram is now cultivated commercially in some parts of the world, most supplies are still collected from the wild in the mediterranean region, and particularly in southern Italy. The nature of both the volatile oil composition and to some extent the plant's appearance depends on where it is cultivated. The southern European product is far more pungent and bears little resemblance in flavour to that from the cooler north.

The generic name *Origanum* is from the Greek *oros* and *ganos* meaning mountain glamour, or joy of the mountain, after the attractive appearance and aroma of the bushy flowering plant; *vulgare* means common.

Description Erect hairy aromatic perennial, frequently bushy, on horizontal root-stock, to 75 cm tall. Leaves glabrous, opposite and decussate, entire or obscurely toothed, petiolate, pointed, broadly ovate 1.5–4.5 cm long, upper leaves often reddish. Flowers rose-purple, sometimes pink to whitish, 6–8 mm long, bracteoles purple, borne on short spikes or corymbose clusters, appearing late summer to mid-autumn.

Distribution European native; also in Iran, Middle East and Himalayas. Introduced to Far East. On dry, usually calcareous or gravelly but nutrient-rich soils in warm positions; especially hedgebanks, woodland clearings and peripheries, roadsides; to 2000 m altitude.

Cultivation Wild. Collected commercially in southern Italy, cultivated commercially in North America. Propagate from seed sown in late spring on warm site, later thinning to 30 cm apart. Several forms exist including a variegated form with golden leaves.

Constituents Essential oil (0.5%) comprising thymol (to 15%), origanene, carvacrol; bitter principles; tannic acid; resins.

Uses (dried flowering plant, occasionally oil) Expectorant; antiseptic; antispasmodic; carminative; tonic; stomachic; anti-inflammatory.

Useful specifically for gastro-intestinal or respiratory disorders; particularly coughs associated with upper respiratory tract infection, and colic or indigestion. May be used externally in baths, inhalants or poultices where an antiseptic action is required. Weakly sedative and of some benefit in nervous headaches or irritability. Aids digestion.

Wide commercial and domestic culinary use as a flavouring, especially in meat dishes and stuffings.

Oil and herb used in cosmetic industry.

May be used as a tisane (*Thé Rouge*); once used to flavour beer.

Oxalis acetosella L OXALIDACEAE

Wood Sorrel Irish Shamrock

Oxalis is from the Greek for sour, after the taste of this small attractive herb which contains quite high concentrations of oxalic acid and its salts. It was cultivated from at least the fourteenth century as a major sauce herb, but it was displaced after the introduction of the unrelated French Sorrel (*Rumex scutatus* L).

Description Stemless perennial on scaly rhizome,

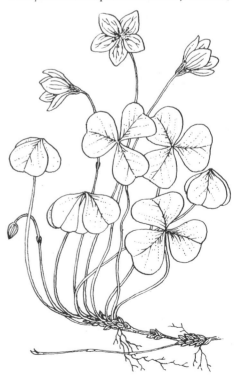

reaching 5–8 cm. Pale green leaves composed of 3 obcordate leaflets on long petiole. Flowers 5-petalled, white tinged with purple veins and yellow flecks at corolla base, solitary on long peduncles; appearing late spring to early summer.

Distribution Native to Europe, north and central Asia, Japan; introduced elsewhere. On acidic, humus-rich moist soils in mixed or deciduous woodland shade, to 2000 m.

Cultivation Wild plant. Cultivated by root division in spring.

Constituents Oxalic acid and potassium oxalate, to which the taste is due; mucilage; vitamin C.

Uses (fresh leaves and root-stock) Diuretic; weakly antipyretic.

Once used internally as a spring tonic (especially in Iceland), in fevers, and after excess alcohol consumption. Now principally used as an external application for the treatment of scabies, and as a gargle. Small quantities only of the leaves may be used in salads or sauces.

Contra-indications Large quantities are POISONOUS. To be avoided by those predisposed to gout, rheumatism or renal calculi.

Paeonia officinalis L PAEONIACEAE
Peony Common Peony

The Peony was first used very early in medical history and is named after Paeon, the physician of the Greek gods. Known as *paeonia*, it was included in many very early medicinal recipes and one, accredited to Pliny, combined this herb with Mint (*Mentha* spp.) and Chick Pea (*Cicer arietinum* L) for the specific treatment of both kidney and bladder stones, which, it was claimed, the mixture would dissolve.

After the sixteenth century the medicinal status of *P. officinalis* declined rapidly in Western folk medicine, but the herb is still retained in Chinese traditional medicine today.

Description Perennial on thick, knotted, dark, root-stock, producing stout succulent stem 60 cm–1 m tall. Leaves biternate or ternate, with ovate-lanceolate leaflets, 3 cm wide, dark green above and lighter beneath. Single red, or occasionally pink or whitish, flower; large and attractive and composed of 8 petals and 5 petal-like sepals, to 20 cm diameter. Appearing early summer to early autumn.

Distribution Native to southern Europe from France to Albania, and western Europe. Widely introduced as garden ornamental elsewhere.

Cultivation Wild. Propagated by division of root-stock in early autumn or from seed sown in spring on deeply-dug, well-manured soil. Once established, it must not be moved. Several forms exist, including *Alba plena*, *Rubra plena* and *Rosea plena*.

Constituents Benzoic acid (5%) l-asparagin; essential oil; an alkaloid; a ketone, paeonol; a heteroside. The alkaloid is vasoconstrictive; stimulates uterine contractions, and may increase blood coagulation.

Uses (dried root-stock) Vasoconstrictor; antispasmodic; diuretic; sedative; emmenagogue. Formerly used specifically in the treatment of both renal and gall-bladder calculi. Also once used for a variety of other conditions including those of a nervous origin, gastric disorders, varicose veins and haemorrhoids. May be effective in the latter condition, but now rarely used.

Contra-indications POISONOUS, the flowers especially so. Only to be used by medical personnel.

Panax pseudoginseng Wallich ARALIACEAE
Ginseng

Ginseng is so well known in both the East and West that it has become the most widely used of all medicinal herbs. The Koreans and Chinese have employed it as a panacea for centuries. This is reflected in its botanical name, *Panax* from *pan* meaning all, and *akos* meaning remedy. It was so highly prized in the Orient that not only did emperors monopolize the rights to harvest the roots, but wars were fought over them.

The word *Ginseng* is derived from *Jin-chen* or *Schin-seng*, meaning man root or like a man, after the peculiar human shape of the root. In commerce various grades exist depending on shape, age and colour. Red Korean Ginseng is one of the most expensive and sought-after types, and Ginseng production in Korea is carefully controlled by the government.

The wide range of effects on human physiology claimed by Chinese physicians have only recently been tentatively acknowledged by Western pharmacologists who have created a new term, adaptogen, to explain the normalizing effect of the active ingredients.

Panax pseudoginseng was formerly classified as *P. ginseng* C. A. Mey and *P. schinseng* Nees. Russian scientists claim that another member of the Araliaceae family, *Eleutherococcus senticosus* or Siberian Ginseng, possesses similar adaptogenic properties to Ginseng.

A related species, *Panax fruticosum* L, is used in some Polynesian Islands as both a food and medicine.

Description Perennial 60–80 cm tall on aromatic, frequently bifurcated, spindle-shaped root-stock; bearing persistent fleshy scales at stem base. Single erect stem, unbranched and reddish, bearing whorl of 3 or 5 palmate leaves, the leaflet thin, finely serrate, gradually acuminate, 8–13 cm long. Flowers greenish-yellow, small, few, in single terminal peduncled umbel; appearing mid to late summer and followed by bright red drupe-like berry on elongated peduncle.

Distribution Native to China (Manchuria) and Korea. In damp, cool, humus-rich woodland.

Cultivation Wild, but becoming rare. Cultivated on an increasing scale commercially in Korea and China, from seed and carefully selected seedlings, by a complex horticultural procedure involving specially prepared seed-beds, transplantation and shading. Harvested up to 9 years after planting.

Constituents Volatile oils, comprising sapogenin and pañacen (stimulating the central nervous system); a saponin, panaxin; panax acid; ginsenin (with hypoglycaemic activity); a glycoside, panaquilon (acting as a vasoconstrictive stimulant); ginsennosides; phytosterols; hormones; vitamins B_1 and B_2; mucilage; several other substances; all combining to produce a complex total effect.

Uses (dried root) Tonic; adaptogenic.
Used in a very wide range of conditions, but particularly of benefit where increased mental

and physical efficiency is required, or where the patient is exposed to internal and external physiological stress factors – such as ageing, surgery or disease.

Contra-indications Large doses may cause depression, insomnia and nervous disorders. Do not combine with any herbal remedies containing iron, or with Indian or China teas (*Camellia* spp.).

Panax quinquefolium L ARALIACEAE
American Ginseng
This has the same general properties as *Panax pseudoginseng*, its Oriental relative, and from 1718, when first exported to China by Canadian Jesuits, until the end of the nineteenth century it was so heavily collected that it is now practically unknown in its natural wild habitat. Most supplies are today cultivated in Wisconsin and exported to the East; some probably return to the United States and Europe fraudulently described as the more expensive Chinese or Korean root. There is little evidence that any North American Indian tribes beside the Chippewas or Ojibwas used the herb to the same extent as the Chinese.
Description Perennial .12.5–45 cm tall on aromatic, occasionally bifurcated, spindle-shaped root-stock, bearing thin scales at stem base which are shed during growth. Stem simple, erect, unbranched and reddish, bearing whorl of 3 or 5 palmate leaves; the leaflets obovate, thin, coarsely serrate, abruptly acuminate, 8–13 cm long. Flowers pink, small, few, in single terminal, peduncled umbel; appearing late summer and followed by a cluster of red drupe-like berries on elongated peduncle.

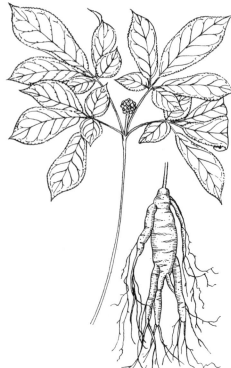

Distribution North American native from Quebec to Minnesota. Exclusively in cool, humus-rich woodlands.
Cultivation Formerly wild. Now extremely rare. Cultivated commercially in the same way as *Panax pseudoginseng*.
Constituents Similar to *Panax pseudoginseng* Wallich.
Uses (dried root) Tonic; adaptogenic. Similar to *Panax pseudoginseng* Wallich.

Papaver rhoeas L PAPAVERACEAE
Corn Poppy Field Poppy/Flanders Poppy
Corn Poppy petals have been collected as a colouring agent since at least the fifteenth century, and were employed from the earliest times as a medicine. *P. dubium* L is often substituted for this species, its action being similar.
Description Slender erect branched annual to 90 cm; hairy stem bearing deeply pinnate, sessile, short leaves with lanceolate segments. Flowers to 5 cm diameter, solitary, deep red with purplish flecks at the base (occasionally white), on long peduncles. Appearing early to late summer, followed by ovoid capsule.
Distribution Native to Europe and Asia, naturalized in North America and introduced elsewhere. In fields, arable land, on roadsides, especially after soil disturbance. On either chalky soils or loam, in warm positions; to 1700 m altitude.
Cultivation Wild plant.
Constituents (flower) Pigments comprising the anthocyanins, mecocyanin and cyanidol; mucilage; traces of the crystalline alkaloids, rhoeadine, rhoeagenine and rhoearubine.
Uses (fresh, dried flowers rarely) Sedative; antispasmodic; diaphoretic.
Of benefit in colic, anxiety, tonsillitis, bron-

chitis and particularly irritable coughs. Principally used as a colouring agent for medicine and wine.
Seed is sprinkled on bread, biscuits and cakes. Poppy seed oil is used in cooking.

Papaver somniferum L PAPAVERACEAE
Opium Poppy
The abuse of this medicinal plant and its products has caused considerable human misery and a great deal of governmental effort has gone into controlling its cultivation and distribution.
America and other nations have recently attempted to dissuade Turkish farmers, for example, from cultivating it on so large a scale, for it presents a formidable problem of drug abuse – and is therefore an extremely lucrative crop.
The Opium Poppy has, however, provided the greatest of all pain killers, morphine – a substance which has not been artificially synthesized – and opium which has been employed in medicine in the eastern mediterranean, the Middle East and western Asia, since the earliest times. Extraction of the opium or latex is achieved by cutting the green capsule with a small sharp implement and scraping off the soft material which will exude within the following 24 hours.
Opium syrup was particularly advocated in the treatment of coughs by an eleventh-century Arabian physician, Mesue, and as late as the seventeenth century this preparation was still widely known as *Syrupus de Meconio Mesuae*.
The plant's specific name *somniferum* means sleep inducing.
Description Glaucous annual from 60 cm–1.25 m tall; stem rigid, seldom branched and then

only at the base, sometimes slightly hairy; bearing glossy, cordate, unequal, coarsely dentate leaves, 10–25 cm long, the upper leaves usually clasping. Flowers 4-petalled, 7.5–10 cm wide, entire, of variable colour; usually white or lilac with pink or purple markings. Sometimes red or purple. Appearing late summer to early autumn and followed by ovoid, glabrous, then woody, capsules.

Distribution Native to Middle East, south-east Europe, western Asia. Introduced elsewhere. On shallow loamy or chalky soils in sunny situations; especially wasteland as escape.

Cultivation Cultivated plant, especially in Turkey, India and China. Occasionally wild as an escape. Possibly derived from *Papaver setigerum* and developed by centuries of cultivation. Seed is mixed with 4 parts of sand and sown from mid-autumn to late spring; thinning to 25 cm apart.

Constituents (capsules) At least 25 alkaloids mainly comprising morphine (0.1–0.3%), also codeine, papaverine, narcotine, meconic acid, thebaine, narceine. (latex) 25% alkaloid content, and 12% morphine; (seeds) Oil (to 60%); lecithin.

Uses (dried latex, ripe seeds, seed oil) Narcotic; sedative. Opium has traditionally been used in the relief of pain, diarrhoea and certain forms of cough, and is now the source of purified morphine and other pain-killing alkaloidal drugs. An infusion made from powdered capsules of the Poppy was once applied externally to sprains and bruises.

Ripe seed (which does not contain harmful substances) may be used in curries or sprinkled on bread and cakes. The seed oil provides two products: a culinary oil (olivette), and an artists' oil.

Dried capsules are used in dried flower arrangements.

Contra-indications DANGEROUS. To be used only by medical personnel.

Parietaria diffusa Mert. & Koch URTICACAE
Pellitory of the Wall Pellitory
This plant has been used for centuries and was described as a medicinal plant by Pliny and as a vegetable by Theophrastus.

It is commonly found on ruins and old walls, hence its name *parietaria* from the Latin *paries* meaning a wall. As it was a favourite of the apothecaries and herbalists – who used it almost exclusively for urinary complaints – it was formerly an official herb and therefore classified as *P. officinalis* L.

Pellitory contains an unusually large quantity of sulphur.

Description Perennial with reddish, hairy stems, erect and spreading or sometimes decumbent; 20–75 cm tall. Leaves alternate, petiolate, entire, ovate to lanceolate, mostly acuminate, softly hairy. Flowers greenish, unisexual, female terminal, male lateral; appearing mid-summer to mid-autumn.

Distribution European native. Beneath or in the crevices of old walls; occasionally in hedgerows. To 700 m altitude.

Cultivation Wild. May be grown on low stone walls. Divide root-stock in mid-spring, plant in cracks with peaty soil.

Constituents Sulphur; tannic acid; bitter principles; flavones; potassium and calcium salts; mucilage. Diuretic action due to the presence of potassium salts and flavones.

Uses (dried or fresh flowering plant) Demulcent; diuretic.

Employed in the treatment of cystitis, with or without bladder stones, and less frequently in pyelitis. The fresh plant is much more effective than the dried herb.

Contra-indications To be avoided by hay fever sufferers; this is one of several species shown to cause allergic rhinitis and possibly hypersensitivity pneumonitis.

Passiflora incarnata L PASSIFLORACEAE
Passion Flower Maypop
Passiflora species are predominantly of subtropical American origin, and several have been employed traditionally for a variety of complaints. This herb was introduced in 1867 in the United States for its effective sedative properties, and has been retained in certain national pharmacopoeias; it is also a popular folk medicine and constituent of some proprietary herbal sedative preparations.

Passion-flower, from the Latin, *passiflora*, is named after the supposed symbolic association between the anatomical and numerical arrangement of the flowers and the elements of the crucifixion.

Description Perennial vine on strong, woody, hairy stem 6 m to 10 m tall, climbing by means of axillary tendrils. Leaves serrate, 3-lobed, cordate, petiolate, 7.5–12.5 cm long. Flowers attractive, white, with pink or purple calyx, 4–7.5 cm wide, appearing early to late summer and followed by edible, yellow, ovoid fruit 5 cm in diameter.

Distribution Native to southern United States. Introduced to Bermuda and elsewhere. On

loamy, nutrient-rich soils in full sun.
Cultivation Wild. Occasionally cultivated; the commercial sources of the edible passion fruit or Granadilla are *Passiflora edulis* Sims, or less commonly *P. ligularis* Juss. *P. caerulea* L is the most common species grown as a climbing shrub in warmer temperate zones.
Constituents (fruit) Ascorbic acid; flavonoids; citric and malic acids; amylopectin; fixed oil. (flowering plant) Alkaloids comprising harmine, harmol, passiflorine; a cyanogenic heteroside; flavonoids; passiflortannoid; maracugin.
Uses (dried fruiting and flowering tops, fruit) Antispasmodic; sedative; anodyne.
Principally of benefit in the treatment of nervous tachycardia, anxiety and insomnia; also used in certain types of convulsion or spasmodic complaints such as epilepsy. Its anodyne effects are employed in various neuralgias.
The fruit is edible, refreshing, tonic and employed in commercial drinks in some countries.
Contra-indications Sedative. To be taken only under medical supervision.

Pastinaca sativa L UMBELLIFERAE
Parsnip Wild Parsnip

The Parsnip (a fourteenth-century name) was once a major Roman foodstuff being called *pastinacea* after the Latin word *pastus* for food. It was largely replaced by the Carrot in the eleventh century, probably because of dangers of mistaking it for related but poisonous species of the Umbelliferae family.
Description Thick-rooted biennial, 50–120 cm tall, with hairy, robust, grooved stem becoming hollow. Leaves pinnate or bipinnate with ovate or oblong, sessile, toothed leaflets 5–10 cm long. Greenish yellow flowers in compound umbels appearing mid to late summer.
Distribution Eurasian native. Naturalized in

New Zealand, Australia, North America and Uruguay and introduced elsewhere. In deep nitrogenous or calcareous soils on wasteland and meadows. To 1000 m.
Cultivation Wild plant. Extensive commercial cultivation for the edible root, especially the cultivar *P. sativa* var. *sativa hortensis* Ehrh. Requires deeply dug loamy soil. Sow seed in spring and lift root in autumn.
Constituents (root): Protein; starch; vitamin C (0.03%); pectin; essential oil; a furo-coumarin, bergaptene (to 0.2%).
Uses (fresh leaf, root) Diuretic; aromatic; nutritive; mild sedative.
Traditionally employed in urinary disorders as a diuretic, and to promote appetite.
Principally used as a root vegetable; the leafy tops may be cooked and eaten. Root extract employed to flavour schnapps.
Contra-indications May cause photodermatoses; gloves should be worn when handling leaves.

Pelargonium graveolens L'Hérit GERANIACEAE
Rose Geranium Pelargonium

In the rose-scented geranium group the species most commonly cultivated in temperate gardens and homes is *P. graveolems*. Other species which are grown commercially as sources of oil of Geranium include *P. capitatum*, *P. radens* and *P. odoratissimum*; and these may be employed for similar domestic and culinary purposes.
Almost all scented Geraniums – or more correctly Pelargoniums – are South African natives. They were introduced to England from Cape Province in 1632 but were largely unknown until 1847 when their potential in perfumery was recognized by the French. Oil of Geranium is an essential ingredient of certain perfumes for men, and some of the finest quality used for this purpose comes from Rhodesia and Réunion.
Pelargonium is derived from the Greek for stork's bill after the fruit's shape.
Description Bushy aromatic perennial, becoming woody, to 1 m. Leaves long-petioled, hairy, 5–7 lobed, circular to cordate-ovate, margins dentate. Flowers 2.5 cm wide, pink, unscented, sessile or nearly so, on short-peduncled, dense umbels.
Distribution South African native. Introduced elsewhere. On dryish, well-drained, loamy soils in full sun.
Cultivation Wild. Widely cultivated as a house plant. Cultivated commercially in the warmer south-west mediterranean region, central and southern Africa and Réunion. In cooler temperate zones grow as tender perennial, sinking pots in the garden during the summer, and bringing plants indoors before threat of frost. Easily propagated from cuttings taken in late summer and struck in a peat and sand mix. Several cultivars exist, and the aroma varies from lemon to apple.
Constituents Volatile oil, comprising mainly geraniol, also linalol, geranyl tiglate, citronellol, citronella forminate and iso-menthone.
Uses (fresh or dried leaf, oil) Aromatic; astringent. Not used medicinally in Europe; in Africa the roots of certain *Pelargonium* species are employed in the treatment of diarrhoea.

Fresh leaves can be added to cakes before baking; to sweet fruit dishes, and cold summer dishes.
The oil is of importance in the perfumery industry, and is often used as a substitute for oil of Rose.
Dried leaves may be employed in a variety of scented articles, and cosmetic bath preparations.
An attractive house plant.

Petasites hybridus (L) Gaertn., May & Scherb. COMPOSITAE
Butterbur Bog Rhubarb

The botanical name is derived from the Greek *petasos*, meaning a large Greek hat that was thought to resemble the shape of the Butterbur leaf. In French the plant is known as *chapeau du diable* – devil's hat.
The common name Butterbur may indicate that butter was once wrapped in these large leaves.
In 1685 Schröder described several preparations from this plant for use against the Plague: they included the juice extracted from the root; an alcoholic extract; the fresh leaves and flowers; and an oil distilled from the whole plant. Butterbur is now only seldom used in folk medicine.
Description Semi-aquatic perennial on thick, creeping, pinkish rhizome. Flowers appear before the leaves, from mid-spring to early summer, on 10–40 cm long, stout, scaly, hollow, purplish stems. Male and female flowers appear on different plants; both flowers are a pinkish violet on spike-like racemes, but the former are 7–12 mm wide and short-stalked, and the latter are 3–6 mm wide and long-stalked. Leaves, appearing towards the end of flowering, are large, 10–90 cm wide, long stalked, woolly underneath, deeply cordate and roundish.
Distribution European native; on wet, calcareous and stony soils, beside streams, rivers, in ditches or flooded pasture.
Cultivation Wild.
Constituents Inulin; helianthenine; tannic acid; mucilage; an essential oil; petasine and

petasitine; an alkaloid.

Uses (dried rhizome, occasionally fresh or dried flowers and leaves) Vulnerary; astringent; weak diuretic; expectorant; antispasmodic; weak emmenagogue.

Principally used homeopathically in the treatment of neck pains and headache. Fresh leaves and flowers may be applied as a poultice to wounds. Rhizome may be employed in combination with other inulin-containing remedies for certain eruptive skin conditions. Once used as an antispasmodic in coughs, urinary tract infections and for stammering.

Petroselinum crispum (Mill.) Nyman
UMBELLIFERAE
Parsley
The Greeks differentiated between Marsh Celery or Smallage (*heleio selinon*) and Rock Celery or Parsley (*petros selinon*). Both types were associated with death and funerals and only later on in Roman times were they used as food. Pliny stated that every sauce and salad contained what was then known to the Romans as *apium* – or Parsley. Today Parsley is the best known of all garnishing herbs in the West, and a number of varieties exist. Columella (A.D. 42) was the first to mention a curly form – the type now favoured in English-speaking countries. It lacks, however, the hardiness of plain-leaved varieties, though it is less likely to be confused with the highly poisonous Fool's Parsley (*Aethusa cynapium*). At least three other forms are commonly cultivated: the Neapolitan or celery-leaved; the fern-leaved; and the Hamburg or turnip-rooted. Parsley root is still retained in the

Portugese, Yugoslavian and Czechoslovakian pharmacopoeias, and the seed is found in Swiss, French and Portugese pharmacopoeias. The botanical name for this herb has changed several times; it has previously been classified as *Petroselinum hortenso* Hoffm., *P. sativum* Hoffm., *Apium petroselinum* L, *A. crispum* Mill., and *Carum petroselinum* Benth.

Description Biennial or short-lived perennial on stout vertical taproot; stems solid, branching, to 75 cm tall (usually 30 cm). Leaves deltoid, pinnate, segments 1–2 cm long, cuneate-ovate, stalked, much curled (depending on cultivar). Flowers small, greenish-yellow or yellowish, in flat-topped, 2–5 cm wide compound umbels, appearing mid-summer to early autumn; followed by 2.5 mm long, ribbed, ovoid fruit.

Distribution Native to northern and central Europe. Introduced and naturalized elsewhere, including some subtropical zones (such as the West Indies).

Cultivation Wild. Extensively cultivated horticulturally and commercially. Propagate from seed sown in drills in early spring to early summer. Remove flower-heads to encourage leaf growth. Requires rich, moist, open soil in partial shade or full sun; a good watering during hot weather and protection under cloches during winter. Germination is often poor and slow (to 8 weeks) and may be encouraged by pouring boiling water in drills immediately after sowing. The plain-leaved varieties tolerate extremes of cold and dryness better than the curly-leaved varieties.

Constituents Essential oil comprising apiol, apiolin, myristicin, pinene; flavonoids; a glucoside; apiin; provitamin A; ascorbic acid. Action largely due to the apiol content of the essential oil, which stimulates the appetite and increases blood-flow to the digestive tract, uterus and mucosae.

Uses (fresh or dried leaves, dried root, dried seed, occasionally oil) Diuretic; emmenagogue; stomachic; carminative.

Effective in dysmenorrhoea, amenorrhoea, as a diuretic, anti-flatulent and to stimulate the appetite.

The use of the leaf for culinary purposes is well known. The leaf was formerly used as a tea (Parsley tea). May be chewed to destroy garlic odour on the breath. Dried stems of use as a green dye.

Contra-indications The oil should only be used under medical supervision. Very large doses of either the oil or the leaf may cause abortion. They may also cause polyneuritis. Apiol and myristicin can induce fatty degeneration of the liver, and gastro-intestinal haemorrhages.

Petroselinum crispum var. *tuberosum* Crovetto
UMBELLIFERAE
Turnip Rooted Parsley Hamburg Parsley
This variety of Parsley was probably first developed in Holland since it was once called Dutch Parsley. Fuchs described it as *oreoselinum* in Germany in the mid-sixteenth century, and the name Hamburg Parsley was used by Mawe in 1778. Philip Miller (1691–1771), the curator of the Chelsea Physic Garden, introduced it to England in 1727, but it was only

popular there for a century – from 1780 to 1880. The plant is still frequently found in France and Germany in vegetable markets.

It is also described botanically as *P. crispum* var. *radicosum* Bailey and *P. sativum* var. *tuberosum* Bernh.

Description Similar to *P. crispum* but leaf segments usually not curled or crisped, and taproot is fleshy, 5 cm wide and 12.5 cm long.

Distribution North and east European cultivated plant.

Cultivation Cultivated horticulturally and commercially particularly in Holland, France and Germany.

Seed is sown in early spring on deep, rich, well-dug soil; watered well during dry weather; and roots harvested from mid-autumn onwards. Frost resistant.

Constituents Similar to *P. crispum*; the root also contains bergapten.

Uses (cooked root) Not used medicinally. Cooked as a vegetable; or used in soup mixes. Flavour resembles both Celery and Parsley.

Peumus boldus Molina MONIMIACEAE
Boldo Boldu
This native of the Chilean Andes is still retained in several South American and European pharmacopoeias, and is employed predominantly for liver disease. The leaves, which are the only parts used in medicine, were first tested in Europe in 1869 by the French physician Dujardin-Baumez.

Other botanical names for Boldo, which is the local Chilean name, included *Boldoa fragrans* Gay and *Ruizia fragrans* Pavon.

Description Aromatic, dioecious, evergreen shrub 5–6 m tall; leaves shortly petiolate, grey-green, coriaceous, entire, somewhat revolute, ovate or elliptical, upper and lower surfaces slightly pubescent, upper surface covered with small papillae. Flowers small, pinkish, on open terminal racemes.

Distribution Chilean native. Introduced elsewhere. Especially on sunny slopes.

Cultivation Wild. Limited cultivation in Morocco and elsewhere.

Constituents Volatile oil (to 2%) comprising mainly eucalyptol, also ascaridol; alkaloids, comprising mainly boldine (to 0.1%); a glycoside, boldin (boldoglucin or boldina). Cholagogue action due to the presence of boldine. Antihelmintic action due to ascaridol.

Uses (dried leaves, occasionally bark) Cholagogue; choleretic; stomachic; sedative; diuretic; sternutatory; antihelmintic. Formerly used as a tonic where quinine was contraindicated; in rheumatism; and in certain urinary tract infections, including gonorrhoea. Of benefit in the treatment of hepatic congestion and gallstones; used to stimulate the secretion and release of bile, and hence to aid digestion, and as a tonic in gall-bladder disease. The powdered leaf may be used to induce sneezing.
The aromatic fruit pulp can be eaten.
Bark was once used in tanning.
Contra-indications Large doses cause vomiting.

Physalis alkekengi L SOLANACEAE
Bladder Cherry Chinese Lantern
Dioscorides called the herb *phusalis* or *strychnos halikakabos* and considered it a sedative. Although several other *Physalis* species are used for jams, they are now seldom of medicinal interest.
Description Perennial (often grown as annual) on creeping rhizome, reaching 20–110 cm. Leaves entire, ovate, petiolate to 8 cm. Flowers solitary, whitish, nodding, appearing early summer to late autumn and followed by red globose berry enclosed in paper-thin, orange-red calyx.
Distribution Native from central and south-east Europe and western Asia to Japan. On dry calcareous soils in vineyards and wasteland, to 1500 m altitude.
Cultivation Wild; frequently as a garden escape. Cultivated as an ornamental from seed sown as early as possible, or under glass. Requires warm position. Also propagated by division.
Constituents (fruit) Vitamin C; organic acids including malic and citric; a bitter substance, physaline; pectin; pectinase; glucose.

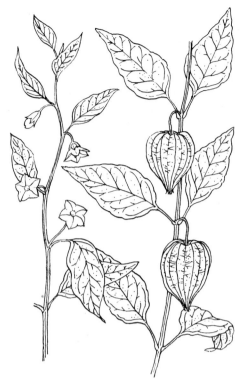

Uses (fruit, rarely leaves) Diuretic; antipyretic; mild sedative; nutritive; laxative. Formerly employed in the treatment of renal calculi, rheumatism, arthritis and gout. The fruit may be eaten in small quantities or used in jams, and the whole plant (except the root) is used in certain diuretic wines.
Contra-indications Large quantities may cause diarrhoea.

Physostigma venenosum Balfour LEGUMINOSAE
Calabar Bean Ordeal Bean/Esere Nut
Calabar Bean is named after the area in southeast Nigeria, and near to the modern Port Harcourt, where the plant is most commonly found.
It is known locally as *esere*, hence one of its common names – Esere Nut. The plant's cotyledons were once used in trials by ordeal in Africa in which the accused had to drink the powdered bean. An explanation for the fact that the innocent generally survived and the guilty died is that in the former case the entire quantity was drunk thereby inducing violent vomiting and purging which removed much of the poison; while the guilty person sipped the potion, allowing rapid absorption of the alkaloids from the gastro-intestinal tract and therefore subsequent death from cardiac arrest. It was introduced to Europe in 1840 by Daniell, and its medicinal properties were recognized in 1860. The plant has no place in modern medicine, and physostigmine (its chief constituent) has now largely been replaced by neostigmine.
Description Perennial on climbing woody stem (to 5 cm thick) reaching 15 m tall. Leaves large, ternate, pinnate; flowers purple, 3 cm wide, produced on long pendulous axillary racemes, each possessing 30 or more flowers; appearing early to mid-spring, and followed by

a dehiscent oblong pod 16 cm long, and containing 2 or 3 seeds to 3 cm long.
Distribution Native to west coast of Africa, especially Nigeria, Cameroun, Togo, Dahomey; introduced to Brazil and other tropical countries. On swampy river banks.
Cultivation Wild, and collected commercially in West Africa. Ripe seed germinated and plant grown in greenhouses in temperate zones.
Constituents Alkaloids comprising mainly eserine (physostigmine) to 0.3%, also calabarine; starch (to 50%); proteins (to 23%).
Uses (cotyledons from ripe seed) Miotic. Now used exclusively in opthalmology – to contract the pupil in the eye, and decrease intro-ocular

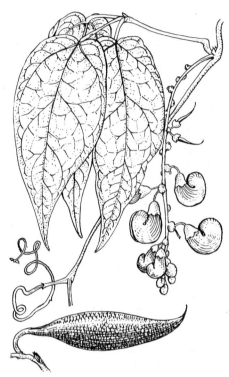

pressure in glaucoma. Formerly employed in tetanus and rheumatism. Used as a source of physostigmine, a parasympathomimetic alkaloid used in some of the above conditions and in the treatment of myasthenia gravis (a neuro-muscular disease), and to induce peristalsis in post-operative gastro-intestinal debility. Calabarine and physostigmine exert opposite effects; the action of the seed is therefore frequently different from that of pure alkaloids. Once used in veterinary medicine.
Contra-indications Very POISONOUS. Death may be caused by cardiac arrest or respiratory paralysis.

Phytolacca americana L PHYTOLACCACEAE
Poke Weed Poke Root/Pigeonberry
Phytolacca is derived from the Greek *phyton* meaning plant and the French *lac* (a reddish pigment), reflecting the berries' ability to produce a crimson dye.
The herb was introduced to American settlers by Indians to whom it was known as *pocan* or *cocum* and from which the name Poke Weed originates. Traditionally Poke Weed was used as an emetic and as a remedy for venereal

diseases, but by 1830 Geiger had discovered other medicinal attributes.

Because of its complex chemical constituents the herb has received considerable scientific attention, and among other things it has been shown to possess a mitogenic phytohaemagglutin called Poke Weed mitogen factor (PWM) which is employed for immunological purposes in modern medicine.

Another factor, which has the ability to destroy snails, is being examined in Africa as a possible agent to control the carrier of Bilharzia, a disease caused by a parasite which invades and destroys many body organs and which is contracted by washing in water containing certain snails.

Description Perennial with thick, smooth hollow purplish stem, 1.25–3.5 m tall, on large fleshy branched root. Leaves unpleasantly scented, petiolate, alternate, entire, ovate-lanceolate or oblong, 10–30 cm long, acute at both ends. Flowers white or sometimes pinkish, 7.5 mm wide, bisexual, on many-flowered terminal, then lateral, racemes from 5–20 cm long. Appearing late summer to mid-autumn and followed by purple-red, globose berries to 1 cm diameter.

Distribution North American native, from New England to Texas and Florida. Introduced elsewhere, particularly in the mediterranean region. Especially on rich, light soils in newly cleared land, field edges, roadsides.

Cultivation Wild. Cultivated on a market-garden scale in Carolina and elsewhere in the United States. Propagated from seed sown in spring or from root division in spring or autumn. Prefers sunny situation on deeply-dug, nutrient-rich, well-drained soils. A winter crop of vegetable leaf may be obtained by lifting roots in late autumn and planting closely in a box of damp peat, kept indoors; leaf may be cut when 15 cm long.

Constituents (root) Neutral principle, phytolaccin; alkaloidal substance, phytolaccine; phytolaccic acid; phytolaccatoxin (cyanchotoxin)

and a hydrolysis product, phytolaccagenin; jaligonic acid; carboxy and dicarboxy oleanenes; various steroids and saponins; potassium salts. (berries) Saponins (to 25%); mucilage; tannic acid; phytolaccinic acid; red pigment, caryophylline. (leaf) Anti-viral protein, called PAP and similar to interferon; rubber; fatty oil. Note: the exact chemical status and nature of phytolaccin and phytolaccine are not fully known.

Uses (dried root, occasionally young cooked leaves) Emetic; purgative: narcotic; sternutatory; molluscicidal; spermicidal; fungicide; anti-rheumatic; anti-catarrhal. Root principally used internally in the treatment of throat infections associated with swollen glands; acting particularly on the lymphatics. Also used in chronic rheumatism and upper respiratory tract infections. Externally it is applied as an ointment or poultice in fungal infections, ulcers, haemorrhoids and scabies. Juice from the berries was once applied externally to ulcers and tumours, but it is not very effective. In Hungary the root is employed as an abortifacient, and in Mauritius it is considered to be a sedative.

After special treatment the berries may be used to colour wine and confectionery. They have also been used as a colouring in artists' paint.

Contra-indications Toxic and dangerous; it should only be used by medical personnel. To remove harmful substances it is important to soak in salt water, and cook well with 2 changes of water. The use of the young cooked plant, however, is not advised. When handling the mature plant gloves should be worn. May cause haematological abnormalities, violent emesis and possibly death.

Picea abies (L) Karst. PINACEAE
Norway Spruce

Picea is the ancient Latin name for a tree which is now the most commonly planted conifer in North America and Europe. It yields a light but strong timber. Norway Spruce is locally employed in the manufacture of spruce beer by fermenting with yeast the leaves and twigs in a sugar solution.

Description Monoecious evergreen tree to 40 m tall; bark reddish brown, branches pendulous, pubescent or glabrous, bearing quadrangular leaves 14–18 mm long. Female cones cylindrical-oblong to 18 cm, woody and pendulous. Male cones catkin-like.

Distribution Central and north European native. Introduced elsewhere.

Cultivation Wild. Extensively grown for timber. Numerous horticultural cultivars used as ornamentals.

Constituents Resin comprising α – and β – picea-pimarolic, piceapimarinic and piceapimaric acids and juroresene; also volatile oil.

Uses (resin, Burgundy pitch, wood) Burgundy pitch was formerly used in counter-irritant plasters for the treatment of lumbago, rheumatism and chronic bronchitis.

Young tips (the spray) used in beer manufacture in north Europe.

The timber, white deal, is of great economic importance and a main source of paper pulp.

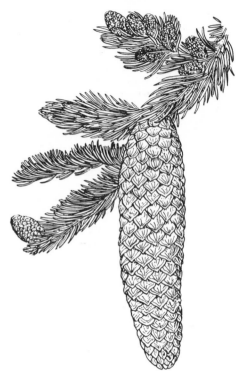

Picrasma excelsa (SW.) Planchon SIMARUBACEAE
Quassia Jamaican Quassia/Bitter Ash

Quassia was a generic name given by Linnaeus to *Quassia amara* L in honour of a Guyanan slave called Quassi who had used the wood from this 2 m-high shrub to treat fevers. *Quassia amara* L or the Bitter Wood of Surinam (Surinam Quassia) was therefore introduced to Europe (1756) and entered the London Pharmacopoeia in 1788.

By 1791 however the much larger, but closely related, West Indian tree, *Picrasma excelsa* (then known as *Quassia excelsa* Swartz) had been shown to possess very similar properties and this so-called Bitter Wood of Jamaica was imported to England. It replaced Surinam Quassia in the London Pharmacopoeia of 1809, but in several other countries – including Holland and Germany – *Quassia amara* has remained to this day the official Quassia. The Indians use another related plant, *Picrasma quassioides* Benn. for exactly the same purposes.

Description Ash-like tree to 20 m tall; leaves opposite, entire, unequally pinnate; the leaflets pointed at both ends, ovate. Flowers inconspicuous, greenish, appearing late autumn to early winter; followed by shiny black drupes.

Distribution Native to West Indies, particularly Jamaica (on lower mountains and plains), St Vincent and Antigua.

Cultivation Wild. Trees felled and sawn into logs 2 m long for export for quassia chip manufacture and for local pharmaceutical processing.

Constituents Resin comprising α- and β-piceasin, isoquassin (picrasmin) and neoquassin, to which the action is due.

Uses (stem wood) Bitter tonic; stomachic; insecticide. A powerful non-astringent bitter of benefit in loss of appetite due to gastric debility. Stimulates the gall-bladder and gastric secretions Once used as an enema to eradicate threadworm, and as an ingredient of lotions to destroy pediculi and other parasites. Roasted, powdered wood once employed as a Hop substitute to render ale bitter.

Infusions of Quassia chips, sweetened with sugar, or used alone, may be used as a fly killer. Of service as a horticultural insecticide destroying red spider, woolly aphids and greenfly.

Contra-indications Large doses irritate the stomach and cause vomiting.

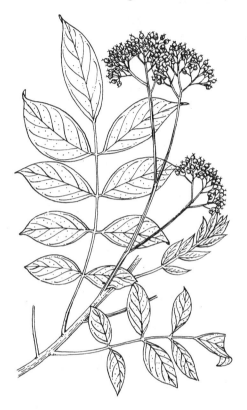

Pimenta dioica (L) Merr. MYRTACEAE
Allspice Pimento/Jamaica Pepper
Most of the European supplies of Allspice come from Jamaica where plantations of natural woodland consisting predominantly of these trees are called Pimento walks. The berries are harvested by hand when green and unripe. and then either sun or kiln-dried.

The name Pimento derives from the Spanish *pimienta* or *pimiento* meaning pepper, after the similarity in shape to peppercorns. *Pimienta* itself comes from the medieval term *pigmentum* meaning spicery.

The spice was first imported to Britain in the early seventeenth century and variously called *Pimienta de Chapa* and *Pimienta de Tabasco*, before Ray in 1693 described it as Allspice because of its combination of the flavours of cinnamon, nutmeg and cloves.

Botanically it has been classified as *Myrtus dioica* L, *M. pimenta* L, *Eugenia pimenta* DC, and *Pimenta officinalis* Lindl. – the last name emphasizing that the plant was included in the official British Pharmacopoeia from 1721 to 1914.

Description Aromatic evergreen tree to 12 m, resembling a large Myrtle; leaves petiolate,

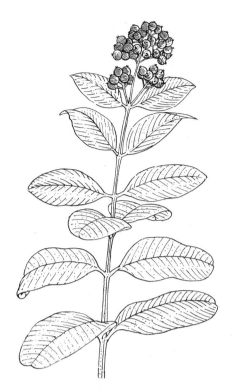

entire, glossy and leathery; oblong-lanceolate to 12.5 cm long. Flowers small (to 7.5 mm wide) white, in many-flowered cymes borne in the upper axils. Appearing mid-summer to early autumn and followed by dark brown, globose, 6 mm wide, 2-celled berries.

Distribution Native to Central America, Mexico, West Indies. Introduced to Indonesia. Prefers hilly environments on calcareous soils.

Cultivation Wild. Cultivated commercially in Central America; collected commercially in Jamaica. May be propagated by cuttings or layering, but in northern zones only grown as a non-flowering greenhouse ornamental.

Constituents Volatile oil (to 4.5%) comprising mainly eugenol (to 65%), also cineole, phellandrene, caryophyllene.

Uses (dried unripe berries, oil) Carminative; aromatic stimulant. Used as the source of oil of Pimento, which was once employed as a carminative. Powdered berries are of benefit in flatulence, dyspepsia and to disguise the taste of disagreeable medicines. They may also be incorporated in stimulant lotions and plasters. Principally used as a flavouring in rice, curries, puddings and cakes, and in pickling.

The tree provides wood which was once much used in the manufacture of umbrella handles and walking sticks.

Pimpinella anisum L UMBELLIFERAE
Anise Aniseed
Aniseed is one of the most ancient of spices and was cultivated by the Egyptians and later by the Greeks and Arabs. The early Arabic name was *anysum* from which was derived the Greek *anison* or *anneson* and the Latin *anisum*. Dioscorides considered that Egyptian Aniseed was second only to that grown in Crete.

In the Middle Ages it was largely used as a spice and as a carminative medicine, but it

also entered into the composition of several classic aphrodisiac mixtures. In recent years its use as a flavouring has declined because of its high cost, and it is often replaced by Chinese Anise (*Illicium verum* Hook).

Description Aromatic, pubescent annual on thin root, to 75 cm tall. Stems erect, bearing long-petiolate, simple, coarsely-toothed, reniform lower leaves, 2.5–5 cm long, and 2 or 3 lobed, cuneate, entire or toothed upper leaves. Flowers whitish, small, numerous in open, thin, compound umbels; appearing late summer to early autumn, and followed by brownish, ribbed, aromatic, ovate fruit.

Distribution Indigenous to Egypt, the Levant and parts of the eastern mediterranean. On dry poor soils in sunny situations.

Cultivation Wild, or occasionally wild as an escape. Widely cultivated commercially in many warm countries, particularly India, Turkey, south mediterranean region, Mexico, Chile and Soviet Union. Propagate from seed sown in spring, later thinning to 30 cm apart; cannot be transplanted successfully. Will not produce ripe seeds in cold northern zones.

Constituents (seed) Volatile oil (to 3.5%) comprising mainly anethole (to 85%), methyl chavicol (estragol) (to 15%); also fixed oil (to 20%); starch; choline; sugars; mucilage. Action mostly due to volatile oil content.

Uses (ripe seed, fresh leaf, occasionally oil) Mild expectorant; carminative; galactagogue; weak diuretic; laxative; antispasmodic.

Especially effective in flatulence or flatulent colic. Aids digestion and improves the appetite by promotion of gastric secretions. Stimulates the mammary gland secretions and acts as a cough suppressant. Used in the treatment of bronchial catarrh. Used in combination with other laxatives. Once employed in asthma powders.

The oil may be combined satisfactorily with

liquorice in cough lozenges, or used alone as an antiseptic.

Important in manufacturing industries as a flavouring for food, liqueurs. Fresh leaf may be used in salads. Seed is added to vegetable curries, or chewed to sweeten the breath. It is occasionally used in perfumery, for example. as a constituent of eau de Cologne.

Pimpinella saxifraga L UMBELLIFERAE
Burnet Saxifrage

This somewhat variable herb is widely distributed throughout much of Europe but was not certainly used by the ancients – although it may be the *kaukalis* which Dioscorides referred to in his writings.

German physicians used it particularly from the Middle Ages onwards and it appeared in a number of pharmacopoeias including those of Augsburg (1640), Württemberg (1741) and Prussia (1799–1829).

In seventeenth-century Germany is was an ingredient of 'magic powders'.

Description Perennial on unpleasantly smelling taproot. Stem 30–100 cm tall, strong, slightly hairy, finely furrowed; bearing few 1 or 2-pinnate leaves, with ovate to lanceolate segments, 1–2.5 cm long. Flowers white or pink in compound umbels to 5 cm diameter. Appearing late summer to early autumn.

Distribution Native to Europe, Middle East and Siberia. Introduced and naturalized in New Zealand and the United States. On dry, grassy, shallow, stony and calcareous soils in warm situations to 2500 m altitude.

Cultivation Wild.

Constituents Volatile oil (to 0.4%) comprising coumarinic substances including isopimpinellin and pimpinellin; saponosides; bitter principles; resin; tannic acid.

Uses (dried root, occasionally fresh root) Expectorant; vulnerary; diuretic; stomachic; antiseptic; weak galactagogue; weak sedative. May be used in combination with other remedies for genito-urinary infections. Alone it is of benefit in the treatment of respiratory tract catarrh, upper respiratory tract infections and throat infections – in the latter case it

may be used as a gargle. It promotes gastric and mammary gland secretions when taken internally.

Formerly employed as a mild sedative and externally as a poultice or bath to treat wounds. The young fresh leaf can be included in salads. The oil has limited use in certain liqueurs as a bitter flavouring.

Pinus mugo var. *pumilio* (Haenke) Zenari
PINACEAE
Dwarf Mountain Pine

This variety of Mountain Pine is the source of a pure essential oil which is variously described as Pumilio Pine Oil, Pine Needle Oil and Oleum Pini Pumiliones. The oil is retained in the Swiss, Rumanian, Yugoslavian, Hungarian, Austrian and Czechoslovakian pharmacopoeias, and it is especially popular in Swiss, Italian and Hungarian medicinal use.

Pumilio Pine Oil is produced by distillation of the fresh young needles (which are shown in the illustration, below). It has been used since at least the seventeenth century.

In Britain, Dr Prosser James described its beneficial action in 1888 for certain respiratory diseases, and suggested its use in an atomizer to disinfect sickrooms.

Description Low prostrate shrub with glabrous, dark brownish, erect branchlets, and a grey somewhat scaly bark. Leaves to 3.5 cm long, stiff, needle-like, crowded in clusters or fascicles, bright green. Cones dark brown to yellowish, almost sessile, deciduous and dehiscent, ovoid to 4 cm long.

Distribution Native to the mountains of southern and central Europe. Rarely introduced elsewhere. Often on light, sandy or rocky soils.

Cultivation Wild plant infrequently cultivated horticulturally as an ornamental.

Constituents (oil) Esters (4–10%) comprising

mainly bornyl acetate. (leaves) Esters; resins; small quantities of glycosides; unknown substances.

Uses (fresh leaves) Stimulant; counter-irritant and sometimes appears to possess slight anaesthetic properties. Inhaled as steam, the oil is of benefit in the treatment of coughs, laryngitis, chronic bronchitis, catarrh, asthma and other respiratory diseases since it exerts dilatatory action on the bronchi, the oil may be taken internally in small doses in the form of lozenges, syrups, or on sugar. The infusion of leaves is inhaled in the treatment of similar respiratory disorders.

Piper betle L PIPERACAE
Betel Betel Leaf

Betel chewing is a habit among Malays almost as popular as tobacco smoking among Europeans. The method consists of rolling up a slice or Areca Nut (*Areca catechu* L) with a little Lime (Chunam) (made by burning seashells), inside a leaf of Betel, and then slowly chewing the mixture – called a quid.

Chavica siriboa Miq. is sometimes used as a substitute for Betel Leaf.

Description Shrub, climbing by adventitious rootlets; stems semi-woody, enlarged at nodes, bearing entire, or undulate, thick, glossy, broadly ovate, slightly cordate leaves on 2.5 cm long petioles. Flowers yellowish in dense pendulous cylindrical spikes to 5 cm long; followed by fleshy fruit.

Distribution Indigenous to India, Ceylon and Malaysia. Introduced elsewhere. Requires hot and moist environment, in partial shade.

Cultivation Wild. Cultivated in India and the Far East.

Constituents Essential oil (0.2–1.0%) comprising cadenene, chavicol, chavibetol and sesquiterpenes; also sugars; starch; tannic acid;

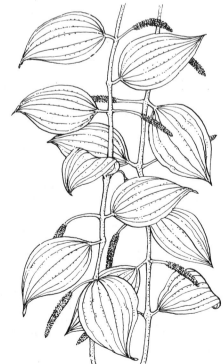

acid; diastase (to 2%).

Uses (leaves, oil) Stimulant; antiseptic; carminative; sialogogue; tonic; stomachic.

Leaves commonly employed as a masticatory in the East; they act as a general tonic, promote salivary and gastric secretions, aid digestion, decrease perspiration and increase physical endurance.

Piper cubeba L PIPERACEAE
Cubeb Cubebs/Tailed Pepper
Cubeb was the East Indian name for this spice

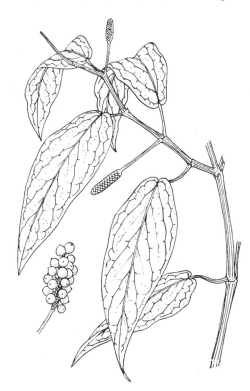

which as early as the tenth century was recognized by the Arabs to be a product of Java. Some authorities consider that the Arabic word *kababe* was a collective term which referred to a number of similar cubeb-like fruit. Indeed, even in modern times the peppercorn-like berries are frequently adulterated with inferior Piper species such as *Piper crassipes, P. ribesioides, P. mollissimum* and *P. muricatum.* The spice has enjoyed varying popularity. In the thirteenth century it was commonly found in Europe as a medicine and as a condiment, but by the end of the seventeenth century it was both uncommon and expensive. In England it had fallen into almost complete disuse by the early nineteenth century, but was reintroduced in 1815 after verification of its therapeutic effects by Army medical officers serving in the Far East.

Description Climbing perennial or shrub; stems smooth and flexuous, bearing glabrous entire, acuminate, petiolate, oblong or ovate-oblong, coriaceous and obliquely cordate leaves. Flowers dioecious, in spikes, and followed by brownish globose fruit to 6 mm diameter.

Distribution Native to south-east Asia, especially Sumatra and Java. Introduced elsewhere.
Cultivation Wild. Cultivated commercially in

Ceylon, India and the East Indies.

Constituents Volatile oil (5–20%) comprising cubebic acid (to 1%), cubebin, cadinene, several terpenes and sesquiterpenes; resin; fixed oil; starch; calcium and magnesium malate. Action largely due to cubebic acid which has a local irritant and stimulant effect on mucous membranes.

Uses (dried unripe fruit, occasionally oil) Antiseptic; diuretic; stimulant; expectorant; stomachic; carminative. Once used in the treatment of genito-urinary tract infections, including gonorrhoea. May be of benefit in cystitis, indigestion, and if incorporated in lozenges, can be used for coughs, bronchitis and respiratory complaints. Formerly employed in the United States in asthma cigarettes. Principally of use as a condiment; the flavour resembles Allspice, and is suitable for sauces and fruit dishes.

Piper nigrum L PIPERACEAE
Pepper Black Pepper
Historically one of the most important spices which has been very highly prized since the earliest days of East-West trade. It has been used as a form of currency: during the siege of Rome (A.D. 408) part of the city's ransom was paid in Pepper berries, and a thousand years later 'pepper rents' were commonly paid to landlords. The quest for Pepper by European nations led them to discover a maritime route to the East. During the Middle Ages much of the wealth of Venice was derived from its Pepper trade.

In England the control of the spice trade was in the hands of the Guild of Pepperers (or *Piperarii* – derived from *Piper* or Pepper) from as early as 1154; this Guild was later to become incorporated with the Grocers Company, which in turn eventually lost its control over drugs and spices to the apothecaries. *P. nigrum* is also the source of White Pepper. Instead of picking the unripe berries and drying them to produce the Black variety, the fruit is allowed to ripen on the vine and then soaked to remove the dark skin (pericarp). White Pepper was known to Theophrastus and his Greek contemporaries but by the Middle Ages it had lost its popularity. Although still used most White Pepper is now, in fact, decorticated Pepper in that the outer layer is incompletely removed by machinery.

Description Perennial climbing shrub; stem strong and woody bearing glossy, prominently nerved, ovate-oblong to orbicular leaves, to 18 cm long and 12 cm wide, on 2 cm long petioles. Flowers white, usually dioecious, on glabrous spikes from 5–15 cm long. Followed by 6 mm diameter globose, yellow and then red, fruit.

Distribution Native to southern India; introduced to tropical Asia, Malagasy Republic, Brazil. In tropical forests; requires shade and high humidity.

Cultivation Wild. Cultivated commercially in Indonesia, South India, West Indies, Brazil and China; frequently in mixed plantations with other lucrative crops such as Coffee. Will yield a crop for approximately 10 years.

Constituents Volatile oil (to 2.5%), comprising

the alkaloids piperine, piperidine and chavicine; a yellow compound piperettine which hydrolyzes to piperidine and piperettic acid; traces of hydrocyanic acid; resins (to 6%); starch (to 30%).

Uses (dried unripe fruit) Stomachic; carminative; aromatic stimulant; antibacterial; insecticide; diaphoretic.

Stimulates taste-buds and thus causes reflex stimulation of gastric secretions. Employed in atonic dyspepsia. Also stimulates mucous membranes and part of the nervous system, and raises body temperature. May be used as a gargle, and externally as a rubefacient. East Africans use it as an abortifacient. They also consider that the body odour resulting from eating the fruit repels mosquitoes.

Mostly employed as a stimulating condiment and food preservative, as, for example, in sausage meats.

Plantago major L PLANTAGINACEAE
Greater Plantain Rat-tail Plantain/
Waybread
This and some closely related *Plantago* species such as *P. major* var. *asiatica* Decne. and *P. lanceolata* L have a long traditional use in the treatment of sores which has recently been vindicated by modern examination of the plant's action.

The unattractive and tenacious Plantains are the scourge of gardeners, but many are still highly respected in folk medicine from Africa to Vietnam.

Description Perennial. Leaves entire or slightly toothed, long petioled, ovate to elliptic, 5–20 cm long, forming a basal rosette. Leaves prominently 7-veined and no more than twice as long as the petiole. Flowers inconspicuous 3 mm wide, numerous, yellowish-green, with lilac and then yellow anthers; on cylindrical spike 5–40 cm long. Appearing early summer to mid-autumn.

Distribution Native to Europe. Introduced to other temperate zones. Widely distributed on cultivated land, wasteland and roadside. Prefers moist sandy or loamy nutrient-rich soils, but tolerates most conditions.

Cultivation Wild plant. In eastern Europe commercial cultivation of *P. lanceolata* L. has recently begun.

Constituents (leaf) Mucilage; a pentacyclic triterpene, oleanolic acid; a glycoside, aucubin (rhinanthin); the enzymes emulsin and invertin; potassium salts (to 0.5%); citric acid. (seed) Oil (to 22%); a trisaccharide, planteose; aucubin; choline; various organic acids.

Uses (dried leaves, seed) Vulnerary; diuretic; expectorant; astringent; bacteriostatic.

Principally of use as a poultice, ointment or in decoction for the external treatment of wounds, ulcers and bites. Also used as a gargle and as an eye-wash in blepharitis and conjunctivitis.

The plant has the ability to destroy a wide range of micro-organisms, and stimulates the healing process (epithelization).

The leaf may be employed internally to treat diarrhoea, and conversely the seed is of benefit in constipation.

Formerly used to treat various haemorrhages including post-partum haemorrhage; also bronchitis, bronchial catarrh and coughs. An effective diuretic. Employed homeopathically. The young leaf was once used as a pot-herb.

Plantago psyllium L PLANTAGINACEAE
Psyllium Flea Seed

Seeds from several *Plantago* species which have the ability to swell in water due to their high mucilage content have been used for medicinal and other purposes.

P. psyllium and *P. indica* L. seeds are rich in mucilage and both are commercially known

as Psyllium. They have been used since Dioscorides' day, and the specific name is derived from the Greek for flea (*psylla*) – an allusion to the seed's appearance. Apothecaries called the seed *Pulicariae*, from the Latin for flea.

In India *P. ovata* Forskal, commonly known as Ispaghula, is used for precisely the same purposes, and may therefore replace Psyllium.

Description Annual with erect thin hairy stems 10–35 cm tall, bearing sessile, long thin (acicular) grey-green glandular leaves; opposite or in whorls of 3–6 leaves. Flowers small, numerous, white, in globose spikes borne on long peduncles; appearing late spring to late summer, and followed by 2–3 mm long, dark brown glossy seeds.

Distribution Native to the mediterranean region; especially France, Spain and North Africa. On poor, dry sandy soils in full sun.

Cultivation Wild. Cultivated commercially from seed sown in the spring.

Constituents Oil; mucilage (to 10%), comprising xylose, arabinose, galactose, and galacturonic acid, to which its therapeutic action is due.

Uses (seeds) Emollient; laxative.

Used in the treatment of chronic constipation; the seed's mucilage swells considerably in water and the gelatinous mass acts as a bulk purgative. The emollient action makes this herb also suitable for use in severe diarrhoea. It can be used as a soothing eye lotion.

Young leaves may be added to salads.

Employed industrially to dress muslin.

An ingredient of certain cosmetic preparations, such as face masks.

Podophyllum peltatum L BERBERIDACEAE
American Mandrake Podophyllum/
Common May-apple

The name May-apple is derived from the fact that the juicy and acidic fruits are sometimes eaten, and, despite their laxative effects, they were once on sale in some American markets. All other parts of the plant must, however, be considered as poisonous, and the powerful nature of the dried rhizome is emphasized by the size of the therapeutic dose – 0.12 of a gram. American Mandrake was long used as an emetic by the Indians; but its purgative effect was introduced to medicine by Schöpf (1787) who was the physician to German soldiers fighting in the American War of Independence. It first entered the United States Pharmacopoeia in 1820 and is also in the Spanish and Portugese pharmacopoeias – although now only as the source of Podophyllum resin.

The generic name is derived from the Greek for foot-leaf; while *peltatum* means shield-shaped.

Description Perennial on reddish-brown, long (to 2 m), cylindrical rhizome 5–15 mm diameter. Stems simple, erect to 45 cm, bearing 1 or 2, 7–9 deeply lobed drooping leaves, to 30 cm wide. Flowers white, borne singly on nodding peduncle in the stem bifurcation between 2 leaves. Petals fleshy, 6 or 9; stamens 12 or 18; corolla to 5 cm wide. Appearing early summer

and followed in early autumn by 3–5 cm long, ovoid, yellow edible fruit.

Distribution North American native from Texas to Florida and Quebec. On damp nitrogenous soils in open woodland, pastures and near streams.

Cultivation Wild. Collected commercially in eastern North America. May be propagated by division of root-stock in the autumn, or from seed sown in the spring. Requires damp, humus-rich soils, and partial shade.

Constituents Podophyllotoxin and related substances such as picropodophyllin; podophylloresin; quercetin; α- and β-peltatin; starch; flavonoids. Purgative action due to the podophyllotoxin and podophylloresin content.

Podophyllin or podophyllum resin is produced by adding the alcoholic tincture to water.

Uses (rhizome, Podophyllum resin) Powerful purgative; gastro-intestinal irritant; antihelmintic; anti-mitotic. Used locally externally on soft venereal warts and on other warts. Both resin and rhizome have been employed as a purgative in cases of chronic constipation with associated liver complaints, although actual choleretic action is not substantiated. Normally combined with less drastic remedies.

Contra-indications POISONOUS. May cause severe gastro-intestinal irritation or polyneuritis. External application must be carefully restricted to abnormal tissue only; systemic absorption has been shown to cause poisoning. Not to be used during pregnancy. Only to be used by medical personnel.

Pogostemon patchouli Pellet LABIATAE
Patchouli

Patchouli oil has one of the strongest and most distinctive perfumes known and for this reason was traditionally used to scent Indian linen, to distinguish material of Indian origin. Several of the 40 species in the genus *Pogostemon* are now used as a source of Patchouli oil, which has therefore become of somewhat variable quality. Besides *P. patchouli* Pell. (which is also known as *P. heyeanus* Benth. and *P. cablin* (Blanco) Benth.), Patchouli is mostly derived from the Javanese species *P. comosus* Miq. Alternative sources from different genera include *Microtaena cymosa* Prain and *Plectranthus patchouli* Clarke.

Description Aromatic perennial to 1 m tall; stems erect, square, slightly hirsute, bearing opposite, ovate or triangular leaves approximately 3–5 cm long. Flowers whitish, often marked with purple, arranged in groups on terminal and axillary spikes.

Distribution Native to south-east Asia and India; introduced to West Indies and parts of South America. Requires tropical or subtropical conditions.

Cultivation Wild. Cultivated commercially and horticulturally from seed sown in the spring, or by division of root-stock in spring or autumn, or from cuttings taken in late spring. May be grown as a greenhouse plant in temperate zones. Use a rich or medium-rich potting compost, and strike heeled cuttings in high humidity.

Constituents Oil comprising cadinene, stearoptene and related compounds. Obtained from leaves by distillation.

Uses (dried leaves, oil) Antiseptic; insecticide. Not commonly used for medicinal purposes. Once considered to act as a stimulant.

Principally of use as a perfume. The oil may be employed in a wide range of cosmetic preparations, including soaps. It is also used in incense. Leaves can be incorporated in potpourris, scented sachets and other scented articles.

Polemonium caeruleum L POLEMONIACEAE

Jacob's Ladder Charity/Greek Valerian

Polemonium is an ancient name of uncertain origin for a herb which has now largely fallen into disuse. It was known to Dioscorides as *polemonion* and the root was once administered in wine in cases of dysentery, toothache and against the bites of poisonous animals.

As late as 1830 the herb, then called *Herba*

Valerianae graecae, was still retained in some European pharmacopoeias and was employed predominantly as an antisyphilitic agent or in the treatment of rabies.

The common name refers to the ladder-like shape of the leaves.

Description Perennial from 30 cm to 1 m tall; stems erect bearing short, petiolate or sessile, alternate, pinnate leaves. Basal leaves from 7.5–12.5 cm long, long-petiolate, the petioles being winged; 11–21 lanceolate leaflets larger than stem leaves, from 15 mm to 2 cm long. Flowers blue, 5-petalled, 3 cm diameter, in drooping panicles, appearing late to mid-summer.

Distribution European native. Introduced to temperate zones.

Prefers damp soils near streams in the partial shade of woodland.

Cultivation Wild, usually rare and localized. Found as a garden escape. Cultivated horticulturally from seed sown in spring or by division in the autumn. Requires rich, moisture-retaining soil and the addition of lime.

P. caeruleum var. *lacteum* Benth. has white flowers; *P. caeruleum* var. *himalayanum* Baker has larger lilac-blue flowers. Both may be found in cultivation as Jacob's Ladder.

Constituents Unknown.

Uses (dried flowering plant, dried root) Weak diaphoretic. Once considered to possess blood-purifying qualities, but now no longer used for medicinal purposes.

Principally of horticultural use in formal and historical gardens.

Polygala vulgaris L POLYGALACEAE

Common Milkwort

In chalky areas and in continental Europe the very similar Bitter Milkwort (*P. amara* L) is the

species commonly found; it has the same properties as *P. vulgaris* but it is more bitter and hence acts as a bitter tonic. Early writers decided that *P. vulgaris* was the *polygala* and *polugalon* of Pliny and Dioscorides respectively – both from the Greek meaning much milk – but this cannot be certain and several Milkwort's now retain the traditional virtue of being galactogogues.

Description Perennial 10–30 cm tall, with erect or decumbent stems. Leaves alternate, evergreen, obovate to lanceolate, 5–35 mm long. Flowers usually blue, occasionally pink or whitish, in loose racemes; appearing early summer to early autumn.

Distribution Native to Europe; on grassland, heathland, mountain pastures, in sandy, well-drained, but humus-rich soils to 2000 m altitude.

Cultivation Wild. Propagate from seed sown in

spring on the soil surface; do not cover with soil or germination will be poor.

Constituents Essential oil, comprising gaultherine and other compounds; saponins; polygalic acid and senegine; mucilage; resin.

Uses (dried whole plant, dried root) Expectorant; diuretic; laxative; stomachic.

Traditionally considered to be a galactogogue, but this is unsubstantiated. Of use in bronchitis and pulmonary complaints, often combined with other remedies; but not effective in asthma as once supposed.

The leaves and root make a crude soap which is similar to *Saponaria officinalis* but less effective.

Polygonum bistorta L POLYGONACEAE

Bistort Snake Root/Snakeweed

Bistort belongs to the knotweed genus, many members of which are characterized by their swollen or jointed stems. *Polygonum* itself means many-kneed from the stem's shape.

Bistorta describes the rhizome and is from the Latin for twice twisted, after the snake-like shape of the underground parts. It used to be known as *Serpentaria* or *Serpentaria rubra* (after the red colour within the blackish rhizome) which has led to some confusion since both *Artemisia dracunculus* L and *Arum maculatum* L were also called *Serpentaria* in the sixteenth and seventeenth centuries.

There are over 200 species of *Polygonum* and this one was not introduced into medical practice until the Renaissance; the leaf, however is still included in the Swiss Pharmacopoeia and the rhizome in the pharmacopoeias of France and Russia.

It was certainly an important food in the spring in northern countries from earliest times – sometimes even being cultivated as a garden herb.

Description Perennial on thick, somewhat flattened and twisted S-shaped rhizome; stem erect 25–50 cm or occasionally to 1 m tall. Radical leaves broadly ovate or lanceolate, lighter and hairy beneath, 5–15 cm long, outline wavy; stem leaves sparse, smaller, triangular-acuminate. Petioles variable in length and triangular in section; leaves folded longitudinally before opening. Flowers pale pink or rarely white, numerous, small (4 mm diameter), in dense solitary, cylindrical terminal spikes of 10–15 mm diameter. Appearing mid-summer to early autumn.

Distribution European native. On moist siliceous nutrient-rich grassland, mixed woodland, fenland and alpine mats. Particularly on higher ground, and frequently near water.

Cultivation Wild plant.

Constituents Tannic acid (to 20%); oxalic acid; vitamin C; starch; action due to the astringency of the tannins.

Uses (dried rhizome) Strong astringent; anti-inflammatory; vulnerary.

Useful in decoction or infusion for diarrhoea or as a gargle in aphthous ulcers, stomatitis and gingivitis. Applied externally to cuts or sores

and to haemorrhoids. The powdered rhizome acts as a styptic. Once used in the treatment of tuberculosis (action uncertain).

The root is edible after it has been soaked in water and then roasted.

Young shoots and leaves may be boiled and eaten as spring greens.

Used in veterinary medicine.

Polypodium vulgare L POLYPODIACEAE
Polypody Root Common Polypody/Brake Root

Both the generic and common names of this fern refer to the branching habit of the rhizome; the Latin *polypodium* means many-footed.

Dioscorides knew the drug and prescribed it as a purgative. He also used the pulverized fresh mucilaginous root as a poultice for sprained or fractured fingers. It is now rarely used and in the past it was usually only used for its expectorant action, which is weak. A related Peruvian Polypody, *P. calaguala* Ruiz – whose

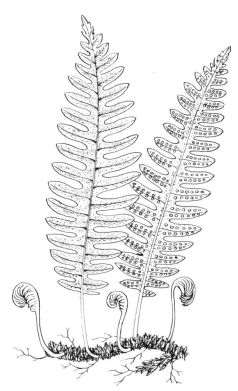

common name is Calahualae – was shown in the 1930s to possess better expectorant qualities than this species.

Description Perennial fern on long creeping somewhat flattened rhizome to 10 mm thick, bearing numerous brown scales, and from which the stipes grow to 10–50 cm. Leaves smooth, deeply pinnate, with 20–40 lanceolate, alternate and opposite, obtuse or semiacute sometimes curved, segments; midribs prominent. Sporangia in light brown circular sori arranged either side of main segmental nerve.

Distribution Native to Europe, western Asia; introduced to North America and other temperate regions. Frequently found on old walls, rocky ground, woodland, ruins and old

decaying tree trunks. Requires damp, shady sheltered conditions.

Cultivation Wild. Several varieties cultivated for horticultural purposes; most of these forms being characterized by attractive foliage.

Constituents Essential oil; mucilage; sugars; tannic acid; bitter resins; a saponoside, polypodine; various mineral salts. Cholagogue action largely due to polypodine.

Uses (dried rhizome) Cholagogue; expectorant; laxative; antihelmintic.

Small doses promote the appetite; stronger decoctions are useful in the treatment of chest infections, coughs, and bronchial catarrh. Large doses act as a mild laxative and antihelmintic with some action against tapeworms.

Populus candicans Ait. SALICACEAE
Balm of Gilead Poplar Buds

The descriptive term Balm of Gilead has been used for a number of different plants. One of the first and possibly the original Balm of the Bible was the oleo-resin obtained from *Balsamodendron opobalsamum* Kunth. – also called the Balm of Mecca. Miraculous properties were once attributed to this aromatic substance but it is now obsolete in Europe and most authorities consider it is extinct in its former Indian and Egyptian homes, although it may survive locally in the Middle East.

Canada Balsam from *Abies balsamea* Marshall was also once called Balm of Gilead, but the commercial product is now derived from *P. candicans* (which is also known as *P. balsamifera* var. *candicans* Gray and *P. gileadensis* Rouleau) and from the Balsam Poplar, *P. balsamifera* L. (also called *P. tacamahacca* Mill.). It is probable that several other substitutes from the Poplar family (such as *P. tremuloides* Michx.) are known as Balm of Gilead.

Description Tree to 20 m (occasionally to 30 m), spreading with open and irregular top; leaves

dark above, lighter and hirsute beneath, cordate, alternate, petiolate, broad-ovate or deltoid, 10–15 cm long. Flowers in drooping scaly catkins to 15 cm long. Winter leaf buds sticky, resinous and highly aromatic.
Distribution Uncertain origin. Introduced and naturalized in several temperate countries. Frequently beside rivers.
Cultivation Wild. Cultivated horticulturally as aromatic garden ornamental.
Constituents Oleo-resin; salicylic compounds including salicin and salicin benzoate; buds yield to 40% of an alcohol-soluble extractive.
Uses (dried or rarely fresh leaf buds, occasionally oleo-resin) Antiseptic; rubefacient; expectorant.
Used internally in the treatment of upper respiratory tract infections, particularly coughs, laryngitis and bronchitis. May be employed in ointments for external application to relieve the local pain and irritation of arthritis, cuts and bruises. An excellent gargle for sore throats.
The buds can be used in a range of scented articles where a heavy resinous balsamic aroma is required.

Portulaca oleracea L PORTULACACEAE
Purslane Wild Purslane/Yellow Portulaca
Purslane has long been used as a foodstuff in India and the Middle East, and was introduced into cultivation in Europe in the Middle Ages. It was first grown in England in 1582 but was probably well-known in Italy and France long before this as Ruellius described both the wild and erect cultivated garden form in 1536.
It is still collected from the wild in Africa, India and the Far East and used for culinary and medicinal purposes. The related plant *P. quadrifida* L is used in South Africa as an emetic by the Zulu.
Description Annual or biennial with fleshy prostrate or decumbent stems to 15 cm; somewhat pinkish, and bearing opposite, fleshy, spatulate, sessile leaves 1–2 cm long. Flowers small (7.5 mm), yellow, sessile, single or in groups of 2 or 3, appearing in late summer; the petals soon fall and reveal a small seed capsule.

Distribution Native from Greece to China. Introduced elsewhere. On dry, sandy, nitrogen-rich weedy soils in full sun.
Cultivation Wild. Cultivated horticulturally for centuries in the Middle and Far East. A number of varieties and cultigens have been developed from this wild species. Propagate from seed sown successively from late spring to early autumn on light, well-drained soil; water well and harvest 6–8 weeks after sowing. Leaves of the cultivated varieties may be less sharp than the wild plant.
Constituents Vitamin C (700 mg per 100 g fresh plant); potassium salts (1% in fresh, 70% in dry plant); urea; oxalic acid; carotenoid pigments; alkaloids (0.03%); glucoside; β-sitosterol; volatile oil; resins; organic acids (to 1%); sacchariferoid (2%). The combined action being predominantly diuretic and tonic.
Uses (fresh herb) Diuretic; tonic; anti-scorbutic. Due to its high vitamin C content the plant was once an important remedy for scurvy. It has also been used in a variety of pulmonary and skin diseases. The seed and root are reported to be antihelmintic but this has not been proved. It is a useful diuretic when used fresh and may be incorporated with other remedies for the treatment of urino-genital infections. The leaf has vasoconstrictive properties, and in conditions of low blood pressure can be used to induce more vigorous contractions of the heart.
Extensively used in several subtropical countries as a cooked vegetable and a salad herb.

Portulaca oleracea var. *sativa* (L) DC.
PORTULACACEAE
Garden Purslane Green Purslane/Kitchen-garden Purslane
Garden Purslane was popular in north-west Europe from the end of the sixteenth century until the end of the eighteenth century, but in English speaking countries it is now rarely grown.
Several varieties were developed from the Wild Purslane of which the Green, Golden and large-leaved Golden were the best known. Only the Green and Golden varieties are now easily obtained, the latter sometimes erroneously being described as a separate species, *P. sativa* or the Yellow Purslane. The true Yellow Purslane is *P. lutea* Soland and is found in New Zealand.
The common name is from the old Latin name for the plant *porcilacca*; while *oleracea* means a vegetable garden herb used in cooking.
Description Annual. Similar to *P. oleracea* L but a taller plant reaching 50 cm, with thicker stems and bright green succulent spatulate leaves.
Distribution Widespread in temperate and subtropical zones. Probably developed in the Middle East or southern Europe. Prefers nitrogen-rich, well-drained dryish soils in full sun.
Cultivation Only found in the wild as a garden escape. Propagate as for *P. oleracea* L. Plant 15–20 cm apart in rows 30 cm apart. If sufficient water is given, 2 or 3 gatherings will be possible from each plant. A winter and early

spring crop can be obtained by successive plantings on hotbeds or in frames. Grown semi-commercially in France, Italy and Holland.
Constituents Similar to *P. oleracea* L.
Uses (fresh herb) Not used for medicinal purposes. Principally eaten cooked but may also be used sparingly in salads; it has a sharp taste. The stem and leaves are pickled for winter use. A traditional ingredient of the French soup *bonne femme* and the Middle East salad, *fattoush*.
The attractive golden-leaved variety may be used for horticultural purposes in formal herb gardens.

Potentilla anserina L ROSACEAE
Silverweed Wild Tansy
There are more than 300 species in the genus *Potentilla*, most of which are found in the northern temperate zones, and Silverweed is one of the most easily recognized with its silky-silver leaf undersides. This characteristic led to both its current common name and the earlier names *Argentina* and *Argentaria* (from *argent* meaning silver).
The generic name is from the Latin *potens* meaning powerful after the medicinal action of the group, most of which contain high percentages of tannin and are thus strong astringents.
Anserina comes from the Latin *anserinus* meaning pertaining to geese, since the birds were thought to be particularly partial to the leaves; many animals are happy to graze on the plant. The Silverweed has been identified as the *Myriophyllon* of Dioscorides who suggested boiling the plant in salted water for the treatment of haemorrhages.
Description Silky perennial 20–40 cm tall, on short, thick root-stock from which arise long creeping stolons (to 80 cm long) which root at the nodes. Radical leaves 5–25 cm long, compound, pinnate, silvery-white and hairy beneath; 14–24 leaflets, 1–6 cm long, alternately large and small, oval, deeply dentate.

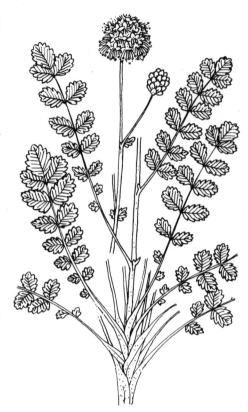

Flowers 5-petalled, golden yellow, to 2 cm diameter, borne singly on long stems arising from the basal rosette. Appearing mid to late summer.

Distribution European native. Introduced elsewhere. On nitrogen-rich, loamy, undisturbed damp soils; roadsides, railway embankments, damp pastureland to 1500 m altitude.

Cultivation Wild.

Constituents Tannins; choline; resins; flavones; an alcohol, tormentol; starch.

Uses (dried flowering plant, dried leaves, occasionally root-stock) Astringent; antispasmodic; tonic; stomachic.

Used in the treatment of diarrhoea, painful menstruation (weak action), and as a digestive aid in indigestion. Formerly used to treat various haemorrhages including those arising from haemorrhoids; as a douche in leucorrhoea, and for uterine spasms. Externally it may be applied to cuts and wounds, and it is of use as a gargle in mouth complaints such as ulcers. Employed homeopathically. The roots may be roasted, boiled or eaten raw.

Potentilla erecta (L) Raüsch. ROSACEAE
Tormentilla Common Tormentil
The red colouring matter found in the root-stock of this herb appears to be identical with a substance known as ratanhia-red present in the root-bark of *Krameria triandra* Ruiz and Pav. or Peruvian Rhatany, an astringent plant which was introduced to Europe in 1796 by Hipolito Ruiz and which has now largely replaced Tormentilla in several official prepar-

ations. Many authorities have noted that Rhatany is preferred only for economic reasons, since the plants possess similar actions. It is coincidental that Rhatany was brought to the notice of Ruiz by the women of Lima who used it to preserve their teeth, while Tormentilla was long used as an astringent tooth powder. *P. erecta* was apparently not widely used in medicine until the sixteenth century when it first found favour in the treatment of colic; the name Tormentilla is derived from the Latin *tormina* meaning colic.

It is still employed widely in European folk medicine, and occasionally in the manufacture of artists' colours.

Description Perennial, 10–40 cm tall on thick (to 3 cm), woody, long (to 20 cm) rhizome, reddish internally. Stems prostrate or more usually erect, thin, branched, bearing sessile, 5-lobed stem leaves, with 1–2 cm long, narrow leaflets and long stalked, 3-lobed, broadly ovate, basal leaves, with 5–10 mm long leaflets. Flowers yellow, only 4-petalled, 10–15 mm wide, carried singly on long (10–30 cm) thin peduncles, arising from stem-leaf axils. Appearing from early summer to early autumn.

Distribution Native to Europe, West Asia and Siberia; rarer in the mediterranean region. On light, acidic, damp soils, particularly heathland, fenland, open deciduous and coniferous woodland, and often in hilly regions. To 2200 m altitude.

Cultivation Wild plant.

Constituents Catechol-tannins (to 20%), which on storage convert to phlobaphenes; an alcohol, tormentol; a glycoside, tormentilline; starch; sugars; a bitter, chinovic acid (or quinovic acid) also found in Cinchona bark.

Uses (dried root-stock) Astringent; haemostatic; anti-inflammatory; vulnerary.

A powerful remedy in severe diarrhoea, largely due to its high tannin content. Principally used to much benefit externally as an infusion on cuts, wounds, abrasions and burns, including sunburn. The plant promotes epithelization. It is also used as a lotion for topical applications to haemorrhoids, frostbite, and as a gargle in throat and mouth inflammations. The powdered root-stock is an excellent styptic.

A root extract is used in certain forms of schnapps.

The roots provide a red dye.

Once used in tanning.

Contra-indications A powerful astringent; must be used internally with care. Prolonged contact with the skin should be avoided, as it may cause scarring.

Poterium sanguisorba L ROSACEAE
Salad Burnet Garden Burnet
It has been cultivated as a salad herb at least since Lyte recorded it in *Dodoens' Herball* of 1578, but was also known as *Sanguisorba minor* from the time of Fuchs (1542). The Great Burnet (*Sanguisorba officinalis* L) was preferred as the official medicinal plant, probably because it is larger; both species, however, possess similar properties.

Sanguisorba means either blood-ball or blood stopping after both the appearance and action of the inflorescence and whole plant.

Description Perennial on woody root-stock 20–70 cm tall, forming a clump of branching grooved stems bearing leaves subdivided into 7–11 serrate lobes, oblong or orbicular. Flowers greenish or reddish brown, small, in a dense rounded terminal panicle to 15 mm diameter; appearing early to mid-summer.

Distribution Native to Europe and Asia; introduced and sometimes naturalized elsewhere. On dryish porous calcareous grassland, woodland edges, roadsides, in warm situations to 1700 m altitude.

Cultivation Wild. Cultivated as a salad herb from seed sown in spring or autumn. Remove the flowers to encourage production of leaf. Suitable as an edging plant in formal herb garden designs.

Constituents Vitamin C; essential oil; tannins; flavones; a saponoside.

Uses (whole fresh or dried plant, fresh leaf; rarely dried root-stock) Astringent; vulnerary; haemostatic; carminative; digestive.

Chewing the leaf assists digestion, while infusions of the whole plant are of use in treating haemorrhoids or diarrhoea. The root decoction is an excellent haemostatic and can be used on all cuts and wounds. Traditionally considered of benefit in the menopause, but this is unsubstantiated.

Primula veris L PRIMULACEAE
Cowslip Paigle
The Cowslip obtained its name by corruption of 'cowslop' from the old English *cu-sloppe*, signifying its occurrence in meadows fre-

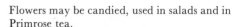

quented by domesticated animals. Changing agricultural practices, however, have led to its rapid disappearance in parts of Europe, and attempts to cultivate it on a commercial scale in eastern Europe have proved uneconomic. Tradition maintains that the Cowslip arose from the ground where St Peter dropped his keys, hence the English, French and German common names, Keys of Heaven, *Clef de St Pierre* and *Schlüsselblumen*. The generic name Primula is from the Latin *primus* meaning first after its early flowering in the spring.

Description Soft-pubescent perennial on short, stout rhizome surrounded by leaf bases and producing long thin rootlets. Leaves obtuse, ovate-oblong, finely hairy and crenate, 5–20 cm long, narrowing at the base into a winged petiole, equally long as the leaf blade. 1–30 deep yellow flowers marked with orange, 10–15 mm diameter, on a nodding umbel surmounting a 10–30 cm long stalk (scape). Appearing late spring to late summer.

Distribution Native to northern and central Europe, Iran. Introduced and sometimes naturalized elsewhere. On porous calcareous soils in meadows and pastures, mixed or deciduous woodland; preferably in warm dryish situations. To 2000 m altitude.

Cultivation Wild. May be propagated from seed sown as soon as ripe, or by division of root-stock in autumn. The Oxlip *P. elatior* (L) Hill is frequently mistaken for the Cowslip but may be distinguished by its lack of orange marking and its possession of a seed capsule longer than the calyx.

P. veris var. *Kleynii* Hort. is found in cultivation; it has darker yellow to salmon coloured flowers.

Constituents Vitamin .C; saponins (to 10%); flavonoid pigments; a volatile oil, primula camphor; the heterosides primulaveroside and primveroside; enzymes; mineral salts.

Uses (dried root-stock, dried flowers and calices, occasionally dried leaves) Expectorant; antispasmodic; weak diuretic; weak laxative.

Of benefit in inflammatory conditions of the respiratory tract, bronchitis and coughs; frequently used in the form of a syrup. Once used to treat pneumonia and traditionally thought to be a remedy for palsy and paralysis.

The flowers are used as a weakly sedative tea;

also in the manufacture of home-made wines, and are candied and used as cake decorations.

Contra-indications Some members of the Primulaceae, but particularly *Primula obconica* Hance, possess the quinone, primin, which causes a particular form of contact dermatitis called primula sensitivity, characterized by a violent vesicular eruption on the fingers and forearms. Allergic individuals should avoid the plants.

Primula vulgaris Huds. PRIMULACEAE
Primrose
The Primrose is so popular in spring that it is now almost extinct close to large urban areas. It has in fact always been heavily cropped by man, not so much as a medicine but rather as a base for home-made drinks, conserves, cosmetics or just for their attractive appearance and subtle smell. They are to the north Europeans the epitome of spring, and are well named since the word Primrose comes from the Latin *prima rosa*, meaning the first rose (of the year).

The genus *Primula* comprises more than 400 species which hybridize readily and are an important horticultural group. This species, for example, hybridizes with *P. veris* L to produce the so-called Common Oxlip.

Description Perennial on short thick root-stock Leaves wrinkled, blunt, obovate-spatulate, hairy beneath, glabrous above, crenulate, 8–20 cm long, narrowed into a petiole shorter than the leaf blade. Flowers pale yellow, occasionally purplish, 3–4 cm wide, solitary on pubescent pedicels to 20 cm long. Appearing early spring to early summer.

Distribution European native. On rich, damp soils in shady woodland, hedgerows, grassland.

Cultivation Wild plant. Propagate by division on heavy or medium loam in semi-shade or sun.

Constituents Saponins; volatile oil.

Uses (dried root-stock, fresh flowering plant) Expectorant; antispasmodic; diuretic; anodyne.

Used as an expectorant in bronchitis and other respiratory infections. The tisane may be of benefit as a mild sedative in anxiety and insomnia. Formerly used in rheumatic disorders and in ointments for skin wounds and blemishes.

Flowers may be candied, used in salads and in Primrose tea.

Leaves once boiled as greens.

Contra-indications The same precautions apply as for *Primula veris*.

Prunella vulgaris L LABIATAE
Self Heal Heal-all/Woundwort
A common weed throughout America and from western Europe to China. Its easy availability led no doubt to its commonest use in stemming blood flow resulting from domestic accidents and fights; hence the common names Carpenter's Herb, Touch and Heal, Sicklewort, Hercules Woundwort, and the plant's historical pre-eminence as a vulnerary herb. It has other uses: the Chinese, for example, discovered its antipyretic and diuretic actions and still use it in gout in conjunction with other remedies.

Sixteenth-century adherents of the Doctrine of Signatures saw the throat in the shape of the flower and introduced it to treat diseases of the throat such as quinsy and diphtheria. Hence its modern generic name *Prunella* which is derived via Brunella and Braunella from the German for quinsy (*Die Braüne*). It is still called *Brunelle commune* and *Gemeine Brunelle* in France and Germany respectively.

Description Aromatic perennial with creeping rhizome on square erect or decumbent stems to 60 cm. Leaves either entire or toothed, petiolate, opposite and decussate, oblong-ovate, 3–7.5 cm long. Flowers violet-purple

(occasionally pink) 8–15 mm long, borne in leaf axils on compact spikes to 4 cm long. Appearing mid-summer to mid-autumn.

Distribution Native to Europe, Asia and North America; introduced elsewhere. On moist, loamy, well-drained soils in grassland, pastures, open woodland; preferably in sunny situations.

Cultivation Wild. Propagate from stem cuttings taken in spring or summer and rooted in a peat and sand mix; or by division of clumps. The pink flowered form is sometimes called *P. vulgaris* var. *rubrifolia* Beckhaus., while a white variety may be found as *P. vulgaris* var. *leucantha* Schur.

Constituents Tannins; volatile oil; an alkaloid; bitter principles; unknown substances.

Uses (dried flowering plant) Vulnerary; astringent; antiseptic; carminative.

Commonly used as a mouthwash, gargle and external wash in the treatment of sore throats, irritation and inflammation of the mouth, ulcers, cuts, burns, wounds and bruises. Once considered a specific against diphtheria. Rarely used internally and then only in cases of mild diarrhoea or flatulence. It acts as a weak bitter tonic.

Strong infusions of the dried powdered herb are effective styptics.

Prunus avium L ROSACEAE
Wild Cherry Common Wild Cherry/Gean

The fruit of *P. avium* are smaller than those of the cultivated Cherry varieties but, unusually for wild European fruits, they are quite sweet. The tree is, therefore, understandably called Sweet Cherry in the United States yet rarely so described in its native home.

It has doubtless long been of domestic importance since its stones have been discovered in Neolithic remains. This species has also provided the stock for the table Cherry while the Morello or Sour Cherry comes from *P. cerasus* L. *Prunus* is an ancient name for the plum, while *avium* is the Latin for bird, which readily eat the fruit. The word cherry can be traced back to an Assyrian base *karsu*; the Greek name for it was *kerasos*.

Description Deciduous tree 10–20 m tall; bark smooth, reddish, peeling off transversely in strips; branches ascending bearing dark green, dentate, alternate somewhat variably shaped leaves, 10–15 cm long, but usually oblong-ovate to oblong-obovate, and pubescent beneath. Flowers white, 5-petalled, 3 cm wide, on long glabrous pedicels to 4 cm; appearing late spring to early summer with the first leaves, and followed by globular or cordate fruit which are first yellow, then red and finally purple.

Distribution Native to Europe, western Asia; introduced elsewhere. In deciduous woodland.

Cultivation Wild – the species from which the cultivated Cherry was developed. It is used for grafting purposes in fruit-tree nurseries. Many different ornamental forms exist with double flowers, variegated leaves, weeping growth and attractive foliage. The variety *P. avium*

var. *Juliana* (L) Schübl. and Martens provides the Heart Cherries, and *P. avium* var. *duracina* (L) Schübl. and Martens the Bigarreau Cherries, of which the best known are Napoleon and Windsor.

Constituents (fruit stalks) Tannic acid; potassium salts; flavonoids. (fruit) Organic acids; provitamin A; tannins.

Uses (fruit, dried fruit stalks) Diuretic; astringent.

Many parts of the tree have traditionally been used for a variety of medicinal purposes. Today only the dried fruit stalks are available commercially, for use in folk medicine as a diuretic.

They also have some effect in cases of mild diarrhoea.

The fruit is used domestically for home-made conserves and commercially in liqueur manufacture (kirsch).

The wood is a valuable timber.

Prunus dulcis (Mill.) D.A. Webb ROSACEAE
Almond

The Almond tree has been in cultivation in Asia for thousands of years and is mentioned in Genesis. It was introduced to Europe by the Greeks who knew of more than 10 kinds of the seed which was then known as *amugdale*, and from which the Latin term *amygdala* was derived. The Romans called them *Nuces graecae* or Greek Nuts, and they have been cultivated in Italy from a very early date. They do not seem to have been grown in France until the eighth century and were not grown in north-west Europe until the late Middle Ages; the first tree was planted in England in the early sixteenth century. Elizabethan cooking, however, used large quantities of the seed, and 'Almond water' was frequently called for and used much as we now use milk in certain recipes. The botanical classification of the plant is complicated and very many different names will be found; *Prunus amygdalus* Batsch. and *Amygdalus communis* L are the commonest, but have now been superseded.

Description Bush or tree from 3–7 m tall, with glabrous light-coloured branches, and narrow, glabrous finely dentate, acuminate, oblong-lanceolate leaves 7.5–10 cm long, with gland-bearing petiole. Flowers pink or white, usually solitary, 3–4 cm wide, sessile, appearing mid to late spring either with or before the first leaves; followed by oblong-ovoid light green pubescent fruit, to 4 cm long containing 2 seeds.

Distribution Native to southern and central Asia, especially Persia. Introduced to south-Europe 2500 years ago; now widespread and frequently naturalized. To 3000 m altitude.

Cultivation Wild. Widely cultivated, and is the original species from which many varieties have been developed. The Bitter Almond is *P. dulcis* var. *amara* (DC) Buckheim (formerly *P. amygdalus* var. *amara* (DC) Focke), and the Sweet Almond is *P. dulcis* var. *dulcis* (DC) Buckheim (formerly *P. amygdalus* var. *sativa* (F.C. Ludw.) Focke). Other varieties and cultigens provide fruit of different shapes and sizes. The tree is somewhat frost sensitive and should be planted on well-drained soil in full

sun in a warm position.

Constituents (seed) Protein (to 20%); edible fatty oil (to 65%); enzymes, mainly emulsin; vitamins A, B$_1$, B$_2$B$_,$, B$_6$, E and PP (nicotinamide); mineral salts. (Bitter almond seed contains up to 4% of a toxic glycoside, amygdalin).

Uses (oil, seed) Demulcent; nutritive; emulsifying agent. Sweet Almond oil is predominantly used to prepare emulsions in which other herbal remedies may be suspended, particularly for cough mixtures. The sweet oil is used externally in massage oils and internally as a laxative. Bitter Almond oil was once used as a flavouring in pharmaceutical preparations and externally in demulcent skin and sunburn lotions, and is now used in the perfumery, liqueur and confectionery industries. Almond flour was formerly used in diabetic foodstuffs. Both oils are widely used in cosmetic and toilet preparations.

The seed is used in many sweet and savoury dishes.

Contra-indications The raw Bitter Almond seed contains cyanide derivatives and is POISONOUS.

Prunus laurocerasus L ROSACEAE
Cherry Laurel Cherry Bay/
Common Cherry Laurel

The Cherry Laurel is now most commonly found as an ornamental hedge, and has never been of great importance medically although some Spanish and Swiss physicians once promoted it as a sedative. In Britain it was noticed first by Madden in Dublin (1731) following fatal poisoning by Irish cooks who mistakenly thought it could be used as a Bitter Almond flavouring. Its action is due to the presence of cyanide derivatives, which may be fatal even in small quantities.

The plant was introduced to European botany by Pierre Belon and Clusius between 1550 and 1580.

Description Variable evergreen bush or small tree usually 3–4 m (occasionally 6 m) tall. Leaves shiny, dark green, oblong, alternate, obtuse or occasionally retuse, short-petioled, 7.5–12.5 cm long. Flowers strongly scented, white, in slender racemes to 10 cm long, appearing late spring to early summer and

followed by dark purple conical fruit to 15 mm long.

Distribution Native to south-east Europe, and western Asia to Iran. Introduced and often naturalized elsewhere. Frequently in valleys in hilly regions.

Cultivation Wild. Introduced as an ornamental bush and successfully grown in areas where neither the summers nor the winters are too extreme. Frequently used in hedging, when it should be pruned carefully with secateurs rather than generally clipped. May be propagated by cuttings taken in summer.

Constituents The glycosides prulaurasin (laurocerasin) and prunasin, which are decomposed in water by the enzyme prunase to release hydrogen cyanide, benzaldehyde and glucose. Cherry Laurel water is manufactured from the leaves by distillation.

Uses (Cherry Laurel water, very occasionally leaves) Sedative; antispasmodic.

The water was once used in the treatment of nausea and vomiting, as a flavouring agent, and, much diluted, as an eye lotion. It is now obsolete in most countries. The leaves can only be applied externally in small quantities in a mixed poultice for the temporary relief of pain.

Contra-indications Very POISONOUS. To be used internally only under medical supervision.

Pulmonaria officinalis L BORAGINACEAE
Lungwort Jerusalem Cowslip/Jerusalem Sage

This herb's common names variously refer to the white spots on its leaves, the change in its flower colour from pink to blue, or more frequently to its former application in lung diseases. Hence the generic name *Pulmonaria* which is derived from its medieval Latin name of *pulmonaria*, and, by translation, Lungwort. Lungwort's reputation far exceeded its therapeutic action, however.

Description Hairy perennial on creeping rootstock, reaching 30 cm tall; stems hairy and unbranched bearing few, alternate, sessile, white-spotted, oval and slightly pointed leaves to 7.5 cm long. Flowers blue, pink, purplish or white, primrose-like, to 2 cm long in terminal cymes; appearing spring to early summer. Flowering stem dies down in late summer and is replaced by a rosette of basal, long-petioled, auriculate-cordate leaves.

Distribution Native to Europe; introduced elsewhere. On well-drained calcareous soils in mixed woodland and thickets; to 1000 m altitude.

Cultivation Wild. Propagate by rootstock division in autumn or after flowering.

Constituents Mucilage; tannins; mineral salts, especially potassium and silica; saponins; allantoin.

Uses (dried flowering plant) astringent; diuretic; emollient; weak expectorant. Of use in the treatment of diarrhoea, haemorroids and some gastro-intestinal problems; also of some benefit in respiratory disorders such as bronchial catarrh.

Leaves once used as a pot herb.

Punica granatum L PUNICACEAE
Pomegranate

Pomegranates are mentioned in many ancient writings and have been depicted in various forms of illustration from the days of the Egyptians.

Both the fruit rind and root bark were used medicinally by the ancients, and Pliny and Dioscorides specifically mentioned the root decoction as being effective in the destruction of tapeworms. Yet, although various parts of the plant – such as the fruit rind – can be traced in the writings of the apothecaries and druggists, the valuable root bark apparently fell into disuse for 2000 years until the nineteenth century. In 1807 Buchanan and then Fleming reintroduced it following observations of its use in India.

The generic word *Punica* is derived from the Latin *malum punicum* meaning the apple of Carthage, which is one of its early names while *poma granata* (and hence pomegranate) means apples with many seeds.

Description Deciduous tree or shrub to 6 m tall, with spiny tipped branches; leaves opposite, sub-opposite or clustered, glabrous, entire, oblong or oval-lanceolate with pellucid areas, 2.5–6.0 cm long, narrowing at the base to a very short petiole.

Flowers orange-red, waxy, 4–5 cm long and wide, followed by large brownish-red or yellowish edible fruit (4–8 cm diameter) containing numerous seeds and soft pink pulp.

Distribution Native to Asia, particularly Afghanistan, Persia and the Himalayas. Naturalized in the mediterranean region, India, South America, southern United States, and parts of south and east Africa.

Cultivation Wild. Cultivated commercially and horticulturally. Both this species and a dwarf form, *P. granatum* var. *nana* (Pers.) are grown in temperate zones as greenhouse ornamentals.

Constituents (fruit rind) Yellow bitter colouring matter; gallotannic acid (to 30%). (root bark) Alkaloids (to 0.9%), comprising mainly pelletierine, pseudopelletierine, isopelletierine and methylisopelletierine, to which the antihelmintic action is due; also tannins (to 20%). (leaf) Ursolic and betulic acids; various triterpenes. (fruit) Invert sugar (10–20%); glucose (5–10%); citric acid (0.5–3.5%);

boric acid; vitamin C.

Uses (dried fruit rind, fresh or dried root bark, fresh leaf, fresh fruit) Astringent; antihelmintic; antibacterial. The rind is a powerful astringent which is used in decoction in the treatment of dysentery and diarrhoea, and as an infusion for colitis or stomach ache. Also used as a douche in leucorrhoea. The bark is effective in the removal of tapeworms (more effective when fresh), and has been used as an emmenagogue.

The leaf has antibacterial properties and is applied externally to sores.

The fruit is bitter and refreshing; of commercial importance both as the whole fruit and in fruit drinks.

Pyracantha coccinea M.J. Roem. ROSACEAE
Firethorn Everlasting Thorn

Although closely related to the genus *Crataegus* some of whose species provide valuable heart remedies, the Firethorn is now employed only as an ornamental. *Pyracantha* is from the

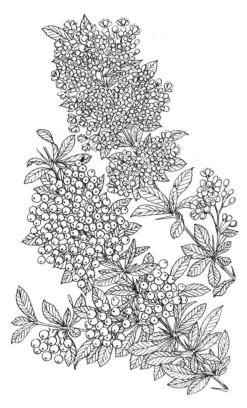

Greek for fire and thorn after the red fruit and shiny branches.

Description Much branched evergreen shrub or small tree to 5 m. Leaves dark green, acute, crenate-serrate, narrow-elliptic, 1.5 cm–5 cm long. Small, white flowers in large corymbs, appearing early summer and followed by red or orange berries which last through the winter.

Distribution Native from south Europe to western Asia. Escaped and naturalized in North America and elsewhere.

Cultivation Wild. Cultivated as ornamental or wall shrub, often espaliered. Hardy on well-drained soils. Propagate by ripe wood cuttings under glass, by seed, or by layering. Prune back hard to promote branching. Dislikes transplanting.

Constituents Cyanogenic glycosides.

Uses No longer used for medicinal purposes; the fruit is purgative but toxic.

Of use as a winter ornamental for hedges or walls.

Quercus robur L FAGACEAE
Oak English Oak/Pedunculate Oak

No plant has been of greater symbolic, religious and magical importance in Europe than the Oak tree, and its esteem has been traced back to the earliest Indo-Germanic religions. No other plant has provided more in the construction of buildings, ships, weapons and fine furniture. Oak's strength and durability were unequalled, and as a result the vast Oak forests of Europe have been virtually destroyed. Although its bark provides an excellent astringent medicinal remedy, only herbalists used it to much extent, the apothecaries and others preferring more exotic and costly drugs.

Description Round-topped deciduous tree to 40 m tall; bark first smooth, later developing fissures; leaves 5–12.5 cm long, oblong-ovate with 3–7 lobes each side, petiole short (to 1 cm). Small, greenish-yellow staminate flowers in thin catkins; pistillate flowers in spikes in leaf axils; appearing late spring to early summer, and followed by ovoid or oblong fruit on peduncles 3–7.5 cm long.

Distribution Native to North Africa, Europe and western Asia; introduced elsewhere. In forests, mixed woodland, on clay soils; from lowlands to mountainous regions.

Cultivation Wild plant. Planted commercially on estates and forestry land for timber. The variety *Q. robur* var. *fastigiata* DC has a more columnar appearance while the Durmast or Sessile Oak (*Q. petraea* (Matt.) Lieblein) has a less spreading and less branched growth, and sessile fruit. Several forms of *Q. petraea* exist.

Constituents Tannins (to 20%); a glycoside, quercitrin.

Uses (dried bark, occasionally dried leaves and fruit) Astringent; anti-inflammatory; antiseptic.

Used as a gargle for throat disorders; as a douche in leucorrhoea; externally as a lotion for cuts, burns, abrasions, and for application to haemorrhoids.

Used internally for haemorrhoids, diarrhoea and enteritis. Once used as a tonic tea.

Roasted acorns have been used as a coffee substitute.

Valuable timber.

Bark was once the most important agent for tanning leather; and also provided a variety of dyes, the colour depending upon the mordant used.

Ranunculus ficaria L RANUNCULACEAE
Lesser Celandine Pilewort

The fig-like shape of the swollen root-tubers of this plant led to the specific epithet *ficaria* from *ficus* or fig. Earlier herbalists considered the same structure to resemble piles and by association they were used, with much success, in the treatment of haemorrhoids.

Members of the genus *Ranunculus* are not popular in folk medicine because of their poisonous and acrid nature, and all species should be handled with care and only used externally.

The Latin *ranunculus* means a little frog and it was given this name since many of the 250 species in the group are aquatic or are found in very wet habitats.

Description Perennial with hollow, erect or prostrate branched stem, on several clavate or fusiform root-tubers; 5–25 cm tall. Leaves cordate, occasionally toothed, glabrous, petiolate and sheathed at the base, glossy; 1–4 cm long, the stem leaves being smallest. Flowers yellow, 2–3 cm diameter with 8–12 petals, solitary, appearing mid to late spring on long peduncles.

Distribution Native to Europe, North Africa and western Asia. On rich nitrogenous soils in wet situations; in woodland, meadows, ditches. Prefers shade.

Cultivation Wild plant. Propagate from root-tubers planted in the autumn, 5 cm deep, in damp rich soils.

Constituents Vitamin C; anthemol; tannins.

Uses (fresh herb, occasionally dried herb) Astringent. The plant is specifically used in the preparation of ointments for external application to haemorrhoids.

The acrid and vesicant juices from the sliced tubers were once applied to warts.

Very young leaves were once eaten to prevent scurvy.

Contra-indications POISONOUS in the fresh state; not to be used internally. Handling the bruised plant may cause skin irritation.

Raphanus sativus L CRUCIFERAE
Radish

This well-known salad herb has been in cultivation for so long that its origin is uncertain, but it probably originated in China where many varieties exist today including a long-rooted, winter-harvested Chinese Radish, or Daikon (a Japanese name), which is sometimes cultivated in the West.

Some authorities believe that *R. sativus* (*sativus* means cultivated) is a cultivated variety of the Wild Radish or Wild Charlock (*R. raphanistrum* L), a widespread and troublesome weed.

Radishes have certainly been grown since the time of the Pharaohs, and the Greeks and

Romans knew several varieties including the *syriacan* (or round Radish) and the *radicula* or *radix* (the common long Radish) the latter meaning simply root and being the source of the common name, Radish.

The black Radishes which are the varieties now employed in homeopathic medicine were probably developed in Spain in the Middle Ages.

Description Annual or biennial on fleshy root of variable shape and colour; stem glaucous 60–90 cm bearing lyrate-divided, petiolate leaves with a large terminal segment. Flowers dark-violet, white-veined, in racemes appearing summer and followed by 3–7 cm long fruit (a silique).

Distribution Worldwide on most soil types.

Cultivation Cultivated plant; found wild as an escape. Many cultigens exist, all of which are raised from seed sown thinly on moist, friable soils in an open position. Time of sowing depends on variety; but usually best sown every three weeks.

Constituents An antibiotic glycoside, glucoraphenine; mineral salts; vitamin C; oxalic acid. The seeds contain linoleic and linolenic acids.

Uses (fresh root, fresh leaves, root juice, fresh young seed pods) Antibiotic; bechic; tonic; carminative; choleretic; nutritive.

Of benefit in the relief of dyspepsia and used to promote salivation. Formerly employed in the treatment of coughs and bronchitis. May be used in combination with other remedies in the treatment of liver conditions especially where bile secretion is inadequate. Also used homeopathically.

The root and young leaves are eaten as a salad herb, and the young seed pods may be pickled.

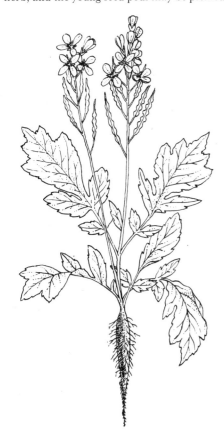

Rhamnus catharticus L RHAMNACEAE
Buckthorn

So common a plant with so drastic an effect as this powerful purgative has doubtless been used for a very long time. The Anglo-Saxons certainly recorded it in the ninth century, when it was known as Waythorn or Hartsthorn, while the thirteenth-century Welsh physicians of Myddvai used its fruit boiled with honey. Three hundred years later Gerard was to recommend boiling them with broth; they are rarely taken alone, and even when Syrup of Buckthorn was first included in the London Pharmacopoeia in 1650 (it had appeared almost a century earlier in the German pharmacopoeias) it was mixed with Nutmeg, Cinnamon, Aniseed and Mastich (the latter a gum from *Pistacia lentiscus* L). The characteristic spine on the branches has led to most of its names: Crescenzi and Gesner called it *Spina cervina*; Cordus, *Cervi spina*; Matthiolus, *Spinus infectoria*; and Caeselpinus, *Spina cervatis*. Dodoens knew it as *Rhamnus solutivus*.

The plant is now rarely used for medicinal purposes, but home dyers still employ the bark as a golden-brown dyestuff.

Description Deciduous bushy shrub from 2–4 m tall, occasionally to 6 m. Branches spreading irregularly, and often tipped with a spine; bark reddish-brown and glossy. Leaves opposite, acute or obtuse, margins finely dentate, ovate, 3–6 cm long, 2–5 cm wide. Flowers small, greenish-yellow; usually unisexual, in delicate clusters in leaf axils, appearing late spring to mid-summer, and followed by 7.5 mm diameter globose, fleshy, black fruit (drupe).

Distribution Native to north-west Europe, northern Asia, eastern North America. Widespread in scrub, woodland, forests, on calcareous soils to 1200 m altitude.

Cultivation Wild. Planted on farmland as hedging. Cuttings taken in summer are easily rooted.

Constituents Vitamin C; frangula-emodin; shesterine; chrysophanol; rhamnosterin; rhamnicoside; rhamnicogenol; a fluorescent pigment, rhamnofluorin; other yellow pigments.

Uses (2 year old bark, fruit) Purgative; diuretic. Only employed in the treatment of chronic constipation; usually in association with other remedies. Juice from the fruit was once used in veterinary medicine as a laxative.

The fruit and bark can be used as sources of dyes.

Contra-indications Strong purgative action; to be taken with great care.

Do not use fresh bark.

Rhamnus purshiana DC RHAMNACEAE
Cascara Sagrada Sacred Bark

Cascara sagrada means sacred bark and this was the name first given to the tree by Spanish-Mexicans who noted the American Indian use of the bark as a laxative and tonic.

The tree was mentioned in the eighteenth-century American materia medicas but first described botanically in 1814 by Pursh – hence the plant's specific name. Use of the bark in conventional medicine began in 1877 and a year later a nauseous and bitter fluid extract for use in chronic constipation was available pharmaceutically. This extract was exported to Europe and it was not until 1883 that the bark itself was made available outside the United States of America. It has been conclusively demonstrated that the crude bark is

very much more effective as a purgative than any commercial preparation made from the bark; the official dried and liquid extracts are for example only 15 per cent as active. The bark is retained in many national pharmacopoeias.

Description Deciduous tree to 10 m. Bark dark grey, smoothly wrinkled. Leaves in tufts at branchlet tips; 5–15 cm long, elliptic to ovate-oblong, either rounded or acute. Flowers in umbels, stalked, appearing spring and followed by black, globose fruit of 7.5 mm diameter.

Distribution North American native from British Columbia to Washington state. In coniferous woodland, on mountain ridges and canyon walls.

Cultivation Wild plant.

Constituents Anthraquinone glycosides (6–9%), comprising cascarosides A, B, C and D and other glucosides, to which the action is due.

Uses (dried stem bark, at least 6 months old)

Purgative; bitter stomachic. May be used in small doses as an appetite stimulant. In large doses it acts as a laxative or a mild purgative. Sometimes the tincture is applied to childrens' fingernails to deter them from biting their nails.

Rheum officinale Baill. POLYGONACEAE
Rhubarb

This is not the garden species commonly grown for its edible leaf stalks, that one being *R. rhabarbarum* L. The garden Rhubarb was introduced to western Europe in 1608 and was first cultivated at Padua botanic gardens by Prosper Alpinus; it was widely grown by the end of the eighteenth century, but the root has never been used owing to a substance (the glycoside, rhaponticin) which exerts a hormonal effect on humans.

Rheum officinale, however, is one of two main species, the dried rhizomes of which have been important medicinally in China since around 2700 B.C. Both have been imported into Europe since the time of the early Greeks. Dioscorides described the drug as *rheon* or *rha*, hence the modern names. Because the main centre for trading in the drug has changed over the centuries, both this and other species have been variously described as Turkey, East Indian and Muscovitic rhubarbs. The plant was introduced to Europe in 1867 and limited cultivation led to further names such as English, German, Bucharest, Dutch and French rhubarbs.

Description Perennial on thick rhizome, reaching 3 m tall. Leaves to 1 m wide, round-elliptic, basal, 3–7 lobed. Flowers white small, numerous, in panicles on tall, stout, hollow, finely grooved stem. Appearing mid to late summer.

Distribution Native to Tibet and west China, introduced elsewhere. On deep, rich, moist soil at altitudes of 3000–4000 m.

Cultivation Wild. Cultivated in the East.

Constituents Tannins; anthraquinone derivatives of aloe-emodin, chrysophanol, emodin and rhein (to 10%).

Uses (dried rhizome) Mild purgative; astringent; bitter.

Principally employed alone or in combination with other remedies in the treatment of chronic constipation. In small doses it may be used to treat diarrhoea, gastro-intestinal catarrh, and to stimulate the appetite.

Added to tonic wines as a bitter.

Contra-indications Not to be used by individuals with renal or urinary calculi.

Rheum palmatum L POLYGONACEAE
Rhubarb Chinghai Rhubarb

R. palmatum and some varieties such as *R. palmatum* var. *tanguticum* (L) Maxim., and *R. palmatum* var. *palmatum* (L) Maxim., are now, and possibly always were, the main sources of medicinal Rhubarb.

R. palmatum was introduced to European gardens in 1763, earlier than *R. officinale* Baill., and like that species was cultivated commercially. It is still cultivated in Russia and Germany, but the Chinese product is superior. In the Chinese herbal Pen-King (2700 B.C.) the drug was called *Ta-huang*, meaning the great yellow, after its colour and reputation, and this name was retained for 2000 years by the traders who collected it in Tibet and the province of Kansu. *R. palmatum* is now called Chinghai or high-dried Rhubarb.

Description Perennial on thick rhizome, reaching 2 m tall. Large leaves in basal clumps, cordate at base, orbicular and palmately lobed. Flowers reddish to greenish-white, small, numerous, in clusters on tall, stout, hollow, finely grooved stem. Appearing mid to late summer.

Distribution Native to north-east Asia. On

deep, rich, moist soils at altitudes of 3000–4000 m.

Cultivation Wild. Cultivated commercially in China, Russia, Germany and Central Europe. Requires moist, deep, well-manured soil; propagated from root division and root cuttings, rarely from seed. Occasionally grown as garden ornamental.

Constituents Tannins; anthraquinone derivatives of aloe-emodin, chrysophanol, emodin and rhein (to 10%).

Uses (dried rhizome) Mild purgative; astringent; bitter.

Principally employed alone or in combination with other remedies in the treatment of chronic constipation. In small doses it may be used to treat diarrhoea, gastro-intestinal catarrh, and to stimulate the appetite.

Added to tonic wines as a bitter.

Contra-indications Not to be used by individuals with renal or urinary calculi.

Ribes nigrum L SAXIFRAGACEAE
Blackcurrant

A well-known fruit formerly collected from the wild in northern Europe and now extensively cultivated commercially and horticulturally. Although it was once used in folk medicine for throat infections it is now not considered to be of medicinal importance and finds greatest use in the food and drinks industries.

Ribes is an old Arabic name and the specific epithet *nigrum* means black, referring to the colour of the wild fruit. Today green, yellow and white forms are grown, and many cultivars have been developed.

Description Aromatic perennial shrub to 2 m, lacking spines and bearing 5-lobed, rounded, long-petiolate, alternate or clustered leaves. Flowers 4–10, greenish-white in pendulous racemes in leaf axils. Appearing late spring to early summer and followed by spherical, soft berries.

Description Native to north and central Europe, and west Asia. Introduced and naturalized in North America. On moist, loamy, slightly acidic soils in woodland.

Cultivation Wild. Cultivated commercially and horticulturally for fruit. Several cultivars exist. Propagation by cuttings taken in autumn. Prefers cool, humid climate and clay soils provided they are well drained. Constant pruning is essential to good cropping.

Constituents Anthocyanin pigments; vitamin C; pectin; sugars; various organic acids; essential oil.

Uses (fresh or dried leaves, fruit) Nutritive; diuretic; astringent; tonic.

The leaves may be used as an infusion to treat

diarrhoea; they are also weakly diaphoretic and have been included in cold remedies, and to treat urinogenital infections.

Once employed in the treatment of rheumatism. The fruit is of value to those suffering from hypertension, or possessing capillary fragility; and can be used in an infusion as a gargle for sore throats. Leaves can be used as a tea substitute. Fruit widely used in conserves, jams, drinks, cordials and liqueurs as well as eaten fresh.

Ricinus communis L EUPHORBIACEAE
Castor Oil Plant Wonder Tree

The Castor Oil Plant was certainly known to the Egyptians who employed the seed oil as an unguent base and also in lamps. Theophrastus, Dioscorides and other Greeks also knew both the plant and the oil, but considered the latter unfit for culinary use and suitable only for external application medically – a tradition maintained for the following 1500 years

and faithfully reproduced in the sixteenth-century herbals of Turner and Gerard. Up to the end of the sixteenth century European supplies of the oil came from the East, notably India, but for a period of 200 years the supply declined for some reason and in much of Europe it was only used infrequently.

The oil was reintroduced to medicine in 1764 by Canvane who had noted its use in the West Indies where it was called *Palma Christi* and *agno casto* by the Spanish, (hence Casto oil, and then Castor oil).

Since the 1780s it has been retained as a purgative in many pharmacopoeias.

Description Very variable annual herb or perennial tree from 2–15 m tall, usually 4 m. Leaves simple, alternate, long-petioled, 5–11 lobed, glossy, to 1 m wide. Flowers monoe-

cious; male below, female above; both without petals and in panicles. Followed by a smooth or spiny capsule, 3 cm in diameter.

Distribution Native to India, tropical Africa; distributed throughout tropical and many temperate regions. On most well-drained soils in full sun.

Cultivation Wild. Cultivated commercially in many countries especially South America, India, Africa, Italy. Grown as a house plant in cool, northern temperate zones, or outside in protected sites. Prefers well-drained clay or sandy loams. Propagate from seed planted in early spring or under glass, transplanting in early summer. Many cultivars exist.

Constituents (seed) Protein (to 26%); fixed oil (to 50%) comprising ricinoleic, oleic, linoleic, stearic and hydroxystearic acids. One of the protein substances in the whole seed is a toxic albuminoid, ricin, to which the poisoning is due.

Uses (seed oil, steam treated seed cake) Purgative.

Principally used to treat chronic constipation but also in acute diarrhoea caused by food poisoning. Applied as an enema to remove impacted faeces.

Used externally as an emollient and a vehicle for various ointments. Soothes eye irritations. The oil is not suitable for cooking, but is used in the manufacture of paints, varnishes and soap. The seed cake (steam treatment destroys the poison, ricin) is employed as a fertilizer.

Contra-indications Whole seeds are toxic; not to be used internally. Large doses of the oil may cause vomiting, colic and severe purgation.

Rosa canina L ROSACEAE
Dog Rose Dog Briar

The Rose more than any other flower symbolizes the zenith of beauty in the plant kingdom, and since man started cultivation its scent has been most highly esteemed. The Dog Rose, however, was so common throughout Europe (Pliny thought Britain was called Albion because it was covered with the white rose – *alba* meaning white) that it has generally been treated with familiarity and contempt.

The epithet Dog is only incidentally derogatory, coming originally from the *cynorrodon* of Pliny and *Rosa canina* of the Middle Ages after a supposed ability of the root to cure 'mad-dog bites', or rabies. Apothecaries employed the briar balls or galls of the Dog Rose as a diuretic and the rose-hips were used as a tart fruit from the earliest times. The latter became medicinally important only in the Second World War as a rich source of vitamin C.

Description Climbing and trailing prickly perennial shrub to 3 m. Leaves alternate, ovate to elliptic, to 4 cm long, serrate, acute or acuminate. Flowers aromatic, large, white or pale pink on long pedicels, appearing mid to late summer. Followed by 15 mm-long, fleshy, scarlet false fruits (hips).

Distribution Native to Europe, North Africa, western Asia; introduced and naturalized elsewhere. On porous soil in hedgerows, woodland, thickets to 1600 m in altitude.

Cultivation Wild.

Constituents Vitamin C (to 1.7%); vitamins B, E, K; nicotinamide; organic acids; tannins; pectin.

Uses (rose-hips, leaves) Tonic; laxative; diuretic; astringent.

The leaves may be used as a laxative or in poultices to aid wound healing.

Rose-hips, usually used as a tisane or in the form of the seedless purée, are an excellent source of vitamin C, a tonic, and useful in lethargy. The seeds were once used as a diuretic. The hips are used in conserves and jams.

Rosa eglanteria L ROSACEAE
Sweet Briar Eglantine

This is a vigorous grower and possesses a strong fragrance which can be smelled at a distance, characteristics which led to its use as a hedging plant from early times.

The common and specific names come from the medieval Latin *aculentus* meaning thorny. Formerly classified as *Rosa rubiginosa* agg. and subdivided into two species, *R. rubiginosa* L and *R. micrantha* Borrer ex Sm., but now considered as *R. eglanteria*.

Description Perennial shrub 1–2 m tall. Leaves orbicular to elliptic, to 3 cm long; pubescent

and rusty-coloured beneath. Flowers 1–3, bright pink, strongly scented, to 3 cm wide, appearing mid to late summer and followed by round scarlet false fruit (hip).
Distribution Native to Europe, west Asia, introduced and naturalized elsewhere. In hedgerows and woodland edges.
Cultivation Wild plant. A cultivar, *Duplex*, with double flowers is grown horticulturally.
Constituents Tannins; essential oil.
Uses (flowers) Astringent.
No longer used medicinally. In some countries it is employed in the treatment of diarrhoea and colic.
A useful hedging plant in large gardens.

Rosa rugosa Thunb. ROSACEAE
Japanese Rose Turkestan Rose
This is one of the most hardy of all roses and is in addition both disease resistant and a profuse and continuous bloomer. The scent is rich and

somewhat clove-like and is considered superior to Sweet Briar as a hedge plant. The hips may be used as a source of vitamin C.
Description Perennial to 2 m. Very prickly stems. Leaves subdivided into 5–9 elliptic leaflets to 5 cm long. Flowers scented, white to rose, to 7.5 cm diameter, followed by large red or orange hip to 3 cm diameter.
Distribution Native to Japan and China.
Cultivation Wild. Widely cultivated as a large number of attractive hybrids, and varieties include Max Graf, one of the lowest growing roses, obtained by crossing *R. rugosa* with *R. wichuraiana* Crép.
Constituents (hips) Vitamin B, C, E, K; nicotinamide; organic acids; tannins; pectin.
Uses Rarely used for any purpose other than as a hedge plant.

Rosmarinus officinalis L LABIATAE
Rosemary
The common and generic names are derived from the early Latin *ros maris* or dew of the sea, from its habit of growing close to the sea and the dew-like appearance of the blossom at a distance. From earliest times its medicinal virtues were recognized and it has always been a popular aromatic plant.
The oil was first extracted by distillation in

about 1330 by Raymundus Lullus, and it is still extensively used in perfumery. One of the most famous cosmetic preparations containing the herb was the Queen of Hungary's water. The apothecaries used Rosemary in a wide range of preparations including waters, tinctures, conserves, syrups, spirits and unguents; but today only the oil is included in the pharmacopoeias, while the leaf remains popular in folk medicine.
Description Aromatic, evergreen perennial shrub to 180 cm, usually 100 cm tall. Branches somewhat pubescent when young, becoming woody. Leaves simple, opposite, leathery, tomentose beneath, to 3.5 cm long. Flowers pale blue or rarely white to pink, small, in short axillary racemes, appearing late spring to early summer.
Distribution Native to mediterranean coast.
Cultivation Wild. Collected commercially from the wild and cultivated only as a garden plant. Requires well-drained soil and warm, wind-sheltered position in cooler regions. May be grown in pots. Propagate by stem cuttings or seed. Various cultivars are grown of which the most useful is the prostrate form, (sometimes called *R. prostratus* Hort.).
Constituents Essential oil (to 2%) comprising 2–5% esters (mainly bornyl acetate) and 10–20% free alcohols (mainly borneol and linalol); organic acids; choline; saponoside; heterosides; tannins.
Uses (fresh or dried leaves, oil) Tonic; diuretic; aromatic; stomachic; carminative; antispasmodic; cholagogue; antiseptic; emmenagogue.
A leaf infusion has a wide variety of internal applications as indicated. The oil may be used externally as an insect repellant, in various soothing embrocations, and diluted as an antiseptic gargle. It is particularly effective in neuralgia.
Wide culinary use of the leaf in meat dishes.
The oil is employed widely in the cosmetic industry.
Leaf may be used in bath mixtures and aromatic preparations.
Contra-indications The oil should not be used internally. Extremely large doses of the leaf

are toxic, possibly causing abortion, convulsions, and very rarely, death.

Rubia tinctorum L RUBIACEAE
Madder Dyer's Madder
Both the early Greek name *Erythrodanon* and the Latin name *Rubia* come from a stem-word meaning red, since this has traditionally been the source of a brilliant red permanent dye Adrianople Red or Turkey Red, later called alizarin.
By the end of the nineteenth century the process of maddering wool or cotton consisted of various steps including scouring in mild alkali, steeping in oily emulsions, washing in sheep dung, galling with oak galls, treating with alum and finally maddering with powdered and partially fermented roots.
The dried roots were first exported from southeast Europe and Turkey to other parts of Europe, and cultivation then commenced near the cloth centres of France, Holland, Germany and, less commonly, England. Even though it has long since been replaced by synthetic alizarin, it is still grown as a medicinal plant in central Europe and west Asia.
The Wild Madder (*Rubia peregrina* L) provides a rose-pink dye.
Description Climbing perennial, 60–100 cm tall, on long, fleshy, much-branched rootstock. Leaves in whorls of 4–8 on stiff, prickly stem; usually sessile, lanceolate, 5–10 cm long, tipped and spiky at the margins. Flowers small, greenish-yellow, in both axillary and terminal cymes; appearing mid-summer to early autumn, followed by globose, purple-black berry.
Distribution Native to south-east Europe, Asia Minor; introduced to central and north-west Europe, and locally naturalized. On well-drained alkaline soils in full sun or partial shade to 1000 m altitude.
Cultivation Wild. Propagated from seed sown spring or autumn, or by root division. Prefers deep, friable soils.
Constituents Heteroside anthraquinones (comprising mainly ruberythric acid) to which the medicinal action is mainly due; sugars; pectin. The colouring matter includes madder red (alizarin), madder purple (purpurin),

madder orange (rubiacin), and madder yellow (xanthine).

Uses (root, rarely leafy stems) Choleretic; tonic; antiseptic; diuretic; vulnerary; emmenagogue; laxative; antispasmodic.

The powdered root is of much value in the dissolution and elimination of renal and bladder calculi; the remedy also acts as a prophylactic against stone formation. May be used externally to aid wound healing.

The leafy stem in infusion can be used to treat constipation.

Root is employed as a dye.

Rubus fructicosus agg. ROSACEAE
Bramble Blackberry
While the Raspberry was named after a sweet red French wine, *raspis*, the common fruit of the 1000 or more varieties and species grouped under the name *R. fructicosus* were simply blackberries, and the plant itself was the brom or thorny shrub, hence bramble.

In German the plant is still called *Brombeere*. Like raspberries they have been picked and eaten for thousands of years and today in much of industrialized Europe Blackberry picking is now the last ritualistic seasonal collecting of wild plant food still practised.

Description Variable shrub with woody, biennial stems densely covered with prickles. Leaves palmate or ternate, and petiolate. Flowers white to pink in compound inflorescence appearing mid-summer to early autumn and followed by fleshy, black, edible fruit.

Distribution European native; especially in hedgerows, wood edges and gardens. On moist soils to 2400 m in altitude.

Cultivation Wild. Introduced near habitation and often rampant.

Constituents (fruit) Vitamin C; organic acids; pectins. (leaves) Tannins; sugars.

Uses (dried or fresh leaves, fruit, rarely flowers) Astringent; tonic; diuretic.

Leaves may be used in decoction as a gargle or douche and externally on ulcers. They have been accredited with (as yet unsubstantiated) antidiabetic activity.

Wide culinary use of the fruit. The root provides an orange dye.

Rubus idaeus L ROSACEAE
Raspberry
Like so many wild fruits the Raspberry has been known and used since prehistory in Europe, fragments of the berry being found in archaeological excavations of Swiss villages. Cultivation began in the Middle Ages, and the many European raspberry cultivars are all developed from this wild species. Prior to 1866 (at which time over 41 varieties were known in the United States of America) all American types were also from *R. idaeus*. They are now also developed from *R. ulmifolius* Schott, *R. ursinus* Cham and Schlechtend, *R. occidentalis* L. *Rubus* is from the Latin for red, and *idaeus* means 'of Mount Ida', after its abundance on Mount Ida.

Description Upright or bent perennial 90–150 cm tall, with varying degrees of prickles or sometimes entirely lacking them. Leaves glabrous above, grey tomentose beneath, compris-

ing 3 or 5 ovate leaflets. Flowers small, 1–6 in drooping panicles in terminal axils, appearing early to mid-summer, followed by aromatic fleshy cone-shaped red to yellow fruit.

Distribution Eurasian native, introduced and widespread. In woodland clearings and edges, especially deciduous woodlands. On light soil, moist and rich in nutrients, to 2000 m in altitude.

Cultivation Wild. Numerous cultivars propagated by suckers or root cuttings. Canes should be removed after fruiting to allow new ones (primocanes) to develop. Tolerates most soils.

Constituents (leaf) Fragarine and other substances, acting in isolation as both uterine muscle stimulants and relaxants. (fruit) Citric acid; vitamin C; pectin.

Uses (fresh or dried leaves, fruit) Astringent; oxytocic; nutritive; laxative.

The leaf is of proven value during confinement, if taken regularly and in small doses as an infusion – it eases and speeds parturition. In larger doses the leaf is of benefit in painful menstruation and also in diarrhoea. In large amounts the fruit is mildly laxative.

The fruit was formerly employed in a variety of pharmaceutical and herbal products as a flavouring and colouring.

Edible fruit is of economic importance.

Used in wines, liqueurs, vinegars, syrups, and for other confectionery, culinary and some cosmetic purposes.

Rumex acetosa L POLYGONACEAE
Sorrel
All sorrels are acidic and sour-tasting, and in former times were popular ingredients of sauces, especially those for fish. The common name is derived from *sur* meaning sour, via the old French *surele*.

The plant's acidity is due to both its vitamin C and its oxalic acid and oxalate salts (mostly potassium hydrogen oxalate).

These latter substances are responsible for the occasional cases of Sorrel poisoning caused either by *R. acetosa* or by *R. acetosella* L, occurring in both man and animals. The herb has, nevertheless, long been used as a salad and vegetable and was cultivated in the fourteenth century or even earlier. By the eighteenth century, however, it was largely replaced by *R. scutatus* L in horticulture. The plant was known to the apothecaries as *Herba Acetosa* and was included in many dispensatories from the fifteenth to the nineteenth centuries.

Description Perennial 50–150 cm tall, nearly glabrous. Leaves rather thick, oblong-lanceolate to 10 cm long, the upper ones sessile. Flowers small, reddish-brown on slender, loose inflorescence to 40 cm long, appearing early summer to early autumn.

Distribution European native; also found in northern Asia. In meadowland on nitrogen-rich, damp, loamy soils to 2500 m in altitude.

Cultivation Wild plant. May be propagated by root division in autumn.

Constituents (leaf and juice) Oxalic acid and potassium binoxalate (to 1%); tartaric acid; vitamin C. (rhizome) A hyperoside, quercetin-3-D-galactoside; anthracene; oxymethylanthraquinone; tannins (to 25%).

Uses (fresh leaf, rhizome) Diuretic; laxative; tonic; antiseptic; bitter.

The root decoction is used as a bitter tonic and as an astringent in diarrhoea; also as a diuretic; it is not suitable for use in either young or very old people.

The leaf may be employed in poultices to treat certain skin complaints, including acne.

The young leaf is edible fresh or cooked.

Contra-indications Very large doses are POISONOUS, causing severe kidney damage. The herb should not be used by those predisposed to rheumatism, arthritis, gout, kidney stones or gastric hyper-acidity. The leaf may cause dermatitis.

Rumex crispus L POLYGONACEAE
Yellow Dock Curled Dock/Rumex
In ancient writings both this species and another common weed, the Broad-leaved Dock (*R. obtusifolius* L) have been used for the same medicinal purposes, and more recently they have been shown to possess similar chemical constituents.

R. obtusifolius was known as *Lapathum* or *Lapathum acutum* from the fourteenth century, while the Yellow Dock was called *Lapathum crispum*. In the development of physiomedicalism in the early nineteenth century in America, *R. crispus* was used for obstinate skin complaints, while in Europe *R. obtusifolius* was used for the same condition. Today *Rumex* is found in English herbals, and *Lapathum* in European ones.

Description Perennial 50–100 cm tall on stout rootstock. Leaves with undulate edges, lanceolate, large, crispy. Flowers greenish, small, in whorls along a somewhat branched inflorescence, appearing mid-summer to mid-autumn.

Distribution Eurasian native, widely distributed in temperate and subtropical countries as a weed. In any rich, heavy soil in weedy places, to 1500 m altitude.

Cultivation Wild. Propagate from seed.

Constituents (root-stock) Oxymethylanthraquinone (to 0.2%); emodin (to 0.1%); chrysophanic acid; volatile oil; resin; tannins; rumicin; starch; thiamine. The combined action is both astringent and purgative, and is described as tonic laxative.

Uses (root-stock, young leaves, rarely seed) Purgative; cholagogue; tonic; astringent. Of much value both internally and externally in skin complaints, especially where the cause is associated with constipation or liver dysfunction. May be applied to ringworm, scabies and urticaria, the parasites probably being destroyed by the rumicin content.

In small doses it is stomachic and tonic, and in China it is considered antipyretic.

The powdered root-stock in water is employed as a gargle for laryngitis and as a tooth powder in gingivitis.

The seed is highly astringent and may be used in cases of diarrhoea.

Young leaves may be eaten as greens, but water should be changed twice during cooking.

Contra-indications May cause dermatitis. Excessive doses produce nausea.

Rumex scutatus L POLYGONACEAE
French Sorrel Garden Sorrel
While *Rumex alpinus* L or Monk's Rhubarb is the most physiologically active of the European species of *Rumex*, the French Sorrel is probably the least, and since it in addition possesses a mildly sour, lemony taste it has become the most popular of the edible sorrels. Once established its deeply-growing roots may be difficult to eradicate.

Description Perennial, low-growing and glaucous, 10–50 cm tall. Leaves petiolate, hastate, fleshy. Flowers small, reddish, unisexual, appearing mid to late summer.

Distribution Native to Europe and Asia; introduced elsewhere.

Cultivation Wild. Cultivated as a salad herb in any rich, moist soil. Propagate from seed sown in spring, thinning to 30 cm apart and

removing flower-heads to promote leaf. Water well in hot weather. Tolerates partial shade or full sun, and can be grown under cloches to provide leaf throughout the year.

Constituents Oxalates, in small quantities.

Uses (fresh leaf) Diuretic.
Not used medicinally but moderate amounts of the leaf are diuretic.
May be used with discretion in salads.

Contra-indications Not suitable for those predisposed to kidney stones.

Ruscus aculeatus L LILIACEAE
Butcher's Broom Box Holly/Jew's Myrtle
This unusual member of the Lily family was associated with the meat trade from the sixteenth to the nineteenth centuries, first as a crude repellent barrier to vermin and animals,

then as a broom or twitch to scrub chopping blocks, and finally as a decoration for meat at festive times. It bears scarlet berries at Christmas time, and the evergreen twigs are now used in florists' winter decorations.

It is related to Asparagus and starts with young edible shoots which can be eaten in a similar way. The ancient names of Butcher's Broom included *Bruscus*, *Eruscus* and *Hypoglosson*; Dioscorides recommended the rhizome in cases of kidney stones.

Description Erect evergreen perennial 30–90 cm tall. The leaves are minute and bract-like and subtend the 4 cm-long, spine-pointed, ovate, leaf-like cladodes. Flowers whitish or pinkish, minute, solitary or clustered, attached to the cladode midrib, appearing mid-autumn to late spring and followed by red or yellow globose berries reaching 15 mm in diameter.

Distribution Native from the Azores to Iran, including north-west Europe and the mediterranean region. Introduced elsewhere. In woodland thickets on poor, dry soil among rocks. To 600 m in altitude.

Cultivation Wild. Grown horticulturally, and collected on a small commercial scale.

Constituents Essential oil; saponoside; resin; potassium salts.

Uses (dried root-stock, young shoots, rarely leaves) Antipyretic; diuretic; vasoconstrictive. Rarely used medicinally, but of value in some problems associated with venous circulation. Traditionally used in the treatment of haemorrhoids, gout and jaundice.

The young shoots have been used in spring salads in the same way as Asparagus.

Contra-indications Not to be used by individuals with hypertension.

Ruta graveolens L RUTACEAE
Rue Herb of Grace/Herbygrass
Rue is an ancient and important medicinal plant of undoubted effectiveness which deserves wider use by medical personnel; yet, besides folk medicine application and use in Chinese herbal medicine, it is now only retained in the Swiss Pharmacopoeia.

It had wide therapeutic application traditionally and was also included as a major ingredient of the poison antidotes of Mithridates. Its

beneficial effects led to its pre-eminence as a protector against witchcraft and magic; the name was once thought to be derived from the Greek *reuo* meaning to set free after its general effectiveness. The ancients, however, knew it both as *hrute* and *peganon* and Dioscorides further differentiated between a sharper 'mountain peganon' and a 'garden peganon'. *Ruta* is now thought to be derived from *hrute*, and hence the word Rue.

Writers after Dioscorides also emphasized the plant's effect on the uterus and the nervous system, and many, such as Bock in the fifteenth century and Lemery in the eighteenth, differentiated between the wild and garden herbs in medicinal application. Hahnemann introduced its use in homeopathy in 1818.

Since the flavour of Rue is strong and distinctive and the plant has to be used with care, it has not enjoyed popular use in recent times; maintaining the tradition of its employment in the old Mead known as sack, however, it is included in the Italian grape spirit *Grappa con ruta*.

Description Aromatic semi-evergreen perennial, glabrous and glaucous herb or subshrub to 1 m. Deeply subdivided alternate leaves with spatulate or oblong 15 mm long segments.

Flowers yellow in terminal corymbose inflorescence, appearing summer to early autumn.

Distribution Native to southern Europe, as far north as the southern Alps. In sheltered positions on dry rocky or limestone soils.

Cultivation Wild. Collected commercially from the wild. Grown horticulturally and propagated from seed sown in the spring, from cuttings taken in spring, or by careful division. Prefers full sun and well-drained soil. The cultivar *variegata* with variegated leaves, and the variety var. *divaricata* (Ten.) Wilk., with bright yellow-green leaves, are also grown in herb gardens.

Constituents Volatile oil (to 0.6%), comprising various ketones, but mainly methylnonylketone (to 90%), also limonene, cineol, methyl acetate; resin; tannins; the rhamno-glucoside, rutin; coumarin; fixed oil; bergapten; xantotoxin; alkaloids; ascorbic acid; furo-cou-

marins; several other active substances.

Uses (dried or fresh leaf, rarely juice) Emmenagogue; abortifacient; antihelmintic; stomachic; diaphoretic.

Principally active on the uterus and in small doses beneficial for the relief of dysmenorrhoea; it acts as an emmenagogue.

Increases blood-flow to the gastro-intestinal system, aids in colic and acts as a stomachic. Of much value in certain autonomic nervous system disorders; traditionally employed in epilepsy. Externally used to treat skin diseases, to aid wound healing, in neuralgia, rheumatism and as an eye lotion. Also as a gargle. Leaves may be used, with discretion, in salads as a flavouring.

The oil is employed in the perfumery industry.

Contra-indications Must be used only by medical personnel. Must not be used at all by pregnant women as it is an abortifacient. Large doses are toxic, sometimes precipitating mental confusion, and the oil is capable of causing death. Handling the plant can cause allergic reactions or phytophotodermatitis.

Salicornia europaea agg. CHENOPODIACEAE
Glasswort Marsh Samphire
A herb of the salt marshes of Europe, especially found in the north and west, and one which – as its common name suggests – was employed as a source of materials used in glass manufacture. It replaced the southern *Salsola soda* L which had been exported northwards up to the sixteenth century. Its other common name indicates it was eaten in the same way as Samphire (*Crithmum maritimum* L).

It is now rarely, if ever, used. It is also known botanically as *S. herbacea* L.

Description Succulent annual or biennial with green leaves, and green or dull red uniformly candelabra-shaped stems, to 10 cm tall. Leaves

opposite, joined along their margins forming 'segments'. Flowers minute, greenish, borne on fleshy spikes, appearing early to mid-autumn.

Distribution European native. On salt marshes and mud flats.

Cultivation Wild.

Constituents Large proportion of mineral salts.

Uses (fresh plant) Diuretic.

Rarely used medicinally.

May be eaten either raw, or cooked with a knob of butter.

Salsola soda L CHENOPODIACEAE
Saltwort
Both this species and the closely related *S. kali* L were once important in the manufacture of glass, and large amounts of the mineral-rich

ash were exported from southern Europe and North Africa under the name Barilla. In north-west Europe *Salsola* species were replaced over 300 years ago by the abundant local Salicornias, but in France and Italy they continued to be of both commercial and, to a lesser extent, medicinal importance until the nineteenth century. The herb was never included in German pharmacopoeias, since superior remedies are numerous. The plant is no longer used.

Description Decumbent annual with spreading stems to 60 cm; leaves to 4 cm long, fleshy, sessile, simple and cylindrical; flowers usually solitary, greenish and insignificant. Appearing late summer to mid-autumn.

Distribution Native to mediterranean region. On sandy seashores.

Cultivation Wild plant.

Constituents Mineral salts, particularly large quantities of sodium sulphate; alkaloids, salsoline and salsolidine.

Uses (fresh or dried plant) Diuretic. No longer employed medicinally.

Salvia officinalis L LABIATAE
Sage
The Sage family is a large group of horticultur-

ally important plants which consists of over 750 species widely distributed throughout the world. Some are also of culinary use, others medicinal and at least one central American species is a powerful hallucinogen, traditionally employed in religious and magical rites.

The most important and best known is *Salvia officinalis*, which has been cultivated for millenia. Its ancient names include *elifagus, elelispha-kon* (the latter named by Dioscorides), *lingua humana, selba* and *salvia*. The name *salvia* is from the Latin *salvere*, meaning to be in good health; and the old French *saulje* gives us the modern common name.

At one time Sage was included in a brew called Sage Ale, and Sage tea was also a popular drink. The Chinese once preferred it to their local teas and exchanged their product with the Dutch for Sage tea, bartering on the basis of weight for weight.

Description Subshrub from 30–70 cm tall; stem woody at the base, branched, quadrangular, white and woolly when young. Leaves oblong, 3–5 cm long, usually entire, glandular or rugose, grey-green, petiolate. Flowers violet-blue, to 3 cm long, between 5 and 10 arranged on terminal spikes. Appearing early summer to early autumn.

Distribution Native to southern Europe, notably the mediterranean region. On limestone soils in full sun slopes, to 750 m altitude.

Cultivation Wild. Collected commercially from the wild, especially in Yugoslavia (Dalmatian Sage). Wide horticultural use and several varieties commonly grown. In northern countries Narrow-leaved Sage is grown from seed in late spring, flowering early summer to early autumn. Broad-leaved Sage does not flower in cool regions and cannot be raised from seed; use cuttings taken in late spring or early summer. Red-leaved Sage (Purple or Red Sage), Variegated Sage and Tricolor Sage (variegated and tipped with purple) are all grown from cuttings or by layering. Old leggy plants should be earthed up in spring and rooted cuttings cut off and planted out in autumn. Replace every 4–7 years.

Constituents Volatile oil (to 2%) comprising mainly thujone and cineol but including numerous other substances; also tannins; organic acids; rosmarinic acid; oestrogens;

bitter compounds including picrosalvine.
Uses (fresh or dried leaves, oil) Antiseptic; antifungal; anti-inflammatory; astringent; carminative; emmenagogue; choleretic; weak hypoglycaemic.

Wide medicinal application; especially effective as an anti-sudorific in cases of excessive sweating, and also to reduce lactation. Useful in liver disease, respiratory tract infections, and in nervous conditions such as anxiety or depression. Red Sage is an effective antiseptic gargle and may be used as a douche in leucorrhoea, or in baths to treat skin problems. It was traditionally employed in female sterility.

The oil is employed in both the pharmaceutical and culinary industries.

Salvia sclarea L LABIATAE
Clary Clary Sage/Muscatel Sage

Clary Sage is also known as Muscatel Sage since it is now almost exclusively grown commercially as the source of Muscatel oil, which is used in flavouring and in the perfumery industry. The leaves were once mixed

with Elderflower and employed in flavouring wines, and Clary wine itself was a sixteenth-century aphrodisiac. The name Clary comes from the Latin *clarus* after the use of its mucilaginous seeds to clear the eye of grit.

Description Erect biennial 30–120 cm tall, flowering stems bristly. Leaves simple, aromatic, pubescent, petiolate, broad-ovate, 15–22 cm long. Flowers white, lavender and pink, attractive, numerous, on terminal panicles. Appearing early summer to late autumn.

Distribution Native to southern Europe on dry limey or sandy soils, to 1000 m altitude.

Cultivation Wild. Grown commercially and horticulturally from seed sown thinly in spring. For blooming each year allow some plants to self-seed, or plant every year.

Constituents Essential oil (to 0.1%) comprising

linalol and esters; choline; saponine; tannins; mucilage.
Uses (seed, fresh or dried leaves, oil) Antispasmodic; stimulant; emmenagogue.

The seed becomes mucilaginous in water and may then be used to extract foreign bodies from the eye. The leaves in infusion may be used as a gargle, douche, skin wash for ulcers and cuts, and in small doses may be taken to promote appetite. It reduces sweating. Its principal employment is as the source of the oil, and it is most commonly used in herbal medicine to treat vomiting.

Oil is of value in the perfume and flavouring industries.

A decorative garden plant.

Sambucus ebulus L CAPRIFOLIACEAE
Dwarf Elder Danewort

Of the 20 or so species in the genus *Sambucus* the Dwarf Elder is the most active pharmacologically, and unlike its close relative the Elder (*S. nigra* L) its fruit should be considered as poisonous. The dark purple berries are certainly violently purgative; in the Middle Ages both these and the root or root bark were used as such – although ancient Greek physicians did not recommend their use.

Early names included *chamaiakte, atrix* and *ebulus*, the last stemming from the Latin *ebullire* meaning to bubble out, and possibly describing its purgative action.

Grigson in *The Englishman's Flora* traces the origin of the common name Danewort and shows it has nothing to do with the spilled 'blood of the Danes', from which the herb was once thought to grow; it is, in fact, derived from the *danes*, or diarrhoea, caused by the plant.

The Anglo-Saxons and Gauls employed Dwarf Elder berries as a blue dye, and this is now the main use for the herb.

Description Strong-smelling herbaceous perennial to 120 cm, on creeping rhizome. Stems numerous, grooved, bearing long-pointed, oblong, serrate, leaflets 5–15 cm long. Flowers in flat-topped, broad cymes, white to pink; appearing late summer to early autumn and followed by small black fruit.

Distribution Native to Europe, North Africa, Asia; introduced elsewhere. On damp soils,

wasteland, grassland or roadsides, to 1400 m altitude.
Cultivation Wild plant.
Constituents Essential oil; anthocyanins; tannins; organic acids.
Uses (root bark, fresh berries, flowers) Purgative. Rarely used owing to its drastic action. The fruit produces a blue dye.
Contra-indications The berries should not be taken internally.

Sambucus nigra L CAPRIFOLIACEAE
Elder

The Elder has been used continuously since the days of the Egyptians and probably before, and it is still included in certain modern cosmetic preparations as well as retaining its popularity in folk medicine. Elder flowers and Peppermint infusion is the medicine of choice for the treatment of colds in many country homes in Europe.
The plant has several uses, and some believe that every part of the Elder has some use. None is more popular than elderberry wine, while Elder flowers soaked in lemon juice overnight provide a most refreshing summer drink. Probably out of respect for its usefulness, the plant has been attributed with a variety of magical virtues, and many different European spirits were thought to inhabit it. In some

places old people still doff their caps at the plant or refuse to burn it.
It was known to the ancients as *rixus, ixus* and *akte,* but mostly as *sambucus* which gives us its modern generic name.
Description Shrub or small tree to 10 m tall; leaves dull green, subdivided into 5 elliptic, serrate acuminate leaflets, 3–9 cm long. Flowers white, 5 mm diameter, numerous, in flat-topped cymes to 20 cm diameter; appearing mid-summer and followed by numerous edible, purple, globose fruit to 8 mm diameter.
Distribution Native to Europe, North Africa, western Asia. Introduced elsewhere. In hedgerows, woodland edges, on nitrogen-rich soils. To 1000 m altitude.
Cultivation Wild plant. Usually propagated by suckers or cuttings. Prefers moist soils.

Some horticultural varieties exist, such as white, golden-yellow, variegated, or deeply dissected forms.
Constituents Essential oil comprising terpenes; the glucosides, rutin and quercitrin; alkaloids; tannins; vitamin C; mucilage; anthocyanins. The combined action is predominantly diaphoretic.
Uses (fresh or dried flowers, fruit, leaves, root bark, stem pith) Diaphoretic; laxative; antispasmodic: diuretic; emollient.
Mostly of use in combination with Peppermint and Yarrow in the treatment of colds and nasal catarrh, or alone as a gargle in throat infections.
Also of value with other remedies in constipation, haemorrhoids, rheumatism, bronchitis and cystitis. The flowers are sometimes used as an ingredient of eye lotions. Young buds can be pickled, and the flowers can be eaten raw or used in various drinks including wines. Fruit valuable in conserves, pies, jams and also wines. They can be used in home dyeing.
Wide cosmetic use of the flowers.

Sanguinaria canadensis L PAPAVERACEAE
Bloodroot Red Puccoon/Tetterwort

Another common name for this small pretty herb is Indian Paint since it was one of the body stains (and clothing dyes) used by the Red Indians.
Introduced to medicine via folklore, it was used as a domestic remedy for gastric complaints. It was described by Geiger (1830) as having an action similar to Foxglove (*Digitalis purpurea* L), and a century later in the *Hager-Handbuch* as an emetic similar to Ipecacuanha. These are powerful properties for a domestic remedy, and the rhizome should not be used except under medical supervision, since in large doses it can be fatal.
Sanguinaria describes the red colour of the rhizome and juice. It is the only species in the genus.
Description Perennial to 30 cm on thick rhizome; one leaf, basal, palmately lobed, petiolate, and only appearing when flower dies. Stem is a smooth scape to 20 cm, terminated by white, sometimes pinkish, flower. Solitary flower to 4 cm wide, appears midspring to early summer, followed by 3 cm-long oblong capsule.
Distribution North American native. On moist, rich soils in woods and woodland slopes in the shade.
Cultivation Wild. Introduced as a shady wild garden ornamental. Propagate by division in the autumn. A cultivar 'multiplex' with double flowers is found horticulturally.
Constituents Alkaloids comprising sanguinarine, protopine, chelerythrine, α- and β-homochelidonine, also chelidonic acid; an orange resin; gum; starch; sugars.
Uses (dried rhizome) Expectorant; emetic; antipyretic; spasmolytic; cardio-active; stimulant; topical irritant; cathartic; antiseptic.
The fresh juice is caustic (escharotic) and has been used against warts. The powdered drug has also been used externally to treat certain skin complaints and as a snuff in nasal polyps.

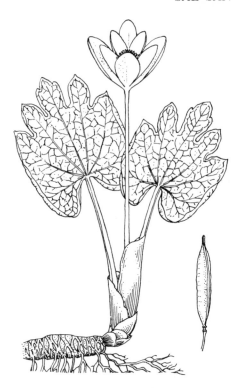

Principally employed in chronic bronchitis as an expectorant, and in cases of deficient capillary circulation.
May be used, much diluted, as a gargle in sore throats.
Contra-indications POISONOUS. Medical use only. The therapeutic dose is very small; large doses are toxic, causing violent vomiting, and possibly death.

Santolina chamaecyparissus L COMPOSITAE
Lavender Cotton Cotton Lavender/
French Lavender

This southern European native was introduced to cooler northern climates (which it tolerates well) in the sixteenth century, largely to be used in the low, clipped hedges of formal knot gardens. It was also valued as an ingredient of scented sachets to repel moths in clothes drawers. Other than this the herb has not received much attention, although its vermifugal properties have been recognized from the earliest times.

The Greeks knew it as *abrotonon* and the Romans as *habrotanum*, both referring to the tree-like shape of the flowering branches – a characteristic also indicated in the modern specific name.

Description Perennial evergreen shrub 20–50 cm tall; much branched with silver-grey, tomentose leaves to 4 cm long, subdivided into small, thin segments. Flowers bright yellow, numerous, but in solitary rounded capitula at the tips of branchlets; appearing mid-summer to early autumn.

Distribution Spain to Albania; North Africa; introduced elsewhere and locally escaped. On dry rocky soils in full sun, to 1000 m altitude.

Cultivation Wild. Cultivated horticulturally from cuttings taken late summer, autumn or early spring, and rooted under glass in a peat and sand mix. Well-drained soil in full sun is required in cool climates. Clip in mid-spring to shape.

Constituents Essential oil; bitter principles; unknown substances.

Uses (dried flowering stems, leaves) Vermifuge; antispasmodic; weak emmenagogue. Rarely used medicinally.

Leaves may be included in insect-repellent sachets.

Principally of use as a decorative evergreen garden shrub. Especially suitable as a low hedge.

Saponaria officinalis L CARYOPHYLLACEAE
Soapwort Bouncing Bet

As both the common and generic names suggest, the boiled leaves and roots of this herb may be used as the source of a somewhat astringent lather suitable for cleaning woollen fabrics. How long the herb has been used as a natural soap (its cleaning properties being due to the presence of saponins in the plant) is uncertain. It is not known how widely it was employed, but it may have been known to the Assyrians and is certainly still used both in the Middle East and rarely in the West for cleaning old and delicate tapestries.

Dioscorides probably knew *Saponaria officinalis* as *Struthion* while in the Middle Ages it was variously called *Herba Philippi*, *Sapanaria* or *Herba fullonis*. The latter name indicates that those who fulled cloth (that is, the fullers who cleaned and thickened it) used it as a cleaning agent, and from this William Turner in his *The Names of Herbes* (1548) called it 'Soapwort'.

Soapwort has to be treated in special ways before it can be used medicinally and it has been implicated in the poisoning of both animals and man, a property once recognized in its use as a fish poison.

Description Perennial, sparingly branched, on rhizome bearing erect, finely pubescent stems 30–40 cm tall. Leaves opposite, ovate-lanceolate, usually 7 cm long, 3-veined. Flowers pink or whitish to 4 cm wide in dense terminal clusters; appearing mid-summer to mid-autumn.

Distribution Native to Europe and western Asia.

Introduced and naturalized elsewhere.

On moist but well-drained soils in wasteland and roadsides, to 1500 m altitude.

Cultivation Wild. Grown horticulturally from seed sown in mid-spring, or by division. Tolerates poor soils.

Constituents Saponins (to 5%), comprising saporubin and saprubrinic acid; gums; flavonoids; vitamin C; vitexin.

Uses (fresh leaves, dried root-stock) Diuretic; laxative; cholagogue; choleretic; expectorant. Once used in the treatment of certain skin conditions, including psoriasis, eczema, and acne. In India the specially prepared root-stock is considered a galactagogue, and elsewhere it has been employed as an expectorant in respiratory complaints. Fresh leaf is principally used as the source of a soap to clean old fabrics.

Contra-indications To be used internally only under medical supervision.

Sarothamnus scoparius (L) Wimmer ex Koch
PAPILIONACEAE
Broom Scotch Broom

Formerly classified as *Cytisus scoparius* (L) Link and known as *Genista* in the early herbals, this useful medicinal herb was employed by all the major European schools of medicine and is still in demand in folk medicine. It was the emblem of the Norman conquerors of England. *Cytisus* was the Greek name for a type of clover, which, in fact, it hardly resembles at all.

Description Deciduous shrub to 3 m; with many erect slender glabrous 5-angled branches bearing short-petioled obovate or oblanceolate acute leaves, 5–10 mm long. Flowers usually appear alone in the axils, pale or bright yellow, 2-lipped, 2.5 cm long, appearing spring and summer.

Distribution Central and southern European native; naturalized in the United States. On wood fringes, roadsides, in clearings to 500 m altitude. Calcifugous.

Cultivation Wild plant; grown horticulturally, the variety *Andreanus* has yellow flowers with dark crimson wings.

Constituents Several alkaloids, including sparteine; flavonoid pigments; a glycoside, scoparin; mineral salts; bitter principles; tannin; volatile oil. Action largely due to sparteine

which lessens irritability and conductivity of cardiac muscle.

Uses (dried flowering herb) Diuretic, purgative, anti-haemorrhagic.

Of use in the treatment of tachycardia and functional palpitation, especially when the blood pressure is lowered. Some oxytocic activity, and therefore cannot be used in pregnancy. Constricts peripheral blood vessels, and of benefit in profuse menstruation.

Seeds once served as a Coffee substitute, and the flowers and buds were pickled and eaten as Capers.

Twigs used for basket manufacture.

Bark yields fibre suitable for manufacture of paper and cloth.

Formerly used to tan leather, and leaves yield a green dye.

Contra-indications Large doses paralyze the autonomic ganglia; to be avoided in pregnancy and hypertension.

Sassafras albidum (Nutt.) Nees LAURACEAE
Sassafras

This tree is considered by many authorities to

have provided the first of the American medicinal plant drugs to reach Europe. Its action was noticed by Monardes during an expedition to Florida (1564), and in 1574 the wood was imported to Spain.

It was known firstly by the native Indian name *pavame*, and also the French *sassafras*. From 1582 the Germans called it *lignum floridum* and Fennel Wood, as well as *lignum pauame* after its origin and the fennel-like aroma of the bark. The tree was grown in England as early as 1597. An Italian, Angelus Sala, first extracted the Sassafras oil by distillation, and it was this product which in modern times has been used most frequently. It is now under scrutiny for possible toxicity problems, and in many countries it has been withdrawn as a flavouring.

Description Aromatic deciduous tree to 30 m tall. Leaves variable, lobed or entire, alternate, ovate to 12 cm long, darker above. Flowers greenish yellow, on clustered racemes to 5 cm long; followed by dark blue fruit with fleshy red pedicel. Leaves attractively coloured in autumn.

Distribution North American native from central to southern states.

Cultivation Wild.

Constituents (oil, to 3%) comprising safrole (to 80%), phellandrene and pinene.

Uses (root wood, root bark, oil rarely) Aromatic; carminative; stimulant; diaphoretic; diuretic. The inner root bark in decoction is mildly aromatic and carminative and has been used for gastro-intestinal complaints, and in association with purgatives in constipation. The wood shavings were formerly administered with Guaiacum and Sarsaparilla (*Smilax ornata*) in decoction to induce sweating.

The oil is rubefacient and destroys lice, although safer remedies for both purposes are preferred. Pith from the stem forms a demulcent mucilage in water and can be used in eye lotions.

Oil is used in food flavouring (now under review), tobacco flavouring and perfumery. Sassafras tea is made from the wood shavings.

Contra-indications Oil should not be used internally as it causes liver and kidney damage. May irritate the skin if used externally.

Satureja hortensis L LABIATAE
Summer Savory

This is sometimes incorrectly named as *Satureia hortensis*. It is now most commonly used as a culinary herb, the name Savory emphasizing its culinary use. It has been employed in food flavouring for over 2000 years and probably longer than Sage. The herb also possesses effective medicinal properties including a stimulant effect which led to its former use as an aphrodisiac. Some authorities believe that this effect was the origin of the old name *Satureia* meaning satyr. The Italians were among the first to introduce this as a garden herb, and it has been in cultivation since the ninth century.

Description Annual, 30–40 cm tall, pubescent, erect and branched. Leaves acute, entire, 3 cm long. Flowers rose, lilac or white, in a sparsely-flowered inflorescence, appearing late summer to mid-autumn.

Distribution Native to eastern mediterranean region, and south-west Asia, introduced to South Africa, America and elsewhere. On dry chalky soils, rocky hills, roadsides; to 800 m altitude.

Cultivation Wild. Collected commercially from the wild. Cultivated from seed sown in spring.

Constituents Essential oil (to 1.5%) comprising mainly carvacrol and cymene; phenolic substances; resins; tannins; mucilage.

Uses (fresh or dried leaves, dried flowering tops) Antiseptic; expectorant; carminative; stomachic; stimulant; antihelmintic; diuretic. Principally of use in gastric complaints, to aid digestion or stimulate appetite. Possesses a beneficial antihelmintic action, and can also be used as an antiseptic gargle. Once considered an effective aphrodisiac although this is probably only due to its stimulant effect.

The oil is used commercially as a flavouring, as is the leaf which is an important constituent of salami.

Satureja montana L LABIATAE
Winter Savory

This has the same properties and uses as Summer Savory and is collected commercially both for the leaf and for the oil extracted from the leaves. The flavour of Winter Savory is, however, both coarser and stronger, but it has the advantage of being a hardier plant and a perennial evergreen, thus providing fresh leaf for winter flavouring in warmer climates.

Winter Savory is also called Mountain Savory, hence its specific name *montana*.

Description Shrubby evergreen perennial 10–40 cm tall, woody at the base, branched and forming a compact bush. Leaves sessile, entire, oblong-linear or oblanceolate, 15–30 mm long. White or pink flowers, in terminal flowering spikes appearing early summer to early autumn.

Distribution Native to south-east Europe and North Africa; introduced elsewhere. On dry chalky soils, rocky hills and mountains to 1500 m altitude.

Cultivation Wild. Collected commercially from

the wild. Grown from seed sown in poor, well-drained and chalky soils in early to mid-autumn; or propagated by division in spring or autumn.

Constituents Essential oil (to 1.5%) comprising mainly carvacrol and cymene; phenolic substances; resins; tannins; mucilage.

Uses (fresh or dried leaves, dried flowering tops) Antiseptic; expectorant; carminative; stomachic; stimulant; antihelmintic; diuretic. Principally of use in gastric complaints, to aid digestion or stimulate appetite. Possesses a beneficial antihelmintic action, and can also be used as an antiseptic gargle. Once considered an effective aphrodisiac although this is probably only due to its stimulant effect. The oil is used commercially as a flavouring, as is the leaf which is an important constituent of salami.

Scrophularia nodosa L SCROPHULARIACEAE
Knotted Figwort

Figwort is an interesting medicinal plant which deserves closer modern examination. Like the Foxglove, which is also a member of the Scrophulariaceae, it possesses cardio-active substances which lead to increased myocardial contraction. It is not used in heart therapy however, and its main employment in folk medicine is a dermatological one, where its action on the liver is traditionally considered to benefit skin problems. Nineteenth-century research also indicated a hypoglycaemic action, and for a time the root was included as an antidiabetic agent. The plant's names indicate still older, traditional uses. Figwort and the apothecaries' name *Ficaria major* refer to the ancient application against the *ficus* (Latin for fig) or piles; while *Scrophularia* is from *scrophula* (Latin for goitre and tuberculosis of the cervical lymph nodes), since it was used in complaints characterized by swelling, such as tumours and mastitis.

Description Square-stemmed, strong-smelling perennial, 40 to 120 cm tall, on tuberous rhizome; leaves opposite, undivided, decussate, ovate and glabrous. Flowers greenish-brown, to 1 cm long in panicles appearing mid-summer to mid-autumn.

Distribution European native. In wet woodland,

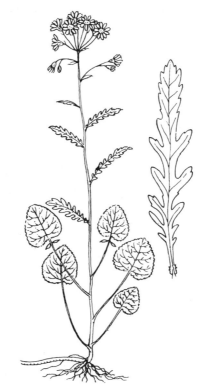

fenland hedgerows, ditches, near streams. To 1700 m altitude. On nutrient-rich loamy, but porous, soils.
Cultivation Wild plant.
Constituents Cardio-active glycosides; saponins, comprising mainly diosinine; hesperetin; vitamin C; palmitic and malic acids; unknown substances.
Uses (dried root-stock, dried flowering tops) choleretic; diuretic; cardio-active; vulnerary; weak hypoglycaemic.
Used in poultices for the external treatment of wounds, burns, ulcers and haemorrhoids. Formerly used externally and internally in glandular disorders, mastitis and tumerous conditions. Also used externally and internally in chronic skin diseases such as eczema.
Contra-indications Owing to its action on the heart it should only be used under medical supervision.

Sedum acre L CRASSULACEAE
Biting Stonecrop Yellow Stonecrop or Wall-pepper
The Wall-pepper, named after its habitat and taste, has never been considered of much medicinal importance, and even some of the ancient writers warned against its internal use. It was, however, included in some sixteenth-century apothecaries' remedies for intestinal parasites, and was known then as *vermicularis*. Similar, related plants were used for the same purpose and by 1741 the Württemberg Pharmacopoeia specified '*Vermicularis flore flavo*', the yellow-flowered *Vermicularis*. In 1830 its possible employment in epilepsy had been recognized, but it was rarely used for this purpose because the irritant substances it contains caused blisters.
Description Fleshy perennial on creeping or decumbent stems forming mats 5–20 cm tall. Leaves 3–4 mm long, thick, sessile, numerous, cylindrical, arranged closely along the stem. Flowers yellow, to 15 mm wide, sparse, in terminal cymes; appearing mid-summer to early autumn.
Distribution European native; introduced elsewhere. On poor, dry, warm, calcareous or stony soils, or sand; especially on old walls,

rubble, embankments and roofs.
Cultivation Wild.
Constituents Alkaloids including semadine; glycosides; mucilage; unknown substances.
Uses (fresh leaves) Rubefacient; hypotensive; irritant.
Use of the fresh plant must be restricted to external application for local treatment of warts and corns; it should be diluted with water to aid wound healing. The plant cannot safely be used in the treatment of hypertension. May be employed homeopathically.
Contra-indications Not to be used internally. External use may cause blistering.

Senecio aureus L COMPOSITAE
Golden Ragwort Liferoot/Squaw Weed
Senecio aureus is also called Female Regulator and indeed most of its uses were traditionally concerned with female complaints. American

Indian women formerly made a tea from the plant which they used before or during childbirth, and to treat conditions such as leucorrhoea. The herb never attracted much attention however, and it was only included in the early nineteenth-century American *Eclectic Materia Medica*; Hale introduced a homeopathic preparation, however, of the fresh flowering plant in 1875. The plant contains toxic substances which have been implicated in cattle poisoning, and it is, therefore, now seldom used.
Description Perennial on thick horizontal root, reaching 30–60 cm tall. The stem is grooved, erect and brown-streaked; basal leaves alternate, long petioled, obtuse, toothed, 3–15 cm long. Stem leaves oblong or lanceolate, lyrate or pinnatifid. Flowers golden-yellow to 2 cm wide, in corymbs, appearing early to midsummer.
Distribution North American native; on nutrient-rich wet soils, near to streams, in marshland.
Cultivation Wild.
Constituents Alkaloids; tannins; resin; unknown substances.
Uses (fresh or dried flowering plant and root) Emmenagogue; diaphoretic; tonic; diuretic; anti-haemorrhagic.
Once used in the treatment of certain internal haemorrhages, especially pulmonary haemorrhage; in female complaints and in childbirth; in genito-urinary tract infections. Considered to be a tonic in debility following illness.
Contra-indications To be used only by medical personnel. May prove toxic.

Senecio vulgaris L COMPOSITAE
Groundsel
This common weed is known to most European gardeners as an unwelcome intruder in the vegetable plot, or wherever soil has been disturbed. Dioscorides called it *erigeron* and considered it had cooling properties, a statement echoed 1600 years later by Culpeper who thought the herb of value in all diseases caused by 'heat'. In the sixteenth and seventeenth centuries Groundsel was frequently used in various conditions, but it evidently fell out of fashion, since in 1780 Hagen wrote that 'it had formerly been used . . .'. Dr Finazzi reintroduced the herb in 1824 for liver diseases, and a century later its folk medicinal application included it being used in amenorrhoea and dysmenorrhoea. It is now known that, like its American relative *S. aureus*, it possesses toxic alkaloids which after prolonged or large dosage damage the liver.
The English name Groundsel, (from the old English ground swallower) and the French name *Toute-venue*, emphasize the weed's vivacity.
Description Annual 4–60 cm tall; stems erect, succulent, purple at the base. Leaves pinnatifid, with irregularly toothed lobes, short-petioled or half-clasping. Flowers yellow, the flower-heads to 4 mm diameter in cylindrical involucre, on terminal dense corymbose clusters; appearing throughout the year.
Distribution European native, introduced else-

where. Widespread and common on wild and cultivated soils, to 2000 m altitude.
Cultivation Wild.
Constituents Alkaloids including senecionine; mucilage; tannins; resin; various mineral salts; unknown substances.
Uses (entire flowering plant) Emmenagogue; astringent; vulnerary; haemostatic. Used in homeopathy. Once used in various conditions associated with blood circulation or haemorrhages, and in problems of menstruation. Now very rarely employed, except externally as a wash for cuts.
Popularly used to feed caged birds.
Contra-indications Large doses are dangerous and can damage the liver; to be used only under medical supervision.

Serenoa repens (Bartr.) Small PALMAE
Saw Palmetto Sabal
The generic name *Serenoa* is named after Sereno Watson, an American botanist (1826–1892); *repens* means creeping, and refers to the habit of the stems. This habit leads to dense stands of Saw Palmetto growing along the coastal plains of Florida and Georgia in the United States of America.
American Indians used the ground-up seed as food and considered the fruits were sedative and tonic. They were, therefore, included in some orthodox pharmacopoeias from 1830 for about 100 years, but their use is now restricted to folk medicine. Saw Palmetto refers to the saw-toothed edges of the leaves of the palm. It was formerly known as *S. serrulata* (Michx.) Hook.
Description Palm, usually low and shrubby, 1–2 m tall, sometimes to 6 m tall, with prostrate and creeping, branching stem, often underground. Leaves very deeply divided (to 20 segments), 75 cm wide, green or glaucous. Flowers inconspicuous, on a branched cluster, followed by succulent purple drupes (fruit) soon drying, darkening, and shrinking to 18 mm long.
Distribution North American native, on coastal

plains from Florida and Texas to South Carolina. In swampy, low-lying land on well-drained soils.
Cultivation Wild. Sometimes transplanted as a garden cover plant.
Constituents Fixed oil (to 1.5%) to which the action is due.
Uses (partly dried ripe fruit) Tonic; stimulant; expectorant; nutritive; sedative. Although the general action is mildly sedative, the fruits have a local stimulant action on the mucous membranes of both the respiratory and genito-urinary systems. The overall action is considered tonic, especially following illness. Principally used therefore in chronic and sub-acute cystitis, bronchitis, catarrh, and as a tonic tea. Considered to be of benefit in sexual debility and atrophy of the testes, but this is unsubstantiated.

Sesamum indicum L PEDALIACEAE
Sesame Benne/Gingelli
Sesame is still widely cultivated for its seed which yields the valuable Sesame or Gigelly oil – an edible oil with similar properties to those of Olive oil. The name Sesame can be traced back through the Arabic *Simsim* and Coptic *Semsem* to the early Egyptian *Semsemt*, a name mentioned in the Ebers Papyrus (*c.* 1800 B.C.) which indicates how long man has known and used the herb.
Description Erect, strongly smelling, finely pubescent annual to 90 cm tall. Leaves variable, simple above, lanceolate or oblong, alternate or opposite. Flowers purple to whitish, to 3 cm long, sub-erect or drooping, solitary, axillary. Followed by 3 cm-long capsule containing numerous flat seeds.
Distribution Native to the tropics.
Cultivation Widely cultivated in Africa, Asia and America, on sandy loam; the seed being sown broadcast and harvested within 4

months. *S. indicum* L yields white or yellowish seed and the expressed oil is suitable for both culinary and medicinal purposes. The black or brown seed from *S. orientale* L (now classified as a cultivar of *S. indicum* L) gives an oil which is considered suitable for industrial purposes.
Constituents Fixed oil (to 55%) comprising glycerides of palmitic, stearic, myristic, oleic and linoleic and other acids; a phenolic substance, sesamol; sesamin; choline; lecithin; nicotinic acid; calcium salts.
Uses (seed, seed oil, fresh leaves rarely) Nutritive; laxative; emollient; demulcent. Fresh leaves may be used as a poultice, as may the seeds. The ground seed when mixed with water can be used to treat bleeding haemorrhoids, and can be taken for genito-urinary infections when combined with other remedies.
Seeds are of benefit in constipation, and Indians consider a decoction acts as an emmenagogue.
The oil has wide medical, pharmaceutical and culinary application.
Sesame seed paste (tahini) is used in spreads, sauces, casseroles and pâtés.
The seed is used to decorate and flavour bread.

Silybum marianum L Gaertn. COMPOSITAE
Milk-thistle Marian Thistle/
Wild Artichoke
Dioscorides described this herb as *silybon* but from early Christian times both Latin and common names have normally included the name of the Virgin Mary, after an old tradition that the white veination on the leaves came from her milk. From this there arose the belief that the plant affected lactation – for which there is no modern evidence. The herb is

effective upon the liver, however, a property it shares with another species of the Compositae Family, the Artichoke; and, like the Artichoke, the flower receptacle can be eaten.

Milk Thistle was formerly cultivated quite widely, not only for the receptacle but also for the young stalks, leaves and roots – the latter resembling Salsify (*Tragopogon porrifolius* L). In the eighteenth century the young shoots were thought to be superior to the best cabbage.

Medicinally the herb was often used in place of the Blessed Thistle (*Cnicus benedictus* L) and for a long time the seed was considered a specific for stitches in the side.

Description Annual or biennial; 30–150 cm tall with erect, prominently grooved, seldom branched stem. Leaves large, oblong, shiny, variegated and very spiny; sessile or clasping. Flowers violet-purple, thistle-like in a hemispherical capitula to 5 cm long; usually solitary and surrounded at the base by long spiny appendages.

Appearing late summer to early autumn.

Distribution Native to central and west Europe; introduced and naturalized in California and elsewhere. On dry rocky or stony soils in wastelands, fields and roadsides to 600 m altitude.

Cultivation Wild plant. Easily grown from seed; prefers sunny situation and well-drained soil.

Constituents Essential oil; tyramine; histamine; bitter principles; a flavonoid, silymarine.

Uses (powdered seed, fresh and dried leaves, whole and dried flowering plant, fresh root, fresh young stems and shoots, fresh receptacle) Choleretic; cholagogue; bitter tonic; hypertensive; diuretic.

The whole herb is of value in the stimulation of appetite and to assist digestion. The powdered seeds taken in emulsion are markedly choleretic and of use in certain cardiovascular disorders. They also act prophylactically against travel sickness. Formerly used in the treatment of leg ulcers and varicose veins.

Young leaves, shoots, peeled stems, receptacles and roots can be cooked and eaten.

Contra-indications The seed should be used only by medical personnel.

Sinapis alba L CRUCIFERAE
Mustard White Mustard

The ancient Greeks and Romans used Mustard as a spice, usually ground up and sprinkled over food. The development of the now universally known condiment began in France in the seventeenth century, and today over half the world's supply comes from Dijon. White Mustard is closely related to the Wild Charlock (*Sinapis arvensis* L), and is much less pungent than Black Mustard. There was no medicinal differentiation between the various types of Mustard seed until the London Pharmacopoeia of 1720.

Description Branched annual to 1 m high; slightly hairy stems; leaves generally oval and lobed. Flowers small, bright yellow, appearing mid-summer to early autumn. Seed yellowish in colour, in bristly pods.

Distribution Native to southern parts of Europe and western Asia. Introduced elsewhere.

Cultivation Wild plant. Cultivated commercially on wide scale.

Constituents A glycoside comprising sinalbin; an enzyme, myrosin, which interact in the presence of cold water when the seed is crushed.

Uses (seed, leaves) Stimulant, irritant, emetic. Less powerful than Black Mustard and used in combination with it for similar purposes. Powerful preservative, effective against moulds and bacterial growth; used for this reason in pickles. Young leaves used in salads.

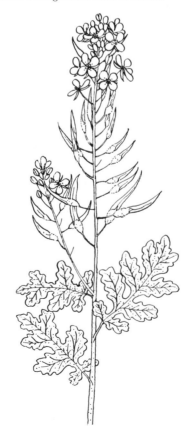

Sisymbrium officinale (L) Scop. CRUCIFERAE
Hedge Mustard

This herb was the *erysimon* of Dioscorides who prescribed it (combined with honey) against deadly poisons and a host of other diseases and pestilences. The Greek name was retained in the apothecaries' *Herba erysimi*, and even by Linnaeus who classified it as *Erysimum officinale* –

recognizing in that name the fact that Hedge Mustard had long been an official plant, and effective as an expectorant.

Traditionally, and in practice, the herb or juice may be used fresh to restore the voice in hoarseness or in complete loss, and for this reason it became known as the Singer's plant.

Description Annual on branched, erect stem 30–90 cm tall, with 5–8 cm long basal leaves deeply pinnatifid and toothed; stem leaves thinner and hastate. Flowers small, pale yellow on long racemes, appearing early summer to mid-autumn.

Distribution European native; in hedgerows, roadsides, railway embankments, most wasteland and weedy places and occasionally on walls. To 1700 m altitude.

Cultivation Wild. Once cultivated as a pot-herb.

Constituents Sulphur-containing compounds; cardenolides.

Uses (fresh flowering tops, fresh juice) Expectorant; bechic; stomachic; tonic; diuretic; laxative.

Useful in bronchitis, pharyngitis, tracheitis, and as a tonic.

May be used with discretion in sauces; formerly eaten as a vegetable but the flavour is strong and disagreeable in large quantities.

Contra-indications As it has an effect on the heart it is not suitable for the very young, old or those with cardiovascular problems.

Smilax ornata Hook. f. LILIACEAE
Sarsaparilla

Sarsaparilla was introduced to Seville, Spain, between 1536 and 1545 from Mexico, and it soon received attention as a potential remedy for syphilis – particularly following the reports of successful treatment using the herb's roots by Pedro de Ciezo de Leon in the 1540s. The plant was established as an official drug by the mid-sixteenth century and remained official until the early twentieth century.

Initially it was given various names, including Zarzaparilla, Zarza-Parrilla, Salsa Parilla and *Sarmentum indicum,* and by 1685 three main sorts, Mexican, Honduran and that from the province of Quito were being exported to Europe in large quantities.

By the nineteenth century Sarsaparilla was established as a valuable alterative and tonic for use in rheumatic, syphilitic, scrophulous, and chronic dermatological problems, and many different types of root were reaching Europe. These included Honduran, Guatemalan, Brazilian, Jamaican, Mexican and Guayaquil Sarsaparillas. Of these, the so-called Jamaica Sarsaparilla (exported via Jamaica but actually from central America) was the only sort once allowed in the British Pharmacopoeia.

The root is now retained in few national pharmacopoeias, and besides folk medicinal use, it is only employed as a vehicle and flavouring agent for medicines, or as a soft drink flavouring.

Description Dioecious, woody vine climbing by means of paired stipular tendrils. Stems prickly arising from rhizomatous root-stock, from which numerous thin, cylindrical roots also arise. Leaves alternate, variable. Flowers greenish to white, followed by berries.

Distribution Native to Central America, especially Costa Rica. In humid forests, swamps, and river-banks.

Cultivation Wild. The thin rootlets are usually collected from the wild.

Constituents Sarsaponin, a glycoside; sarsapic acid; sitosterol-d-glycoside; fatty acids; sugars; resins.

Uses (root) Alterative; diuretic; tonic. This remedy is ineffective in syphilis and is now considered of low therapeutic value. It does assist in the elimination of urea and uric acid, however, and is thus of value in gout; it is of

some benefit in rheumatism. Evidence suggests it is more effective in warmer climates. Employed as a pharmaceutical flavouring agent. Used in soft drinks.

Smyrnium olusatrum L UMBELLIFERAE
Alexanders Black Lovage/Horse Parsley
Because of superficial similarities with other members of the Umbelliferae family, Alexanders is also known as Black Lovage, Wild Celery, and Horse Parsley. A medieval name *Petroselinum Alexandrium* or the Rock Parsley of Alexandria echoes these similarities and gives us the name Alexanders.

It was known to Theophrastus as *hipposelinon* and occasionally as *petroselinon,* the latter name usually being applied to Parsley. A related plant, *S. perfoliatum* L, which had similar properties and uses was given the Greek name *Smyrnion* and from this the generic name of Alexanders is obtained. Both plants were official from the earliest times, and the root

and seed remained so until 1830 in much of Europe.

Alexanders has been most important as a culinary herb however, and its cultivation was described by Pliny and Columella in the first century A.D. Even Galen considered it more important as a food than a medicine. The leaves, the upper part of the roots, stem and shoots were most often used, but the flower buds were also added to salads. Like Celery the herb was blanched to remove bitterness. Due to the whims of fashion, Alexanders largely disappeared from gardens in the mid-eighteenth century, but it is worthy of modern cultivation.

Description Glabrous biennial, 50–150 cm tall on solid, furrowed stem. Lower leaves to 30 cm long, compound, stalked, with broadly ovate segments to 6 cm long. Flowers yellow-green in sub-globose umbels to 10 cm wide appearing early to mid-summer and followed by aromatic black seed.

Distribution Native to west Europe, mediterranean region, and naturalized elsewhere; on moist soils in hedge banks, rocky soils, cliffs, specially close to the sea.

Cultivation Wild plant. Cultivated on most soils

in a sunny position from seed sown in the autumn. Its cultivation is similar to Celery.

Constituents Unknown.

Uses (seed, dried and fresh root, fresh stems and leaves) Stomachic; diuretic.

Now rarely used medicinally, the seed soaked in wine was formerly considered an emmenagogue, while the leaves were antiscorbutic in days when vitamin C was unavailable. The root is mildly diuretic and a bitter, thus promoting appetite. The seed is stomachic, and was once thought to be of benefit in asthma. The fresh juice may be used on cuts and wounds.

Seed may be crushed and used with discretion as a condiment.

Leaves, stem, root and shoots may be boiled and eaten. The fresh blanched stem and flower buds can be eaten raw.

Solanum dulcamara L SOLANACEAE
Nightshade Bittersweet/Woody Nightshade
The Solanaceae family consists of over 1700 species, some of which are of considerable economic importance – such as the Egg-plant, Pepino, and Potato. Others are of horticultural interest and several have been employed for medicinal purposes in all parts of the world. Many, such as this species, have very poisonous berries due to their glycoalkaloid content. This irritant substance partially breaks down, however, in solution to yield steroidal alkamine aglycones which have an effect on the nervous system. Various parts of the plant (excluding the berries) have therefore been used appropriately in medicinal practice since as early as the thirteenth century. The specific use of the herb's stem was introduced in Germany in the sixteenth century when it was called *Dulcis amara,* literally sweet bitter, after the taste which is first bitter, then sweet (due to the chemical changes mentioned above).

Its medical use has almost disappeared in the last 30 years although it is included as a food flavouring provided the solanine content in the final food product is not more than 10 mg per kg.

Description Shrubby perennial usually 60–170 cm tall, sometimes climbing or trailing to 4 m tall. Leaves ovate, pubescent, petiolate, entire

2 or more basal lobes; to 10 cm long. Flowers violet, spotted green, with bright yellow anthers; numerous in long-stalked cymes, appearing mid-summer or mid-autumn. Followed by ovoid, scarlet-red fruit to 12 mm diameter.

Distribution Widespread. Native to Europe, Asia, and North America. On wasteland, weedy places, stream edges, and woodland; on damp nutrient-rich soils.

Cultivation Wild plant.

Constituents Alkaloids (to 1%) comprising solaceine, solaneine and solanine; glycosidal and non-glycosidal saponins comprising dulcamaric and dulcamaretic acids.

Uses (dried stems) Expectorant; diuretic. Formerly employed in decoction to treat asthma, catarrh, rheumatism and bronchitis, and especially of benefit in dermatological problems such as eczema, psoriasis and pityriasis. May be used homeopathically.

Contra-indications All parts of the plant are POISONOUS; to be used only by medical personnel.

Solidago virgaurea L COMPOSITAE
Golden Rod

The common name refers to the herb's appearance. It is an attractive plant and has been taken into cultivation as a useful late-flowering ornamental.

The herb is not certainly mentioned in ancient writings and there is evidence that it was particularly promoted by the Arabs in the Middle Ages, since to fifteenth and sixteenth-century Italians it was known as *Erba pagana* and the Germans called it *Consolida Saracenia*. Golden Rod has principally been used as a wound herb, hence the name *consolida* from the Latin to make whole – and hence its generic name. Traditionally it was employed both externally and internally. Clarke introduced an extract of the fresh flowers to homeopathic medicine in 1902, and in 1949 it was discovered by Hager that Brazilians used the closely related herb *S. microglossa* DC as a wound plant, too.

Description Erect perennial to 1 m tall; on knotted rhizome. Stems usually sparsely branched, sometimes unbranched. Leaves altern-

ate, pubescent, the basal ones obovate to oblanceolate and petiolate, to 10 cm long. Upper leaves smaller and becoming sessile. Leaves either dentate or entire. Flowers golden-yellow, to 15 mm wide, arranged in terminal panicles; appearing late summer to late autumn.

Distribution Native to Europe, North Africa and Asia. Introduced elsewhere. In woodland clearings, wood edges, grassland; on deep porous acid and calcareous soils, to 2800 m altitude.

Cultivation Wild plant. Propagated horticulturally by division in spring or autumn, or from seed sown in spring. Prefers open conditions, and soils which are not too rich.

Constituents Essential oil; flavonoids; tannins; saponins; various organic acids comprising mainly citric, tartaric and oxalic acids; unknown substances.

Uses (dried flowering plant) Anti-inflammatory; expectorant; vulnerary; astringent; weakly diuretic.

Of much use applied externally in poultices or ointments to assist tissue healing; used internally for the same purpose, and also in urinogenital inflammations or to treat chronic skin problems.

Formerly taken as an adjuvant (assisting agent) with other remedies, of benefit in asthma, arthritis and rheumatism.

Rarely used in cases of diarrhoea. Its ability to reduce cholesterol levels is not clinically substantiated.

Spigelia marilandica L LOGANIACEAE
Pink Root Carolina Pink/Worm Grass/ Indian Pink

The generic name of this once popular North American Indian remedy for round-worms is taken from Adrian van der Spiegel, a physician from Brussels who died in Padua in 1625, in whose honour it was called *Spigelia*.

The herb was particularly favoured in the southern States by the Cherokees, to whom it was known as *unsteetla*. It was introduced to medicine in the 1750s by Dr Garden and Dr Chalmers; it was included in the United States Pharmacopoeia, and continued to be used in orthodox medicine until 40 years ago. The name Pink Root comes from the internal colour of the root-stock. It was formerly classified as *Lonicera marilandica* L.

Description Perennial on twisted root-stock, from 30–60 cm tall. Leaves opposite, entire, acuminate, sessile, ovate to ovate-lanceolate, somewhat pubescent beneath; 5–10 cm long. Flowers very attractive, 3–5 cm long, deep red outside, yellow inside, carried on erect, one-sided terminal cymes; appearing early to late summer.

Distribution North American native; from southern New Jersey to Florida and Texas; in rich, deep soils at the edges of woods and in woodland clearings.

Cultivation Wild plant.

Constituents An alkaloid, spigeline; bitter principles; resin; volatile oil; fixed oil; tannins; the action is mostly due to the spigeline content, which is a slightly toxic substance.

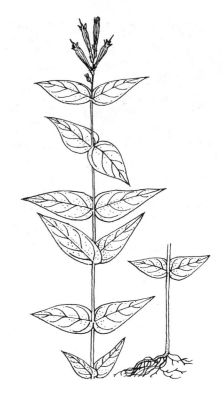

Uses (dried or fresh roots and rhizome, rarely fresh leaves) Antihelmintic; narcotic.

Once specifically used to expel round-worms; the action only being effective when purgation takes place. It was, therefore, usually administered in conjunction with a purgative.

In small quantities the powder is thought to be of use in the treatment of nervous headache. The remedy is incompletely studied, but may be of benefit in certain nervous complaints.

The leaves may be used, with discretion, as a stomachic tea; they do not contain the same quantity of active substances as are found in the root-stock.

Stachys officinalis (L) Trevisan LABIATAE
Betony

This is an interesting example of a herb which was attributed with magical properties from the earliest times when it was used medicinally, and which for some time retained an important place in folk medicine even though its value is now being seriously questioned. The Egyptians were the first to attribute Betony with magical properties, and it was the most important magical plant of the Anglo-Saxons, being mentioned as one of the medicinal plants in the eleventh-century work, the *Lacnunga*. Dioscorides knew it as *kestron* while the Romans called it *vettonica*, from which the old name *betonica* is derived. It was previously known as *Betonica officinalis* L.

Today opinions differ as to its value; some authorities consider it is only an astringent bitter (it was once an ingredient of bitter tonics), while others believe it is sedative. It is, however, now chiefly employed in herbal smoking mixtures and herbal snuffs, as well as occasionally being used in folk medicine.

Description Perennial with square stems; reach-

ing 30–60 cm tall. Basal rosette of cordate, dentate, slightly hairy, long-petiolate and strongly-nerved leaves. Flowers pink or purple, in a dense, terminal spike surmounting a long stalk; appearing mid-summer to mid-autumn.

Distribution European native; on sandy loams in wood clearings, meadowland, to 1500 m altitude.

Cultivation Wild plant.

Constituents Tannins (to 15%); bitter substances; saponosides; glucosides; alkaloids comprising betonicine and stachydrine.

Uses (dried flowering tops, root-stock rarely) Astringent; stomachic; emetic; purgative; vulnerary; sternutatory; bitter; sedative.

The root may cause purgation and is not usually employed.

The herb is an effective bitter tonic and useful in diarrhoea and for external application to wounds.

It may possess a mild sedative action of benefit in headaches and anxiety states, but is best taken with other remedies.

The dried leaves may be used as a tea substitute, and are included in smoking and snuff mixtures.

The fresh plant provides a yellow dye.

Stellaria media (L) Vill. CARYOPHYLLACEAE
Chickweed
Chickweed is this herb's English name, *herbe à l'oiseau* its French name, *Vogelmiere* its German, and in medieval Latin *morsus gallinae* (hen's bite) – all of these emphasizing the association with birds.

It has long been used as a bird feed, and in winter it provides one of the few sources of fresh seed for them. Indeed, it is as a foodstuff for animals and poor country folk that it has received most attention; the ancient writers ignored it and it has few, if any, medicinal applications.

Stellaria is from the Latin *stella* meaning a star, after the flower shape; while *media* serves to distinguish this plant from both larger and smaller relatives as it means middle.

Description Vigorous annual, but rapidly propagating and found throughout the year. Stems much-branched, decumbent and ascending, very straggly, 10–40 cm tall. Leaves ovate-acute, long-petioled, 3–20 mm long; some leaves ovate and sessile. Flowers small, white, numerous on downwardly pointing stalks. Appearing early spring to mid-winter.

Distribution European native; distributed worldwide, and often naturalized as a weed of importance. On all moist, cultivated land and wasteland to 2000 m altitude.

Cultivation Wild plant.

Constituents Mineral salts including calcium and potassium salts; saponins.

Uses (fresh stems and leaves) Vulnerary.

The crushed plant may be used in poultices; once rubbed on arthritic joints to relieve discomfort. Used homeopathically in the treatment of rheumatism.

Principally used as a salad herb or may be cooked as a vegetable with a knob of butter added.

Stillingia sylvatica Gard. EUPHORBIACEAE
Queen's Delight Queen's Root/Yaw-root
Queen's Delight receives its generic name from Dr Benjamin Stillingfleet, after whom it was named.

The use of the herb as a specific against syphilis was established in the southern United States well before 1828 when it was introduced

to medicine by Dr Symons. It was soon an official drug in the United States Pharmacopoeia, and entered European pharmacopoeias; its action is markedly reduced if old tinctures or roots are employed, and it was found to be a better expectorant than an antisyphilitic. It is still retained in folk medicine and proprietary herbal products as an alterative.

Its leaves are often marked with chancre-like (like syphilitic lesions) spots – which may have originally suggested its use in syphilis.

Description Glabrous, perennial subshrub to 90 cm tall, on thick, creeping root-stock. Stems clustered and regularly branched. Leaves very variable in form; from ovate to oblong or lanceolate, sessile or short-petioled, toothed, green to red, 3–11 cm long. Flowers monoecious, yellow, without petals, in dense, terminal spikes to 12 cm long; male flowers in clusters, female solitary. Appearing late spring to mid-autumn.

Distribution North American native; from Virginia to Florida and Texas. In sandy, light, dry soils in full sun.

Cultivation Wild plant.

Constituents Volatile oil (to 4%); fixed oil; an acrid resin, sylvacrol; tannins; calcium oxalate; cyanogenic glycosides; starch. The combined action is mildly irritant.

Uses (dried or fresh root-stock, not more than 12 months old) Expectorant; emetic; purgative; laxative; sialogogue.

Principally used now as an alterative in chronic skin problems, liver infections and urino-genital infections. In small doses it is laxative, and in large doses it is emetic and purgative.

Of benefit as an expectorant in pulmonary disorders.

Styrax benzoin Dryander STYRACACEAE
Benzoin Gum Benjamin
It was first noted by Ibn Batuta following his visit to Sumatra in 1325 to 1349, and he called it Java Frankincense (or Luban Jawi in Arabic). The Arabic name was altered to Banjawi, Benzui, Benzoin and Benjamin over subsequent centuries.

The resin was imported to Europe following Garcia de Orta's description of the drug (1563), and in the list of taxes levied at Worms in 1582 it was listed as *Asa dulcis* (Sweet Asa) – a name retained until the 1850s.

By 1800 the antiseptic properties of Benzoin had been fully recognized and both Simple and Compound Tinctures of Benzoin were regularly employed as preservatives in a wide range of medicinal and cosmetic preparations, and the resin is still used today in herbal preparations.

Description Tree to 7 m tall; leaves simple, elliptic to orbicular, entire or slightly dentate. Flowers white, several, in drooping clusters on 2 cm long pedicels.

Distribution Native to south-east Asia, especially Sumatra; in mixed forests close to rivers.

Cultivation Wild and cultivated commercially. The resin is obtained by tapping 7–10 year old trees and scraping off the whitish exudation from the bark. Trees can be so treated for up to

20 years, before they die.

Constituents Balsamic acids (to 60%) comprising esters of cinnamic and benzoic acids; benzoresinol; benzaldehyde; styrol; vanillin; and several related substances. The combined action is predominantly antiseptic.

Uses (resin) Carminative; antiseptic; diuretic; mildly expectorant.

Used internally as a genito-urinary antiseptic, and as an expectorant in chronic bronchitis. Principally of benefit as an antiseptic in poultices and plasters, and also applied directly to the skin as an antiseptic tincture. The tincture is an excellent preservative, suitable for various pharmaceutical and cosmetic preparations.

It can be used diluted as a mouth wash.

Used in incense and aromatic products.

Succisa pratensis Moench. DIPSACACEAE
Devil's-Bit Scabious

The second part of this herb's common name refers to the fact that it has been used in the treatment of scabies and similar skin conditions in which scratching is characteristic. It was formerly classified as *Scabiosa succisa* L.

This may have been introduced through the theory of the Doctrine of Signatures, since most members of the Dipsacaceae have scratchy seed heads; the Fuller's Teasel (*Dipsacus sativus* (L) Honk.) is the most extreme example of this, and the bracts were once used to tease or scratch up the nap on cloth.

Devil's-Bit is an old prefix from a traditional story in which the devil bit part of the root off. The herb is not very effective medicinally and is rarely used today.

Description Perennial on short, erect root-stock; stem erect 15–100 cm tall, usually glabrous. Basal leaves narrowly elliptic to obovate-lanceolate, to 30 cm long, arranged in a rosette; stem leaves narrower and rarely toothed. Flowers dark blue, occasionally white, numerous, arranged in globular, involucral heads, terminating a long stalk. Appearing late summer to late autumn.

Distribution Native to North Africa; Europe; western Siberia; introduced and naturalized in north-east United States and elsewhere. On moist soils in woods, pastures, fenland, and marshes. To 1800 m altitude.

Cultivation Wild plant.

Constituents Saponins; a glucoside, scabioside; starch; tannins; mineral salts.

Uses (dried root-stock; rarely flowers and juice) Expectorant; diuretic; antihelmintic; vulnerary; astringent; stomachic.

Now rarely used; the root-stock was formerly considered of benefit as an expectorant in bronchitis. A decoction may be used externally to relieve itching of the skin (pruritus) or to aid wound healing or ulcers. Also used homeopathically.

Symphytum officinale L BORAGINACEAE
Comfrey Knitbone

Comfrey has received much attention in recent years both as a medicinal plant (providing a source of vitamin B_{12} and the cell-proliferant allantoin) and as a potential source of protein. Certain strains of the herb contain almost 35 per cent total protein, which is the same percentage as that of soya beans, and 10 per cent more than that of Cheddar Cheese.

Attempts to extract the protein in a form suitable for human consumption and to develop the plant as a food source in underdeveloped countries have so far been unsuccessful.

Comfrey is, however, an important animal feed in some parts of the world, and in Africa, for example, it is increasing in importance. It is also grown as an organic compost and mulch. It is not certain that this species was the *symphiton* of Dioscorides, but it probably was the Roman *conferva* (from the verb meaning to join together), the name from which both the medieval *Consolidae maioris* and common name Comfrey are derived.

Comfrey was once one of the main herbs used in treating fractures and hence the alternative name Knitbone. The pounded root forms a mucilaginous mass which can be bound around a fracture and which, when dry, holds the bone in place.

Description Perennial, 30–120 cm tall, on thick brownish-black root-stock. Leaves and stem erect, with stiff hairs. Lower leaves to 25 cm long, petiolate, lanceolate, hairy beneath. Upper leaves narrower. Flowers purplish, pinkish or yellowish-white, in crowded terminal cymes; appearing early summer to early autumn.

Distribution Native to Europe, Asia; introduced and naturalized elsewhere. On rich, wet soils near rivers, streams, in ditches, on low-lying meadowland. To 1500 m altitude.

Cultivation Wild. Propagated by division in spring and autumn, or by root cuttings from spring to autumn. Tolerates most conditions, but requires regular watering on dry soils.

Constituents Mucilage; allantoin (to 0.8%); tannic acid; resin; traces of alkaloids comprising consollidine and symphyto-cynoglossine; sugars; essential oil; choline. The cell-proliferant action is due to the allantoin content.

Uses (fresh or dried root-stock, fresh or dried leaves) Astringent; demulcent; cell-proliferant; vulnerary; weak sedative.

Root used internally in the treatment of gastric and duodenal ulcers and diarrhoea; leaf used in pleurisy and bronchitis.

For wounds, bruising, ulceration and dermatological complaints the leaves or macerated root are applied as a poultice, lotion or decoction. Considered of benefit in neuralgia and rheumatism, applied externally. Occasionally used externally in the treatment of varicose veins.

Dried leaf is a tea substitute.

Fresh leaf used as a vegetable; in animal feeds; in composting and mulching.

Symplocarpus foetidus (L) Nutt. ARACEAE
Skunk Cabbage Polecat Weed
This herb has an unusual appearance and, as
its common names suggest, an awful smell
when bruised.
It has been classified botanically in several
different genera, notably *Ictodes*, *Pothos*,
Arum, and *Dracontium*, but it is now included
as the only species of the genus *Symplocarpus*.
Skunk Cabbage root and seed were introduced
to Europe in the early nineteenth century from
American folk use, and although included in
the United States Pharmacopoeia for a short
time they did not attract much attention since
superior antispasmodics were available. It is,
however, retained in folk medicine.
Description Foetid, hardy perennial on large
tuberous root-stock and long rootlets. Stemless. Leaves (produced after the flowers) ovate-
cordate, 45 cm long and 30 cm wide, smooth,
entire, long-petioled (to 25 cm). Inflorescence
is a fleshy ovoid spathe to 15 cm long, purple-
brown, mottled with yellow, covering a black
oval spadix; appearing early to mid-spring.
Distribution North-eastern North American
native; also in north-east Asia; in swamps and
boggy land.

Cultivation Wild.
Constituents Resin; fixed oil; volatile oil; sugars;
gums; unknown acrid substances.
Uses (dried root and rhizome) Antispasmodic;
expectorant; diuretic; emetic; mild sedative.
Of use in the treatment of various respiratory
complaints, including asthma, bronchitis,
whooping cough, hay fever, respiratory
catarrh.
The leaves can be used fresh as a vulnerary.
Root-stock formerly employed in the treatment of certain nervous disorders; also used to
treat snake bites.
Contra-indications Slightly narcotic; medical use
only. The fresh plant may cause blistering.

Syzygium aromaticum (L) Merr. & Perry
MYRTACEAE
Clove-tree
The dried unopened flower buds, known as
Cloves, are derived from a tree originally
growing only on the 5 small islands comprising
the Moluccas proper. For this reason they were

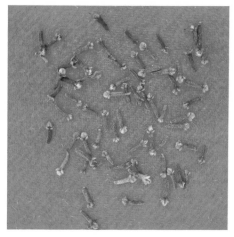

first mentioned in the writings of Chinese
physicians, and an early custom of the Han
dynasty (266 B.C. to A.D. 220) was to retain a
Clove in the mouth when addressing the
emperor, presumably to counteract halitosis.
Pliny mentioned a spice called *caryophyllon*,
hence the specific name, and by the fourth
century Cloves were widely used throughout
Europe. In the seventeenth and eighteenth
centuries the spice caused serious trade rivalry
between some European countries, and eventually the French began cultivation in Mauritius. It was first grown in Zanzibar in 1800.
Description Attractive pyramidal evergreen tree
10–15 m tall. Leaves ovate-oblong, 5–12.5 cm
long, smooth and shiny, leathery, acute, and
tapering at the base. Flowers crimson or pale
purple, 7 mm wide, in branched terminal
cymes. Fresh buds pink, but reddish-brown
after sun drying.
Distribution Native to south-east Asian islands,
especially the Moluccas. Introduced to West
Indies, tropical East Africa, China.
Cultivation Wild; cultivated commercially in
tropical maritime countries.
Constituents Volatile oil (15%); gallotannic acid
(13%); caryophyllin; action due to volatile oil.
Uses (dried flower buds, oil) Aromatic stimulant; antispasmodic; carminative; rubefacient; counter-irritant.
Used in the treatment of flatulent colic, and as
a remedy for toothache. Applied externally in
embrocations to relieve neuralgic pain, and in
rheumatism.
A constituent of tooth-powders and tooth-
pastes, as a flavouring agent and antiseptic.
Culinary uses include bread sauce, curry,
mulled spiced wine, liqueurs and stews. Acts as
a preservative in pickles. Used in pomanders.
Contra-indications If applied for toothache, the
oil should not have prolonged contact with the
gums as this may cause serious irritation.

Tamus communis L DIOSCOREACEAE
Black Bryony
The Black Bryony is thought to be the herb
described as the wild or field *Ampelos* (*Ampelos
agria*) of Dioscorides – who prescribed his
remedy externally to treat bruises.
Certainly by the Middle Ages this plant was
called *ampelos melana* (black ampelos), *vitis
nigra* (black vine) and finally *brionia nigra*

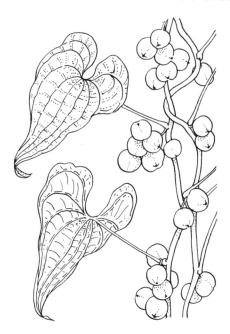

(black brionia) – from which the common
name is derived.
Black Bryony is poisonous, and if the root is
used internally it is violently purgative and
emetic. It has, therefore, never been considered useful medicinally, but Clarke introduced
a homeopathic preparation in 1902 to be used
in sunstroke and rheumatism.
Description Dioecious perennial, on very large
tuber (to 60 cm diameter), producing annual,
twining stems. Leaves entire, cordate, broadly-
ovate, glossy, to 10 cm long, with very long
petioles. Flowers yellowish-green, male stalked, female sessile; both small. Appearing late
spring to late summer, and followed by 12 mm
diameter globose, red berry.
Distribution Native to central and southern
Europe. In hedgerows, woodland clearings,
wood margins, scrubland; on moist, well-
drained, nutrient-rich soils, to 1100 m altitude.
Cultivation Wild plant.
Constituents (root-stock) Mucilage; gums; his-
tamine-like compound; calcium oxalate; unknown substances.
Uses (fresh or dried root-stock) Rubefacient;
resolvent.
Formerly only used externally as a poultice to
treat contusions.
Contra-indications POISONOUS; the berries
can be fatal to children.

Tanacetum vulgare L COMPOSITAE
Tansy
Tansy is also found classified as *Chrysanthemum
vulgare* (L) Bernh. It is now frequently grown
in herb gardens for its attractive and long-
lasting yellow flower-heads, many of which are
used in insect-repelling pot-pourris or other
scented articles.
It has traditionally been used as an insecticide
or insect repellent, and in the Middle Ages was
one of the strewing herbs used on floors.
Tansy was also rubbed over meat to keep flies
away, and one of its old names *arthemisia
domestica* emphasizes its use in the house.
It was also called *athanasia* and *tanacetum*,

names of uncertain association but considered to mean deathless – possibly because the flowers last so long.

Tansy was used until the mid-eighteenth century in certain types of pancakes called tansies. These were eaten at Lent, and the bitterness was meant to remind the eater of Christ's sufferings; they, no doubt, also acted as a useful vermifuge since this has been the herb's main therapeutic use from the days of the first apothecaries.

Description Aromatic, somewhat straggling perennial, 60–120 cm tall, on a rhizome. Leaves pinnate, alternate, to 12 cm long, sub-divided into numerous leaflets which are deeply toothed. Several golden yellow flowers, consisting only of disc florets, in a dense flat or hemispherical corymb. Appearing late summer to early or mid-autumn.

Distribution Native to Europe and Asia; introduced and naturalized elsewhere, especially in north-east North America. On wasteland, wood clearings and undisturbed, nitrogen-rich, loamy soils to 1500 m altitude.

Cultivation Wild. May be propagated by division of old clumps in spring or autumn, or from seed sown in spring or autumn. Tolerates most positions provided the soil is not constantly wet. A variety (var. *crispum* DC) with larger and more finely divided leaves is sometimes preferred in herb gardens.

Constituents Essential oil, comprising thujone (to 70%), and borneol; vitamin C; tannins; resin; citric acid; butyric acid; oxalic acid; lipids.

Uses (fresh or dried flowering stems) Anti-helmintic; insecticide; emmenagogue.

Small doses are effective in the treatment of round-worms. The herb also aids digestion. May be used in infusion as a gargle in gingivitis. The extracted oil was formerly used externally in the treatment of rheumatic pain.

Employed in a variety of insect-repellent sachets and scented articles.

Contra-indications Large doses are irritant and if taken during pregnancy may induce abortion.

Taraktogenos kurzii King FLACOURTIACEAE
Chaulmoogra
This tree is also classified as *Hydnocarpus kurzii* (King) Warb. It is one of several members of the family Flacourtiaceae which yield seed containing a fatty oil. The oil, and the crushed seed, have long been used in south-east Asia to treat various skin diseases, and it has been shown that the active principles of the oil (hydnocarpic and chaulmoogric acids) are strongly antibacterial. For this reason Chaulmoogra is employed in Hindu medicine to treat leprosy.

Description Tree to 20 m tall; leaves glossy, entire, alternate, leathery and oblong-lanceolate, to 20 cm long. Flowers few, in branched axillary cymes, or appearing singly. Followed by rugose, indehiscent, hard, globular fruit to 10 cm diameter; containing numerous seeds in a pulpy mass.

Distribution Native to Burma and Thailand; and now introduced to other regions of tropical

south-east Asia.

Constituents (seed) Chaulmoogra oil, comprising hydnocarpic acid (to 36%), chaulmoogric acid (to 23%), gorlic acid, oleic acid and palmitic acid.

Uses (oil, seed) Antibacterial; alterative; irritant.

The oil is effective in the treatment of lepromatous leprosy, and is still used in the East. Also useful in the treatment of intestinal worms. Seed used externally and internally in various skin diseases. Usually applied as an ointment. In India the seeds are considered to be an alterative tonic.

Contra-indications The oil is irritant and may cause nausea and vomiting, as well as having a slight depressant action on the cardiovascular system.

Taraxacum officinale Weber COMPOSITAE
Dandelion
Although the Dandelion is generally considered to be a ubiquitous weed, it is in fact one of the most useful of European herbs and all parts of the plant can be employed. It is an extremely effective medicinal plant, being possibly the safest and most active plant diuretic and one of the best herbs known to treat liver complaints. Both the leaves and root have long been eaten as salad material, and in the last century cultivated forms with large leaves have been developed as an autumn and spring vegetable; these usually being blanched in the same way as Endive.

Dandelion roots provide (when dried, chopped and roasted) the best-known coffee substitute, and all parts have been employed in fermented and unfermented beers, wines and tonic drinks. Surprisingly the herb is rarely mentioned by the ancient Greeks and Romans, and it is generally considered that the Arabs promoted its use in the eleventh century.

By the sixteenth century it was well established as an official drug of the apothecaries, who knew it as *Herba Taraxacon* or *Herba Urinaria* – the latter term emphasizing its diuretic effect. It was also called *Denta Leonis* (lion's teeth), after the leaf shape, and from which term the common name is derived via the French *dents de lion*.

It is still retained in the national pharmacopoeias of Hungary, Poland, the Soviet Union and Switzerland. The Russian Dandelion (*T. kok-saghyz* Rodin.) was extensively cultivated during the Second World War as a source of rubber, which was extracted from the latex of the roots. Small quantities of a similar latex are found in *T. officinale*.

Description Variable perennial on taproot, to 30 cm tall. Leaves spatulate, oblong or oblanceolate, entire to runcinate-pinnatifid. Flowers yellow, on hollow scapes, appearing late spring to mid-summer.

Distribution Native to Europe and Asia; introduced elsewhere. On nitrogen-rich soils in any situation to 2000 m altitude.

Cultivation Wild. Propagated from seed sown in spring for use as an autumn salad herb. Blanch by earthing up or placing an inverted flower pot over the plant. Grow as an annual to prevent bitterness developing in the plant.

Constituents Taraxacin, a bitter principle; taraxerin, an acrid resin; taraxerol; taraxas-

terol; 3:4 dioxycinnamic acid; flavoxanthin; inulin; citric acid; phenyloxyacetic acid; riboflavin; sitosterol; sitosterin; stigmasterol; coumestrol; vitamins B, C and provitamin A.
Uses (fresh or dried roots, leaves and flowers) Diuretic; cholagogue; choleretic; laxative; bitter tonic; stomachic.

An excellent bitter tonic in atonic dyspepsia; a mild laxative in chronic constipation; a cholagogue and choleretic in liver disease (especially jaundice, cholecystitis and the primary stages of cirrhosis). Considered of benefit as an anti-rheumatic. As a bitter it promotes appetite and improves digestion. A very effective diuretic.

Leaf and root used as a salad; root is a coffee substitute. Flowers used in Dandelion wine, and leaves in Dandelion beer and tonic drinks. The plant is safe to use in large amounts.

Teucrium chamaedrys L LABIATAE
Wall Germander Germander

The genus *Teucrium* consists of about 300 species, many of which are native to the mediterranean region. For this reason it has not been possible to identify definitely this particular species with the *Khamaidrys* of Dioscorides, and it is now considered most probably to be the same as his *Teukrion*.

Both these Greek names have, however, been combined to give the botanical name, and for much of the Middle Ages the herb was known as *Herba chamaedryos*. Germander was also called *Quercula maior* or *Quercula* – names which (like *chamaedryos*) mean ground or little oak, after the shape of the leaf. The common name is derived from *gamandrea* the latinization of *khamaidrys*.

The herb was once a popular medicine used predominantly in digestive or feverish complaints, but it was also much employed in formal herb and knot gardens as an edging plant. There is very little modern information available on Germander, however, and it is little used other than as an ingredient of liqueurs and tonic wines.

Description Small, shrubby, practically evergreen perennial, 10–30 cm tall. Stem erect or decumbent, hairy, marked with purple, bearing oblong to obovate-oblong, toothed leaves,

2 cm long. Flowers purple, rose or rarely white, typically labiate but lacking upper lip, in either loose or dense terminal spikes; appearing early summer to mid-autumn.
Distribution Native to Europe and south-west Asia; introduced elsewhere. On dry chalky soils, in dry thickets, woodland, rocky screes, and old walls. To 1500 m altitude.
Cultivation Wild. Cultivated as an edging plant. Propagated from seed sown in spring; division in autumn; or cuttings from spring to summer. The dwarf cultivar *T. chamaedrys* cv. Prostratum is useful as a carpeting herb.
Constituents Tannins; an essential oil; bitter principles probably including picropulin; sugars including stachyose and raffinose; unknown substances.
Uses (dried flowering plant) Choleretic; antiseptic; antipyretic; tonic; aromatic; diuretic. Principally of use in gall-bladder and digestive disorders. The infusion can be employed to promote the appetite, aid digestion, and dispel flatulence.

Once used in feverish conditions and formerly considered effective in the treatment of gout, although this is unsubstantiated.

Used in the manufacture of liqueurs, vermouths and tonic wines.

May be used effectively as a horticultural edging plant.

Theobroma cacao L BYTTNERIACEAE
Cacao Cocoa-Plant

The Spanish were the first to describe the seeds of this now important economic plant. In the sixteenth century Valdes reported their use as a form of exchange instead of coins (in the Yucatan), and the trees have long been cultivated in northern South America as a source of chocolate. The name itself comes from the Mexican *chocolatl* while *cacao* is from *cacauatl* in the same language.

Both the seed and chocolate itself were known in much of Europe by 1600, and Cacao butter was prepared in 1695 by Homberg in France. The medicinal applications of Cacao butter were promoted by the French and it was soon popular in various cosmetic preparations. It is still retained as a base for medical pessaries, bougies, and suppositories, and forms a vehicle for certain cosmetics – its main value being that it does not go rancid quickly. Both Cocoa and chocolate consist of the fermented and roasted plant seed; they differ in the quantity of sugar and type of additional flavouring (such as vanilla) added to the product.
Description Evergreen tree to 7 m tall. Leaves simple, alternate, glossy and leathery, oblong to 30 cm long, red when young. Flowers small, yellowish-pink, long-stalked in clusters carried directly on branches or the trunk, followed by 30-cm long yellow to brown fruit containing 20–40 3 cm-long seeds.
Distribution Native to Central and South America; introduced elsewhere. In lowland tropics or wet soils.
Cultivation Wild. Cultivated commercially in many tropical countries, especially Brazil and the west coast of Africa. Usually given arti-

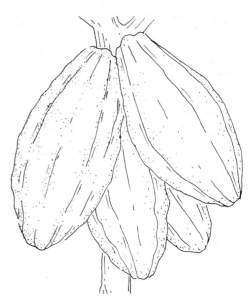

ficial shading or planted under higher trees. Propagated from seed.
Constituents (seed) Fat called Cocoa butter or Theobroma oil; theobromine (1–3%); sucrose and glucose (2.5%); caffeine; mucilage. (fat) Comprises 55% oleopalmitostearin.
Uses (Fat – Cocoa butter, seed products – cocoa and chocolate) Emollient; nutritive; diuretic.

Any medicinal actions of the seed products are due to their theobromine and caffeine content, which act as a mild stimulant and diuretic. Theobromine has no stimulant effect on the central nervous system.

Cocoa and chocolate are now used pharmaceutically to mask unpleasant flavours. The fat is used in pessaries, ointments and as a massage lubricant.

Very wide culinary and confectionery use of the seed products.

The fat is used in cosmetics.

Thymus x *citriodorus* (Pers.) Schreb. ex Scheigg. & Körte LABIATAE
Lemon Thyme

Of the many species and cultivars of Thyme which are available for use in a scented herb garden, one of the most popular is the true Lemon Thyme.

Since it is a cross between *T. pulegioides* L and *T. vulgaris* L there is often confusion with other lemon-scented Thymes, notably some varieties of *T. vulgaris*.

Lemon Thyme is variable in form. It is often found as the silver-variegated cultivar, Silver Queen, which itself ranges in degree and colour of variegation.

Because of its mild flavour Lemon Thyme is a popular culinary herb.
Description Aromatic lemon-scented bushy shrub to 25 cm tall. Leaves glabrous and revolute, varying in colour from dark to light, or silver-variegated, lanceolate to ovate, to 9 mm long. Flowers pale lilac, in small, oblong inflorescence; appearing mid to late summer.
Distribution Cultivated world-wide.
Cultivation Found horticulturally only; propagate from cuttings spring to autumn, or by

division in spring. Requires well-drained soil in a warm position. Winter protection under glass may be necessary for some cultivars in northern climates.
Constituents Essential oil.
Uses (fresh or dried leaves) Not used medicinally.
Widely used as a culinary herb. Used horticulturally as an aromatic ornamental and edging plant.

Thymus serpyllum L LABIATAE
Wild Thyme
As the common name suggests this herb is found wild. It is extensively distributed in Europe and Asia and is found as far north as Iceland. Wild Thyme has been used since the earliest times, and Dioscorides called it *herpyllos*; the Romans knew it as *serpyllum*. Both ancient names refer to the prostrate, snake-like growth habit of the plant. Wild Thyme exists in many forms with variations in colour, growth habit and leaf size; many different varieties are, therefore, found as Wild Thyme, but all are suitable as a quickly spreading

aromatic carpeting herb for the garden. *T. serpyllum* is also described as Mother of Thyme, Creeping Thyme and, confusingly, Lemon Thyme.
Description Extremely variable, prostrate, mat-forming, aromatic perennial 10–40 cm tall; woody at the base and sometimes a semi-shrub. Flowering stems erect to 10 cm tall bearing 8 mm-long linear to elliptic, almost sessile leaves and pink to purple small flowers arranged in an ovoid, short, terminal inflorescence. Appearing late summer to early autumn.
Distribution Native to Europe, north-west Asia; introduced and naturalized elsewhere. On well-drained sandy soils or sandy loams in dry turf, roadsides, sunny slopes, woodland clearing; to 2600 m altitude.
Cultivation Wild. Propagated by layering in summer or from cuttings taken from spring to autumn.
Constituents Essential oil (to 0.3%) comprising mainly thymol and carvacrol; tannins; saponoside; resins; flavones; bitter principles. Composition varies considerably.
Uses (dried flowering tops, rarely oil) Antispasmodic; antiseptic; expectorant; carminative; bitter aromatic.
Principally employed in digestive complaints, including flatulence and indigestion. Useful in coughs and respiratory tract infection.
May be used as a disinfectant mouth wash, external poultice on wounds, for rheumatic pain, and as a douche.
The oil (Oil of Serpolet) is used commercially in certain pharmaceutical and cosmetic products.
Dried leaves can be taken as a tea, and are used for culinary purposes.

Thymus vulgaris L LABIATAE
Garden Thyme Common Thyme
Thyme is one of the best known and most widely used of the culinary herbs, and to satisfy the demand it is not only collected from the wild in mediterranean areas, but is also cultivated commercially in central and eastern Europe.

The generic and common names come from the Latin *thymum* which in turn derives from the Greek names *thymbra* or *thumon*. It is however, most unlikely that this species was the main one used by the ancient Greeks, more probably they used *Thymus capitatus* Lk.
It is also uncertain when Thyme was first cultivated in northern European countries; some believe the Romans took it to Britain, while there is stronger evidence that it became popular north of the Alps between A.D. 850 and 1250. Certainly by the sixteenth century it was in general cultivation being grown as an annual in the far north.
The German apothecary Neumann first isolated the plant's essential oil in 1725, and this powerfully antiseptic substance is still used in pharmacy and various commercial preparations.
Description Aromatic perennial sub-shrub on somewhat gnarled or tortuous woody stems, 10–30 cm tall; leaves grey-green, opposite, small, entire, linear to elliptic, petioled or sessile, tomentose, to 15 mm long. Flowers lilac to white, small, in dense or loose many-flowered terminal inflorescences, characterized by somewhat larger leaves than those on non-flowering stems. Appearing early summer to late autumn.
Distribution Native to the western mediterranean region and southern Italy; introduced elsewhere. To 2500 m in altitude. On dry soils, either rocky or well-drained, in sunny positions.
Cultivation Wild. Collected commercially from the wild in south-west mediterranean countries; cultivated commercially in Europe, especially Hungary and Germany.
Widely grown as a horticultural or culinary plant. Propagated from seed sown in early summer, by division in spring, or by cuttings or layering from mid-spring to early summer. Grown as an annual in very cold climates. Very variable plant.
Constituents Essential oil (to 2.5%), comprising thymol (to 40%), carvacrol, borneol, cymene, linalol, *l*-pinene, bornyl-acetate; acid and neutral saponins; thiamine; ursolic acid; caffeic acid; tannins; bitter compounds; other active components.
The combined action is antiseptic, and mostly due to the thymol content.
Uses (dried flowering plant, oil) Antiseptic; carminative; vermifuge; rubefacient.
Thyme can be used in a wide range of conditions where its antiseptic properties are required. Particularly beneficial in gastro-intestinal and respiratory complaints.
The oil may be used as an antihelmintic, particularly to destroy hookworm.
Wide use of the oil in commercial, pharmaceutical, flavouring, and cosmetic preparations.
The plant is of great importance as a flavouring and kitchen herb.

Tilia cordata Mill. TILIACEAE
Small-Leaved Lime
The Lime, like the Oak and certain other European plants, was sacred to the Indo-Germanic peoples, and the name Lime is

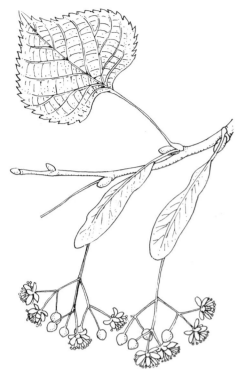

unknown active substances.

Uses (dried flowers and bracts, bark, fresh leaves). Antispasmodic; sedative; diaphoretic; diuretic; expectorant; choleretic.

Flowers principally used in combination with Hawthorn (*Crataegus monogyna* Jacq.) and Mistletoe (*Viscum album* L) in the treatment of hypertension.

They are also of much benefit in feverish chills, respiratory catarrh, indigestion, anxiety states and migraine, and in combination with other remedies in urinary infections. Small doses assist digestion. An infusion can be made for external use on skin rashes, as a gargle, or as a soothing bath. The bark decoction is of benefit in liver disease. Flowers used as a tisane – Linden Tea.

Fresh leaves may be eaten.

Wood used for carving and is also used in charcoal manufacture.

The tree is used (often clipped to shape) as a roadside ornamental.

Toxicodendron toxicaria (Salisb) Gillis
ANACARDIACEAE
Poison Ivy Poison Oak/Hiedra

The genus *Rhus* contains more than 150 species, some of which are grown as orna-

mentals. Recently six species (each commonly known as Poison Ivy or Poison Oak) have been transferred to the genus *Toxicodendron*, and *Toxicodendron toxicaria* was formerly classified as *Rhus toxicodendron* L. It is frequently confused with the closely related *R. radicans* L (now *T. radicans* (L) O. Kuntze) which is considered by some authorities to be a variety of *T. toxicaria*, and having the same properties. Poison Ivy is best known as an agent causing a violent allergic response in susceptible individuals. This allergy occurs either on contact with the

plant or simply by standing close to it.

Its medicinal use was discovered in 1794 by Anderson and Horsfield in America, and it was introduced to Europe by Du Fresnoy in 1798. The leaves and a tincture have been included in various pharmacopoeias and materia medicas until as late as 1941. Now only used homeopathically.

Description Perennial shrub to 2 m containing milky juice. Leaves compound, comprising three thin, acute, rounded and dentate or crenate leaflets, downy beneath. Flowers small, several, greenish, in open axillary, racemose panicles; appearing mid-summer, followed by pale brown globose fruit.

Distribution Native to eastern North America in thickets.

Cultivation Wild plant.

Constituents Tannins, as rhoitannic acid; toxicodendric acid; unknown substances.

Uses (leaves, juice) Narcotic; irritant.

Once used in the treatment of chronic skin problems, rheumatism and paralysis. No longer employed, except in homeopathy.

The juice was formerly used as an indelible ink, and in shoe-creams.

Contra-indications May cause severe contact dermatitis. Not to be used internally.

Tragopogon porrifolius L COMPOSITAE
Salsify Vegetable Oyster/Oyster Plant

The Greek name for Salsify was *tragopogon* which means goat's beard; this gives both the generic name for this species and the family, as well as the English common name for a different herb, *Tragopogon pratensis* L. The French name for *T. pratensis* is, however, *Salsifis des prés*, or Meadow Salsify (although *barbe de bouc* or goat's beard is also used), thus adding to and emphasizing the confusion that surrounds international names.

The medieval names for Salsify were *oculus porci* or pig's eye (which might be a reference to the colour and appearance of the broken root) and *herba salsifica* from the Italian *sassefrica* (meaning the plant which accompanies stones – after its predisposition for rocky land).

The Italians were the first to cultivate Salsify as a vegetable, doing so in the early sixteenth century. By the seventeenth century it had not only been introduced as a vegetable in northern Europe, but also as a flower.

Salsify was largely ignored by nineteenth-century gardeners in favour of the Spanish Scorzonera (*Scorzonera hispanica* L), although both are now used commercially.

The herb has never been of medicinal interest.

Description Attractive hardy biennial to 110 cm, on 25 cm-long edible taproot. Leaves clasped, tapering, pointed and grass-like. Flowers purple, attractive, solitary, opening in the morning, ligulate to 8 cm wide. Appearing early to late summer.

Distribution Native to southern Europe; introduced elsewhere. Naturalized as a weed in North America. On stony but moist soils with some loam, in meadowland to 2000 m altitude.

Cultivation Wild. Propagate from seed sown in spring, thinning to 10 cm apart. Requires well-dug, rich and deep soil which is kept well-

derived from the German base *lind*. A tea made from the flowers is still called Linden Tea. In America the so-called American Linden (*T. americana* L) provides a similar drink – the Basswood Tea (which should, however, only be taken sparingly since it can cause nausea). The Latin name for this and related species was *Tilia*, hence the generic name and the modern French, Italian, and Spanish names *Tilleul*, *Tiglio* and *Tilia*.

The tree has long been planted around houses and in towns as a decorative or shade-plant. It is the lightest European wood in weight as well as being one of the easiest to work in carving. The inner bark fibre was also once used in rope manufacture.

Besides the use of its blossom in a pleasant herbal tisane, Lime has an important place in folk medicine and eastern European medicine as a remedy for high blood pressure. For this purpose the flowers of *T. platyphyllos* Scop. (Large-leaved Lime) and *T. x europaea* L (a hybrid between *T. platyphyllos* and *T. cordata*) are also collected for medicinal application.

Description Deciduous tree or, rarely, shrub 15–40 m tall. Trunk straight, smooth when young. Leaves to 6.5 cm, orbicular, petiolate, serrate. Flowers aromatic, yellowish, in either erect or pendulous cymes of 5–10 flowers, appearing mid to late summer, followed by globose fruit.

Distribution European native, in mixed or deciduous woodland especially in sandy or stony soils in warm position; to 1600 m altitude.

Cultivation Wild. Introduced in towns as an ornamental tree. May reach 1000 years old.

Constituents Volatile oil (to 0.02%) comprising several compounds including farnesol; mucilage; manganese salts; flavonoid glycosides; saponins; polyphenols; tannins; other

watered. Lift roots in autumn or leave during winter in the soil. Readily self-sown.
Constituents Unknown.
Uses (fresh taproot) Nutritive; diuretic; bitter. Although not used medicinally, the root acts as an appetite stimulant, and there is some evidence that it may have a beneficial effect on the liver.
Roots cooked and eaten as a vegetable.
Leaves may be used sparingly in salads.

Trifolium pratense L LEGUMINOSAE
Red Clover
Red Clover is a short-lived perennial (sometimes incorrectly described in seed lists as an annual or biennial) which is of great importance as a forage and cover crop in agriculture. It is often incorporated in short-term leas (arable land under pasture) with Italian Ryegrass (*Lolium multiflorum* ssp. *multiflorum*

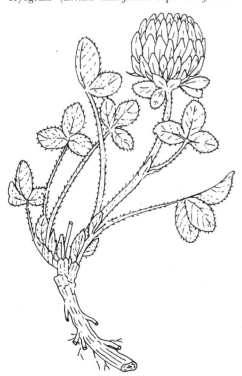

(Lam.) Husnot). The herb was known to the ancients as *triphyllon* and *trifolium*, after its 3 leaves, but it was not widely used medicinally, only occasionally being used as a vulnerary.
After its introduction to America it soon became naturalized and American Indians both ate it and used it medicinally – in ointments for external sores and internally in skin disease. It appears to have re-entered British herbal use from American folk medicine in the nineteenth century.
Description Short-lived perennial to 50 cm tall, on large branched root. Stems short and hairy, being ovate to obovate, leaflets to 5 cm long, in long-petioled, trifoliate leaves. Flowers rose-purple or white in ovoid, dense heads to 3 cm long; appearing early summer to early autumn.
Distribution European native; introduced and naturalized elsewhere. Widely distributed in fields, beside roadways, on deep, rich, dry or moderately moist soils.
Cultivation Wild. Grown agriculturally as a fodder crop. Usually sown broadcast on prepared, rolled fields in spring.
Constituents (flower) Salicylic acid; coumaric acid; isorhamnetin; a phytosterol glucoside; trifolianol; a quercitin glucoside; essential oil; a phenolic glycoside, trifoliin; an hydroxymethyloxyflavone, pratol; sugars, including rhamnose; a plant oestrogen, coumestrol.
Uses (dried flower-heads, fresh plant) Alterative; antispasmodic; expectorant; vulnerary.
Flower-heads applied externally in the treatment of ulcers, burns, sores and skin complaints. Used internally to treat chronic skin conditions such as psoriasis and eczema.
Once used in domestic wine-making.
The fresh plant is used for cattle fodder and other agricultural purposes – although it has been known to cause a photosensitive dermatitis in cattle known as trifoliosis.

Trigonella foenum-graecum L LEGUMINOSAE
Fenugreek Foenugreek
Like Red Clover (*Trifolium pratense* L) this herb is a fodder crop and the specific name *foenum-graecum* is Latin for Greek hay emphasizing its agricultural use, and the fact that it has been used for this purpose since the earliest times.
Benedictine monks introduced the plant to central Europe and Charlemagne promoted it in the ninth century. It was grown in England in the sixteenth century. The herb has long been a favourite of the Arabs and it was studied at the School of Salerno by Arabic physicians. Egyptians not only use the seeds for medicinal purposes, but roast them as a coffee and eat both the sprouting seed and the fresh leaves as a vegetable. Indians also use the leaves as a vegetable and consider the seed not only a spice for curries, but as a source of a yellow cloth dye. The name Fenugreek is simply an abbreviation of *foenum-graecum*.
It is now used more in veterinary than human medicine.
Description Smooth, erect annual to 60 cm. Leaves trifoliate; leaflets 2–2.5 cm long, toothed, oblanceolate-oblong. Flowers whitish, solitary or in pairs in axils, petals deciduous

after flowering, appearing mid-summer and followed by beaked pod, 5–7.5 cm long, containing 10–20 seeds.
Distribution Native to south Europe and Asia.
Cultivation Wild. Cultivated commercially in the Middle East, India, Morocco and elsewhere. Propagated from seed sown in spring.
Constituents (seed) Mucilage (to 30%); trigonelline; choline; flavone pigment; fixed oil; protein (to 20%); lecithin; phytosterols.
Uses (seed, fresh leaves) Aromatic; carminative; tonic. Seed valuable in dyspepsia and diarrhoea.
Used as a spice, or roasted as a coffee substitute.

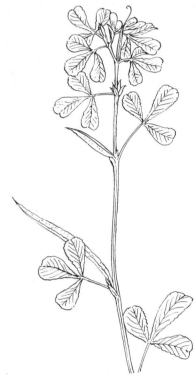

An ingredient of commercial chutneys and the Middle Eastern confectionery, halva. The seeds are celery-flavoured. Fresh leaf may be used in curries, or seed can be sprouted and used as a salad herb.
Seed provides a yellow dye.
Employed as a fodder plant.

Trillium erectum L LILIACEAE
Bethroot Brown Beth/
Squawroot/Stinking Benjamin
The Bethroot (or Wake-Robin) genus consists of about 30 species of attractive spring-flowering liliaceous plants. The generic name refers to the fact that each species produces three leaves and a tripartite flower.
Most are native to North America and traditionally the Appalachian and other Indians used various species to treat a range of female complaints (hence the name Squawroot).
When Rafinesque and others introduced Bethroot to medicine in 1830 it was considered that any species of *Trillium* could be employed, although the Indians considered the white flowering species the most effective.
Millspaugh proposed in 1892 that only *T.*

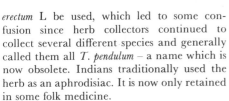

erectum L be used, which led to some confusion since herb collectors continued to collect several different species and generally called them all *T. pendulum* – a name which is now obsolete. Indians traditionally used the herb as an aphrodisiac. It is now only retained in some folk medicine.

Description Perennial to 50 cm tall, on short, thick root-stock; 3 leaves, sessile, rhomboid, to 21 cm long in terminal whorl, subtending a pedunculate solitary, somewhat nodding, attractive flower to 5 cm wide. The colour ranges from white to brownish purple. Appearing late spring.

Distribution North American native, from Quebec to North Carolina. In shaded woodland, on moist rich soils.

Cultivation Wild.

Constituents Volatile oil; gum; tannins; fixed oil; a saponin, trillarin.

Uses (dried root-stock) Astringent; emmenagogue; antispasmodic; emetic; expectorant. Used in uterine haemorrhages, metrorrhagia, menorrhoea, leucorrhoea. The poultice is applied to ulcers and sores.

Considered to be an astringent tonic and of use post-partum; and an alterative of benefit in chronic skin conditions.

Tropaeolum majus L TROPAEOLACEAE
Garden Nasturtium Indian Cress
Nasturtium is a well-known garden ornamental which is a perennial although it is grown as an annual.

It was introduced to Spain from Peru in the sixteenth century and reached Gerard in London in the 1590s; it was unknown in central Europe, however, until 1684 when Bewerning promoted it as a vegetable and medicine.

The herb was known from its introduction as *Nasturcium indicum* or *Nasturcium peruvianum*; hence it became *Nasturtium indicum* or Indian Cress. The seed, flowers and leaves are now eaten for their spicy taste in salads, and the pickled flower buds provide the best substitute for capers. It is now rarely used medicinally, but it is still collected commercially in some countries.

Description Somewhat succulent perennial, grown as an annual in cool climates. Climbing and twining to 3 m tall – dwarf forms only reaching 40 cm. Leaves reniform to orbicular 5–20 cm wide, entire, glossy, alternate, long-petioled. Flowers spurred, to 5 cm wide, from orange to white, occasionally red or mahogany; appearing from early summer to first frosts.

Distribution South American native, especially Peru and Bolivia.

Cultivation Wild. Cultivated widely as an ornamental, and rarely as a drug. Propagated from seed sown in late spring to early summer in rich soil in sunny situation. Dwarf and double-flowered cultivars are found. Some double-flowered forms cannot be raised from seed. Harvest seed before pods lose their green colour.

Constituents (seed) A glycoside, glucotropaeoline, which hydrolyzes to yield an antibiotic and an essential oil. Principal action is antibiotic.

Uses (fresh leaves, flowers, seeds, pickled flower buds) Antibacterial; antimycotic.

Used in infections of the genito-urinary and respiratory systems.

Principally employed as a salad herb or as a caper substitute.

Used as a garden ornamental.

Turnera diffusa Willd. var. *aphrodisiaca* (Ward.) Urb. TURNERACEAE
Damiana Mexican Damiana/Turnera
Damiana is principally a tonic tea which has long been used by the Mexicans who call it *hierba de la pastora*.

It was introduced to Europe from American folk medicine in the early twentieth century and recommended as a tonic and aphrodisiac – formerly being incorporated with other supposed aphrodisiacs or agents considered of benefit in sexual debility. It has not been studied extensively but appears to be useful in various disorders such as depression. Related members of the genus *Turnera* are also used as tonics in tropical America and Africa (such as the Yellow Alder, *T. ulmifolia* L) indicating the presence in the group of a tonic constituent or constituents.

Description Aromatic, pubescent, shrubby perennial to 60 cm tall. Leaves simple, petiolate, obovate, pale green, dentate, to 2.5 cm long. Flowers small, yellow, axillary, attractive, appearing early to late summer, followed by small, globular, many-seeded capsule.

Distribution Native to subtropical North America, especially Mexico, California and Texas. On dry, sandy or rocky soils in full sun.

Cultivation Wild plant. May be propagated from seed sown in spring, division in spring or autumn, and from cuttings taken in summer and rooted in a peat and sand mix.

Constituents Volatile oil (to 1%) comprising damianin; also fixed oil; gum; tannins (4%); starch; two resins.

Uses (dried leaves) Tonic; laxative; mild stimulant.

Principally of benefit as a tonic in depression and similar anxiety neuroses. In atonic constipation the infusion initiates peristalsis and acts as a laxative. It has a specific irritant and hence stimulant, effect on the mucosa of the genito-urinary tract, and therefore possibly acting as an aphrodisiac.

Small doses aid digestion.

Tussilago farfara L COMPOSITAE
Coltsfoot Son-before-father
Named after the leaf shape, Coltsfoot is still one of the most important herbal remedies for the treatment of coughs. The Greeks knew it as *bechion* and the Romans as *tusilago*, both names referring to the 'cough plant' and from which the modern medical terms bechic and (anti-) tussive are derived. Even in the days of Dioscorides Coltsfoot was smoked to relieve coughing, a tradition maintained in its modern

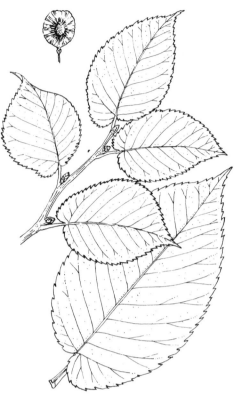

incorporation as the basic ingredients of herbal smoking mixtures. The leaves and flowers are now normally administered in the form of an infusion.

Description Perennial on creeping stolons reaching 8–30 cm tall. Flowers yellow, to 4 cm wide, in solitary capitula, appearing early to late spring on purplish, woolly and scaly scape 12 cm long, later elongating and bearing numerous achenes covered with a pappus of white hairs. Leaves appear from late spring; basal, long-petioled, tomentose beneath, orbicular-cordate, sinuate, 10–18 cm wide.

Distribution Native to Europe, north and west Asia, North Africa; introduced and naturalized in North America and elsewhere. On moist, loamy soils in wasteland and uncultivated places, to 2400 m altitude.

Cultivation Wild. Collected from the wild. Propagated by seed, by root cuttings or division. A moist soil is essential. The herb may become rampant, and care is needed to restrict its growth in gardens.

Constituents Mucilage; tannins; inulin; a bitter glycoside; essential oil; potassium and calcium salts; saponins.

Uses (dried leaves and flowers, rarely fresh leaves, fresh juice) Expectorant; demulcent; anti-inflammatory.

Used in the treatment of irritating coughs and respiratory disorders such as bronchitis and laryngitis; applied externally as a poultice to ulcers and sores.

Fresh leaves eaten as a salad herb rarely.

Fresh or dried flowers used in wine-making.

Leaves formerly smoked to relieve coughing, and now included in herbal tobaccos.

Ulmus rubra Mühlenb. ULMACEAE
Slippery Elm Red Elm
Slippery Elm receives its common name from the feel of the moistened inner bark (the secondary phloem), which is the only part now used medicinally. North American Indians have long used the bark tea as both a laxative and treatment for diarrhoea, and the root tea to assist childbirth. Since the bark has been used as a mechanical abortive it is now only available commercially in the powdered, and hence harmless, form.

Slippery Elm drinks, some including malted constituents, are still popular nutritive medicines following gastro-intestinal illnesses.

Formerly called *U. fulva* Michx.

Description Small or medium-sized tree reaching 20 m tall; leaves dark green, simple, rough above and pubescent below, serrate, 12 cm long, obovate to oblong. Flowers inconspicuous in clusters, appearing spring followed by flat, conspicuous 1-seeded samara.

Distribution North American native from Florida to southern Canada. In moist woodland and stream edges; also rarely in dry situations. Prefers poor soils.

Cultivation Wild plant. Inner bark collected in spring.

Constituents Mucilage, on hydrolysis yielding 3-methyl-galactose.

Uses (dried powdered inner bark) Demulcent; emollient.

Used in poultices, or as a decoction for diarrhoea or constipation.

Employed commercially and domestically in nutritive, convalescent drinks.

Urginea maritima (L) Baker LILIACEAE
Squill Sea Onion/White or Red Squill
The Squill is a powerful medicinal plant which has been in almost continuous use from the time of the earliest Greeks to the present. To Dioscorides it was known as *scilla*, hence the common name. There is some evidence that the bulbs were used to beat to death scapegoats or ritual victims in very early Greece in order to placate the gods of fertility. Certainly the large, heavy bulbs have strong magical associations as well as having therapeutic uses. Two varieties were known, the white and red (the colour referring to the bulb scales, not the flowers); both belong to the species *U. maritima*, but the red is more active and preferred by both the early Arab physicians and later French apothecaries. It is now the variety used in certain rat poisons.

White Squill is retained in several national pharmacopoeias, but in view of its action on the heart it is unsuitable for use by other than the medical profession.

Description Bulbous perennial to 150 cm tall; leaves fleshy, glaucous, basal, to 10 cm wide and 40 cm long. Flowers white or rose, in racemes terminating a leafless scape; appearing autumn.

Distribution Native to mediterranean region from Spain to Syria; also Canary Islands and South Africa. On dry sandy soils specially near to the sea, in full sun; but also to 900 m altitude.

Cultivation Wild plant.

Constituents (red and white varieties) Glycosides (mainly scillarin A and B) to which the action is largely due; mucilage (to 11%); a carbohydrate, sinistrin; and other substances. Red Squill, in addition, contains the rat poison scilliroside.

Uses (dried bulb) Expectorant; emetic; irritant; cardio-active.

Used in the treatment of chronic (but not acute) bronchitis.

Employed as a constituent of rat poisons.

Contra-indications Very POISONOUS; to be used only by medical personnel.

Urtica dioica L URTICACEAE
Stinging Nettle Nettle/Common Nettle
The Nettle is now a common and painful stinging weed which appears wherever land is disturbed by man and left derelict. In the past, however, it has variously been used in cloth manufacture, as a food, and medicinally. It was once even cultivated in Scotland, Denmark and Norway.

The use of the plant in cloth manufacture only stopped in the first quarter of the twentieth century but can be traced back to the Bronze Age – and is recorded in the common name, nettle, from an old word meaning to twist (and hence make fibre).

Greeks knew it as *akalyphe* and Romans as

urtica – but the ancients probably used the annual *U. pilulifera* L (or Roman Nettle) rather more, since it is native to southern Europe. Both this species and the Small Nettle (*U. urens*), which is also an annual, have the same values as *U. dioica*.

Description Dioecious perennial, from 80–180 cm tall, stems bristly, sparsely branched, bearing opposite and decussate, acuminate, deeply serrate, petiolate and ovate leaves to 14 cm long. Flowers minute, in pendulous axillary racemes, appearing mid-summer to mid-autumn.

Distribution Widespread; Eurasian native. On wasteland, especially damp and nutrient-rich soils which have previously been disturbed by man; to 2700 m altitude.

Cultivation Wild plant. Cultivated only rarely for medicinal purposes, and as a source of

commercial chlorophyll.
Propagated from seed, or by root division in spring.

Constituents (leaves) Histamine; acetylcholine; formic acid; gallic acid; tannins; 5-hydroxy-tryptamine; vitamins A and C; mineral salts including calcium, potassium, silicon, iron, manganese and sulphur; other active substances; unknown components.

Uses (fresh or dried leaves, root-stock rarely) Astringent; anti-haemorrhagic; diuretic; galactagogue.

The Nettle has many therapeutic applications, but is principally of benefit in all kinds of internal haemorrhages; as a diuretic; in urticaria, jaundice, haemorrhoids; a laxative; and it is used in dermatological problems including eczema.

The powdered leaf used as a snuff stops nose bleeds.

It has been shown to lower the blood-sugar level and also to lower the blood pressure slightly.

Used to promote hair growth rarely, and fresh branches applied externally in rheumatism.

Young shoots and leaves cooked like Spinach.

A commercial source of chlorophyll.
Used in paper and cloth manufacture.

Vaccinium myrtillus L ERICACEAE
Bilberry Whortleberry/Huckleberry
The genus *Vaccinium* includes several species which are grown as ornamentals as well as others which provide such edible berries as the Blueberry, Cranberry and Bilberry.

V. myrtillus has many common names and there is much confusion in the genus (which contains about 150 species) because of the free exchange of the same common name between various species. It is not possible, therefore, to identify definitely this species in ancient writings, but it was an official medicinal plant from the sixteenth century and known then as *vaccinia* and *mora agrestis*. The specific name refers to the Myrtle-shaped leaves.

The fruits have long been a popular food, and are still collected for this purpose.

Description Subshrub 30–60 cm tall, deciduous and glabrous on thin creeping and rooting

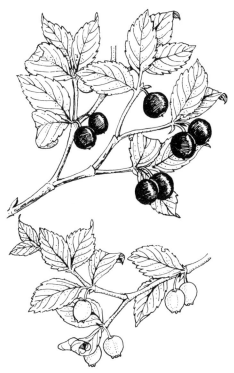

stems. Leaves alternate, bright green, finely dentate, oval, to 3 cm long. Flowers pale greenish-pink, small, solitary, appearing in leaf axils from late spring to late summer, followed by globose purple fruit.

Distribution Native to Europe and northern Asia; in humus-rich, acidic, damp soils in woodland, forests, moorland and fenland, to 2600 m altitude.

Cultivation Wild. Propagated as ground cover in shady positions on damp and acidic soils – either peaty or sandy. Grown from rooted cuttings.

Constituents (fruit) Organic acids; pectin; sugars; mineral salts; tannins; vitamins A and C; arbutin; anthocyanin pigments.

Uses (fresh fruit, leaves rarely) Astringent; antiseptic; tonic.

Fruit used in the treatment of diarrhoea. Leaves have a weak hypoglycaemic action, and have been used in combination with other remedies in the treatment of diabetes.

Principally employed as a nutritive, rather tart fruit in conserves and syrups, or eaten raw. Also distilled to flavour certain liqueurs.

Valeriana officinalis L VALERIANACEAE
Valerian Common Valerian/Garden Heliotrope
Several different species of *Valeriana* have been used in European medicine of which *V. officinalis* L, *V. celtica* L, *V. dioica* L and *V. phu* L, were the most important. The latter species was probably the herb known as Phu to the ancients while *V. celtica* was referred to as *Nardus celticus*.

Valeriana officinalis was particularly promoted by the Arab physicians and the name Valeriana first appears in the tenth century.

Tincture of Valerian was employed in the First World War to treat shellshock, and the rhizome and roots are still retained in several national pharmacopoeias. The root was once included in various recipes and was also used to scent linen.

Description Glabrous perennial 20–150 cm tall, on aromatic root-stock. Stems lightly grooved. Leaves pinnate to 20 cm long, leaflets either entire or toothed, lanceolate. Flowers white or pinkish, small, in terminal inflorescence appearing mid-summer to early autumn.

Distribution Native to Europe and west Asia; naturalized in North America. In grassland, ditches, damp meadowland, close to streams, on nutrient-rich soils to 2000 m altitude.

Cultivation Wild. Propagated by division of root-stock in spring or autumn, or from seed sown in spring.

Constituents Essential oil (to 1%) comprising various components (which include monoterpene valepotriates) and which in combination are sedative and antispasmodic.

Uses (dried root-stock) Sedative; stomachic; antispasmodic; carminative.

Of benefit in the treatment of a wide range of nervous disorders and intestinal colic. Used in combination with other remedies in the treatment of hypertension. Useful in insomnia and migraine, nervous exhaustion and anxiety

states. The root was once used, in small quantities, as a culinary flavouring.
Contra-indications The drug should not be taken in large doses for an extended period of time.

Vanilla planifolia Andrews ORCHIDACEAE
Vanilla

Vanilla was introduced to Europe by the Spanish in the early sixteenth century following their observation of its use in Mexico by the Aztecs for flavouring chocolate. Early names included *Araco aromatico, banillen* and *vainillen*.

It was employed in the seventeenth century, chiefly in France, both for chocolate manufacture and scenting tobacco, and in the eighteenth century it was included for the first time in several pharmacopoeias – as an aromatic carminative. Vanilla pods are now mainly employed in flavouring. West Indian Vanilla is from *V. pompona*.

Description Epiphytic orchid with stout stems, and oblong-lanceolate leathery, fleshy, short-petioled leaves to 20 cm long. Flowers yellow and orange to 5 cm long, followed by aromatic fruit to 18 cm long.

Distribution Native to tropical America; introduced and cultivated elsewhere.

Cultivation Wild. Widely cultivated in Mexico, Madagascar and elsewhere; in high humidity under shade, on poles or tree trunks.

Constituents Vanillin (to 2%); aromatic substances.

Uses (dried cured seed-pods (Vanilla beans)) Aromatic carminative.
Rarely used for medicinal purposes other than as a pharmaceutical flavouring.
Principally employed as a culinary and commercial flavouring and in cosmetics.

Veratrum viride Ait. LILIACEAE
American White Hellebore
Green Hellebore

Veratrum viride was formerly classified as *V. eschscholtzii* A. Gray. The European White Hellebore is *V. album* L. Both these species and another European plant, *V. nigrum* L (the Black Hellebore) have long been used as arrow poisons as they are very toxic.

The Red Indians used *V. viride* as an ordeal poison, and it was introduced to American medical practice in the late eighteenth century when British supplies of *V. album* were cut off by the War of Independence. Green Hellebore was once an American domestic remedy for removing lice from the hair – combing it through in the form of a strong decoction.

The herb contains alkaloids which drastically depress the action of the heart and reduce blood pressure. Its use is now strictly limited to veterinary practice.

Description Rhizomatous, unbranched perennial to 2 m, on thick root-stock. Leaves alternate, ovate to elliptic, to 30 cm long. Flowers in terminal panicles, greenish, to 2.5 cm wide, appearing late spring to late summer.

Distribution North American native, on wet soils in woodland, beside streams, or on low-lying meadowland.

Cultivation Wild plant. Propagated by root-stock division in spring or autumn.

Constituents Several alkaloids (to 1.5%) including veratrine, jervine and veratrosine; glycosides.

Uses (dried rhizome) Hypotensive; toxic; emetic; purgative.
Rarely used for any medicinal purpose. Once employed to reduce blood pressure associated with toxaemia during pregnancy. A decoction

is anti-parasitic and can be used by veterinary personnel for animal use.

Contra-indications Very POISONOUS; only to be used by medical personnel.

Verbascum thapsus L SCROPHULARIACEAE
Mullein Aaron's Rod

The common name, Mullein, is derived from the Latin *mollis* meaning soft, after the large ear-like leaves – the herb is also variously known as Donkey's Ears, Bunny's Ears and Bull's Ears.

Mullein's tall, spire-like flowering stem was once used as a taper, having first been dried and then dipped in tallow. There is evidence that at one time it was one of the supposed magical herbs of the ancients.

Various species of *Verbascum* have been employed medicinally, the most important, historically, being *V. thapsiforme* Schrad. and *V. phlomoides* L. Mullein is now grown mostly as a decorative plant.

Description Erect, very soft and woolly biennial, to 2 m tall. Leaves grey-green, forming a basal rosette in the first year, eventually reaching 30 cm tall. Flowers yellow, sessile, in clusters, on dense, erect 2.5 cm-wide spikes appearing mid-summer to early autumn.

Distribution Eurasian native; naturalized in some temperate zones. On stony, shallow, well-drained, nitrogen-rich soils in wasteland and woodland clearings.

Cultivation Wild. Propagate from seed sown as soon as ripe or in the spring. Will not tolerate cold, wet conditions.

Constituents Mucilage; essential oil; saponosides.

Uses (dried or fresh leaves, dried flowers) Emollient; weakly sedative; expectorant.
Principally employed with other remedies in the treatment of respiratory disorders.

The leaves have been included in herbal smoking mixtures, and used in domestic cosmetic preparations.

The flowers provide a pale yellow dye. An attractive horticultural ornamental.

Verbena officinalis L VERBENACEAE
Vervain

Like Betony, Vervain has a long and well-documented history of association with the magic and sorcery of the Celtic and Germanic peoples of Europe. It also seems to have been considered sacred by the Greeks and Romans however, being known as *Herba sacra* and *Herba veneris*. Not surprisingly for a herb with alleged magical properties, Vervain was used in numerous complaints and it became an official drug. By 1830, however, Geiger stated that in Germany it was seldom used. It still has a place in folk medicine.

Description Perennial 35–80 cm tall, glabrous or nearly so, on erect, ribbed, angular stem; loosely branched and only sparsely leafy. Leaves petiolate, ovate, some pinnatifid, to 6 cm long. Flowers small, lilac, at the tips of long stalks. Appearing summer to late autumn.

Distribution Native to the mediterranean region; established elsewhere. On roadsides, wasteland, on nutrient-rich soils to 1500 m altitude.

Cultivation Wild. Propagated from seed sown in spring. Requires full sun.

Constituents Mucilage; tannins; saponins; essential oil; verbenaloside; the glycosides, verbenaline and verbenine; unknown substances.

Uses (dried flowering plant) Tonic; astringent; diuretic; diaphoretic; galactagogue; emmenagogue; vulnerary; antispasmodic.

Used in the treatment of nervous complaints such as depression, and with other remedies in chronic skin complaints. Considered to have a specific benefit to the uterus, but this is unsubstantiated.

Used externally to treat wounds.

Veronica beccabunga L SCHROPHULARIACEAE
Brooklime Water Pimpernel

Brooklime has a similar (but more bitter) taste to Watercress, and in former times was eaten as a salad herb. Its sharpness may have led to another common name Mouth Smart – or more probably this English name was a translation of the Flemish *beckpunge* and German

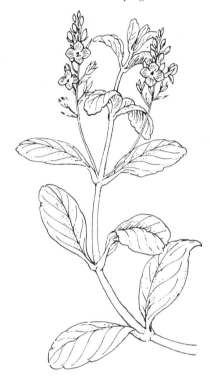

Bachbunge which mean the same.

To the apothecaries it was known as Herba Beccabunga (hence the modern specific name) and *Anagallis aquatica* or Water Pimpernel – from the similarities between Brooklime's flowers and those of the Scarlet Pimpernel (*Anagallis arvensis* L) although they differ in colour.

Description Semi-aquatic succulent perennial, 10–60 cm tall, with hollow, creeping, easily rooted stems. Leaves opposite, short-petioled, oblong to ovate, to 5 cm long, crenate-serrate. Flowers small, blue, in loose short, axillary racemes, appearing early summer to mid-autumn.

Distribution Native to Europe, Asia, North Africa; introduced elsewhere. In streams and ditches to 2600 m altitude.

Cultivation Wild plant.

Constituents Tannins; a glucoside; unknown substances.

Uses (fresh or dried flowering plant, fresh leaves) Diuretic; stimulant; weakly antipyretic; bechic; stomachic.

Rarely used medicinally. Formerly used in liver problems, haemorrhoids, gastro-intestinal complaints, and applied externally to ulcers. Fresh leaves may be eaten sparingly.

Veronica officinalis L SCROPHULARIACEAE
Speedwell Fluellen

Fluellen is probably the older of the two common English names, and it is derived from the old Welsh *llysiau Llywelyn* – the herb of St Llywelyn.

The name Speedwell is given to the entire family, as well as to this species. In America it is also known as Low Speedwell and Gypsyweed – one of many herbs with the latter name. As *Herba Veronica majoris* this plant became official in the Middle Ages and had a reputation as a healing herb – including the ability

to treat a variety of skin complaints. It was also used in a wide range of syrups and elixirs, for respiratory and stomach problems; it became less important by the mid-nineteenth century and it was then mostly used as a tea substitute. The French give it the name *thé d'Europe* – European Tea.

Description Low-growing pubescent perennial, often forming mats of prostrate rooting stems. 10–40 cm tall. Leaves opposite, serrate, ovate or oblong, to 4 cm long, with short petioles or sessile. Flowers pale blue, small, attractive, in dense, erect racemes. Appearing early to late summer.

Distribution Native to Europe, Asia, North America; in scrubland clearings, moorland, coppices, hedgerows, heaths; on acidic, sandy or loamy soils, to 1000 m altitude.

Cultivation Wild.

Constituents A glycoside, aucuboside; resins; bitter principles; tannins; unknown substances.

Uses (dried flowering plant) Expectorant; stomachic; vulnerary; galactagogue; diuretic. All the actions are weak and the plant is no longer of medicinal interest.

Principally employed as a tea substitute in herbal tea mixtures.

Veronicastrum virginicum Farwell
SCROPHULARIACEAE
Culver's Root Black Root/Physic Root
Formerly classified as both *Veronica virginica* L
and *Leptandra virginica* Nutt., this tall American
herb is closely related to the Speedwell family
or Veronicas.

Its popularity as an Indian remedy is reflected
in another common name, Bowman's Root;
the Seneca Indians once used its root as a tea to
cause vomiting for ritualistic and medicinal
purposes.

Although it was formerly included in the
United States Pharmacopoeia it is not now
widely used.

Its botanical name *Veronicastrum* is derived
from *veronica* (which itself was named after St
Veronica) and *astrum* or star – after the
arrangement of the leaves.

It was first introduced to Europe in 1714.
Description Perennial to 2.25 m on horizontal
blackish rhizome. Stem erect, smooth and unbranched bearing 15-cm long lanceolate, or
oblong-lanceolate, dentate, and shortly petiolate flowers in whorls of 3–5 or occasionally 9.
Flowers white, pink or blue, 7 mm long, numerous, on short pedicels, arranged in dense
terminal spike-like racemes. Appearing mid-
summer to mid-autumn.

Distribution North American native from
Massachusetts to Florida and Texas, on a
variety of soils from dry to rich and wet; but
especially in moist meadows and river banks.
Cultivation Wild. May be propagated by
division of rhizomes after flowering in late
autumn, or in mid-spring. A purple variety is
also known.
Constituents Gum; resin; a phytosterol, veros-
terol; volatile oil; citric acid; mannitol; a
saponoside; a volatile alkaloid; a bitter

principle; leptandrine, to which the action is
largely due.
Uses (dried rhizome and root) Purgative;
emetic; cholagogue; tonic.
Small doses are valuable as a stomachic tonic,
in diarrhoea, dyspepsia and atony of the
gastro-intestinal system. Promotes the flow of
bile from the gall bladder. Boiled in milk it
acts as a laxative; larger doses are purgative or
emetic.
Contra-indications In large doses or when used
fresh it acts as a drastic purgative and may
cause vertigo and bloody stools.

Viburnum opulus L CAPRIFOLIACEAE
Guelder Rose Cramp Bark/
Cranberry Tree
This is an attractive plant and several cultivars
are found as horticultural ornamentals. As the
name Cranberry Tree suggests, the fruit have
been used like Cranberries but they do not
really compare in quality and they must be

cooked before they are eaten – the raw fruit
contains a substance, viburnine, which can
cause severe gastro-intestinal disorders.
In Norway and other Scandinavian countries a
liquor has been distilled from the fruit. *V.
opulus* has numerous common names: Guelder
Rose is from the Dutch *Geldersche roos* since the
tree was introduced from Guelders, on the
German border, to England in the sixteenth
century. Strictly, Guelder Rose is *V. opulus* var.
roseum L (or *V. opulus* L var. *sterile* DC) and is a
sterile, thus non-fruiting, ornamental (found
in horticultural lists as the Snowball Tree).
The herb was rarely employed in north and
west European medicine, but it was popular in
the early nineteenth century in America – it is
still included, however, in the Polish, Rumanian and Russian pharmacopoeias.

Description Shrub to 4 m tall, branches glabrous and erect; leaves 3–5 lobed, opposite,
petiolate, dentate. Flowers white, in pedunculate cymes to 9 cm wide, appearing early to
mid-summer; followed by scarlet, then purple,
fruit.
Distribution Native to Europe, North Africa,
northern Asia; introduced elsewhere, often as
an ornamental. In woodland clearings, on wet
loamy soils to 1200 m altitude.
Cultivation Wild plant. Propagated from seed or
hardwood cuttings; several cultivars are grown
as ornamentals.
Constituents (bark) Tannins; isovalerianic acid;
resin; viburnine.
Uses (dried stem bark) Sedative; spasmolytic.
Of benefit in functional uterine disorders, as a
uterine sedative; menopausal metrorrhagia,
miscarriage, and dysmenorrhoea.
Fruit may be cooked and eaten, or used as a
dye.
Contra-indications Fresh berries are POISON-
OUS.

Viburnum prunifolium L CAPRIFOLIACEAE
Black Haw Sweet Viburnum/Stagbush/
American Sloe
V. prunifolium has similar constituents, properties and uses to *V. opulus* L, but differs in that
the part used medicinally is usually the root
bark rather than the stem bark. Its fruit are
also sweeter than those of *V. opulus* – hence the
name Sweet Viburnum. Black Haw continues
to be used in folk medicine and is retained in
several pharmacopoeias; other species are
similarly used, besides *V. opulus*, and they include *V. nudum* L. (the Possumhaw Viburnum)
and *V. rufidulum* Raf. (the Southern Black
Haw) – the latter being found in the Mexican
Pharmacopoeia.
Description Deciduous shrub to 5 m tall;
branches spreading. Leaves dull-coloured,

opposite, petiolate, ovate to elliptic, finely toothed to 7.5 cm long. Flowers small, white, in sessile cymes to 10 cm wide, appearing late spring to early summer, and followed by purple oval fruits.

Distribution Native to North America from Connecticut to Florida.

Cultivation Wild plant.

Constituents (root bark) Tannins; isovalerianic acid; resin; viburnine.

Uses (dried root bark) Sedative; spasmolytic. Of benefit as a uterine sedative in dysmenorrhia, and threatened miscarriage. Once taken as a tonic tea, and considered to be of benefit in asthma.

Contra-indications Uncooked fruit is POISONOUS.

Vinca major L APOCYNACEAE
Greater Periwinkle Periwinkle

The Periwinkle family consists of about 12 species of trailing evergreen shrubs. The genus Vinca (from the old Latin name *Vinca peruinca* from which the common name is derived) formerly included the Madagascan Periwinkle, *Vinca rosea* L, (now classified as *Catharanthus roseus* (L) G. Don) which is an important medicinal source of anti-leukaemic drugs. Both the Greater and the Lesser Periwinkle (*V. minor* L) have long been considered as magical and medicinal plants, but *V. major* was generally preferred, and it is still used in folk medicine.

Various cultivars of *V. minor* are grown as garden ornamentals.

Description Trailing evergreen perennial 30–90 cm tall. Long prostrate stems bearing dark green, shiny, ovate, short-petioled, obtuse or acute leaves to 4 cm long. Flowers pale blue to 4 cm wide, solitary on hollow stalk appearing mid to late spring.

Distribution European native, in mixed woodland in loamy calcareous soils, well-drained, to 1200 m altitude.

Cultivation Wild. Used as ground cover in shady positions; propagate by division or stem cuttings taken in spring or autumn.

Constituents Tannins; alkaloids, including pubescine, vinine and vincamine; flavonoids; pectin; organic acids; several mineral salts; vitamin C; rubber; ursolic acid. The flower contains robinoside.

Uses (flowering plant) Hypotensive; vasodilator; hypoglycaemic; astringent; vulnerary; sedative.

Generally used to stop bleeding, both externally and internally, as in metrorrhagia and menorrhagia. Also used in nervous conditions such as anxiety states and subsequent hypertension.

The herb possesses many other uses. It reduces blood pressure and dilates both coronary and peripheral blood vessels. There is also a marked effect on smooth muscle. Can be used as a tonic, bitter and in catarrh. Employed traditionally in Africa to treat Diabetes mellitus. Note: diabetes must only be treated by medical personnel.

Viola odorata L VIOLACEAE
Sweet Violet

The name Sweet Violet describes both the smell and colour of the flowers, and the plant has been cultivated for over 2000 years as both a colouring agent for drinks and syrups, and as a source of perfume. It is still grown in southern France for the perfume industry. At the turn of the century Violet Water and other Sweet Violet perfumes were one of the most popular of all scents in England (although Violet-scent was also obtained from *Iris germanica* L).

Early names included *viola purpurea*, *viola glaucia* and the Greek *ion agrion*. (The aromatic principle is known as ionine or irone.) The generic name is taken directly from the old Latin name.

Various parts of the plant are still used medicinally but their actions differ. The rootstock is now the part most commonly employed.

Description Perennial on long stolons, 10–15 cm tall, on short rhizome. Stemless. Leaves reniform to cordate-ovate, petiolate. Flowers attractive, scented, to 2 cm wide, usually violet, also white or pink; appearing mid to late spring.

Distribution Native to Asia, North Africa, Europe; introduced elsewhere on damp calcareous soils in shady woodland, scrubland, hedgerows, wood clearings; to 1000 m altitude.

Cultivation Wild. Propagated from offsets replanted in late winter or early spring in a peat and sand mix, under glass; or divide in spring. Requires shade, rich soil and moisture. Various cultivars may be found.

Constituents Saponins; a glycoside, violarutin; methyl salicylate; mucilage; vitamin C; an alkaloid, odoratine; anthocyanin pigments; an aromatic substance ionine or irone; salicylic glycosides.

Uses (dried leaves and flowers, fresh flowers, dried root-stock) Emetic; purgative;

hypotensive; expectorant; diuretic.

Leaves and flowers are principally employed in the treatment of respiratory disorders, especially chronic naso-pharyneal catarrh and bronchitis. Used in cough mixtures, and once employed in the treatment of rheumatism. Used as a gargle in inflamed buccal mucosae. Flowers used to colour medications; candied in confectionery, and used widely in perfumery.

Contra-indications In large doses the root is emetic and purgative.

Viola tricolor L ssp. *arvensis* Murr. VIOLACEAE
Heartsease Wild Pansy/Field Pansy

This herb with three-coloured petals (white, yellow and purple) became the *Herba Trinitatis* of the Middle Ages, and was later given the similarly descriptive specific name *tricolor*.

Heartsease is still official in some eastern European countries and remained so in Germany until 1926; it is now no longer cultivated medicinally. Various cultivars do however remain important horticultural ornamentals as edging plants. The name Pansy is from the French word *pensée*, meaning thought or remembrance, and Wild Pansy is still called *Pensée sauvage* in France. In the traditional language of flowers the purple form meant memories, the white loving thoughts and the yellow souvenirs. Hence Heartsease was a plant received in happy memory to ease the heart-break of separation.

Description Variable, annual or short-lived perennial, somewhat straggly and branched to 25 cm tall. Leaves opposite, ovate to lanceolate, dentate, with lobed stipules. Flowers purple, white, yellow or a combination of these colours. Most frequently yellowish in the wild plant. Appearing mid-spring to late autumn.

Distribution European native. Naturalized in North America. Introduced elsewhere. On wasteland, in fields, hedgerows, rarely in mountain pastures; on acidic soils. To 2000 m altitude.

Cultivation Wild. This species is one parent of the cultivated Garden Pansy (*V.* x *wittrockiana* ssp. *tricolor*) which is found in several forms. The herb hybridizes readily with related plants. Propagate from seed sown in spring or as soon as ripe. Requires rich, damp soil.

Constituents Salicylic acid and salicylates; saponins; flavonic glycosides including violaquercitin; a blue chromoglucoside, violanin; a bitter principle, violin (which acts as an emetic); rutin and related rutins; traces of volatile oil.

Uses (dried flowering plant, fresh juice, dried flowers) Diuretic; antipyretic; tonic; laxative; anti-inflammatory.

Used as a blood-purifying agent especially in chronic skin complaints and rheumatism. Stimulates the metabolism and induces perspiration, and therefore employed in feverish conditions. Of benefit in indigestion and urino-genital inflammatory conditions. Used as a gargle or lotion to aid wound healing, ulcers and sores. A valuable horticultural plant.

Contra-indications Large doses or prolonged use may cause allergic skin reactions.

Viscum album L LORANTHACEAE

Mistletoe

The Loranthaceae family comprises 20 genera and almost 1500 species of mostly parasitic plants which are widely distributed around the world. The species of medicinal interest in Europe is *V. album*, although since the plant is collected from the wild the resultant drug may also contain other species – notably *V. album* L ssp. *abietis* (Wiesb.) Abrom., *V. album* ssp. *album* L, *V. album* L ssp. *austriacum* (Wiesb.)

Vollm., and *Loranthus europaeus* L.

The parasite, Mistletoe (which contains chlorophyll) is found on different deciduous trees and commonly the Apple. It has been shown that the constituents of the Mistletoe may vary according to the host plant on which it is found. This may explain the ancient druidic belief that the drug from the Oak was most valuable (itself thought to be magical by the Druids).

Mistletoe is currently being examined for possible anti-cancer effects. It contains substances called lectins which may combine with certain cancer cells; the chemistry and pharmacology of the plant is very complicated, however, and no definitive results have yet been demonstrated in humans.

Description Woody perennial evergreen; stems to 1 m long and regularly branching. Leaves leathery, light green, blunt, narrow and obovate, to 8 cm long. Flowers sessile, unisexual, in short, almost sessile axillary inflorescence, appearing mid-spring to early summer and followed by 1-cm diameter white, sticky fruit.

Distribution Native to several regions from north-west Europe to China, including Iran and parts of the mediterranean region; rarely found on conifers, but common on some deciduous trees.

Cultivation Wild. Semi-cultivated in some places by the inoculation of tree bark (in Apple orchards, for example) with the squashed ripe fruit.

Constituents 11 proteins; a lectin (with a D-galactosyl specificity); a toxin, viscotoxin; alkaloids; many other supposedly active compounds.

Uses (dried branches and leaves) Hypotensive; cardio-active; diuretic; sedative.

Used in combination with other remedies to treat hypertension, and associated, nervous complaints. Considered anti-neoplastic (dem-

onstrated in some animals but not humans). Used pharmaceutically in certain preparations.

Employed in winter decorations.

Vitex agnus-castus L VERBENACEAE

Chaste Tree Monk's Pepper/Agnus Castus

Vitex agnus-castus is also called Indian Spice, Sage Tree, Hemp Tree and Wild Pepper – the latter reflecting the name *piper agreste* of the Middle Ages (*agreste* meaning wild). It was also called *viticis* and *agnus-castus* from which the botanical name is derived.

Athenian women used to put the leaves in their beds, and later monks in Europe used the ground-up seed as pepper – in both cases the purpose was to ensure chastity (hence Chaste Tree and Monk's Pepper). It is now known that the seeds contain hormone-like substances which reduce libido in the male and are of benefit to women with certain hormonal problems. Chaste Tree is now included in several gynaecological formulations. The branches are used in basket making in southern Europe.

Description Aromatic shrub or small tree to 6 m tall. Leaves opposite, palmately compound, divided into 5–7 lanceolate leaflets, each to 10 cm long. Flowers small, lavender or lilac, in dense cymes to 15 cm wide, in panicles to 30 cm long.

Distribution South European native; introduced and often naturalized in warm regions. On sandy or loamy, well-drained soils in full sun.

Cultivation Wild. Propagated from seed sown in spring, by layering in spring to summer, or from young woody cuttings under glass. Several cultivars are grown for decorative purposes, including the white variety *Alba* Westn.

Constituents Several hormonal substances.

Uses (dried fruit) Anaphrodisiac (in males)

Principally employed in gynaecological conditions including depression in menopause. May be used sparingly as a condiment.

The drug was introduced in 1849 by King following long use by Red Indians as a local and general stimulant. It was once included in remedies for alcoholism, but is now used only in folk medicine.

Sometimes incorrectly found classified as *Xanthoxylum*.

Description Aromatic shrub or small tree to 3 m. Leaves to 30 cm long, subdivided into 5–11 ovate leaflets. Flowers greenish-yellow appearing in late spring before the leaves; arranged in axillary clusters.

Distribution North American native especially in the east. Usually in rich woodland on moist soils.

Cultivation Wild.

Constituents Resins; alkaloid-like substances; a phenol, xanthoxylin.

Uses (dried stem and root bark, rarely fruit) Stimulant; counter-irritant; diaphoretic; carminative.

Used in atonic dyspepsia; in combination with other remedies in respiratory catarrh, and more frequently with other remedies of value in chronic skin disease and rheumatism. Decoction used externally on ulcers.

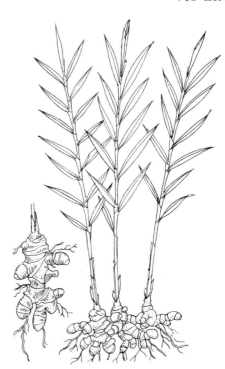

Zanthoxylum americanum Mill. RUTACEAE
Prickly Ash Toothache Tree

Several *Zanthoxylum* species have a medicinal action, notably Prickly Ash and the Southern Prickly Ash (*Z. Clava-Herculis* L). They are called Prickly because of their stem and petiole spines; and the other common name refers to the Red Indian use of the bark for toothache. In this respect the therapeutic use seems to be that of a powerful counter-irritant, and it is not a cure.

Zingiber officinale Roscoe ZINGIBERACEAE
Ginger

Before Roscoe reclassified this well-known plant, it had been called *Amomum zingiber* L, a name reflecting the old Arabic name *Amomum Zerumbeth*. The term *amomum* had been used to describe certain aromatic spices – the Round Cardamom, for example, is still called *Amomum compactum* Soland. ex Maton.

Ginger was long known as Zingiberis however, and the Greeks had imported the rhizome from the east for centuries before Dioscorides described its medicinal uses. In the Far East it had also long been employed; in China it was, and still is, an important drug, and Green Ginger in syrup was a delicacy from the fifteenth century. Ginger is now grown commercially throughout the tropics – from Australia to Jamaica – and many types and grades are available. The Spanish were importing Ginger from Jamaica before the mid-sixteenth century, and Jamaican Ginger is still considered the best for culinary use.

Description Perennial, creeping plant, on thick tuberous rhizome, producing an erect annual stem 60–120 cm tall. Leaves 1–2 cm wide, 15–30 cm long, lanceolate to linear-lanceolate. Flowers greenish marked with purple, in radical spikes (to 7 cm long) on 30 cm-long peduncles.

Distribution Native to south-east Asia; introduced and widespread in several tropical countries. To 1500 m altitude.

Cultivation Cultivated plant. Propagated from rhizome cuttings, planted on rich, well-drained loam.

Constituents Volatile oil (to 3%), comprising camphene, phellandrene, zingiberine, and many other substances; resin; starch; gingerol; shogaol – the latter two substances being pungent.

Uses (fresh or dried rhizome) Stimulant; carminative; aromatic; sialogogue; anti-emetic. Very valuable in flatulent colic, dyspepsia and atonic dyspepsia. Often used as an adjunct to other remedies for general tonic or stimulant purposes, or to purgatives to prevent griping. Rubefacient when applied externally in the fresh state.

Very wide culinary uses in many domestic and commercial preparations.

Contra-indications Large doses should be avoided by patients suffering from any skin complaint.

ACKNOWLEDGMENTS

Acknowledgments are due to the following sources for photographs used in this book: A-Z Collection, Bernard Alfieri, M Bavestrelli, C Bevilacqua, Pat Brindley, R J Corbin, Brian Furner, Iris Hardwick Library, G E Hyde, IGDA, Leslie Johns & Associates, A P Paterson, Derek Reid, Harry Smith Collection, H Veiller, Weed Research Organization. The drawings on pages 14–155 are by Michael Stringer and Roberto Campagna. We are also grateful to Mark Constantine, Ivan Day and Ian Tribe for their assistance.

ORGANIZATIONS

The following organizations offer membership, information and details of suppliers. Those marked (*) offer a regular publication such as a magazine and services of particular benefit to those with an interest in herbalism. A stamped addressed envelope or international reply coupon will usually secure details of what each one offers.

The Herb Society of South Australia Inc.
P.O. Box 140, Parkside, S. Australia, 5063.

The Queensland Herb Society*
23 Greenmount Avenue, Holland Park, Brisbane, Queensland, Australia.

The British Herbal Medicine Association
The Old Coach House, Southborough Road, Surbiton, Surrey, England.

The Garden History Society*
12 Charlbury Road, Oxford, England.

The Herb Society*
34 Boscobel Place, London, SW1, England.

Société de Recherches et de Diffusion de Plantes Medicinales
8 rue St Marc, Paris 2e, France.

Bundesfachverband der Heilmittelindustrie e. V.
D–5000 Koeln, Glockengasstrasse 1, Germany.

Verband der Reformwaren-Hersteller (VRH) e.V.
D–6380 Bad Homburg v.d. H.
Hessenring 73, Postfach 2320, Germany.

The Chinese Medical Practitioners Association
170 Johnston Road, Hong Kong

The Icelandic Nature Health Society
Laufasvegi 2, Reykjavik, Iceland.

Associazione Nazionale Commercianti Produtti Erboristici
Via Massena 20, 10128 Torino, Italy.

Associazione Nazionale Erboristi e Piante Officinali (ANEPO)*
Via E. S. Piccolomini 159, 53100 Siena, Italy.

The Botanical Society of Japan
c/o University of Tokyo, 3 Hongo, Bunkyo-ku, Tokyo, Japan.

The Auckland Herb Society
P.O. Box 20022, Glen Eden, Auckland 7, New Zealand.

The Tasmanian Herb Society
12 Delta Avenue, Taroona, Tasmania, 7006.

The American Horticultural Society*
901 N. Washington Street, Alexandria, Virginia 22314, U.S.A.

The Herb Society of America*
300 Massachusetts Avenue, Boston, Massachusetts 02115, U.S.A.

The Society for Economic Botany
c/o Dr. A. D. Marderosian, Philadelphia College of Pharmacy and Science, Philadelphia, Pennsylvania 19104, U.S.A.

The following organizations offer either training in medical herbalism or include herbalism as part of other courses:

National Herbalists Association of Australia (Queensland Chapter)
Montville Road, Mapleton, Queensland, Australia 4560.

The Academy of Natural Healing Pty Ltd.
7 The Esplanade, Ashfield, New South Wales, Australia 2131.

The General Council and Register of Consultant Herbalists Ltd and The British Herbalist Union Ltd
93 East Avenue Bournemouth, England.

The National Institute of Medical Herbalists Ltd
20 Osborne Avenue, Jesmond, Newcastle, England.

The Chinese Medicine and Acupuncture Research Centre
22nd floor, 322–324 Nathan Road, Kowloon, Hong Kong.

Swedish Herbal Institute (Svenska Örtmedicinska Institutet KB)
Bellmansgatan 11, 411 28 Göteborg, Sweden.

American Foundation for Homeopathy
Suite 428–431, Barr Building, 910 17th Street, N. W., Washington D.C. 20006, U.S.A.

National College of Naturopathic Medicine
1327 North 45th Street, Seattle, Washington 98103, U.S.A.

School of Natural Healing
P.O. Box 352, Provo, Utah 84601, U.S.A.

BIBLIOGRAPHY

Introduction
Altschul, S von Ries, *Drugs and Foods from Little-Known Plants* (Harvard University Press, Cambridge, Mass. 1973)
Baker, H G *Plants and Civilization* (Macmillan, London 1970)
Budge, Sir E W *The Divine Origin of the Craft of the Herbalist* (Culpeper House, London 1928)
Clarkson, R E *Herbs and Savoury Seeds* (Dover Publications, New York 1970)
Crockett, J U and Tanner, O *Herbs* (Time-Life Books, London and New York 1977)
Dawson, W R *A Leechbook or Collection of Medical Recipes of the Fifteenth Century* (Macmillan, London 1934)
Genders, R *Scented Flora of the World* (Robert Hale & Co., London 1977)
Grieve, M A *A Modern Herbal* (Penguin, Harmondsworth, Middx. 1974)
Grigson, G *A Dictionary of English Plant Names* (Allen Lane, Harmondsworth, Middx, 1974)
Grigson, G *The Englishman's Flora* (Paladin, St Albans, Hertfordshire 1975)
Hedrick, U P *Sturtevant's Edible Plants of the World* (Dover Publications, new York 1972)
Heffern, R *The Herb Buyer's Guide* (Pyramid Books, London 1973)
Hemphill, R *Herbs and Spices* (Penguin, Harmondsworth, Middx. 1966)
Huxley, A *Plant and Planet* (Allen Lane, Harmondsworth, Middx. 1974; Viking Press, New York 1975)
Kreig, M *Green Medicine* (Harrap, London 1965; Rand McNally, Chicago, Illinois 1964)
Levy, J de Bairacli *Herbal Handbook for Everyone* (Faber & Faber, London 1972)
Lust, J B *The Herb Book* (Bantam Books, London 1975; Des Plaines, Ill. 1974)
Mabey, R *Food for Free* (Collins, London 1972)
Mabey, R *Plants with a Purpose* (Collins, London 1977)
Mességué, M *Of Men and Plants* (Weidenfeld & Nicolson, London 1972)
Phillips, R *Wild Flowers of Britain* (Pan Books, London 1977)
Pirie, N W *Food Resources: Conventional and Novel* (Penguin, Harmondsworth, Middx. 1969)
Stearn, W T *Botanical Latin* (David & Charles, Newton Abbot, Devon 1973; Hafner Press 1966, distrib. Macmillan, Riverside NJ.)
Swain, T (ed.) *Plants in the Development of Modern Medicine* (Harvard University Press, Cambridge, Mass. 1972)
Thorwald, J *Science and Secrets of Early Medicine: Egypt, Mesopotamia, India, China, Mexico, Peru* (Thames & Hudson, London 1962)

History
Altschul, S von Ries *'Exploring the Herbarium'* (*Scientific American*, vol. 236, May 1977)
Arber, A *Herbals, their Origin and Evolution* (Cambridge University Press 1938)
Clair, C *Of Herbs and Spices* (Abelard-Schuman, London, New York, Toronto 1961)
Gerard, J *The herbal or Generall Historie of Plantes*, 1597 edition (Minerva Press, London 1974; Walter Johnson, Norwood, NJ. 1974)

Le Strange, R *A History of Herbal Plants* (Angus & Robertson, London 1977)
Sanecki, K N *The Complete Book of Herbs* (Macdonald & Jane's, London 1974; Macmillan, New York 1974)
Singer, C *'The Herbal in Antiquity'* (*Journal of Hellenic Studies*, vol, 47, Macmillan, London 1927)

Medicinal uses
British Herbal Medicine Association *British Herbal Pharmacopoeia* (London 1973)
Brooker, S G and Cooper, R C *New Zealand Medicinal Plants* (Unity Press, Auckland 1961)
Bryant, A T *Zulu Medicine and Medicine-Men* (C Struik, Cape Town 1966)
Burlage, H M *Index of Plants with Reputed Medicinal and Poisonous Properties* (Austin Press, Austin, Texas 1968)
Chopra, R N *Indigenous Drugs of India* (Arts Press, New Delhi 1973)
Croizier, R C *Traditional Medicine in Modern China* (Harvard University Press, Cambridge, Mass. 1968)
Huard, P and Wong, M *Chinese Medicine* McGraw-Hill, Maidenhead, Berks., and New York 1968)
Keys, J D *Chinese Herbs; their Botany, Chemistry and Pharmacodynamics* (Charles E Tuttle, Rutland, Vermont 1976)
Martindale, W *The Extra Pharmacopoeia*, 26th Edition – ed. N W Blacow (The Pharmaceutical Press, London 1972; distrib. Rittenhouse Book Distributors, Philadelphia, Penn.)
Millspaugh, C F *American Medicinal Plants* (Dover Publications, New York 1974)
Nelson, A *Medical Botany* (Churchill Livingstone, Edinburgh 1951)
Vogel, V J *American Indian Medicine* (University of Oklahoma Press, Norman, Oklahoma 1970)
Webb, L J *Guide to the Medicinal and Poisonous Plants of Queensland* (Bulletin 232, Center for Scientific and Industrial Research, Melbourne 1948)
Wren, R C *Potter's New Cyclopaedia of Botanical Drugs and Preparations* (Health Science Press, Holsworthy, North Devon 1973; Harper & Row, New York 1972)

Domestic and cosmetic uses
Arlott, J *The Snuff Shop* (Michael Joseph, London 1974)
Brooklyn Botanic Garden Record *Plants and Gardens* (New York 1973)
Buchman, D D *Feed Your Face* (Duckworth, London 1973)
Hériteau, J *Pot Pourris and Other Fragrant Delights* (Lutterworth Press, Guildford, Surrey 1975)
Huson, P *Mastering Herbalism* (Abacus, Tunbridge Wells, Kent 1977; Stein & Day, New York 1974)
Plummer, B *Fragrance* (Robert Hale & Co., London 1976)
Poucher, W A *Perfumes, Cosmetics and Soaps* volumes 1–3 (Chapman & Hall, London 1936)
Redgrove, H S *Scent and all about it* (Heinemann, London 1928)

Rimmel, E *Book of Perfumes* (Chapman & Hall, London 1867)
Ritchie, C *Candle Making* (Hodder & Stoughton, Sevenoaks, Kent 1976)

Cultivation
Brownlow, M E *Herbs and the Fragrant Garden* (Darton, Longman & Todd, London 1978)
Hay, R and Synge, P M *The Dictionary of Garden Plants* (Ebury Press & Michael Joseph, London 1973)
Herb Society, The *Growing Herbs* (London 1977)
Hewer D G and Sanecki, K N *Practical Herb Growing* (G Bell & Sons, London 1969)
Hunter, B T *Gardening without Poisons* (Hamish Hamilton, London 1965)
Loewenfeld, C *Herb Gardening* (Faber & Faber, London 1964)
Perring, F (ed.) *The Flora of a Changing Britain* (Botanical Society of the British Isles Conference Report No. 11, 1972)

Periodicals
ACTA PHYTOTHERAPEUTICA, ten editions per year 1954–1972. Scientific journal on botanical medicine. In 1973 merged with the *Quarterly Journal of Crude Drug Research*. Back copies, Swets & Zeitlinger B V, Publishing Dept., 347 b Heereweg, Lisse, The Netherlands.
ECONOMIC BOTANY, quarterly; economic and medicinal plants, including food crops. Available from: The Society for Economic Botany, The New York Botanical Garden, The Bronx, NY 10458, U.S.A.
GARDEN HISTORY, quarterly; historical, horticultural and etymological information; often of relevance to herbalism. Editor: Dr Christopher Thacker, French Studies, The University, Reading, Berkshire, England.
PLANTS AND GARDENS, quarterly; some editions contain data on domestic and horticultural aspects of herbs. Available from: Brooklyn Botanic Garden, Brooklyn, NY 11225, U.S.A.
QUARTERLY JOURNAL OF CRUDE DRUG RESEARCH, quarterly; scientific aspects of crude drugs, both animal and plant, and their derivatives. Articles in English, French and German; published since 1961. Back copies and subscriptions: Swets & Zeitlinger B V, Publishing Dept., 347 b Heereweg, Lisse, The Netherlands.
RIVISTA DI ERBORISTERIA, quarterly; medical herbalism. Editor: Dr Angiolo Severi, Via E S Piccolomini 159, 53100 Siena, Italy.
THE HERB GROWER, quarterly; mainly horticultural aspects. Available from: Herb Grower, Falls Village, Conn, 06031, U.S.A.
THE HERBAL REVIEW, quarterly; all aspects of herbs and herbalism. Available from: The Herb Society, 34 Boscobel Place, London SW1, England.
THE HERBALIST, annually; non-medical aspects of herbalism. Available from: The Herb Society of America, 300 Massachusetts Avenue, Boston, Mass. 02115, U.S.A.

INDEX OF COMMON NAMES